On the Skirmish Line Behind a Friendly Tree

The Civil War Memoirs of William Royal Oake

✻ 26th Iowa Volunteers ✻

Edited by Stacy Dale Allen

FARCOUNTRY
PRESS

Helena, Montana

ISBN13: 978-1-56037-322-3
ISBN10: 1-56037-322-9

© 2006 Farcountry Press
Front matter and back matter text © 2006 Stacy Dale Allen

Cover photos: William T. Sherman's troops tearing up railroad
track in Atlanta, Georgia (background), Library of Congress;
William Royal Oake (inset), *Sabula Gazette*.

For more information on our books, write Farcountry Press,
P.O. Box 5630, Helena, MT 59604; call (800) 821-3874;
or visit www.farcountrypress.com.

Cataloging-in-Publication data is on file
at the Library of Congress

Created, produced, designed and printed in the United States.

11 10 09 08 07 06   1 2 3 4 5 6 7 8 9 10

———✦

For the United States Volunteers who served
in the Clinton County Regiment.
Your record of service found its voice in the
selected memory of William Royal Oake.

To interpret your intertwined history
has been an honor.

—Stacy Dale Allen

———✦

This book is dedicated to the fourth generation
of Oakes and their families.

Gregory Donald Oake
Douglas William Oake
(sons of Cyril D. Oake)

Patricia Ann Sazma Outzen
Barbara Lou Sazma Green,
Beverly Jean Sazma Price
(daughters of Elsie Oake Sazma)

Colleen Kay Oake
(daughter of Lloyd F. Oake)

Special thank you to Beverly Ann Oake
(mother of Gregory and Douglas)
for submitting this journal for publication.

———✦

Table of Contents

Acknowledgments

By Stacy Dale Allen

Numerous friends, colleagues, archivists, professionals, and one irreplaceable family member have provided valuable assistance as I researched and edited this remarkable Civil War memoir over a two-year period.

My own intimate knowledge of the subject matter proved a great advantage in researching this memoir, and my body of work experience as a historian with the National Park Service and personal interest in the history of the American Civil War has taken me on every prominent field of battle and along the actual routes of movement for the numerous campaigns in which William Royal Oake had participated. My personal library and several significant depositories of documents located nearby provided the vast majority of source material needed to research the period. Unfortunately, the need to attend to my agency management responsibilities did not permit time for personal travel to investigate some historical or geographical issues relevant to the Oake story. Although it would have been extremely useful in developing a more thorough understanding of the author's childhood, making a trip to England to visit the place of his birth was not possible. Outside of an opportunity to briefly revisit a number of the killing grounds and campaign routes in Tennessee, Georgia, and the Carolinas, the major journey of discovery was conducted in the fall of 2003, when I traveled with my wife, Diane, to Iowa. We visited local libraries and historical societies in order to track down historical documents and visit the many sites in Clinton and Jackson counties that held relevance to the pre-war and post-war experiences of William Royal Oake. This travel was absolutely necessary to flesh out the soul and substance of the citizen soldier whose war activities were the primary subject of the memoir.

Given the limitations of travel to conduct research, the traditionalist historian in me was forced to reexamine the value of the internet as a repository for historical data. Suffice to say, I was most impressed by the quantity and quality of the source material discovered. I wish to extend my gratitude to the website developers, coordinators, and technical staff of these websites. The most helpful sites were those for Ancestry.com/MyFamily.com, Inc., the Cambridgeshire Family History Society, the Dullingham History Group, Old Courthouse Museum of Vicksburg, State Historical Society of Iowa, National Archives and Records Administration, and the National Park Service's Civil War Soldier and Sailor System.

I could not have written this book without the much-needed assistance of the editors and staff at Farcountry Press in Helena, Montana. The counsel and support of Charlene Patterson, John Thomas, Kathy Springmeyer, Jessica Solberg, and Kelli Twichel were most appreciated. Especially significant were the copies of materials compiled by Beverly Oake (wife of Cyril Oake, grandson of William Royal Oake) of Davenport, Iowa, which they graciously provided for my use. These initial family history documents proved most helpful in pointing my own research in the right direction.

Fran Buelow, who works in the "Root Cellar" of the Clinton Public Library in Clinton, Iowa, was most gracious and extremely helpful in providing access to microfilm editions of the *Clinton Herald* and in confirming the site location of Camp Kirkwood. Other members of the Clinton library staff assisted with securing local county history sources and in making numerous copies of data from the rare holdings. At the Jackson County Historical Society Museum and Research Library, in Maquoketa, Iowa, Bonnie Wells Mitchell kindly assisted me in the examination of extremely fragile copies of the *Sabula Gazette* and in accessing the county cemetery records. Her generous assistance led to one of the most significant and exciting finds made during the journey to Iowa, which was the discovery of William Royal Oake's obituary and the only photograph of him located during my research. The help that Bonnie and the staff offered with cemetery records facilitated our visit to the gravesites of Royal, Mary Ann, and

Lottie Mae, as well as those of the elder William and Mary Oake.

The efficient staff at the Maquoketa Public Library aided me in locating critical sources on Iowa and Jackson County history. Research in these records led us to the location of the original William Oake homestead in Bloomfield Township, east of Delmar, Iowa, in nearby Clinton County, and thus permitted us to stand on actual ground Royal once plowed, as well as travel the roads he took to enlist in nearby Charlotte and to his first army quarters at Camp Kirkwood in Clinton.

Personnel working at the Sabula Public Library reproduced copies of the obituaries for Lottie Mae Oake and the elder William Oake, provided information on the history of the Island City of Sabula, identified surviving cultural landscape features that were present when William Royal Oake lived in the community, and gave directions to the Evergreen Cemetery, northwest of the city, where we paid a long visit to Royal and his loved ones. Throughout our travels in Clinton and Jackson counties, Diane and I were treated with the utmost kindness, consideration, appreciation, and heartfelt interest by all those we encountered.

I also must extend warmest regards to Mike and Patti Dever of Delmar, Iowa, who currently reside upon the original Oake homestead in Bloomfield Township. They permitted complete strangers the opportunity to view the land that helped shape the character of Royal Oake. Both he and his parents would appreciate the care in which they maintain the old homestead.

Several associates at the National Park Service were, during my research and as always, exemplary of the high regard and trust the American public continues to bestow on them. My oldest agency friend and comrade, Terrence J. Winschel, park historian at Vicksburg National Military Park in Mississippi, coordinated an exhaustive search for what still remains an elusive Vicksburg newspaper account, which reportedly details the potential execution of the Union raiders captured at Deer Creek, briefly referenced by Royal in the memoir. More significantly, my dear friend believed enough in the quality and sensitivity of my research methodology to recommend me for the task of correlating and editing the Oake memoir. His professional advice, skill as a historian, and gifted scholarship provides inspiration; and his unshakeable friendship remains one of the most cherished rewards of my career. The National Park Service staff at the Harpers Ferry Center, Anthony Library, particularly supervisory librarian David Nathanson, provided me with source material from rare publications that otherwise would have been difficult to obtain. A number of my coworkers at Shiloh National Military Park made important contributions. Park rangers Sunny Brook (Garner) Allen, Timothy B. Smith, and Ashley E. Ball helped their technically challenged supervisor scan photographs and documents. Park ranger Thomas Parson read both the introduction and epilogue, identifying grammatical errors and giving sound advice on how to clarify confusing passages. Other members of the ranger staff, including Joe Davis, Jim Minor, Charlie Spearman, and Josh Clemons, listened to their boss interpret the experiences and emotions of volunteer soldiers during the war. These discussions assisted in the development of a greater contextual understanding of William Royal Oake and his unique war experiences. Superintendent Woody Harrell understandingly provided support and approved last-minute requests for leave, which allowed me to stay home and pound the keys to complete the task of writing the introduction and epilogue for the memoir. I commend all the agency employees with whom I proudly serve for the abiding respect they demonstrate daily for the mission of the National Park Service and for the consistent high quality of service they provide the American public.

The person most instrumental in helping me edit this volume is also the most important person in my life, my wife Diane. In addition to enriching my life every day, she proved a most untiring and faithful research assistant on what became a two-year journey of discovery to decipher the history surrounding the remarkable life of William Royal Oake. She ran important errands, patiently listened to my excited interpretations of Civil War soldier life, battles, and campaigns, and walked by my side on roads and fields traveled by citizen-soldier Oake. With every passing day we share, she graciously overlooks my many vices, troubling impatience, occasional bad temper, and extremely colorful farm-boy language. Her generosity, remarkable communication skills, and unpretentious intelligence challenge this flawed Jayhawker to be better than he is—the loving husband and best friend she deserves.

All credit for the remarkable quality and historical value of this book belongs to William Royal Oake. Any liability for inaccurate interpretations or failure to adequately record past human events correctly—without proper clarity and substance—is all mine.

Introduction

It is seldom, indeed, that a subordinate officer knows anything about the disposition of the enemy's forces—except that it is unamiable—or precisely whom he is fighting. As to the rank and file, they can know nothing more of the matter than the arms they carry. They hardly know what troops are upon their own right or left the length of a regiment away. If it is a cloudy day they are ignorant even of the points of the compass. It may be said, generally, that a soldier's knowledge of what is going on about him is coterminous with his official relation to it and his personal connection with it; what is going on in front of him he does not know at all until he learns it afterward.

Ambrose Bierce
"The Crime at Pickett's Mill," 1888

The American Civil War was slightly more than a year old, having already lasted longer than most citizens had anticipated, when William Royal Oake, an eighteen-year-old farmer from Charlotte, Iowa, felt compelled to enlist with the Union in the summer of 1862.

Throughout the Northern states, governors had recently mounted an intensely patriotic campaign to rally support for the war. They sought to enlist the required state quotas of recruits needed in response to the call made by President Abraham Lincoln on July 2, 1862, for 300,000 men to fill the ranks of Union armies. The carnage of recent battles and the unrelenting attrition wrought by disease had either killed or disabled a staggering number of the initial volunteers.[1]

Of the underlying motivating factors that propelled Royal to accept the risks of becoming a soldier while a state of bitter civil war raged among the divided national citizenry, he remained stoically mute. When, a half century later, he reflected upon the momentous decision to enlist, he describes how he simply confided to worried parents that it was what "no more than thousands of others" were doing, stating that he did not think the war would last much longer. Armored with an untrammeled confidence, which routinely seems to shield youthful inexperience from the harsher realities of life, Royal pronounced the belief he would "come out all right" and tramped off to join his regiment, beginning a personal odyssey that would carry him far beyond the peaceful cornfields of Iowa.

The life of William Royal Oake began on February 26, 1844, in the ancient village of Dullingham, England, in the county of Cambridgeshire, about fifty-five miles north-northeast of London. Royal was the son of William and Mary (Riches) Oake, who were likewise natives of England, the former born in Dullingham on June 30, 1813, and the latter from Riddlesworth County, born on May 24, 1814. United in marriage on November 23, 1837, the couple raised seven children in Dullingham, where William engaged in clerical work to support their growing household.[2] Shortly after his parents passed away, William Oake, "being much opposed to a monarchial form of government, determined to emigrate to the United States," and on May 16, 1852, with Mary and their seven children— Elizabeth, Agnes, Nancy, William R. (Royal), George R., Robert R., and the baby Susan—embarked at Liverpool on the sailing vessel *Warbler*. Following what Royal later described "an uneventful and monotonous fifty-three days on the Atlantic Ocean," they ascended the Mississippi to land at the Queen City of the South, New Orleans, Louisiana, on July 8, 1852.[3]

It was midsummer, and the great port city was plagued by a raging epidemic of cholera and scarlet fever. "It was almost miraculous that we escaped its ravages," Royal wrote in 1906, stating his family remained in New Orleans only two days before taking passage on a steamboat north. While en route upriver, the youngest child became ill with cholera and died.

Officials later held the boat for several days at a quarantine ground just outside St. Louis, Missouri, until fears of any further cases of contagious diseases "were dispelled by the healthy conditions of the passengers." The stay in St. Louis proved brief for Royal and his family, as they waited two days for the arrival of the steamer *Brunette*, which was then making the run between St. Louis and St. Paul, Minnesota.

The journey up the Mississippi from St. Louis on the palatial steamer made an impression on the young eight-year-old lad from England, who later recounted how the *Brunette* raced a rival steamer northward, "both boats using the most combustible material that they could get to produce steam and at times it seemed that every plank would shake and tremble by the working of the powerful machinery." At a point just above Le Claire, Iowa, the *Brunette* took the lead, leaving the competitor vessel lost to view. The river journey proceeded more leisurely to its destination, the island city of Sabula, in Jackson County, Iowa, where the boat landed on July 30, 1852.

The family, which had grown with the birth of another child—a daughter named Mary, in Sabula—rented the home known as the "Marshall house" through the fall and winter of 1852 to 1853. The following spring, the elder Oake turned his attention to general agricultural pursuits, devoting his time and energy to the operation of rented farms for the next three years. The tract leased in 1853 was the eighty-acre Westbrook farm, two and one-half miles west of Sabula. The following year the family moved to the Widow Davis farm, north of Sterling, and from 1855 to 1856, they lived on and worked the Widow Killinger farm. At the close of this period, William Oake entered a homestead claim on eighty acres of land from the government that was located along a watershed of Deep Creek in Section 13 within the township of Bloomfield in north-central Clinton County, about nine miles southeast of the town of Maquoketa. For nearly twenty years William worked continually to improve the farm, to which he later added another tract of similar size.[4]

The earliest selected memories of Royal Oake are of the long family journey to America and the formative childhood experiences growing up the son of an Iowa farmer. Of the previous brief eight years he lived in England, he unfortunately left no record. Farm life for a boy in rural Iowa was one of intense physical labor, and Royal was called on to assist his father, brothers, and sisters to work the land, using oxen to cultivate and harvest wheat and corn. However, Royal's childhood was also filled with freedom and boyish adventure. When not assigned rigorous work in the fields, or attending school, and between the ever-constant tasks of daily farm chores, he played with other lads his age, often tramping for hours across the heavily forested hillsides, along thicketed creek bottoms, or to the islands along the Mississippi to hunt the abundant rabbits, squirrels, deer, and ducks. During this early period, the Oake family resided in unpretentious one-room log homes. Royal fondly recalled the many nights he and his siblings lay in their bed, nestled in the cramped attic of the Westbrook cabin, and "watched through the roof the stars twinkling in the heavens"—it was not uncommon to awake in the morning after a fall of snow to find a fresh blanket of the cold white powder covering the bed.[5]

As the oldest son, Royal had a brief childhood. The pressing responsibility to provide for the welfare of the household quite naturally required farmers' sons to become field hands for their fathers, and as he entered his teenage years, Royal's daily activities lost the periods of play and freedom accorded young children and were consumed by a more active role in working and improving the Oake farm. The primary cash crops being raised were corn and wheat, and the annual agricultural year cycled through a consistent process of plowing, planting, cultivating, and harvesting the fields. They used teams of oxen in the early years; later, when they became available in increasing numbers, horses and mules were utilized. The annual harvests were conducted using what Royal termed the "Traveling Machine," or early threshing wagon. Shocks of grain were loaded on board the wagon, which was pulled by teams of draft animals to manipulate the thresher. In this manner the grain was threshed and the straw dispersed throughout the field in an extremely labor-intensive process requiring numerous stops to load more shocks, and then proceeding on to thresh the grain. Once filled with the threshed grain, the wagons required unloading, and the complete cycle was repeated many times until the entire crop had been threshed. Although not nearly as efficient as the later steam-powered threshing machines, Royal stated it worked well for the small crops being planted and harvested in the early days of farming in the region.

Interestingly, Royal appears in the 1860 United States Census twice, once as a seventeen-year-old member of his father's household, listed as a "domestic," and the second instance as a "farm laborer" working for the household headed by S. O. Crum, who with his wife, Flora, and two young children, Lucy and John, managed a large farm in Deep Creek Township, several miles east of the Oake homestead. The census records show that in addition to Royal, Crum also employed two additional laborers and a female servant.[6]

By the time William Royal Oake turned seventeen, seven of fifteen slave states in the South had already seceded from the Union. Commissioners from these seceded states had already met in convention in Montgomery, Alabama, where on February 8, 1861, they adopted a Provisional Constitution establishing a separate Confederate States of America. The following day, they elected Jefferson Davis of Mississippi, Provisional President of the Confederacy. Sixty-three days later, following a thirty-four-hour bombardment, the U.S. Army garrison at Fort Sumter, South Carolina, surrendered to Confederate military forces. Two days later, on April 15, 1861, President Abraham Lincoln issued a proclamation declaring that an insurrection existed. He called for 75,000 militia from the various Northern states to put down the rebellion—thus the old Union lay in ruins and open civil war had erupted among the quarreling sections.[7]

The outbreak of war radically transformed daily existence for thousands of young men of military age in Iowa. However, it appears a strict obedience to parental influence and a sensitivity to the concerns of his father and mother caused Royal to resist the initial call for mobilization to enlist in Iowa's first quota of volunteers in 1861.

A year later, however, after turning eighteen, Royal again moved off the family farm; on March 1, 1862, he hired himself out as a field hand to a farmer named Watts,[8] for whom he was contracted to work for over the course of the next six months for twelve dollars a month and board. Now out on his own, well beyond the parental influence of William and Mary, Royal was plowing a field on a warm day in July when a local recruiting officer by the name of Elijah Frank—canvassing the county in a wagon for the purpose of obtaining enlistments for a new regiment being raised in Clinton—stopped at the Watts farm. Frank was accompanied by two young men who had already enlisted, both of whom Royal was acquainted with, having previously attended school with them years earlier. When asked by Frank if he would join the army, Royal initially refused, citing his contractual arrangement with farmer Watts, which tied him to work the farm until September. Frank inquired if Royal would enlist if Mr. Watts agreed to release him from the contract; the young field hand answered he would. When consulted, Watts reluctantly consented to Royal's premature departure to enlist for war service, but advised, "I don't think you fully realize what you will have to go through as a soldier." Royal departed with Frank and the other recruits, traveling to the nearby hamlet of Charlotte. There, on July 7, 1862, William Royal Oake enlisted as a private in the 26th Iowa Volunteer Infantry. Four days later, on July 11, he formally entered military quarters, being assigned to a permanent camp of recruitment established on the county fairgrounds near the river port city of Clinton.[9]

We will never know the specific reasons why Royal decided to enlist, for he does not state the cause. The mere fact he did not consult with his parents before he enlisted possibly reveals an emerging sense of independence and manhood. While under their direct day-to-day influence, he had remained out of the army. Once he moved outside the bounds of their parental control, having reached the legal age to enlist, he apparently felt compelled to answer the call to duty. In his description of it fifty years later, he expresses his decision to enlist that summer as a simple matter of fact. Could it have been a decision he made in haste, in direct response to mounting societal and peer pressure, being influenced by the fact other young men he knew from the area had already signed up? Or was his decision based on political and economic issues he may have spent considerable time reflecting upon as he labored in the fields over the course of the year since the start of the war?

Royal was a farmer whose individual labors and economic success on behalf of his family, and later his employer, relied on unfettered navigation of the Mississippi River to forward harvests to market. Like thousands of others throughout the Midwest, Royal and his family were directly and adversely affected by secession of the Southern states. The formation of the Confederate States of America in 1861 permanently closed the great river to northern commerce. The highly emotional political discussions and rhetoric Royal would have been privy to and perhaps even participated in, over the course of the last two years, would have championed the economic interests of his profession and the patriotic fever of his community, state, and region. In no instance in the memoir does he take the opportunity to voice his thoughts on the politics of this turbulent time in the United States. Rather he simply demonstrates the blind acceptance common to the people of his region that the Union must be preserved, and when asked to join the army—he does so.

Although he was undeniably innocent and still naïve concerning the brutal truths of war, Royal clearly understood the potential life-threatening consequences of his volunteer enlistment. Published accounts and local conversations concerning recent faraway battles would have foretold the awesome carnage befalling men under arms. At battles at Fort Donelson, Tennessee, and Pea Ridge, Arkansas, fought earlier in the year, Iowa regiments lost a total of 292 officers and 465 men. However, it would be the titanic battle of Pittsburg Landing—or Shiloh, Tennessee, as it was known in Southern accounts—fought a mere three months earlier, where volunteer regiments representing the state of Iowa had sent a total of 6,664 men into the fight, recording a staggering tragic loss of 2,409 Iowans killed, wounded, or taken prisoner as a result of the momentous battle.[10] The impact of this growing list of war casualties involving Iowa volunteers was felt throughout the state and was well chronicled in local, regional, and national newspapers. Any lad trodding in the wake of a yoke of oxen or plowing a cornfield in Iowa that summer would have had much to reflect upon concerning the personal decision of whether to become a soldier or remain a farmer. Suffice it to say, the action he took to join the Union army was a step Royal believed he was justified in taking, whether out of a sense of adventure or maturing patriotism or an all too common male response to the intense pressure that routinely confronts men during a state of military crisis to publicly demonstrate personal courage, duty, and honor through martial action; or perhaps he acted in answer to some undisclosed ideological motivation to do what he believed was the proper thing to do. The decision to become a soldier remained a deeply held private matter that William Royal Oake never felt obligated, even a half century later as he wrote his war memoir, to publicly reveal.

The new recruit from Charlotte, Iowa, stood five feet eight and one-half inches tall, had brown hair, brown eyes, and possessed a fair complexion. We can assume, based on his many years of laboring outdoors, that his youthful features displayed the visible signs of a farmer's tan, being exposed for long hours to both sun and wind; his body strong and robust; and his hands calloused and worn rough from heavy manual labor in the fields.

The records of the adjutant general of the State of Iowa show the ten companies that composed the 26th Iowa Volunteer Infantry were all enrolled in the County of Clinton, although a number of other counties in the state were also represented among the men listed on the original roster. Most of the enrollees were residents of Clinton County. The companies were ordered into quarters at Camp Kirkwood, near Clinton, by Governor Samuel Kirkwood, on dates ranging from July 5 to September 2, 1862. The distances traveled by those joining the regiment—from places of initial enrollment to the muster rendezvous in Clinton—varied from as little as 2 miles to as far as 225 miles. On August 30, 1862, Company A, the one to which Royal Oake was assigned, was mustered into United States service. Company F was the last company mustered, on October 1, 1862, which completed formation of the regiment.[11]

The majority of volunteers mustered in Company A, a total of fifty-seven recruits, came from residences located in other Iowa counties, including four men from Cedar County, one from Dubuque County, thirty-five from Jackson County, six each from Jones and Scott counties, and one man from Worth. Contrary to the general trend in the regiment, only thirty-five of the company's men were from Clinton County. Of these, nineteen recruits, including Royal, resided in Charlotte. Nine were from Lyons and five were from Clinton, with one enlistment each from the towns of Southport and Low Moor. Of the ninety-four men listed on the original muster, only a small minority, twelve in number, including William Royal Oake, were foreign born. Among these, three had been born in Canada, five in England, two in Ireland, and one each in France and Germany. The remainder of the Company A men were natural-born citizens of the United States, with twenty-five men citing nativity in Ohio, twenty-two in New York, seven in Pennsylvania, eight in Indiana, three in Vermont, two each with nativity in Illinois, Kentucky, Michigan, New Jersey, and Virginia, and one each citing birth in New Hampshire, Maryland, and Delaware. One striking example that illustrates just how recently the vast majority of settlers had entered

Iowa is that only two volunteers in the entire company were native born Iowans. The nativity of one enlisted man, Amby M. Harden (or Hardin), was not cited. Six other recruits were officially rejected by the mustering officer for various disabilities. Amazingly, the company would only receive four additional enlistments during the entire war, with these men joining the regiment while it was stationed in winter quarters in January 1864.[12]

While quartered at Camp Kirkwood, the regiment learned the rudiments of drill and discipline, with each day assuming the monotonous regimented routine of soldiering. When all companies were officially mustered into federal service, the organization commonly referred to by local citizenry as the "Clinton County Regiment" departed the state on October 20, 1862, with 920 officers and men enrolled on the muster sheets. Transported south by river steamer, the regiment rapidly descended the Mississippi Valley toward the seat of war.

The long journey William Royal Oake now embarked upon would become the most harrowing, yet equally most rewarding and pivotal experience of his life—an odyssey in which he twice journeys across the Confederacy to the Atlantic Ocean and in each instance makes the long return home to his beloved Iowa. Fifty-one years later, recognizing the importance his military service held for him, Royal would spend the entire winter of 1913 to 1914 writing a detailed memoir of his soldier experiences. With the manuscript nearly complete, written on roughly 400 pages, he looked forward to having the work published in book form for the benefit of his family and old army comrades. Unfortunately, he would never have the pleasure of seeing his war experiences in print, for he passed away shortly after finishing the initial draft.[13] Thus, like so many others who served in the war, the compelling war memories of William Royal Oake joined those held by the great host of forgotten veterans whose record of faithful service rapidly faded upon their death.

Yet eighty-eight years after his passing, the war memoir of William Royal Oake surfaced in the possession of Beverly Ann Oake of Davenport, Iowa. Interested in the story her husband's long-deceased grandfather told within the narrative, Beverly believed the war story Royal had written was worth publishing and contacted the editors at Farcountry Press in Helena, Montana, sending them a copy of the typed transcription in July 2002.

Intrigued by the potential historical value of the memoir, the editors at Farcountry sought the informed advice of Professor Earl Hess at Lincoln Memorial University. Hess believed the document worthy of publication, citing it among the top 25 percent of post-war recollections he had observed. With a busy schedule, Professor Hess stated he would not be able to work on the project, but recommended some knowledgeable historians of the Western theater of the Civil War who possibly might be interested in tackling such a research project, among them Professor Steven Woodworth, at Texas Christian University, and Terrence J. Winschel, veteran park historian with the National Park Service stationed at Vicksburg National Military Park. It was Winschel who, when contacted by Farcountry Press, stated an associate of his working for the National Park Service at Shiloh National Military Park might be able to assist with the Oake manuscript. In that manner, when contacted by Farcountry Press in the spring of 2003, I agreed to review the memoir and begin the task of editing it for publication.

Upon receipt of the transcribed memoir, the historical value of its content quickly became evident. Although William Royal Oake proved to be a most common and average citizen soldier, he was a good writer, and by the time he penned his war memoir, a seasoned and wise man. His observations on the horrors of battle and the ironies that often accompany violent death, as viewed firsthand from within the small deadly space only battle-tested veterans seem to fully comprehend, are strikingly honest and poignant. Throughout the narrative, as Royal tramps across many of the notable fields of battle associated with the war in the western theater, he employs an engaging sense of humor, often chuckling at himself for both the reckless stupidity and often uncommon bravery he displayed in battle. Later, when he matured into a campaign-hardened veteran, grown more self-reliant and less prone to coercive authority, he delights in relating how he learned to employ "the old army game" against his superiors, detailing the many infractions he got away with.

The reader should remember the emotions penned by the author are memories of feelings he expressed roughly half a century after they were experienced. Distanced by this great span of time from the harsh realities of those experiences, Royal had many years to formulate a more structured impression of just how he felt about the war. His feelings about combat, the routine of camp life, or being captured and held as a prisoner of war are quite naturally far more reflective in nature.

Famed author and journalist Ambrose Bierce, one of the more prominent chroniclers to emerge from the Civil War, likewise experienced military service in the Union army, participating in many of the campaigns and battles experienced by William Royal Oake. Based on his own extensive combat experiences, Bierce observed a soldier's knowledge of what occurred about him, while engaged in a given battle, was "coterminous with his official relation to it and his personal connection with it." He further concluded, "what is going on in front of him" the rank and file soldier "does not know at all until he learns it afterward." In writing about the many battles and skirmishes he participated in, Royal ably demonstrates his personal connection to combat. His memories of battle are told from the first-person perspective of a veteran who faced and survived life and death encounters on many a battlefield for which he did not know the broader context surrounding his participation—except the duty of a soldier to obey the orders of his officers and support his comrades in carrying out the immediate task at hand, which was to engage the enemy in their front. Royal writes about battle events that occurred coterminous with his immediate physical and geographical connection to them; but little reference, discussion, or analysis is made in the narrative about the broader contextual perspective. Thus, although he offers gritty descriptions of the military actions he was engaged in, as Bierce provocatively observed, Royal did not know the big picture, the larger context encompassing the combat unfolding before him. It is apparent any significant understanding Royal gained about the context of a given battle was, as Bierce reasoned, learned afterward, and in most instances learned long after the war concluded. Any greater understanding of how his own personal experience related to the overall breadth and scope of battle events was more than likely formed by reading published histories during the decades that followed and through discussions held with comrades about the momentous events they jointly experienced and survived. Only in this manner would Royal begin to forge the broad perspective not readily available to the rank-and-file soldier during the heat of battle.[14]

The battlefield stories related within the narrative offer some memorable vignettes, particularly in respect to Royal's sense of duty as a soldier. It is quite apparent in reading the memoir that the young Iowan felt his first duty was to survive the war. His severest test in battle would be, as was often common for many organizations in the Civil War, the regiment's first experience in combat, at the Post of Arkansas on January 11, 1863. In a massive frontal assault against a fortified Confederate installation, the 26th Iowa Volunteer Infantry suffered its single highest loss in killed and wounded of any engagement it participated in during the entire war. The casualties suffered by the regiment are more notable for being the greatest number of men killed and wounded in the battle, among all the organizations engaged—Union or Confederate. Roughly 55 percent of the battle casualties recorded for the regiment during the entire war fell in that first action fought in Arkansas.[15] The initial test of combat—where his regiment, deployed in close-order battle rank, was called upon to make a frontal assault into a pre-sighted killing zone, over open ground, against an entrenched enemy armed with rifle muskets, and supported by massed field artillery—proved an extremely valuable learning experience for Royal, who survived being struck down, unlike so many of his comrades. As a result of this valuable learning experience, whenever possible, within the context of the tactics being deployed by his superiors, Royal sought the precious advantage of cover on the battlefield, whether it existed within prepared or hastily constructed field fortifications, or by securing for himself a personal "soldier" shelter of convenience. This is ably described in his references to "friendly" trees and boulders he continuously sought out when advancing over the killing field. Yet eleven months later—during a rare instance when he failed to secure adequate cover while his company skirmished across the wooded northeastern flank of Lookout Mountain, Tennessee, on November 24, 1863—Royal was struck in the shoulder by a rifle ball. In an ironic example of the chances of war—some call it soldier's luck—the blanket roll he carried slung over his shoulder provided partial protection and stopped the deadly round from either killing or seriously maiming him, and he remained on duty in the field, having gained further appreciation for the value of individual shelters of convenience like trees or field fortifications on the battlefield.

Battles are fought by scared men who would rather be someplace else. Yet such a close brush with death, one of many he experienced during the war, did not elicit from Royal any testimony of spiritual faith, although it is apparent he believed in a divine power. Statements made in the memoir effectively demonstrate Royal possessed a Christian fatalism common among soldiers during the war—a fatalistic attitude that contained both pessimistic and optimistic overtones.[16] Throughout the memoir the young Iowan expresses a playful optimism about death on the battlefield and the belief his service for country will be rewarded by God should he be struck down. "A good many of our army chaplains advocated and preached the doctrine: That if a soldier fell while battling for his country it mattered not what his views were he would surely enter the gates of Paradise," he said, "and…most of us had accepted that doctrine as gospel truth."

Royal carried and read a Bible throughout the war and even describes how he came into possession of a "very fine velvet bound pocket bible" along the Cape Fear River during the campaign in North Carolina in March 1865. It became a prize he apparently treasured for the rest of his life, yet the increasingly more brutal and violent nature of the war may have led him to privately question the value of Christian doctrine and his own personal faith. There is a brief notable pessimistic acknowledgment of his growing confusion with his gospel teaching, which arises during the period of incarceration he endured as a prisoner of war in the spring of 1863. While being held a prisoner for nearly two months, with no means to divert his mind from the unbearable monotony of prison life, Royal passed the long hours frequently reading his pocket testament, "more than I ever have since," he exclaimed, further testifying, "I attribute my present aversion to it, to the fact that in reading it so much at that time I became glutted and never recovered from its effects."

It is readily observable within the memoir that Royal was no abolitionist. He was fighting to restore the Union, not to emancipate African slaves. His impression was that the war was a rebellion by a section of the country, and he equates the act of secession with treason. In no instance in the memoir does he discuss slavery as being an underlying link to the secession of the South and the resulting war. In no instance does he use the words "freedom," "emancipation," or "slavery," or his sentiments in regard to the status of slavery and human bondage.[17] In only one instance does he use the word "slave" in the memoir, which is a reference made in regards to the hundreds of "freed slaves" who paraded in the Grand Review in Washington, D.C., conducted at the close of war in late May 1865. In this passage he describes how the freed men followed in the wake of Sherman's passing army. It is but within a single sentence in the memoir, where Royal briefly links the plight of African slaves and racial inequality to the conduct of the war. This occurs when he relates his despair and anger, in the spring of 1863, concerning the probable length of time he possibly could be held as a prisoner of war, while waiting formal parole and exchange from Libby Prison to the safety of federal authority. In relating the concern he and fellow captives felt for how long it might take to be exchanged, Royal links the delay to the diplomatic "disagreement between the North and South in regard to status of the Negro soldier in being on the equality with the white troops." Although this acknowledgement by Royal concerning the provocative societal and political complexities that surrounded the enlistment of free men of color and ex-slaves to serve in the Union army does not offer insight concerning his true feelings on the matter, the comment, made late in his life when he wrote the memoir, is enough to illustrate he was aware the issue of emancipation possessed relevance to the war. When hundreds of thousands of volunteers like Royal, white and black—free and ex-slave—invaded the South wearing the blue uniform of a soldier in the United States Army, or served aboard Union ships and gunboats patrolling the Southern rivers and coastline, they "became agents of emancipation by their very presence." The victory they won eliminated chattel slavery from United States society. Therefore, it is reasonable to believe Royal mostly likely comprehended the undeniable link between slavery and the war. Yet like so many of those he served with and fought against, who later took the time to write down their war recollections, he simply chose to virtually ignore and not give voice to the obvious when he authored his selected memories of the conflict during the final winter of his life—his silence on this manner speaks volumes.[18]

Royal also demonstrated he possessed the racial prejudices of the American society in which he was raised and lived. The war marked his first encounter with large numbers of African-Americans. In the census of 1860, with a combined resident population of 18,938 people, only thirteen free people of color were recorded as living in Clinton County. Likewise, in adjacent Jackson County, to the north, only eleven free people of African descent are cited among the 18,493 people residing in the county. Of the 674,913 people residing in Iowa in 1860, only 1,069 were free people of African descent.[19] Thus, although he was aware people of color existed, beyond the brief childhood observations he experienced ten years earlier of the African slaves he viewed when his family entered the United States through the port of New Orleans, William Royal Oake would have little opportunity to know, associate with, or even observe people of African descent in Iowa prior to the war. Therefore, his pre-war knowledge of "Negros," as he referred to them, was probably based on local and statewide political discussions concerning secession, columns commenting about slavery in area newspapers, and possibly popular stylized literary representations of African people, such as those depicted in Harriett Beecher Stowe's provocative *Uncle Tom's Cabin*. That Royal possessed a belief of racial superiority base on his lack of association and knowledge of Africans living in America is undeniable. In his memoir Royal demonstrates within his prose a racial prejudice and antipathy toward the African-Americans he encountered in the South. "One who reads letters and diaries of Union soldiers encounters an enormous amount of antipathy toward Negros," observed historian Bell Irvin Wiley. "Expressions of unfriendliness range from blunt statements bespeaking intense hatred to belittling remarks concerning dress and demeanor," Wiley noted. Several factors contributed to the anti-black feeling in the Union army, and it was Wiley's impression many Northern soldiers "were deeply prejudiced before entering the service." Initial pre-war prejudices sometimes were softened by their experiences in the army, but more often the reverse tended to occur. On their marches through the slaveholding region, Royal and his comrades frequently were not opposed to toying with the numerous slaves they encountered for sake of their own crude amusement. Again Wiley noted in his studies that "prejudice and hostility frequently asserted themselves in abuse," and often "mistreatment was no more than a semi-good-natured playing on the freedmen's gullibility and ignorance." Yet from the perspective of the context of the world and society in which he lived, the comments made in the memoir provide glimpses of the racial opinions and social consciousness of the Civil War generation in which he remains fixed by the boundaries of time as a uniquely common representative.[20]

Royal freely employs the terms "Negro" and "darkey," both commonly used in the period, throughout the memoir to describe the numerous slaves he encountered and observed during his war odyssey. While writing of his regiment's arrival in South Carolina, he observes the dark-skinned slaves, representative of the Gullah people who inhabited the coastal low-country region, and describes them as "the true type of the full blooded African Negro." His impression was that they possessed "the low receding forehead, and short kinky crop of wool, together with the broad and flat nose, which would justify a person in placing them in the monkey family rather than human beings." Without actually giving voice to his inner feelings, Royal states that he believes the slaves he met belonged "to a lower physical order than whites." Yet it must be understood that during his war travels Royal encountered a diversity of culture with which he was unfamiliar. The same antipathy held true in his opinion of Southern whites. The major difference was that the enemy soldiers and civilians he waged war against were of sim-ilar heritage—a white heritage. Thus, he possessed—would always pos-sess—from a cultural perspective, far more in common with those he fought than with the slaves he encountered. In his own way, by document-ing within the memoir the distinctive slave language and cultural attributes he experienced in the South—paraphrasing the statements he heard from people of African descent as expressed in the numerous dialects he encoun-tered during his late Southern odyssey—his observations are a strikingly honest commentary on the unique diversity of culture he was privileged to observe.[21]

As far as is known, the original manuscript prepared by William Royal Oake does not exist. The manuscript upon which this book is based is a typed transcription of the original document. When the original document was transcribed and by whom is not known. It was apparent when reading the transcription that the person who deciphered Royal's script possessed little knowledge of the war period, geography, and names of locations and notable figures. It was decided to note the words thus misspelled, note the initial misspelling in brackets, and then use the correct spelling for the remainder of the manuscript. The word "Zazoo" was consistently used for Yazoo River. Familiar with deciphering and reading written documents from the period, this appears to be a highly probable misinterpretation of the original script, and the proper spelling most likely appeared in the original text. In addition, the transcribed memoir consistently had the words "confederate" and "confederacy" spelled in the lower case. It is unknown whether this was actually the case with the original Oake manuscript. If so, it probably illustrates the dislike Royal felt for what he believed was an illegitimate rebellion and formation of a separate government by the Southern states. A similar usage appears in other published histories of the war period. The decision was made to correct each to the more proper Confederate and Confederacy. Readers will also note several dates in the transcribed manuscript were inaccurate and these are indicated and corrected.

Although Royal showed a remarkable recollection of his personal experiences in several notable war events, it was evident he used available published accounts, memoirs, and records from the period to assist him in writing his manuscript. Some passages and statements in this memoir read virtually verbatim from the source he consulted. One such example is the statement Royal makes at the end of his account detailing the conclusion of the campaign against Atlanta in 1864: "Yes, Atlanta was ours, and fairly won." The use of this statement paraphrases a telegraphic communication that Maj. Gen. William T. Sherman wired to Maj. Gen. Henry W. Halleck on September 3, 1864, which officially advised Halleck, "So Atlanta is ours, and fairly won."[22] The use of these paraphrased statements in no way weakens the war observations made by the author. Royal simply utilized the available war historiography to augment his selected memory of events. We must remember he was writing this for his children and regimental comrades, the latter of which would have known the historic context of these paraphrased passages. In addition, where the original prose possessed complicated grammatical issues, or lack of specific clarity, that might cause confusion for the reader, additional words or brief passages were introduced and set apart using parenthesis to provide a more accurate context and flow to the narrative Royal intended his reader to experience. An epilogue was prepared to fill the biographical void concerning his post-war experiences, and a biographical appendix to the text provides supplementary information on many of the people Royal cites in his memoir; those names are marked with an asterisk.

This personal war history written by an average citizen soldier from Iowa complements other scholarship prepared by men on both sides of the quarrel who honorably served during the Civil War. No book-length regimental history has ever been written to document the organization and war history of the men who served with the 26th Iowa Infantry. Perhaps by publishing this post-war memoir, written by a surviving member of the original "Clinton County Regiment," an unfortunate 140-year-old vacuum will finally be eliminated by giving voice to the selected memories of an honorable soldier of the Grand Army of the Republic—Private William Royal Oake.

CHAPTER NOTES:

Introduction

❧ ──────────────── ❧

1. *Roster and Record of Iowa Soldiers in the War of the Rebellion Together with Historical Sketches of Volunteer Organizations 1861-1866.* 6 vols. (Des Moines, 1910), Vol. 3, 1017. Hereafter cited as *Roster*.

2. Ancestry.com. *Ancestry World Tree Project:* Rebecca, 152 entries [database online].

3. The census cites William (senior) age 37, Mary age 36, Elizabeth age 12, Agnes age 10, Nancy age 8, William R. (Royal) age 7, George R. age 5, Robert R. age 2, and Susan age 5 months. The 1841 census spells Agnes as Agness. *Cambridgeshire 1851 Census Index,* Film HO107/1762, Folio 59B, Surname=Oake, Parish or Town=Dullingham, Cambridgeshire Family History Society, 2001 [database online]. www.cambridgeshirehistory.com.

4. James W. Ellis. *History of Jackson County, Iowa.* 2 vols. (Chicago, 1910), "Reminiscences." W. R. Oake, 1: 542–49.

5. Ibid., 544.

6. The household of William Oake (spelled Oak in the census) is found on Schedule 1. Free Inhabitants in Bloomfield Township, Clinton County, Iowa. August 6, 1860, p. 28. The S. O. Crum household is cited on Schedule 1. Free Inhabitants in Deep Creek Township, Clinton County, Iowa. June 22, 1860, p. 8. The fact Royal is on two census schedules might mean he was only a temporary inhabitant at the Crum farm, working and boarding there as a field hand during the early summer harvest, then returned home prior to the census being taken in his own township. Ibid., Ancestry.com. *1860 United States Federal Census* [database online]. Provo, Utah: MyFamily.com, Inc., 2004. Original data: United States. *1860 United States Federal Census.* M653, 1438 rolls. National Archives and Records Administration, Washington D.C.

7. E. B. Long and Barbara Long. *The Civil War Day by Day: An Almanac 1861-1865.* Doubleday & Co., Inc. (Garden City, New York, 1971), 12, 23–34, 55–60.

8. There are two reasonable probabilities for the identity of the farmer who hired Royal in the spring of 1862. It might have been Baily Watts, age 30, who along with his wife Cynthia, age 31, and month-old son, George, resided on a farm (real estate valued over $1,100 in 1860) in Waterford Township near Charlotte; or it may have been Thomas Watts, age 43, who along with his wife Emeline, age 43, and five children, Isaac (13), Thomas (11), Jane (9), Mary (3), and Emeline (4 months), farmed a large farm (valued at $4,000 in 1860) in Deep Creek Township. The 1860 census cites Watts employed a farm hand by the name of Henry Papen, age 20. Ibid., *1860 United States Federal Census* [database online], The Baily Watts household on Schedule 1. Free Inhabitants in Waterford Township, Clinton County, Iowa. June 21, 1860, p. 53; and the Thomas Watts household is cite on Schedule 1. Free Inhabitants in Deep Creek Township, Clinton County, Iowa. June 22, 1860, p. 43.

9. *Roster* cites his name as Oaks, however the "Muster and Descriptive Roll of Company A, 26th Iowa Infantry" cites it correctly as Oake. The "Muster-in Roll" incorrectly gives Lincolnshire, England, as place of birth—Compiled Military Service Record for William R. Oake, National Archives and Records Administration, Washington, D.C. *Roster* 3: 1085.

10. Byers, S. H. M. *Iowa in War Times* (W. D. Condit & Co., Des Moines, 1888), 102, 120, 145–46; Abernathy, Alonzo. *Dedication of Monuments Erected by the State of Iowa. Commemorating the death, suffering and valor of Her Soldiers on the Battlefields of Vicksburg,*

Lookout Mountain, Missionary Ridge, Shiloh, and in the Confederate Prison at Andersonville. State of Iowa (Des Moines, 1906), 200.

11. *Roster* 3: 1017; *Report of the Adjutant General and Acting Quartermaster General of the State of Iowa. January 1, 1863.* 2 vols. (Des Moines, 1865), Vol. 1, 918–21.

12. Ibid., *Roster* 3: 1017–1112.

13. It was apparent, when reading over the manuscript, Royal most likely had not finished the task of editing the memoir.

14. A contemporary of Samuel "Mark Twain" Clemons, Walt Whitman, and other late 19th-century American literary notables, Ambrose Gwinnett Bierce made his reputation after the war, much of it founded on his experiences as a soldier. Born in Meigs City, Ohio, June 24, 1842, Bierce was reared in Indiana, where he was a clerk in a store in Elkhart, when he enlisted in April 1861, for three months service in Co. C, 9th Indiana Infantry, seeing action in western (now West) Virginia before the regiment disbanded in July. In August 1861, he reenlisted as a private in the reorganized 9th Indiana Infantry for three years service. He rose through the ranks, promoted to sergeant and regimental sergeant-major, before being commissioned a second lieutenant on December 1, 1862. In February 1863, he was promoted to first lieutenant and assigned to the brigade headquarters of Gen. William B. Hazen as topographical engineer. Bierce fought at Shiloh, the siege of Corinth, Stones River, Chickamauga, Chattanooga, and throughout the campaign for Atlanta until he was severely wounded in the head at Kennesaw Mountain, Georgia, on June 23, 1864. He returned to active duty in Tennessee during the fall of 1864, fighting with Hazen's brigade at Franklin and Nashville. While in winter quarters at Huntsville, Alabama, he applied for a discharge, and on January 16, 1865, became a civilian. The violence he experienced during the war forever changed his perception of the human condition, and in postwar years, largely through an association with news magnate William Randolph Hearst, Bierce became a nationally recognized satirist. In 1913 he mysteriously disappeared in Mexico, while covering the insurrection waged by Pancho Villa as war correspondent. One of the more plausible conjectures for his demise is he was accidentally slain, in January 1914, during Villa's famous siege of Ojinaga. *Ambrose Bierce's Civil War.* William McCann, ed. (New York, 1956), iii–xi. For a more recent study of his writings on the Civil War, see *Phantoms of a Blood-Stained Period: The Complete Civil War Writings of Ambrose Bierce.* Russell Duncan and David K. Klooster, eds. (University of Massachuetts Press, Amherst, 2002).

15. Fox, William F., *Regimental Losses in The American Civil War 1861-1865.* (Albany, New York, 1889), 435, 516, 519–20.

16. McPherson, James M. *For Cause & Comrades: Why Men Fought in the Civil War,* (New York: Oxford University Press, 1987), 62–67.

17. McPherson notes "relatively few Union volunteers mentioned the slavery issue when they enlisted." Ibid., 19.

18. For a brillant and provocative scholarly examination of racism and how the politics of memory shaped white perceptions of slavery and emancipation in post-war reconstructed American society, see David W. Blight, *Race and ReUnion: The Civil War in American Memory* (Harvard University Press, Cambridge, 2001). Blight likely would conclude the avoidance displayed by William Royal Oake (by not making any reference to slavery as a cause for the war) is illustrative of a shift in political attitudes and racial prejudice among white Americans, North and South. This is far more reflective of post-war developments in national society than it is of similar social and political attitudes held before the war. Blight reveals that the decades following the conflict witnessed the birth of a culture of reunion among white Americans, which downplayed sectional division and emphasized the heroics of a conflict fought between the noble soldiers of the Union and Confederacy. Virtually lost in this emerging national culture was any recognition of the actual antebellum moral crusades over slavery that triggered secession and ignited the war, the presence and effective participation of African people—slave and free—in prosecuting the war, and the promise of emancipation that emerged from the war. Ibid., 119.

19. Census contains statistical analysis on the previous population census recorded in the state, including the 1860 United States Federal Census. John A. T. Hull. *Census of Iowa for 1880* (Des Moines, 1883), 211–12.

20. Bell Irvin Wiley. *The Life of Billy Yank* (Baton Rouge, 1952), 109, 113.

21. Ira Berlin notes the coastal slave culture Royal encountered in and around Savannah, Georgia, and Beaufort, South Carolina, was marked by the development of distinctive song, dance, and language to black life in the low country—known as Gullah, a variant of Atlantic Creole. Wiley, *The Life of Billy Yank*, 113. For further discussion on the attitudes of Union soldiers toward slavery and emancipation, see McPherson, *For Cause & Comrades*, 117–130. Ira Berlin. *Many Thousands Gone: The First Two Centuries of Slavery in America* (Havard: Cambridge, 1998), 174.

22. Maj. Gen. William T. Sherman to Maj. Gen. Henry W. Halleck, September 3, 1864, in *The War of the Rebellion: A Compilation of the Official Records of the Union and Confederate Armies*. 73 vols., 128 parts (Washington, 1880–1901), Ser. I, XXXVIII, Pt. V, 777.

Major General John A. McClernand.
In January 1863, William Royal Oake served briefly under
McClernand's leadership when his regiment suffered heavy casual-
ties in the bloody assault on the Confederate bastion at the Post of
Arkansas. NATIONAL ARCHIVES

CHAPTER ONE

Enlistment and in Camp

The writer of this little work was born in the village of Dullingham, Cambridgeshire, England, on the twenty-sixth day of February 1844, and in the year of 1852 his parents removed to the United States of America, coming direct to Sabula, Jackson County,[1] Iowa. From 1852 to 1857 they resided in the vicinity of Sabula,[2] [and] in the spring of 1857 Father removed upon some government land he had entered situated in Bloomfield Township,[3] Clinton County,[4] Iowa, where we resided at the outbreak of the Great Civil War between the North and the South.

In the spring of 1862, the writer then a boy just past his 18th year[5] hired out to a farmer for six months for twelve dollars per month with board, commencing March first and ending September first. On July first while plowing corn in a field near the main wagon road, which ran by the farm I saw approaching in a two horse wagon a party of men and they were playing a fife and drum. I waited until they came to where I was when they halted, and I learned that it was a recruiting officer getting recruits for the 18th Iowa Infantry[6] then being raised and going into a rendezvous at Clinton,[7] Iowa. In the wagon were two young men that had enlisted that day and with whom I was well acquainted. One of them in fact had been a schoolmate of mine in 1855 and 1856.

After conversing with them a short time the recruiting officer asked me to join. I thought the matter over for a few moments when I replied I thought I would not enlisted just at present as I had hired out to Mr. Watts (That being my employers name) until September first, and that I did not want to leave him in such a busy time. He replied, "Will you enlist if Mr. Watts is willing to let you off?" After thinking the matter over for a few moments I replied in the affirmative. He then drove up to the house to see my employer, and after a short time returned informing me that Mr. Watts stated that I could do as I pleased although he did not like to lose me just at that time, but that if I thought best to enlist I had his consent, and his best wishes would be for my welfare.

Driving the team with which I had been plowing corn with up to the house I found my employer at work near the house. I asked him if he had told the officer he was willing to let me go. With a smile he looked at me and replied, "Yes I told him so, at the same time Royal I hate to see you enlist. You have given entire satisfaction since you have been with me, and while I can manage to get along for help, I don't think you fully realize what you will have to go through as a soldier."

Unhitching and putting in the barn the team with which I had been working I returned to the house and wrapping up my few needed clothes I told my employer that he could pay what was coming to me to my father, (nearly three months wages), and shaking hands with all of the family I bid them Good Bye.

At this time the recruiting officer was making his headquarters while out drumming up recruits at the home of his brother-in-law Garrett Davenpeet[8] who was running the county Farm[9] near Charlotte,[10] Clinton County, Iowa. At the above named place we stayed the first night, and the next day went to Clinton, Iowa and drew our uniforms.[11]

After being rigged out in a suit of Uncle Sam's blue, and the side of my hat fastened up with a big brass eagle about the size of your hand I thought all I would have to do would be to show Jeff Davis[12] my fighting rig, and the boasted confederacy[13] would at once collapse.

The first two weeks after enlisting I spent most of the time around the country with the recruiting officer in visiting some of my schoolmates assisting him in getting recruits. Right here I will mention that the recruiting officer's name was Elijah H. Frank,* 27 years of age, a native of New York

State, who had for several years prior to the breaking out of the rebellion been engaged in teaching the public schools. Frank was a gentleman in the fullest sense of the word, and beloved by all that was acquainted with him, but was destined to sacrifice his life on the alter of his country, an account of which will be given later on.

On my trips through the country I paid a visit to my parents, who up to this time did not know that I had enlisted. Never will I forget the look my mother gave me when she first saw me as I entered the home. She did not speak for several minutes, but seating herself in a chair gave vent to a fit of sobbing as though her heart would break. After a few minutes she looked up and said, "Royal, why did you do that?" I replied, "Mother it is no more than thousands of others are doing, and I don't think the war will last much longer anyway, and I believe I will come out all right."

My father took it more philosophically, but at the same time thought I had done wrong in enlisting without consulting them.[14]

After remaining at home a few days I returned to camp at Clinton, and most of the two following months of August and September were spent in drilling and learning the manual of arms. Early in August the 18th [Regiment Iowa Infantry] being full (in fact there were twelve companies[15] in camp at the time) its commander[16] received orders to proceed to Sedalia, Missouri, and that two companies would have to remain over for the next regiment, the 26th,[17] that would rendezvous at the same camp. Our Captain S. [Sherman] R. Williams[18] being a little ambitious and thinking that perhaps if his company would be one of two companies that would remain over that perhaps he could get a Majors commission in the 26th Iowa, but as subsequent events show, when the regiment left for the front he still held a Captain['s] commission.

During our stay in our camp at Clinton (Camp Kirkwood,[19] that being the name of the camp, named in honor of the Governor of the State*[20]) occurred one sad incident that threw a gloom over the entire camp. In Company A of which the writer was a member were two brothers Alonzo[21] and George H. [M.] Peck,[22] both of whom lived in the same neighborhood, and attended the same district school as the writer did. As is customary in camps of instruction we had an old cannon that was used in firing at sunrise and at sunset. On one quite frosty morning in the first part of October[23] just before sunrise the writer arose, and walked out of the barracks in which we were to the fire where the Company cooks were preparing breakfast, which was about fifty feet from and directly in the rear of the aforesaid gun. At that time Alonzo Peck came out of the Company quarters walking towards the fire, and when within about six feet of the fire stopped and faced the gun to witness a soldier who just at that moment was in the act of firing it off. Upon being fired it burst into fragments terribly mangling poor Peck,[24] and from which he died on the morning of October 20th, 1862 without regaining consciousness.[25]

On the 18th of September the regiment was presented with a beautiful flag[26] by the Clinton County Agricultural Society, and on September 26th the Irish Ladies of Clinton and vicinity presented Company G 26th (that being an Irish Company) with a beautiful banner. About the 20th of October the Commander of the regiment, [Col. Milo Smith*] received orders to proceed to St. Louis and report to Major General [Samuel R.] Curtis.*[27] Well does the writer remember that memorable occasion of the regiment falling into line, and marching through the streets of Clinton to the steamboat landing to board the good old steamer *Denmark*[28] that was to convey us to St. Louis. It was quite an imposing sight as nearly one thousand men[29] preceded by a fine martial band and flags fluttering in the October breeze marched to the wharf. Upon arriving at the landing it was some little time before we marched on board of the boat the time being spend in shaking hands and bidding friends good bye. Many there were in the regiment that were leaving their wives and young family and in some instances for the last time. At last the boat bell rang, and orders to march on board were given.[30] All being on board the boat swung out on the broad bosom of the Mississippi and while the band played Dixie[31] we gave three times three rousing cheers, which was heartily responded to by friends on shore shaking hankerchiefs [handkerchiefs] and waving us a long good bye, and to many it proved to be a final good bye.

The following is a list of **Field and Staff** [32] of the 26th Iowa with their home address:

Colonel Milo Smith*   Clinton, Iowa
Lieutenant Colonel Samuel G. Magill[33]   Lyons   "
Major Samuel Clark[34]   DeWitt   "
Adjutant Thomas G. Ferreby[35]   Marion   "
Quarter Master Joseph H. Flint[36]   Lyons   "
Surgeon Alijah [Abijah] T. Hudson[37]   Lyons   "
Assistant Surgeon William MacQuigg[38]   Cammanche [Camanche]   "
Assistant Surgeon George F. Weatherell[39]   Mechanicsville   "
Chaplin John McLeish, Junior[40]   Clinton   "
Sergeant Major Joseph D. Fegan[41]   Wheatland   "
Quarter Master Sergeant David M. Cooper[42]   Lyons   "
Commissary Sergeant Henry L. Walker[43]   Clinton   "
Hospital Steward William H. Young[44]   Clinton   "
Hospital Steward John A. Ladd[45]   Wheatland   "
Drum Major Albert Linton[46]   Clinton   "
Field Major Robert Ralson [Ralston], Junior[47]   Clinton   "

Line Officers
Company A
Captain Sherman R. Williams[48]   Lyons   Iowa
1st Lieutenant Asa Franklin[49]   Northwood   "
2nd Lieutenant Alanson D. Gaston[50]   Lyons   "

Company B
Captain James W. Eckles[51]   Fulton Iowa
1st Lieutenant Alva Wilson[52]   Maquoketa   "
2nd Lieutenant Thomas B. Harrison[53]   Maquoketa   "

Company C
Captain George W. Johnson[54]   Clinton Iowa
1st Lieutenant Peter L. Hyde[55]   Clinton   "
2nd Lieutenant James McDill[56]   Clinton   "

Company D

Captain Nathaniel A. Merrell[57]	DeWitt	Iowa
1st Lieutenant James H. Runyon[58]	DeWitt	"
2nd Lieutenant John F. Gilmore[59]	DeWitt	"

Company E

Captain John Lubbers[60]	Clinton	Iowa
1st Lieutenant Edward Svendsen[61]	Clinton	"
2nd Lieutenant Preben Hansen[62]	Clinton	"

Company F

Captain Joel B. Bishop[63]	DeWitt	Iowa
1st Lieutenant William R. Ward[64]	DeWitt	"
2nd Lieutenant Silas Freeman[65]	DeWitt	"

Company G

Captain James H. Heavey[66]	Lyons	Iowa
1st Lieutenant John Quinn[67]	Lyons	"
2nd Lieutenant Philip McCahill[68]	Lyons	"

Company H

Captain Charles M. Nye[69]	DeWitt	Iowa
1st Lieutenant James S. Patterson[70]	DeWitt	"
2nd Lieutenant John Barrett[71]	DeWitt	"

Company I

Captain Edwin A. Wemple[72]	Wheatland	Iowa
1st Lieutenant John L. Steele[73]	Wheatland	"
2nd Lieutenant Edwin W. Bennett[74]	Wheatland	"

Company K

Captain Nelson C. Roe[75]	Lyons	Iowa
1st Lieutenant Nathan D. Hubbard[76]	Lyons	"
2nd Lieutenant Lucius Pomeroy[77]	Lyons	"

After leaving Clinton we ran down to Point Byron,[78] and remained there and at LeClaire [Le Claire][79] until morning. While crossing from the former to the latter place Thomas Montague[80] of Company K fell overboard and was drowned. During the night another soldier Anthony Cain[81] of Company I was missed but at the time it was not thought he had met with a similar fate, but had deserted.[82]

We left LeClaire at daybreak October 21st and arrived at East Davenport[83] at 8 A. M. Here Colonel Smith ordered the Regiment ashore not deeming it safe for his men to remain on board while going through the Rock Island bridge. The Regiment was formed in line, and marched through Davenport to the levee below the bridge. Here Adjutant General [Nathaniel B.] Baker[84] gave us a beautiful silk flag regulation pattern sent to us by the Government as our Regimental colors. It was a noticeable fact that all the time we were in Davenport not a shout or cheer was heard, the boys no doubt fearing that any such demonstration might be taken by the State authorities located there as a compliment for the (efficient) arms[85] furnished us.

At Davenport we took in tow a Barge which made our situation more comfortable. We did not cross over the river to Rock Island until dark. A strong wind blowing against us prevented our progress sooner. Two commissioned officers and squad of men were left by remaining up town too long. On October 22nd we passed Burlington, [Iowa], at daybreak where the Captain of the *Denmark* insisted on leaving one of the two barges we had in tow, and would not yield until told by Colonel Smith that there were pilots and engineers in the Regiment, and unless things were conducted satisfactorily to him he would take possession, and run the institution himself.[86]

October 23rd[87] arrived at St. Louis, [Missouri], about 10 A. M. where we learned that the Regiment had been reported as fully armed and equipped ready for the field, and that a boat was in readiness to take us to Helena, Arkansas. The truth of the matter was eight companies had in fact no arms at all, though they were nominally fully supplies, but the miserable old second-handed muskets given them were worse than none, for the men had no confidence in them.[88] As for equipments, we had no tents, no fatigue suit, no hats, no shirts, no knapsacks, no haversacks, no canteens, and almost nothing.[89] General Curtis however supplied us with all those, and addition to what has been named he also supplied us with wagons, harness mules, beef cattle and promised better arms if they were in the arsenal.

October 24th about 9 o'clock A. M. [we] left the *Denmark*, formed the Regiment, and marched through the streets for a short time to show the boys the City, and the City the boys, as well as to take a little much needed exercise. We came to a halt on the steamer *Imperial*[90] bound for our destination, Helena, Arkansas. We found four Companies of the 24th Iowa, Temperance Regiment,[91] already on board bound for the same point in Rebeldom.[92] The loading of the clothing, equipments and stores occupied all the remainder of that day, and was not then finished.

October 25th the work of loading continued, and was finished about the middle of the forenoon. We were then about to leave, and no better guns yet, when several wagons drove up and commenced to unload a number of strong boxes marked Enfield Muskets, Rifled. A shout went up from our boat, and kept going up for a while, which showed conclusively that the boys of the 26th wanted arms they could fight with, and that fighting to kill was the business they proposed engaging in three years or during the war unless soon discharged.[93]

The companies were marched on shore and relieved of their old muskets. The new muskets were then brought on board and soon we were on our way to the land of cotton.

On Sunday evening October 26th while the *Imperial* was lying at Buford Bend[94] taking on wood, occurred a laughable incident. Mr. Buckner (Cousin of the Secessionist General[95] of that name) owner of the wood yard came on board for the Yankee balm where he was closely questioned, and his answers not precisely coming up to the standard of loyalty he was invited to take the oath.[96] At first he seemed inclined to repudiate the idea, but the significant and persuasive arguments used by the officers induced him to comply, and accordingly, 1st Lieutenant [Asa] Franklin of Company A 26th Regiment taking him by the arm and led him up to Lieutenant [James W.] Strong[97] of the 24th Regiment, where he was fairly initiated into the beautiful rights and benefits of this glorious Union.

Before taking the oath he assured the bystanders that Secessionist script [scrip][98] was good as gold, but when one of the officers of the boat tendered him $15.00 of that trash in part payment for his wood he backed out and said that the U.S. Treasury Notes were better to buy salt with, an article which he stood much in need of. He seemed after coming aboard the boat to be threatened with a regular Mississippi chill, and to add to his discomfort the boys made him believe that one of the Darkies had blown upon him.[99] After enjoying a rich treat and carrying him some five or six miles down the river the boat was landed and he was put ashore to proceed as leisurely as he pleased to his home. A wiser if not a better man.

I had neglected to mention the fact that four companies of the 24th Iowa were also on board of the *Imperial* that Regiment also having received orders to proceed to Helena, Arkansas.

After leaving our Secessionist afore mentioned we continued on our way and without any further incident arrived at our destination Helena,[100] on the morning of October 28th, and after a short time marched ashore to what was to be our camp while in Helena, and which proved to be an old cotton field one mile South of town.

I distinctly remember that occasion of marching through the cotton field, a good share of which had not been harvested, and the little white balls of cotton sticking on the plants was something new to the northern soldier. For several days after our arrival we were kept busy in preparing the ground for our camp, to make it as comfortable as possible as it was supposed that we would remain there for sometime. In fact it was our camp until early in December when all the troops in that vicinity embarked on steamers and went South to take part in the first attack on Vicksburg.[101]

While in camp at Helena a great many of the soldiers were sick, which was a common experience of all Northern troops in the early period of their service, but the conditions which the troops near Helena encountered were uncommonly bad.[102]

Upon our arrival in Helena we were temporarily assigned to the First Brigade, Fourth Division, Army of the South West,[103] General Alvin P. Hovey in command.[104] During our stay in Helena occurred an incident that deprived the Regiment of its lieutenant colonel and major. After a few weeks of camp life our Lieutenant Colonel Magill, Major Clark and our Chief Surgeon Major Hudson decided to make a little trip in the country as a diversion from the monotony of camp life, and after getting a short distance outside of the picket lines were surprised, and Lieutenant Colonel Sam

Magill and the major were captured[105] by the enemy the fleetness of the surgeon's horse enabling him to escape. The colonel and major were paroled shortly afterward when they returned to their homes in Iowa and shortly afterward resigned.

During the month of November the Regiment took part in an expedition to the Talahatchie [Tallahatchie] River,[106] a distance of about 50 [30] miles. The object of the move being to divert the attention of the enemy from [Major] General [Ulysses S.] Grant's* Army [of the Tennessee] [advancing] down along the line of the Mississippi Central Railroad toward Vicksburg.[107] Embarking on board steamboats, [the morning of November 27th], the command under General Hovey[108] proceeded down the river a distance of about 10 miles landing at a place called Old Town[109] from which place the troops marched towards the junction of the Tallahatchie and Cold Water [Coldwater][110] Rivers. After a four days march we reached the junction[111] of the Tallahatchie and Coldwater where we encamped for three days during an exceedingly disagreeable time it raining most of the time, and having no tents and a good many of the troops being new troops and unused to such hardships there was a good deal of suffering and sickness.

As was customary with the troops at the early period of the war every soldier carried a knapsack with woolen blankets overcoat and extra clothing together with haversack canteen gun and equipment made a load of at least fifty pounds more than many of the soldiers were able to carry. The consequence was that there was a good deal of straggling from the ranks of those unable to carry so heavy a load, while many others would throw away blankets, overcoats and extra clothing and the road the entire distance was strewn with discarded clothing.

On our arrival at the rivers above named it rained very hard; we went into camp near an old plantation on which were a good many outbuildings, most of which were set on posts above the ground about two feet, giving plenty of room underneath for chickens and hogs to run under the buildings.

After camping and getting our supper the rain continued to pour down and we were wet to the skin. The writer concluded he would try and hunt some place in the dry to sleep if possible. Going over to the plantation afore mentioned I managed to squeeze in under one of the outbuildings, and while it was not quite as comfortable a bed as I had been used to sleeping in at home in Old Iowa I was protected from the incessant rain and managed to put in a fairly good nights rest. I remember the next morning after crawling out of my bed from under the building of course on going to bed our clothes were wet through and as it was very dusty and dry under the building the dry dust would naturally adhere to our wet clothes. We did not look a bit like the fine military pictures generally displayed in the windows of Uncle Sam's Recruiting Offices. Me thinks that if some of the young men of the present time could have seen our fine military appearance at that time it would have put a crimp in their military aspiration.

Although upon emerging from our sleeping quarters we were covered with the beautiful gray dust of Mississippi soil it soon disappeared as the rain continued and washed it off, and we were soon resplendent in Uncle Sam's coat of blue.

During our first days camp at this place there was no let up to the rain and our camp being in the edge of a canebrake swamp the boys were busy building Indian Tepees to protect them from the rain. We would select four bunches of canebrake about the right distance apart, and tie the tops together—then we would cut and pile more around our frame until the sides were a foot thick, but it would rain through it in spite of us. A short distance from our camp was an old Cotton Gin and quite a lot of refuse cotton, which we carried in our arms to our Tepees for a bed the next night, and while it made a much softer bed than the bare ground we were a sight the next morning. Our clothes being wet the cotton stuck fast, and unlike the dust it would not wash off. We looked like a flock of geese half picked.

After remaining here two days we received orders to march back to the landing at the river, and return to our camp at Helena.[112] After returning to our camp at Helena the usual routine of camp life occupied our time—drill and picket duty—a monotonous duty to a soldier who would always rather be on an active campaign. At our camp in Helena the Regiment was supplied with tents each tent would accommodate five men. In the tent in which the writer was were four others as follows: Elijah H. Frank,[113] Henry Preffer,[114] John McLain [also spelled McLane][115] and George M. Peck, the latter being a brother of Alonzo Peck mentioned earlier[116] in this work as being killed at Clinton, Iowa, and who was also a schoolmate of the writer. Henry Preffer and John McLain were two young Canadians that had in June 1862

Enlistment and in Camp

prior to their enlistment come from their home in Canada to visit friends living in Charlotte, Clinton County, Iowa, and had enlisted in the 26th Iowa. Both of them were fine young men, Preffer being 26 years of age and McLain 24. I will remember one night at Helena after retiring to our tent for the night of a wish that McLain made as follows, "Boys, I wish I knew how many of us five in this tent will return from the war." Poor McLain in less than three weeks time[117] it was the sad duty of the writer as being one of a file of six soldiers to fire over his grave. Poor John after a very short illness with lung trouble his military career was over. This one of the five would never return.[118]

During our stay at Helena Captain S. R. Williams our Company Commander tendered his resignation and returned to his home at Lyons, Iowa, leaving 1st Lieutenant Asa Franklin in command of Company A.

At this time, [Major] General [William T.] Sherman's* headquarters were at Memphis, and [he] was at that time in command of the right wing of the 13th Army Corps[119] aggregating about 40,000 men.[120] About the 18th of December, orders were issued for all troops in the department to embark on board steamboats and proceed to the vicinity of Vicksburg.[121]

After boarding the boats[122] we proceeded leisurely on our way down the river and it certainly was an imposing sight - 150 crafts of all kinds composed the fleet.[123] At night the boats would tie up, running in day light only. When tied up at night it looked like a city on each side of the river as far as the eye could see. The lights from that huge fleet twinkled like the lights of a modern city, while the strains of music from both martial and brass bands as it was wafted over the placid bosom of the mighty river made it a sight and time to be long remembered.

On our journey down the river the army moved by divisions as on land, and every mile or so would be scattered, through the fleet of transports, an Iron Clad [ironclad gunboat][124] with their ports open, and the black muzzles of shotted[125] guns protruding ready if any bands of the enemy saw fit to fire upon the fleet.

About December 24th the fleet reached Milliken's Bend[126] where [next day] a portion of the army landed and broke up the Vicksburg, [Shreveport] and Texas Railroad[127] for a long way. The balance of the army pushed on to a point opposite the mouth of the Yazoo River[128] where another portion of the army landed and broke up the same railroad to within 8 miles of Vicksburg.[129]

On the morning of December 26th the transports led and convoyed by the gunboat fleet under Admiral D. D. Porter* ascended the old mouth of the Yazoo, about 12 miles. On the transports were four divisions of troops, Generals [George W.] Morgan,* [Frederick] Steele,* Morgan L. Smith* and A. J. Smith*.[130]

By noon on the 27th[131] the entire command had disembarked on the south side of the river near the mouth of the Chickasaw Bayou,[132] a small stream which rising near the town of Vicksburg finds its way across the bottom land about midway between bluffs and river.[133]

During the afternoon of the 27th[134] the troops were gotten into position and on December 28th and 29th was fought the Battle of Chickasaw Bayou. It is not the intention of the writer to try to give an account of the battle as that has already been done by abler and parties more competent to do so, and although Sherman's army was repulsed no troops in the world fought better than did Sherman's army at Chickasaw Bayou. The natural condition of the ground itself over which the troops fought, without being defended by an armed and determined foe,[135] was enough to defeat the bravest of brave. To fully understand the situation it will be necessary to give a partial description of the ground over which our army had to advance to attack the enemy.

The Vicksburg and Yazoo City public road ran along the roof of a range of hills[136] that were honeycombed with the enemy's rifle pits,[137] and artillery, while between the Federal troops and said enemy's works the ground was very swampy, in fact at places almost impassable, the condition of the ground being unknown to our officers at the time. The attacking force moved steadily forward under a galling fire until within a short distance of the enemy's first line when they were confronted with aforesaid swamp as well as by a terrific fire from muskets and artillery such as no troops in the world could withstand, but for a short time they held the ground, then gradually fell back, with many a poor fellow left in the swamp never to be found.[138]

Although the 26th Iowa were present at the battle we took no active part being one of four regiments kept back as a reserve to protect the steamboat landing.[139] After the failure of the first attack it was decided by General Sherman to change the position of the troops [Steele's divison], and in conjunction with the Navy to again attempt the rebel position, but owing to a dense fog that prevented the ironclads from getting into position, and not hearing from General Grant who was moving South to cooperate with him, General Sherman decided to abandon the attack and return to Milliken's Bend.[140]

On the morning [evening and night] of January 1 [- 2], 1863, the [remaining] troops [ashore] were embarked and at the middle of the afternoon [January 2] the transports under convoy and protection of the gunboats passed out of the Yazoo River into the Mississippi. At the mouth of the Yazoo River, General Sherman met and reported to [Major] General [John A.] McClernand who had come down the river on the Steamer *Tigress* with orders to assume command of the troops in that department.[141]

On arrival at Milliken's Bend: January 4th [2nd], General Sherman at once relinquished the command to General McClernand, who brought with him an order[142] issued by the War Department dividing the Army of the Tennessee into four separate army corps to be know as the 13th, 15th, 16th and 17th; General Sherman to be in command of the 15th corps; General Frederick Steele to be in command of the First Division of the 15th corps, the division to which the 26th Iowa had been assigned, it being in the 3rd Brigade of said division. The brigade being commanded by Brigadier General John M. Thayer.*

While lying at Millikens Bend General Sherman suggested to General McClernand the advisability of taking a portion of the army and in conjunction with the ironclads under the command of Admiral Porter steam up to Arkansas Post and clean out that "hornets nest," Fort Hindman,[143] situated, on the north bank of the Arkansas River, and about 50 miles from its mouth. General McClernand having heartily approved of the plan, it was decided to embark for that purpose [the] two divisions of the 13th Corps under the command of General Morgan L. Smith and [the] two divisions of the 15th Corps under command of General Sherman, the gunboats under Porter to assist.

Enlistment and in Camp

1. Organized in 1838, the county is named for Andrew Jackson, seventh president of the United States. It is situated west of the Mississippi River, south of Dubuque County, east of Jones County, and north of Clinton County. Before the Civil War, 8,231 people lived in the county, with an estimated 450 residents of Sabula (population 480 in 1854) in 1852. A. T. Andreas, *Illustrated Historical Atlas of the State of Iowa* (Des Moines, 1875), 443. Hereafter cited as *Historical Atlas.* John A. T. Hull, Secretary of State, *Census of Iowa for 1880* (Des Moines, 1883), 508–9. Hereafter cited as *Census.*

2. Located opposite of Savannah, Illinois, Sabula was founded in 1836 and officially surveyed the following year. Initially called Carrollport, and later Charleston, in 1846 the city was renamed Sabula after the Latin word *sabulum,* which means sand, a direct reference to the river-borne surface deposit upon which the small island community was founded and exists today, only a few feet above the annual flood of the Upper Mississippi River. James W. Ellis, *History of Jackson County.* 2 vols. (Chicago, 1910), 1: 522. Hereafter cited as *Jackson County.* *"Island City" Sabula* (Sabula: Bicentennial Days Commission, 1976), 3.

3. Around 1855, Congressional Townships 82 and 83 north, of Range 3 east, located in northern Clinton County, were set off from Brookfield Precinct and named Bloomfield. When first settled by European and American immigrants, the township contained little timber, the rolling terrain instead covered by native tall-grass prairie. The land where William Oake settled his family consisted of 80 acres situated on the northern watershed of Deep Creek, in Section 13, roughly nine miles southeast of Maquoketa, Iowa. *The History of Clinton County, Iowa, Containing A History of the County, its Cities, Towns, Etc.* (Chicago, 1879), 626-27; "Obituary of Wm. Oake," *Sabula Gazette* (May 1903), Miscellaneous files, Sabula (Iowa) Public Library.

4. Named in honor of the two-time governor of the state of New York, DeWitt Clinton, this county (organized by an act of the Territorial Legislature during the winter of 1839–1840) lies in a great eastern bend of the Mississippi River, nearly midway on the eastern boundary of the state, directly west of Chicago. The majority of the population (recorded as being 18,938 in 1860) lived along the river (with only 840 of the county residents living in Bloomfield Township). At the time of the Civil War the county seat was the town of De Witt, situated near the county's geographic center. *Historical Atlas,* 484; *Census,* 211, 462; *Portrait and Biographical Album of Clinton County,* Iowa, (Chicago. 1886), 678. Hereafter cited as *Portrait and Biographical Album.*

5. Royal turned 18 on February 26. He immediately left home, hiring out to work for another farmer the same week.

6. The 18th Regiment Iowa Volunteer Infantry was organized under authority of Special Orders from the War Department, dated May 21–23, 1862. The ten companies composing the regiment were ordered into quarters by Governor Samuel Kirkwood on dates ranging from June 10 to July 21, 1862. The designated rendezvous for the regiment was Clinton, Iowa. The camp of organization and instruction was named "Kirkwood," in honor of the governor. Iowa Adjutant General, *Roster and Record of Iowa Soldiers in the War of the Rebellion.* 6 vols. (Des Moines, 1910), 3: 117. Hereafter cited as *Roster.*

7. Founded in 1834 and christened "New York," the river community had grown substantially over the last 28 years. Situated on the western shore of the Mississippi River, near the midway point of a prominent bend, in 1838 the community was renamed "Clinton" in honor of Governor DeWitt Clinton of New York. The actual "Clinton" rendezvous site for organizing companies of volunteers was located immediately north of Clinton on the southwestern out-skirts of another independent community called Ringwood. Everett A. Strait, "Once Upon a Time," *Clinton Herald*, 3 vols., Vol. 1: 3, 21.

8. This could be Garrett Davenpeck. There is no individual named Davenpeet listed on the 1860 census for Clinton County, Iowa, and the only person residing in the county with a similar last name in 1870 was Garrett Davenpeck, who lived in Weldon Township, a few miles southwest of the town of Charlotte, in neighboring Waterford Township. "Iowa 1870 Federal Census Index, Weldon Township, Clinton County," 452.

9. Often also called "poorhouses," or by the older term, "alms houses," and commonly known as poor—or county—farms in rural agriculture communities. From the early 19th century to the New Deal era, alms houses dominated the structure of public welfare in America, as tax-support-ed residential institutions to which people were required to go if they could not support them-selves. They were started as a method of providing a less expensive (to the taxpayers) alternative to what modern American society knows as "welfare"—what then was called "outdoor relief." Destitute people could request help from the community Overseer of the Poor (sometimes also called a Poor Master), an elected county (or town) official. If the need was great or likely to be long-term, destitute individuals or families were sent to the poorhouse (farm) instead of being given relief while they continued to live independently. On the county farm they worked the land raising crops, produce, and livestock to provide food for residents. Despite the growing level of poverty in the United States, and good intentions of society, this early system of social assistance inspired considerable dread among the poor, who generally used them only as refuges of last resort. Paul S. Boyer, ed., *The Oxford Companion to United States History* (New York: Oxford University Press, 2001), 27; "History of 19th Century American Poorhouses," http://www.poorhousestory.com/history.htm/.

10. The small Clinton County village of Charlotte is cited as Royal's wartime residence on com-pany (enlistment) muster-in rolls. This small hamlet is located on a watershed of Deep Creek in Waterford Township, roughly four and one-half miles southeast of the Oake homestead in Bloomfield Township. *Roster* 3: 1085; *Compiled Military Service Record of William Royal Oake, Co. A, 26 Reg't Iowa Infantry*, "Company Muster-in Roll, National Archives Record Group 77 (Washington, D.C.). Hereafter cited as *CMSR, Wm. Royal Oake.*

11. The "Company Muster-in Roll" cites William Royal Oake, age 18, enlisted on July 7, 1862 (published as July 11 in *Roster* 3: 1085), for three years service as a private in Co. A, 26th Regiment Iowa Infantry. The place of his enlistment is documented correctly as being Charlotte. The muster records his birthplace incorrectly as Lincolnshire, England. He is cited as being a farmer by occupation, and listed being five feet, eight inches in height, possessing brown eyes and brown hair, and as having a fair complexion. Royal received a $25 bounty for his enlistment, along with a $2 premium paid. Company A was officially mustered into the service of the United States on August 30, 1862, by Captain H. B. Hendershott of the Regular Army, who was the mus-tering officer for each company, eight of which, with the field and staff officers, were mustered on September 30, 1862. Company F was the last company to be mustered (October 1, 1862), when the organization of the regiment was complete. *CMSR*; *Roster* 3: 1017, 1085.

12. Jefferson Davis (1808–1889), graduate of the U.S. Military Academy at West Point, veteran of the Mexican War, renowned Mississippi congressman and senator, and previously secretary of war under President Franklin Pierce, then currently serving as president of the Confederate States of America. Mark M. Boatner, III, *The Civil War Dictionary* (New York: David McKay Co., 1959), 225. Hereafter cited as *Civil War Dictionary.*

13. Royal consistently spells Confederacy using a lower case "c" throughout the transcribed manuscript. This is apparently how the old war veteran exhibited a feeling of distain, even at this late period in his life, for what he considered an illegal government formed in open rebellion to the sovereignty of the United States.

14. As already discussed in the introduction to this memoir, it appears William, Sr., and especially Mary Oake undoubtedly exercised considerable pressure to keep their young son from enlisting prior to his eighteenth birthday. However, having left the Oake farm to work as a laborer on a nearby homestead, Royal was finally separated from their parental influence and control for the first time in his life. Although the young man was now of legal age to exercise his own judgment and make decisions for his own welfare, it seems probable that he became caught up in the second wave of patriotism and enlistment fever then sweeping through Iowa during the summer of 1862. With the United States experiencing a second Fourth of July consumed by violent civil war, it is reasonable to consider this young volunteer was manifestly influenced by peer pressure to enlist for military service.

15. The company was the basic organizational unit and was ideally composed of 100 men (97 enlisted men and noncommissioned officers) and commanded by a captain who was assisted by one first and one second lieutenant. A regiment of infantry was made up of ten companies, and a cavalry regiment was composed of twelve companies. Webb Garrison & Cheryl Garrison, *The Encyclopedia of Civil War Usage: An Illustrated Compendium of the Everyday Language of Soldiers and Civilians* (Nashville: Cumberland House, 2001), 53, 210. Hereafter cited as *Civil War Usage*.

16. The regimental commander was 49-year-old Col. John Edwards, a lawyer and legislator from Chariton, Iowa, who previously was appointed a lieutenant colonel on the staff of Governor Kirkwood. Edwards commanded the 18th Iowa from August 1862 until discharged to accept promotion as brigadier general of United States volunteers, November 7, 1864. After the war, President Andrew Johnson appointed him assessor of internal revenue at Fort Smith, Arkansas, from where he later served as a reconstruction period U.S. congressman for the Liberal Republican Party. He later moved to Washington, D.C., earning a living through his legal talents until he died on April 8, 1894, and was buried in Arlington National Cemetery. Boatner, *Civil War Dictionary,* 261; Ezra J. Warner, *Generals in Blue: Lives of the Union Commanders* (Baton Rouge: Louisiana State University Press, 1964), 137–38. Hereafter cited as *Generals in Blue.*

17. Records show that the ten companies of which the 26th Regiment Iowa Infantry was composed were all enrolled in Clinton County. Even though it included men from other counties, the large number of enlistments from within Clinton County caused the regiment to be known locally and across the state as the "Clinton" or "Clinton County Regiment" throughout the war. The county ultimately sent approximately 2,700 men into the field. *Roster* 3: 1017, 1028–1112; *Portrait and Biographical Album,* 681.

18. Born in New York, Sherman R. Williams was 31 years old and residing in Lyons, Iowa, when he mustered in as captain of Co. A, 26th Iowa Infantry on July 28, 1862. Five months later, on December 29, 1862, he resigned his commission while the regiment was temporarily stationed at Helena, Arkansas, and apparently returned to his home in Lyons. *Roster* 3: 1105.

19. The regimental rendezvous was named Camp Kirkwood. Previously, in August 1861, another training camp with the same name was established at Council Bluffs, Iowa. The second Camp Kirkwood was established on the southwestern outskirts of the independent community of Ringwood, which was a short distance north of Clinton. When Ringwood was platted as a city in 1856, a large sector lying between the town and the bluffs farther west of the river was fenced off and designated as a suitable site for fairs and circuses. Although little more than a glorified pasture by 1862, the fairgrounds served as a convenient location to station the incoming companies of recruits. In 1873, a merger was arranged between the two communities, and Ringwood was incorporated as part of the city of Clinton (the city has grown substantially since its founding in 1834 when it was known as "New York," and eventually it adopted, or merged with, three other independent cities: Lyons, Chancy, and Ringwood). Today the original site of the Ringwood fairgrounds (Camp Kirkwood) is located at 10th Avenue North and 4th Street in modern Clinton. Strait, "Once Upon a Time," 1: 3, 21. Steve Meyer, *Iowans Called to Valor: The Story of Iowa's Entry into the Civil War* (Garrison, Iowa: Meyer Publishing, 1993), 44.

20. The governor of Iowa, Samuel Jordan Kirkwood, was born in Harford City, Maryland, on December 20, 1813. A lawyer and public official in Ohio, Kirkwood moved to Iowa City, Iowa, in 1855, to become a farmer and miller. Highly regarded for integrity and financial good sense, Kirkwood soon won election to the state senate in 1856. Elected governor in 1860 and 1862, he was particularly active in organizing and raising Iowa's allotment of soldiers for the United States Army. Throughout his tenure as governor, he repeatedly urged President Lincoln toward emancipation and the use of "black soldiers." Though Kirkwood favored conscription, under his direction Iowa was one of the few states able to fulfill troop quotas without resorting to the draft. After the war he served as a U.S. senator and as secretary of the interior in the James A. Garfield administration. He died in Iowa City, Iowa, on September 1, 1894. Patricia L. Faust, ed., *Historical Times Illustrated Encyclopedia of the Civil War* (New York: Harper & Row, 1986), 420. Hereafter cited as *Encyclopedia of the Civil War*.

21. William Alonzo Peck was 28, a native of New York and a resident of Charlotte, when he enlisted July 20, 1862. *Roster* 3: 1086. For all biographical citations from this point on, unless an individual resided in another state or country, the reader should make note the town or county cited as residence upon their enlistment is (or was) located in the state of Iowa.

22. Alonzo's younger brother, George M. Peck, age 21, was born in Michigan and enlisted July 11, 1862. George died of disease on March 4, 1863, and is buried in the National Cemetery in Memphis, Tennessee. *Roster* 3: 1086.

23. The tragic accident occurred on Sunday morning, October 12, 1862. *Clinton Herald*, Saturday, October 18, 1862.

24. The brief notice in the *Clinton Herald* reports Private Peck was struck by one piece of the cannon, which shattered his right leg below the knee, and states that it was doubtful that amputation could be avoided. The newspaper incorrectly reports that it was the younger George Peck who was wounded.

25. *Roster* 3: 1086, incorrectly cites that Private William Alonzo Peck was killed September 17, 1862, "by bursting of cannon" in Clinton, Iowa. However, the *Report of the Adjutant General and Acting Quartermaster General of Iowa* (Des Moines, 1863), I: 920 (hereafter cited as *AGI*), agrees with Royal's post-war memory that the mortally wounded Peck died October 20, 1862.

26. It was quite common for ladies and private/public organizations throughout the North and the South to either sew or arrange the purchase of a commercially produced flag that they presented to the volunteer companies or regiments raised and organized from the community. These formal presentations were routinely accompanied by great public ceremony and heartfelt patriotic display.

27. When the 26th Iowa was ordered to proceed to St. Louis in October 1862, Curtis commanded the Union Department of the Missouri. Warner, *Generals in Blue*, 107–8.

28. The tonnage for the packet steamer *Denmark* is unknown. The vessel had previously served in transporting troops and supplies on the Tennessee River in the spring and summer of 1862. Charles Dana Gibson and E. Kay Gibson, *The Army's Navy Series: Dictionary of Transports and*

Combatant Vessels, Steam and Sail, Employed by the Union Army, 1861-1868 (Camden, Maine: Ensign Press, 1995), 84. Hereafter cited as *Dictionary of Transports and Combatant Vessels.*

29. The total number of enlisted men and company officers at the completion of the regimental muster in early October was 899. Early additional enlistments of 11 more volunteers brought the number up to 910. With the addition of field officers and staff, the aggregate strength of the "Clinton County Regiment," at the time it boarded the packet *Denmark* to leave the state on October 20, was 920 officers and enlisted men. *Roster* 3: 1017.

30. The *Denmark* had been expected to arrive at 11 A.M., but it did not dock until 5 P.M. It took nearly five hours before the entire regiment was aboard and the overcrowded packet steamer got under way and began its descent of the Mississippi around 10 P.M. The regimental war correspondent, a member of the 26th Iowa who signed published letters as "J. S. P." (Probably Lt. James S. Patterson, Co. H.—Ed.), wrote on October 26, "the boat furnished us was entirely insufficient for our regiment. The barges were loaded with grain, so that one of them could not be made use of by the regiment at all. The companies got confused and mixed up in the crowd and jam of getting on board, and it was found impossible to separate them that night (October 20–21)." *Clinton Herald*, October 25, 1862; J.S.P. to *Clinton Herald*, October 26, 1862, published November 1, 1862. Hereafter cited as J.S.P. to *Clinton Herald.*

31. The unofficial anthem of the Confederacy, "Dixie" was written by noted minstrel performer Daniel Decatur Emmett in New York City. The song was copyrighted in 1860 and quickly became popular throughout the country. Played at Confederate President Jefferson Davis's inauguration in Montgomery, Alabama, on February 22, 1861, it rapidly became the theme song of the South. It was never adopted as an official anthem because many in the South believed the upbeat song lacked dignity. Its being performed that fall evening as the "Clinton County Regiment" began its long journey south to the seat of war provides a rare glimpse of the patriotic emotions infesting American communities, North and South, at that point of time in the conflict. Faust, ed., *Encyclopedia of the Civil War*, 222–3.

32. This is Royal's listing of those men present with the organization upon its departure from Iowa. He does not include later additions and changes to the roster.

33. Born in Pennsylvania, then age 29, Samuel Magill was appointed lieutenant colonel on August 10, 1862. He served with the regiment for only four months, mustering out on December 1, 1862. *Roster* 3: 1028.

34. Samuel Clark, age 35, like his fellow field officers, received his appointment as major on August 10, 1862. He mustered out of the service on December 1, 1862, the same day Lt. Col. Samuel Magill departed. *Roster* 3: 1028.

35. Adjutant Ferreby (spelled Ferreley in *AGI*, 1863-I: 526), age 23, born in New York, was already a ten-month veteran of the war, having enlisted October 19, 1861, as first corporal in Co. H, 14th Iowa Infantry. He was discharged for promotion to first lieutenant and adjutant of the 26th Iowa, August 10, 1862. The valuable officer soon earned promotion to lieutenant colonel and was twice wounded in battle, first at Arkansas Post, Arkansas, and later at Lookout Mountain, Tennessee. Ferreby mustered out February 20, 1865. *Roster* 2: 805; Ibid 3: 1028.

36. Flint, age 36, had been born in Maine. Appointed regimental quartermaster, August 10, 1862, he served in that capacity throughout the war, mustering out June 6, 1865, in Washington, D.C. *Roster* 3: 1028.

37. Forty-two-year-old Abijah T. Hudson was a native of Massachusetts. As regimental surgeon, he tended to the health of the entire organization throughout the war, mustering out when the regiment disbanded, June 6, 1865, in Washington, D.C. *Roster* 3: 1028.

38. Thirty-six-year-old Mac Quigg (spelled MacQuigg in *AGI,* 1863-I: 918) was a native of Pennsylvania. He was appointed assistant surgeon on September 3, 1862, but resigned January 21, 1863, while the regiment was engaged in the river campaign near Vicksburg, Mississippi. Mac Quigg was replaced by Cornelius Teal, age 31, a resident of Keokuk, Iowa, who had been born in England. Teal was appointed assistant surgeon, March 21, 1863, and was discharged from service a year later, May 31, 1864. *Roster* 3: 1028–29.

39. Born in Connecticut, Weatherell was 27 when he was appointed assistant surgeon, September 3, 1862. He completed his service and mustered out June 6, 1865, in Washington, D.C. *Roster* 3: 1029.

40. Born in Massachusetts, McLeish was appointed chaplain at the age of 29, September 9, 1862. He resigned June 11, 1863, being replaced by John Van Antwert, age 43, a resident of De Witt. Chaplain Antwert, a native of New York, was appointed to his post, June 24, 1863, but resigned nine months later, March 5, 1864. *Roster* 3: 1029.

41. Joseph Fegan, age 31, enlisted August 12, 1862, and proved a capable soldier. Promoted sergeant major from second sergeant in Co. I, September 9, 1862, he won promotion to regimental adjutant at Arkansas Post on January 11, 1863, and later to the rank of captain, commanding Co. B, on June 12, 1863. He resigned for promotion, becoming assistant adjutant general of the 1st Division, XV Army Corps, on May 29, 1865. *Roster* 3: 1029, 1054, 1056.

42. Thirty-five-year-old Cooper, a native of Pennsylvania, enlisted August 15, 1862, in Co. A. He was promoted to quartermaster sergeant on September 12, 1862, serving in that capacity until mustered out on completion of service, June 6, 1865, in Washington, D.C. *Roster* 3: 1029, 1040.

43. Born in New Hampshire, Walker, age 29, enlisted as second corporal, Co. C, August 15, 1862. He was promoted to commissary sergeant, September 12, 1862, serving in that capacity until mustering out in Washington, D.C., June 6, 1865. *Roster* 3: 1029, 1107.

44. Age 20, Young would see extremely brief service with the regiment. After enlisting in Co. C on August 19, 1862, he earned promotion to hospital steward, September 12. He became ill later that fall and was sent back to Iowa, where he died of disease on December 1, 1862, at Camanche. *Roster* 3: 1029, 1112.

45. Royal's memory is faulty here. Ladd, age 29 upon enlistment (August 15, 1862), and a native of New York, actually began his service as third sergeant in Co. I. He earned promotion to hospital steward, December 28, 1862, and was discharged the following spring, April 17, 1863, for a field promotion to assistant surgeon, 1st Iowa Cavalry. His service with the cavalry proved short, and he resigned September 27, 1863. *Roster* 3: 1074; *Ibid,* 4: 19.

46. Linton, age 29, and a native of Vermont, was appointed drum major on August 15, 1862. A resident of Scott County, he saw prior service in Co. E, 8th Iowa Infantry, having enlisted on August 10, 1861, and saw action in Tennessee and Mississippi. He was discharged from the 8th Iowa while the remnants of the regiment, those men not killed, wounded, or captured at Shiloh, were stationed at Camp Montgomery, Corinth, Mississippi. Within months of his reenlistment in the 26th Iowa, he was returned to company ranks and assigned to Co. A, December 28, 1862. He was promoted first sergeant, April 1, 1863, eight days prior to being captured at Deer Creek, Mississippi, April 9, 1863. Upon being exchanged as a prisoner of war, Linton was transferred to the Veteran Reserve Corps, December 28, 1864, and later discharged, May 3, 1865, at Indianapolis, Indiana. *Roster* 1: 1150; *Ibid,* 3: 1029, 1072.

47. Ralston, a native of Scotland, was 20 when he enlisted August 9, 1862, as a fifer. He quickly earned promotion to fife major, September 1. He was severely wounded and had a leg amputated as a result of military operations on the Memphis & Charleston Railroad in the vicinity of Barton's Station, Alabama, October 20–29, 1863. Returned to Iowa, he was discharged for wounds, June 25, 1864, at Davenport. *Roster* 3: 1029, 1091; Frederick H. Dyer, *A Compendium of the War of the Rebellion.* (Des Moines, Iowa: F. H. Dyer, 1908; Dayton, Ohio: Morningside reprint, 1978), 597, 664, 1175. Hereafter cited as *Compendium.*

48. See note 18.

49. Lieutenant Franklin's war service began when he enlisted in Co. A, 21st Iowa Infantry, February 8, 1862. A native of New York (records conflict on whether he was 42 or 43 upon enlistment), he was discharged for promotion to first lieutenant, Co. A, 26th Iowa, October 23, 1862. He resigned February 26, 1863. *Roster* 3: 485, 1054.

50. Gaston, age 24 and a native of New York, came to the 26th Iowa from the ranks of the 1st Iowa Cavalry. His original date of enlistment was September 2, 1861, in Co. M, 1st Iowa Cavalry, as company quartermaster sergeant. He was discharged for promotion to second lieutenant of Co. A, 26th Iowa Infantry, on July 27, 1862 (*Roster* 1: 85, cites his date of discharge for promotion as August 12, 1862). When Sherman Williams resigned in late December, Gaston was promoted to captain of the company January 1, 1863. He was wounded May 18, 1863, at Walnut Hills, Mississippi, during Ulysses S. Grant's drive on Vicksburg. He served with the regiment throughout its subsequent field operations and resigned on May 18, 1865. He is buried at Arlington National Cemetery. *Roster* 3: 1057.

51. Eckles, age 35 and a native of Pennsylvania, was appointed captain of Co. B on July 1, 1862. He resigned his commission on June 11, 1863. *Roster* 3: 1052.

52. Wilson, age 36 and a native of New York, was appointed first lieutenant on September 30, 1862. His service with the regiment proved brief, and he resigned his commission on February 26, 1863. *Roster* 3: 1106.

53. Born in England, Harrison was 25 when appointed second lieutenant of Co. B, September 30, 1862. He resigned March 10, 1863, while the regiment was camped at Young's Point, Louisiana. *Roster* 3: 1061.

54. Johnson, a native of New York, was 24 upon his appointment to captain of Co. C, August 5, 1862. He resigned his commission on February 26, 1863. *Roster* 3: 1068.

55. Born in Pennsylvania, Hyde was 38 when appointed first lieutenant of Co. C, August 9, 1862. He was killed in action January 11, 1863, in the assault on Arkansas Post, Arkansas. *Roster* 3: 1062.

56. McDill, age 29 and a native of Pennsylvania, was appointed second lieutenant of Co. C, August 8, 1862. Severely wounded in the assault on Arkansas Post, Arkansas, January 11, 1863, he was transported back to his hometown of Clinton, where he died February 12, 1863. *Roster* 3: 1075.

57. Born in New York, Merrell was 33 when appointed captain of Co. D, August 11, 1862. He was severely wounded while leading his company in the assault on Arkansas Post, Arkansas, January 11, 1863. He resigned from the regiment on April 18, 1863. *Roster* 3: 1080.

58. Runyon was 31 and a native of Ohio. His appointment to first lieutenant of Co. D dates from August 11, 1862. Like many of his comrades, he fell victim to the wave of illness sweeping through the regiment during the winter of 1862–1863, and died of disease aboard the hospital boat *City of Memphis* on February 22, 1863. *Roster* 3: 1091.

59. Born in New Hampshire, Gilmore, age 32, was appointed second lieutenant of Co. D, August 9, 1862, earning promotion to first lieutenant on February 23, 1863, the day after Lieutenant Runyon died. Gilmore resigned his commission on August 8, 1863, at Vicksburg, Mississippi. *Roster* 3: 1058.

60. Lubbers, age 37 and a native of Germany, was appointed captain of Co. E, August 15, 1862.

Enlistment and in Camp

Lubbers earned promotion to major, February 6, 1864, and four months later, June 15, was wounded at Kennesaw Mountain, Georgia. He was promoted lieutenant colonel on May 11, 1865 and unofficially (apparently for war service) promoted to colonel, June 19, 1865. He mustered out when the regiment officially disbanded, June 6, 1865, in Washington, D.C. *Roster* 3: 1073.

61. Like John Lubbers, Svendsen, age 31, had been born in Germany. Appointed first lieutenant on August 15, 1862, he was wounded in the regiment's first battle at Arkansas Post on January 11, 1863. Promoted captain of Co. E, February 7, 1864, he completed his service, mustering out June 6, 1865, at Washington, D.C. *Roster* 3: 1098.

62. A native of Denmark, Hansen was 26 when appointed second lieutenant of Co. E, August 13, 1862. He served for two years, resigning on August 20, 1864. *Roster* 3: 1063.

63. Bishop, age 40, was appointed captain of Co. F, August 14, 1862. He resigned February 26, 1863. *Roster* 3: 1035.

64. A native of New Jersey, Ward was 35 when appointed first lieutenant of Co. F, August 14, 1862. Severely wounded in the assault on Arkansas Post, January 11, 1863, he was promoted captain, replacing Bishop when the latter resigned. The wounded Ward continued to serve until discharged for disability on June 21, 1864. *Roster* 3: 1109.

65. Appointed second lieutenant on August 14, 1862, Freeman, age 38 and a native of New York, served only six months before resigning, February 4, 1863. *Roster* 3: 1056.

66. Born in Pennsylvania, Heavey, age 30, received his captaincy on August 5, 1862. Like many of his comrades, Heavey departed the regiment during the first winter in the field, resigning on February 26, 1863. *Roster* 3: 1064.

67. Quinn, age 30 and a native of Pennsylvania, was appointed first lieutenant, August 8, 1862. Promoted captain, he replaced James Heavey as company commander, February 27, 1862. Wounded slightly on May 19, 1862, at Vicksburg, Mississippi, Quinn served until mustered out June 6, 1865, in Washington, D.C. *Roster* 3: 1090.

68. McCahill (listed MacCahill in *Roster*), born in Canada, was reported to be either 21 or 22 (*AGI*, 1863-I: 937 reports his age as 21) when he accepted appointment as second lieutenant of Co. G, August 8, 1862. Promoted first lieutenant, February 27, 1863, he served until mustered out in Washington, D.C., June 6, 1865. *Roster* 3: 1082.

69. Nye was 34 and a native of New York when appointed captain of Co. H, September 30, 1862. He was promoted major, January 8, 1863, only three days prior to the regiment's first battle at Arkansas Post. Nye resigned June 28, 1863. *Roster* 3: 1084.

70. Patterson, born in Ohio, was 26 when appointed first lieutenant of Co. H, August 4, 1862. He was killed in action, January 11, 1863, at Arkansas Post, Arkansas, and is buried in the National Cemetery at Little Rock. *Roster* 3: 1089.

71. Barrett was appointed second lieutenant of Co. H, August 9, 1862. He was 35 and a native of Ohio. Promoted to first lieutenant on January 12, 1863, filling the vacancy left by the fallen Patterson, he was then promoted captain, June 8, 1863. He never officially mustered as captain because illness forced him from the field. He died of disease in his hometown of De Witt, September 1, 1863. *Roster* 3: 1037.

72. Appointed captain on August 12, 1862, Wemple was 25 and a native of New York. His war service lasted ten months. He resigned in the field during the siege of Vicksburg, Mississippi, June 4, 1863. *Roster* 3: 1111.

73. A Canadian by birth, Steele was 25 when appointed first lieutenant, August 9, 1862. He replaced Wemple, earning a field promotion to captain of the company, June 5, 1863. Wounded severely, November 27, 1863, at Oak Ridge, near Ringgold, Georgia, he died of wounds on December 1, 1863, at Chattanooga, Tennessee, and was buried in the National Cemetery there. *Roster* 3: 1101.

74. Appointed second lieutenant on August 12, 1862, Bennett was 25 and a native of New York. His service with the regiment lasted only six months, and he resigned February 26, 1863. His younger brother, Charles E. Bennett, age 24, earned promotion to corporal on May 1, 1863, completing his enlistment with Co. I and mustering out June 6, 1865, in Washington, D.C. *Roster* 3: 1038.

75. Born in New York, Roe was 37 when appointed captain on September 30, 1862. He served nearly two years as commander of Co. K, resigning his commission July 24, 1864. *Roster* 3: 1094.

76. A native of New York, Hubbard was 30 when commissioned first lieutenant of Co. K, August 11, 1862. He was wounded on November 27, 1863, at Ringgold, Georgia. After his recovery he was promoted company captain, July 25, 1864, and then major on May 11, 1865. He mustered out as the unofficial (not mustered) lieutenant colonel of the regiment on June 6, 1865, at Washington, D.C. *Roster* 3: 1067.

77. Lucien (spelled Lucius in *AGI*, 1863-I: 947) Pomeroy was 26 and a native of Pennsylvania when appointed second lieutenant of Co. K, August 15, 1862. He resigned January 11, 1864. *Roster* 3: 1090.

78. Point Byron, Illinois, is located roughly 20 river miles below Clinton, Iowa. Fisher, *Johnson's New Illustrated Family Atlas,* Plates 55, 62.

79. Le Claire is located across the river in Iowa and downstream from Point Byron. The regimental war correspondent reported the boat tied up at Le Claire until daylight on account of "the Colonel, not being willing to risk his men over the Rapids in a night passage." The rapids referred to were those on the river at Rock Island, Illinois. Fisher, *Johnson's New Illustrated Family Atlas,* Plate 62; J.S.P. to *Clinton Herald*, October 26, 1862.

80. A native of Ireland, Montague, age 30, enlisted in Co. K, August 12, 1862. *Roster* lists him as "Drowned from steamer *Denmark*, October 22, 1862, Le Claire, Iowa." The date of death cited in *Roster* is inaccurate. *AGI*, 1863-I: 949, cites it correctly as October 21, 1862. The incident occurred while the overcrowded vessel (see note 30, J.S.P. to *Clinton Herald*, for the problems of overcrowding reported by the regimental correspondent) negotiated a crossing from Illinois to the Iowa side of the river during the dark hours of the morning. *Roster* 3: 1083.

81. Cain enlisted as fourth corporal on August 12, 1862.

82. A resident of Wheatland, Cain, age 25, had been born in New York. He enlisted August 12, 1862. He is listed as "Drowned from steamer *Denmark*," October 20, 1862, at Le Claire, Iowa. Royal's suspicion of Corporal Cain's possible desertion was also held by other men in the regiment. In correspondence with the *Clinton Herald*, J.S.P. wrote on October 26, 1862, that, "Anthony Cain, of Capt. Wemple's Co., (I), was missing the next morning, and was known to have been on board after we started. It is hardly supposed, however, that he is drowned." *Roster* 3: 1046; *AGI*, 1863-I: 945; J.S.P. to *Clinton Herald*, October 26, 1862.

83. Davenport, Iowa, is located on the western side of the Mississippi opposite Rock Island, Illinois. The river takes a westerly course at this point; thus Davenport is located slightly downstream and north of Rock Island.

84. Baker was appointed adjutant general for the State of Iowa, July 25, 1861. A native of New Hampshire, he graduated from Harvard with honors, studied law in the office of Franklin Pierce (afterward president of the United States), and served in the state legislature, being twice elected as Speaker of the House. He had also won election as governor of New Hampshire. As adjutant general, Baker worked directly under Governor Kirkwood as the man responsible for raising Iowa's quota of volunteers for war service, organizing state regiments and field batteries, outfitting volunteer personnel with uniforms and equipment, and forwarding the mustered organizations into the U.S. Army. S. H. M. Byers, *Iowa in War Times* (Des Moines, Iowa: W.D. Condit & Co., 1888), 56–8. (See the Biographical Appendix for a more extensive summary biography of General Baker.—Ed.)

85. The arms were issued during the week of October 12–18, 1862. An editorial in the *Clinton Herald,* October 18, 1862, noted there were Enfield rifles sufficient to outfit only two companies; the other firearms "were mostly second-hand Austrian smoothbore muskets, which appeared to have been gathered up from some battle-field. Many of them are entirely worthless—more dangerous at the butt than at the muzzle." The rifles were taken by the men in Companies A and B. The other muskets, the editorial reported, "No company would accept." The newspaper went on to comment, "Discipline may require soldiers to take any arms the Government may furnish, but it is not right that our volunteers should be obliged to go into the field with inferior weapons, if better ones are to be had." Royal's company was issued the superior grade Enfield rifle, a muzzle-loading weapon of British manufacture, adopted by the British Army in 1855. The rifle weighed nine pounds, three ounces, with bayonet, and had a bore diameter of .577 inch. It fired a conical bullet and was very accurate at 800 yards, and fairly accurate at 1,100 yards. Nearly one-half million were imported and used by U.S. armed forces during the war. Boatner, *Civil War Dictionary*, 266.

86. Colonel Milo Smith's threat was that he had riverboat men serving in his regiment who could operate the vessel. Undoubtedly, he wished to avoid the tragic overcrowding experienced during the first leg of the transport, and possibly had fears about keeping the *Denmark* afloat, should he not be able to effectively distribute the weight of his 920 personnel among the boat and barges in tow.

87. The "Historical Sketch" for the regiment published in *Roster* 3: 1017, inaccurately cites the 26th Iowa as having arrived at St. Louis on October 25. That date was when Colonel Smith received Curtis's orders to prepare the regiment for transport to Helena, Arkansas. The regimental correspondent reported the 26th Iowa arrived at St. Louis on Thursday, October 23, around 10 A.M. J.S.P. to *Clinton Herald*, October 26, 1863.

88. See note 85 for *Clinton Herald* editorial comments about inferior weapons.

89. The growing difficulties to raise additional quotas of troops for extended war service placed considerable strain on Adjutant General Baker's, and the State of Iowa's, ability to effectively fund and fully equip the new "Hawkeye" volunteer regiments. Given its great distance from Washington, D.C., Iowa had to compete for supplies with all the other Northern states located closer to the seat of government. The state was often provided with the leftover junk refused by military organizations in the East. Throughout the war, it was all too common for regiments, North and South, to experience some measure (either great or small) of unpreparedness. Their training, experience, issued equipment, and transportation often did not measure up to the hardships, rigors, and labors of the men's initial service in the field. Meyer, *Iowans Called to Valor*, 20–9.

90. Type and tonnage for the packet steamer *Imperial* is unknown. The vessel had served to transport federal forces on the expedition to Pittsburg Landing, Tennessee, in March–April 1862. She was later, in September 1863, burned at St. Louis by Confederate agents. The *Imperial* was not in army employment at the time of its destruction. Gibson & Gibson, *Dictionary of Transports and Combatant Vessels*, 159.

91. The 979 men of the 24th Iowa Infantry, commanded by Col. Eber C. Byam, mustered into

U.S. service, September 18, 1862, at "Camp Strong," Muscatine, Iowa. Colonel Byam was a Methodist preacher, as were other officers in the regiment. The 24th Iowa received its famous "Temperance" label when Governor Kirkwood issued a commission to Byam, authorizing him to raise a regiment of soldiers to be called "The Iowa Temperance Regiment," composed of men of temperance principles and habits—"men who touch not, taste not, handle not spirituous or malt liquor, wine, or cider." *Roster* 3: 781; Byer, *Iowa in War Times*, 528; Clarence Kindred, "Historical Data Compiled On Company A, 24th Iowa Infantry, Formed in Sabula, Iowa," Misc. files, Sabula Public Library.

92. This is an allusion to the eleven slave states that seceded and formed the Confederate States of America.

93. See note 85 for description of Enfield rifle muskets. This passage is virtually identical to that of J.S.P. to *Clinton Herald*, October 26, 1862. Royal probably referred to the newspaper articles when he drafted the manuscript.

94. Buford Bend was located on the west side of the river in northeastern Arkansas, just below the southern boundary of Missouri (the "boot-heel"). J.S.P. to *Clinton Herald*, "On Board the Steamer *Imperial*, October 26, 1862," published November 8, 1862.

95. Royal refers to Brig. Gen. Simon Bolivar Buckner (1813–1914) from Kentucky, who surrendered the Confederate garrison at Fort Donelson at Dover, Tennessee, on February 16, 1862. Boatner, *The Civil War Dictionary*, 95. The full identity of "Mr. Buckner" was not found. A large proportion of the Buckner family, including Simon Bolivar Buckner's parents, moved from Kentucky to Arkansas in the decades prior to the Civil War. Arndt M. Stickles, *Simon Bolivar Buckner: Borderland Knight* (Chapel Hill: University of North Carolina Press, 1940), 9.

96. The "Oath of Allegiance" in support of the Constitution of the United States.

97. Strong, born in Kentucky, was 28 and a resident of Marengo, Iowa, when commissioned first lieutenant of Co. E, 24th Iowa Infantry, on August 12, 1862. He resigned April 4, 1863, while stationed at Helena, Arkansas. *Roster* 3: 882. By all accounts, the Iowans were thoroughly amused by the predicament in which they had placed Mr. Buckner. It was their first experience with a true Southerner—someone they considered a genuine "secesh" or secessionist. For another description of the same incident, see J.S.P to *Clinton Herald*, "On Board the Steamer *Imperial*, October 26, 1862," published November 8, 1862.

98. Script was a term applied to paper money. In this instance the paper being questioned is that of the Confederate States of America.

99. The Hawkeyes made him think a slave had informed them that he (Buckner) was a loyal servant to the Confederacy.

100. Helena, Arkansas, situated on high bluffs overlooking the Mississippi River about fifty miles south of Memphis, Tennessee, was located on the only significantly elevated point on the west side of the river below Memphis. Major roads linked the river port with the state capital at Little Rock, ninety miles farther west. National forces from Samuel Curtis's Army of the Southwest, advancing southeastward from Jacksonport, Arkansas, had captured Helena on July 12, 1862. The geographically important location held military value for United States armed forces operating in the valley, as a enclave from where they could mount further incursion southward down the river, or as a depot to support a drive inland against Little Rock. Possession of Helena denied Confederate forces a convenient elevated location for shore batteries to thwart Federal river transportation and army/navy operations along the stretch of the river lying between Memphis and the Confederate stronghold at Vicksburg, Mississippi. Boatner, *Civil War Dictionary*, 392.

101. Royal makes the usual mistake of believing that the campaign to capture Vicksburg, Mississippi, began with the operations mounted under Maj. Gen. Ulysses S. Grant in the late fall of 1862. However, the first effort to take the strategic city took place in the late spring and summer of 1862, when naval expeditions under Rear Admiral David G. Farragut (commanding the Western Gulf Blockading Squadron) and Flag Officer Charles H. Davis (commanding the Mississippi Gunboat Flotilla) converged on Vicksburg by water from the south and north. The effort failed, and both fleets quit immediate operations in front of Vicksburg in late July and retired. The expedition Oake cites the 26th Iowa will soon embark on was the Yazoo River expedition, led by Maj. Gen. William T. Sherman, which culminated in a Union defeat at the Battle of Chickasaw Bayou, north of Vicksburg, in late December. Boatner, *The Civil War Dictionary*, 870–1; Faust, ed., *Encyclopedia of the Civil War*, 784.

102. The experience of the Clinton Regiment, while garrisoned at Helena, was the same as that of all the other units encamped in the vicinity. It suffered much from sickness, the inevitable result of bad weather conditions that prevailed, accompanied by the change from the comforts of sheltered home life to the hardships and exposure to inclement weather that are part of a soldier's life during active field duty. Records for this period show a total of forty-seven officers and men either died from sickness, or were so enfeebled as to render them unfit for further service. They were subsequently discharged from service. *Roster* 3: 781, 1017–18.

103. Created in December 1861, the Army (or District) of Southwest Missouri was commanded in succession by Brig. Gen. Eugene A. Carr (until November 13), and then by Brig. Gen. Willis A. Gorman. Maj. Gen. Samuel R. Curtis commanded the Department of Missouri, headquartered in St. Louis, to which the Army of Southwest Missouri was assigned. This organization was merged into the District of Eastern Arkansas, Department of the Tennessee, commanded by Maj. Gen. Ulysses S. Grant, on December 13, 1862. Dyer, *Compendium*, 540.

104. In mid-December, with merger of the Army of Southwest Missouri into the District of Eastern Arkansas, Department of the Tennessee, the 26th Iowa Infantry was assigned to the 2nd Brigade, 1st Division, District of Eastern Arkansas. Brig. Gen. John M. Thayer commanded the brigade, while Brig. Gen. Frederick Steele commanded the division. General Alvin P. Hovey assumed command of the 2nd Division, District of Eastern Arkansas, at that time. The "Temperance Regiment" (24th Iowa Infantry), was transferred to this division. Dyer, *Compendium*, 540–3.

105. On November 11, 1862, M. P. Sweeny wrote the *Clinton Herald* that the purpose of the three officers being outside the picket lines was to look for a good camping ground. They were approached by three men who wheeled their horses and drew up their guns, demanding their surrender. Surgeon Hudson, who had kept to the rear, was able to spur his horse and, although fired upon and pursued for a mile and a half, escape. M. P. Sweeny to Editor, *Clinton Herald*, "Helena, Arkansas, November 11, 1862," published November 22, 1862. Records published in *Roster* and *AGI*, 1863-I: 927, suggest the probable correspondent was Pvt. Moses T. Sweeny of Co. C, 26th Iowa. Sweeny, a native of Pennsylvania and resident of Clinton, was 39 when he enlisted August 9, 1862. He mustered out of service, May 17, 1865, at Davenport, Iowa. *Roster* 3: 1097.

106. The transcribed manuscript consistently misspells the word Tallahatchie. The correct spelling is used hereafter. The Tallahatchie River drains a considerable portion of north-central Mississippi. The rise of the river is located north of Tupelo in the black prairie district and drains west toward Abbeville, then south-southwest to a confluence with the Yalobusha River at Greenwood, Mississippi.

107. The Army of the Tennessee advanced south on two major fronts: Grant, accompanying the main column (reinforced by his left wing from Corinth, Mississippi), moved south from Grand

Junction, Tennessee, along the line of the Mississippi Central Railroad, while William T. Sherman pushed the right wing southeastward from Memphis. Grant's goal was to use the railroad to supply and support the offensive as it drove south through Grenada toward Jackson, Mississippi, to sever its communications with Vicksburg to the east. Confederate forces opposing the offensive were led by Lt. Gen. John C. Pemberton, commanding the Department of Mississippi and East Louisiana.

108. Hovey temporarily commanded the District of Eastern Arkansas. However, he was presently superceded by Brig. Gen. Frederick Steele, whose command was moved from Pilot's Knob, Missouri, to reinforce Helena. Steele arrived in Helena at the end of the third week of November to discover that Hovey had taken most of the troops in the district and had moved south against the Post of Arkansas. Upon the return of Hovey's aborted expedition on November 21, Steele perfected plans to support Grant's advance by conducting a raid on Grenada, Mississippi. With Steele now in command of the District, Hovey assumed command of the 2nd Division. Edwin Cole Bearss, *The Vicksburg Campaign*, 3 vols. (Dayton, Ohio: Morningside, 1985-86), I: 78–79. Hereafter cited as *The Vicksburg Campaign. The War of the Rebellion: A Compilation of the Official Records of the Union and Confederate Armies*, 73 vols., 128 parts (Washington, 1880–1901), Ser. I, Vol. XIII, 782, 784; Ser. I, Vol. XVII, Pt. II, 874. Hereafter cited as *O.R.*, with the series number and part number(s) of the source are shown with roman numerals, while the volume and page(s) cited are in Arabic (series, volume, part, page). With this system, a citation of *O.R.* Ser. I, Vol. XVII, Pt. II, 874 would be listed as *O.R.* I-17-II-874.

109. Old Town is located on the Arkansas side of the river. The federal convoy of sixteen transports actually tied up on the Mississippi shore at the levee fronting the village of Delta. There were 7,000 men under Hovey's command. Bearss, *The Vicksburg Campaign*, I: 78.

110. Hovey's column advanced southeast, parallel with and south of the channel of the Coldwater River in the northern edge of the Mississippi Delta. His mission was to drive eastward to the Tallahatchie near Charleston and advance his cavalry to Grenada, Mississippi, and cut the Mississippi Central Railroad by destroying the railroad bridges on the Yalobusha River. If successful Hovey, besides cutting Confederate supply lines, would turn the left flank of Confederate forces defending north Mississippi. Bearss, *The Vicksburg Campaign*, I: 79, 86. The spelling of the Coldwater River is corrected from this point on in the memoir.

111. The junction of the two rivers is located about fifteen miles southwest of Panola, Mississippi, in the southeastern corner of Tunica County. From this point the Tallahatchie meanders southward towards its confluence with the Yalobusha. As earlier noted, Oake's memory failed him as to the distance the Federal column actually covered during the four-day march to the Tallahatchie, which was roughly thirty miles and not the fifty he remembered. From his camp on the Tallahatchie, General Hovey dispatched his 1,900-man cavalry brigade, commanded by Brig. Gen. Cadwallader C. Washburn, to conduct the planned raid on the Yalobusha railroad bridges north of Grenada. Although Washburn's troopers did manage to destroy sections of railroad track on the Mississippi & Tennessee and Mississippi Central railroad's, he was stopped short (by weather and increasing Confederate resistance) from reaching the important Yalobusha bridges. Bearss, *The Vicksburg Campaign*, I: 79, 91–93.

112. Hovey's column, rejoined by Washburn on the evening of December 4, departed the Tallahatchie the next morning, accompanied by more than 500 blacks who had escaped enslavement. The heavy rains of the past several days (as described by Oake) caused a number of the area sloughs and bayous to overflow. Thus delayed, Hovey's troops did not reach the delta until the morning of the 7th, where the men embarked on transports and returned to the staging area at Helena. The weather and aggressive Confederate cavalry activities had kept Washburn from destroying the Yalobusha bridges; however, Hovey was satisfied with the raid, pointing out that at a cost of fifteen casualties (one killed and fourteen wounded), his force had marched deep into the heart of the enemy's country, defeating the Confederates in several skirmishes, burned several railroad bridges, cut telegraph lines, torn up sections of track, and destroyed one locomotive and twelve cars. The track damage inflicted was not serious, however, and railroad crews effected repairs within twenty-four hours. The advance made by Hovey toward Grenada from the west had serious repercussions on the Confederate strategic situation in north Mississippi. With their left flank and primary supply line endangered by Hovey's rapid thrust across the delta, the Confederates were forced to abandon their fortified position on the Tallahatchie and withdraw another 50 miles south to the Yalobusha. *O.R.* I-17-I-531-32; Bearss, *The Vicksburg Campaign*, I: 94.

113. See the Biographical Appendix.

114. Preffer, age 26, enlisted as a private on July 7, 1862, at Charlotte, Iowa. The young Canadian died of disease on May 31, 1863, aboard the hospital boat *D. A. January*. *Roster* 3: 1086.

115. McLain (spelled McLane in *Roster*, but McLain in *AGI*, 1863-I: 918), age 24, enlisted as eighth corporal, July 7, 1862, at Charlotte, Iowa. *Roster* 3: 1075

116. See notes 21 and 22.

117. McLain actually died "of disease" at Helena within a week and a half, on December 17, 1862. *Roster* 3: 1075.

118. On August 14, 1864, when Frank dies of wounds outside Atlanta, Georgia, Royal will find himself the last survivor of the five original tent mates. *Roster* 3: 1054.

119. The original XIII Corps dates from October 24, 1862, when all troops in the United States Department of the Tennessee (created October 16, 1862) were assigned to it, and XIII Corps comprised the principle western army command under Ulysses S. Grant. On December 18, 1862, there was a reorganization that created four corps out of what had formerly been one; these were: XIII (new), XV, XVI, and XVII Corps. The new XIII and XV Corps were not organized as such until January 1863. During the period of December 18, 1862 to January 4, 1863, the troops assigned to these two corps were assigned to and engaged in Maj. Gen. William T. Sherman's Yazoo Expedition, and during January 4–12, 1863, in operations against the Post of Arkansas. The "right wing" consisted of four divisions and was "styled the right wing of (General Grant's) Thirteenth Army Corps…," just as Oake cites it. The order on December 18, 1862, named Maj. Gen. John A. McClernand as commander of the new XIII Corps, and Sherman commander of the XV Corps because McClernand was officially absent on furlough. William T. Sherman, *Memoirs of William T. Sherman*, 2 vols. (New York: D. Appleton & Co., 1875), I: 322; Boatner, *Civil War Dictionary*, 194–95, 951.

120. Some 32,000 officers and men, and forty cannon, were assigned to Sherman's Yazoo Expeditionary Force. Boatner, *Civil War Dictionary*, 951.

121. Heavy cannon mounted in shore batteries on the bluffs overlooking the Mississippi River at Vicksburg denied Northern shipping use of that important avenue of commerce. With Memphis and New Orleans occupied by Federal forces, Vicksburg served as the vital link between the eastern and western parts of the Confederacy, what Confederate President Jefferson Davis called "the nailhead that held the South's two halves together." By late 1862 the city sat astride a major route for food, clothing, medicine, and other important supplies, as well as fresh soldiers from the West. Confederate armies operating east of the river depended on that source. Terrence J. Winschel, *Vicksburg: Fall of the Confederate Gibraltar* (Abilene, Texas: McWhiney Foundation Press, 1999), 14.

122. The 26th Iowa boarded the steamer *Tecumseh* (tonnage unknown) for transport downriver. *O.R.* I-17-I-604, 615.

123. The convoy consisted of approximately fifty-five transports, five supply boats, some tugs, and at least thirteen gunboats (ironclad, tinclad, and wooden), constituting a total of perhaps eighty-one vessels participating in the expedition. Not all the gunboats accompanied the convoy, for several of them were already on station off the mouth of the Yazoo River above Vicksburg. The U.S. Navy vessels supporting the expedition, constituting elements of the Mississippi Squadron, were under the command of Rear Admiral David D. Porter. Bearss, *The Vicksburg Campaign*, I: 134, 152.

124. A naval vessel either made completely of metal, or what was the more common case during the Civil War, whose wooden structure (casement sides and/or hull) were covered and protected with metal plating (in some instances iron rails—or railroad track—were used).

125. Cannon loaded and ready to fire.

126. Milliken's Bend was located on the Louisiana side of the Mississippi River, on the south side of a large west-to-east bend in the river, roughly twenty-four river miles (seventeen air miles) upstream and northwest of Vicksburg. The site no longer exists because of subsequent changes in the river channel. The expedition arrived at the bend long after dark on the night of December 24. Federal officers and troops celebrated Christmas Eve aboard the gaily lighted transports. Bearss, *The Vicksburg Campaign*, I: 136.

127. At the time of the expedition, the railroad extended only from De Soto (opposite Vicksburg) west to Monroe, Louisiana—merely eighty miles. During the winter of 1861–1862, floodwaters washed out most of the bridges on the section of the railroad between Delhi and Delta. Confederate authorities held the railroad in such low esteem that no effort was made to repair the damage. The raid on the line was conducted by Brig. Gen. Stephen A. Burbridge's brigade, accompanied by a detachment of the 6th Missouri Cavalry, from A. J. Smith's division. Burbridge's column marched 37 miles to reach the station of Dallas. Bearss, *The Vicksburg Campaign*, I: 155–56.

128. The mouth of the river was located about twelve river miles upstream from Vicksburg. The Yazoo provided the Federals access to landings immediately north of Vicksburg.

129. After the departure of Burbridge's brigade, all the transports, except those assigned to Smith's division, departed Milliken's Bend and headed down the Mississippi. The convoy tied up at Young's Point on the Louisiana shore, where Sherman had Brig. Gen. Morgan L. Smith disembark Col. Giles A. Smith's brigade to break up the railroad near the Hecla plantation. Giles Smith's soldiers accomplished their mission and returned to Young's Point, where they boarded the transports before day's end. Royal does not mention the incident, but around noon on Christmas Day the men of Steele's division were disembarked, mustered, and marched to an open field south of the levee, where they witnessed the execution of two of their comrades. The soldiers had been recently condemned by a court-martial for plundering and burning private property. Bearss, *The Vicksburg Campaign*, I: 157–59.

130. The vessels carrying Morgan's division pulled away from the Young's Point levee at 8 A.M., taking the lead in the ascent of the Yazoo River, followed by transports carrying Steele's men and then by M. L. Smith's troops. A. J. Smith's division had to await the return of Burbridge's brigade, sent ashore at Milliken's Bend to smash the railroad, before joining the convoy on the Yazoo. The transcribed manuscript spells Yazoo as "Zazoo." The editor interprets this mistake in spelling as a probable transcriber error in deciphering Royal's handwriting. The 26th Iowa was brigaded along with the 4th, 9th, 28th, 30th, and 34th Iowa Infantry, plus Co. A, 1st Iowa Light Artillery, under the command of Brig. Gen. John H. Thayer, who supervised the 3rd Brigade in Steele's division. *O.R.* I-17-I-605, 620.

131. The majority of troops were put ashore on December 26. Apparently Oake decided not to

Enlistment and in Camp

mention the change in Sherman's tactical plans, in which he ordered Steele to re-embark Hovey's and Thayer's brigades aboard their transports the night of December 26, and advance them farther upstream to disembark the next day (27th) east of Chickasaw Bayou. On the 26th, the three Federal divisions present disembarked in the bottomlands west of the mouth of Chickasaw Bayou, roughly six miles north of Vicksburg, and along a shoreline lying roughly three miles north of the range of bluffs known as the Walnut Hills. Bearss, *The Vicksburg Campaign*, I: 159–61, 164–65.

132. Between the River Road, located at the base of the bluffs and the Yazoo River, was a triangular belt of bottomland, about five miles across at its base, the apex of which abutted against Snyder's Bluff—a prominent point on the Walnut Hills roughly ten miles northeast of Vicksburg. Except for cleared fields adjacent to the three plantations located in the triangle, this lowland was densely wooded, being intersected by a number of bayous and sloughs. During periods of high water, much of the area was inundated. Two plantations, those of Capt. W. H. Johnson and Mrs. Annie E. Lake, lay west of Chickasaw Bayou, a sluggish body of water bisecting the triangular belt of bottomland. The plantation of Col. Benson Blake lay to the east and north of Chickasaw Bayou, beyond Thompson Lake. Chickasaw Bayou debouches from McNutt Lake, meandering about one mile in a northeasterly direction along the base of the hills. The stream then veers sharply north and discharges into the Yazoo. A quarter mile upstream of the mouth of Chickasaw Bayou lay the discharge of Thompson Lake, a significant body of water lying parallel to and east of the bayou. Northeast of Thompson Lake, Bliss Creek cut through the Walnut Hills to meander across the valley and empty into the Yazoo three miles below Snyder's Bluff. The smaller triangular parcel of land bordered by Bliss Creek, the river, and the bluffs was swampy and contained two small bodies of water—Cypress Lake and Goose Lake. Bearss, *The Vicksburg Campaign*, I: 152–53.

133. Morgan's division landed near the eastern limits of Capt. W. H. Johnson's plantation. The transports with General Steele's division, in which the 26th Iowa was assigned to Thayer's brigade, tied up near the ruins of Captain Johnson's house. M. L. Smith's division went ashore west of Steele's debarkation, while A. J. Smith's troops, when they arrived from Milliken's Bend, were to be put ashore near Bunch's sawmill. From his landing, Steele advanced Brig. Gen. Frank P. Blair's brigade two miles south along a road (called the Johnson Road by General Steele) following a watershed separating Alligator and Long lakes. Bearss, *The Vicksburg Campaign*, I: 158–61; *O.R.* I-17-I-651.

134. The advance against the Confederate line bordering the base of the bluffs south of the river was to start at 7 A.M. on December 27; however, Sherman was forced to modify his plans when A. J. Smith's division failed to arrive from Milliken's Bend and because rain had started to fall during the night. Two of Steele's three brigades would re-embark and be convoyed up the Yazoo and placed ashore on Blake's Levee, near the mouth of Chickasaw Bayou. From this new beachhead, Steele's men would enfilade the levee flanking the Yazoo that sheltered Confederate forces charged with detonating torpedoes (mines) in the river. Steele's division, now constituting the army's left, was to advance south along the levee skirting the east side of Chickasaw Bayou to reach the enemy guarding approaches to Walnut Hills—while coordinating its movements with Morgan's. The brigades of Hovey and Thayer were selected to make this shift. Blair's command remained in his advanced position on Morgan's right. It is now clear from the wording of his order that Sherman, being unfamiliar with the area, actually described the levee flanking Thompson Lake and not Chickasaw Bayou. Not until his men were ashore in the late afternoon of December 27 and filing southward on the assigned levee did General Steele learn of Sherman's geographical error. Instead of flanking Chickasaw Bayou, Blake's Levee skirted the eastern shoreline of Thompson Lake, lying well east of the bayou, separating Steele's force more than one mile from any support by Morgan's left flank. The levee on which Steele's men (including the 26th Iowa) advanced was a wagon's width on top and from twelve to fifteen feet high, bordered by bottomland swamp on either side. The troops were forced to clear trees felled by the enemy, and minor skirmishing erupted in front of the vanguard. That night, owing to the proximity of Confederate forces, Steele did not permit the men to kindle fires. *O.R.* I-17-I-651, 653–54; Bearss, *The Vicksburg Campaign,* I: 164–66.

135. The Confederate force defending fortifications along the Walnut Hills north of Vicksburg were elements of the Department of Mississippi and East Louisiana, commanded by Lt. Gen. John C. Pemberton. The Second Military District, which consisted of the immediate Vicksburg garrison, initially had 5,500 men available to defend the post, under the command of Maj. Gen. Martin L. Smith. To this were added, on December 26, a force consisting of 6,000 men rapidly transferred by rail from Grenada. In tactical command of this Provisional Division deployed to defend the nine-mile-long Walnut Hills line was Brig. Gen. Stephen D. Lee, until Maj. Gen. Carter L. Stevenson arrived late on December 29 and took command. Reinforcements arrived on December 29–30, swelling the Confederate ranks to roughly 25,000 men before Sherman withdrew. Livermore cites a total of 13,792 Confederates participating in the principal fighting on December 26–29, 1862. Boatner, *Civil War Dictionary,* 153–54; Bearss, *The Vicksburg Campaign,* I: 150, 154, 224–26.

136. These are the Walnut Hills. The section bordering Chickasaw Bayou is commonly referred to in historic documents as the "Chickasaw Bluffs." There were actually two roads, the River Road lying at the base of the hills, and another road located on the ridge. Both permitted travel to and from Yazoo City, and provided the Confederates with lateral lines of communication, and both of them were used to shift troops to resist Federal attack. Bearss, *The Vicksburg Campaign,* I: 152.

137. The basic definition is a hole or short, shallow trench, or place of arms, excavated large enough to afford protection for one or more soldiers. The latter was more often the case during the Civil War. Soldiers bastardized the term rifle pit to refer to the long trenches for the protection of entire companies, battalions, regiments, and brigades, which were not short, and sometimes were several hundred yards in length. Garrison & Garrison, *Civil War Usage,* 214; Colonel H. L. Scott, *Military Dictionary: Comprising Technical Definitions; Information on Raising and Keeping Troops; Actual Service, Including Makeshifts and Improved Material; and Law, Government, Regulation, and Administration Relating to Land Forces* (New York: D. Van Nostrand, 1864), 532. Hereafter cited as *Military Dictionary.*

138. The Walnut Hills line, throughout most of its nine-mile length, was fronted by natural water barriers, so much so that there were only five places where enemy forces could reach or advance to the line. Two of the five approaches were fortified by Confederate forces before Sherman arrived in the area. On Christmas Day, Gen. Stephen D. Lee put large fatigue parties to work digging rifle pits, constructing batteries, and felling immense quantities of trees to erect abatis along the remaining unprotected approaches to block Federal forces' advance. The defenses, in addition to the ground's nearly impassable nature, proved formidable. The Confederates concentrated their limited numbers of troops on defending the most obvious approaches, where Sherman's men had restricted areas to deploy and advance. This permitted the Confederates to shoot along extremely narrow fields of fire (frontages). The difficult terrain deprived the attackers of effective artillery support, while the Confederate gunners and supporting infantry broke up pinned-down Federal attack formations with devastating results. Sherman suffered a total of 1,776 casualties— 208 men killed, 1,005 wounded, and 563 missing. The Confederate loss was listed as 57 killed, 120 wounded, and 10 missing, for 187 total casualties. Bearss, *The Vicksburg Campaign,* I: 153; Boatner, *Civil War Dictionary,* 153–54; *O.R.* I-17-I-671.

Enlistment and in Camp

139. Hemmed in by the restraints of the terrain along Blake's Levee, the bulk of Steele's division, brigades of Hovey and Thayer, saw little fighting on December 27–28. Thwarted by geography, on the night of December 28, Steele's division (brigades of Hovey and Thayer) was re-embarked aboard the transports, and moved back downstream to Johnson's plantation. In the severe fighting on December 29, Steele was called upon to support Sherman's attack against the center of Confederate fortifications. At the time, only Thayer's brigade was immediately available to participate, because Hovey's brigade still was making its way to the front. Thus, Steele sent Thayer to Morgan's support. Owing to the difficulty of negotiating the heavily wooded swamp, the 4th Iowa was the only one of Thayer's regiments that managed to storm the fortifications, going into action to the immediate right and front of Col. John F. DeCourcy's brigade of Morgan's division. The remainder of Thayer's brigade (minus the 26th Iowa, which was on detached pioneer duty, laboring to cut open a road) missed a critical turn to the left, and marched by column to the far right, failing to engage. The entire brigade suffered 124 casualties during the expedition, with the 4th Iowa Infantry, tough veterans of Pea Ridge, losing 7 men killed and 105 wounded in the unsupported assault on the Confederate works. The 26th Iowa recorded no loss in the Chickasaw operation, being primarily employed in fatigue or pioneer duty and, as Oake states, also deployed to garrison the landing. *O.R.* I-17-I-652, 658–60; Bearss, *The Vicksburg Campaign*, I: 201–02, 229.

140. Sherman, with the support of Admiral Porter, had conceived a plan to ascend the Yazoo River and conduct a night amphibious assault on the Confederate right at Snyder's (or Drumgould's) Bluff with a force of 10,000 men, consisting mostly of Steele's division. They were to make the initial attack with bayonets fixed and muskets unloaded (a precaution against accidental discharge that might give warning of the surprise attack). On the night of December 31, however, the operation was terminated when dense fog enveloped the area. Grant's advance south along the Mississippi Central Railroad had been stopped by cavalry raids that destroyed his forward supply depot at Holly Springs, Mississippi, and smashed the line of the Mobile & Ohio Railroad in western Tennessee. These raids were conducted by Maj. Gen. Earl Van Dorn (in Mississippi) and Brig. Gen. Nathan Bedford Forrest (in Tennessee). Unable to supply his troops by rail, Grant was forced to abandon his position north of the Yalobusha River and retire fifty miles north, beyond the Tallahatchie River and eventually into western Tennessee. Unable to sustain his portion of the jointly planned Federal offensive, Grant was unable to coordinate with and support Sherman's attack on Vicksburg. This permitted Pemberton to rapidly shift 6,000 men by rail from the Grenada fortifications. Along with reinforcements from Braxton Bragg's army in Middle Tennessee, they arrived in time to adequately defend the threatened Walnut Hills line north of Vicksburg. Oakes is mistaken about Sherman's decision; Sherman received belated word (correspondence dated December 23, 1862) informing him of Grant's withdrawal of the Army of the Tennessee north of the Tallahatchie. David J. Eicher, *The Longest Night: A Military History of the Civil War* (New York: Simon & Schuster, 2001), 389–92; Bearss, *The Vicksburg Campaign*, I: 220.

141. Oakes is in error. McClernand was to command the troops engaged in the downriver expedition, which was organized within Grant's department. Since late summer, McClernand had been absent on an extended furlough, first traveling to Washington, D.C., to confer with President Lincoln and Secretary of War Edwin Stanton concerning his command of a separate and new Union army on the Mississippi. Most recently, McClernand—a widower and Illinois congressman—had been home in Illinois to politic and take time to marry Minerva Dunlop, his first wife's younger sister. When he headed south with his new bride to assume his new command, he believed the troops to be stationed at Memphis. Instead, Grant had ordered these forces south and placed them under Sherman's temporary command for the attack on Walnut Hills. McClernand, senior to Sherman, ranked second under Grant in the overall command structure of the Department of the Tennessee. The *Tigress* was a small sidewheel steamer and veteran of several military operations on the Tennessee, Cumberland, and Mississippi rivers. She was sunk on April 22, 1863, while attempting to run the batteries at Vicksburg. *O.R.* I-17-I-425; Bearss, *The Vicksburg Campaign*, I: 358–59; Gibson & Gibson, *Dictionary of Transports and Combatant Vessels*, 316.

142. Grant forwarded the orders (December 29) to McClernand, who was then in Memphis, that he was to command the downriver expedition. The orders dated to December 18, 1862. They had been seriously delayed when Forrest's cavalry cut the telegraph connecting Grant's headquarters at Oxford, Mississippi, with Columbus, Kentucky, from where they were to have been relayed to Springfield and Memphis. It would be more than a week and a half before McClernand received the communication from Grant, directing him to proceed to the front and assume command of the expedition. By then McClernand was at Memphis, and Sherman was struggling to carry out his attack on the Walnut Hills line north of Vicksburg. Upon his arrival at Milliken's Bend, McClernand issued orders that in effect declared his independence of General Grant and redesignated his command the Army of the Mississippi. *O.R.* I-17-I-432–33, 425; Bruce Catton, *Grant Moves South* (Boston: Little, Brown & Co., 1960), 339; Bearss, *The Vicksburg Campaign*, I: 358.

143. The Confederate bastion was called the Post of Arkansas by the Southern forces. Only the Federals called it Fort Hindman, in reference to Confederate General Thomas C. Hindman.

Brigadier General John M. Thayer.
The 26th Iowa Infantry was assigned to the brigade commanded by Thayer throughout the critical operations to seize Vicksburg, Mississippi, from December 1862 to August 1863. LIBRARY OF CONGRESS

CHAPTER TWO

Battle of Arkansas Post

⤜ ———————————— ⤛

January 11th, 1863, is a day that will long be remembered by all survivors of the 26th Iowa. In writing of this battle I will try and write it in the single interest of truth and although relying upon memory to a great extent I think all participants in that engagement will admit that in the main it is correct. It is said by many historians that every regiment engaged in war has its Waterloo,[144] and such was Arkansas Post for the 26th Iowa Infantry. The writer has been in many battles and over many bloody fields subsequently. Battles in which perhaps a great many more troops were engaged, but I think the terrible realities of war were never more plainly visible than on that battle ground, and writing as I am many years after its occurrence the scenes and incidents of that day are as indelibly impressed upon my memory as if they occurred but yesterday.

Fort Hindman, commonly known as Arkansas Post, was an old French trading post situated on the left or north bank of the Arkansas River about 50 [actually 25] miles from its mouth.[145] This fort was a very strong bastioned work constructed by the Confederates at the head of a horse shoe bend on an elevated bluff which here touches the river and defines for some distance its left bank.

The work had four bastion fronts inclosing a space of about 100 yards square, and a line of rifle pits, about three quarters of a mile in length, extended across a neck of level ground to a bayou on the west and north. In the fort were three kinds of guns: one a three-inch rifled gun, and four six-pound smooth bores mounted at the salients and flanks, and twelve-pound howitzers, and three-inch rifled guns distributed along the rifle pits.[146] Its garrison consisted of about 5,000 men under the command of Brigadier General T[homas] J[ames] Churchill* of the Confederate army. To show its military value from a rebel standpoint I will mention the fact that its commander had received orders from his superior Lieutenant General [Theophilus H.] Holmes* to hold the fort till all were dead. This post had been very annoying to the Federal Army from the fact that the enemy having in their possession a few fleet steamers that could make a dash down the river into the Mississippi, and capture or destroy unarmed transports that were carrying supplies to the Federal Army then located at Milliken's Bend. In fact a few days prior to this time they had captured the little steamer Blue Wing[147] loaded with mail and hospital stores, and had run it up the Arkansas River to their stronghold, Fort Hindman, but upon the capture of that place January 11th, the steamer was recaptured by the Federals.

On the fourth of January the expedition started up White River through the cut off, which unites its waters with those of the Arkansas River,[148] and up the river to Notribs [Notrebe's][149] Plantation about 3 miles below the fort. The troops, consisting of two divisions of the 13th Army Corps, commanded by Brigadier General [George W.] Morgan, and two divisions of the 15th Corps under General Sherman, were all landed on 9th and 10th, and in the evening of the 10th, Steele's Division of the 15th corps was put in motion to try to envelop the enemy's position. Right here I think I passed one of the most tiresome, and disagreeable nights that I experienced in helping to put down the rebellion.

Although only about 3 miles from the enemy's position we were marching and counter marching the entire night - at times being lost in the labyrinth of roads that traversed the heavy growth of timber that covered that swampy region. King Richard of England once said, "My Kingdom for a horse."[150] That night I believe I could have truthfully said, "My prospects in Paradise for a nights rest."[151] What added to our discomfort was the darkness and chilliness of the night.

At an early hour in the morning of January 11th, it being quite dark, we were halted in the road, being in close proximity to the enemy's outposts, well do I recollect that occasion. There were a lot of old brush piles along the road, and on one of them I lay down, and in a few moments was wrapped in the arms of Morpheus.[152] I remember the sun was shining brightly when we were awakened by the rattle of musketry - skirmishing with the enemy having already began. After partaking of a slim breakfast we were soon in line waiting orders.

Towards noon Major [] Hamlin[153] of General Steele's Staff rapidly approached Colonel Milo Smith of the 26th with orders from General Steele for him to move upon the enemy's works. Colonel Smith immediately placed himself at the head of the regiment, and gave the orders: 26th Iowa, on the right into line, and in a few moments the regiment was in its proper position.[154] Then came the order - "Load arms." Buckling his sword belt a little tighter the Colonel gave the order: "26th Iowa Forward."

Time can never efface from my memory that momentous occasion; we were about three hundred yards from the enemy's line of rifle pits that were plainly visible. The timber that had formerly covered the intervening space having been about all cut down by the enemy, thus giving them a good view of the column coming over that comparatively level stretch of ground.

At the command, "Forward," with a fine alignment, and Old Glory glistening in the bright sun light the regiment sprang forward on its deadly mission. One incident in connection with this engagement I will remember. Just at the right of our regiment as we formed in line stood an old fashioned rail corncrib filled with corn, while behind it under its shelter every inch of which was taken up by skulkers[155] from the different commands that had been ordered into battle, and as the shells began to fly quite lively they could not be shamed out of their place of supposed safety, and as we took a look at them as we marched forward we wished that a few of the enemy's shells would strike the old corncrib, and scatter the cowardly curs. Forward went the 26th[156] and shot and shell flew thick. The enemy reserving musketry fire until every shot would count, upon the capture of the fort we found that quite a number of the enemy were armed with double barrel shot guns, each cartridge containing one ball and three buck shot,[157] making a terrible weapon to fall at short range.

As we pressed forward rapidly closing the intervening distance between the opposing forces we became aware of the fact that other troops had already been engaged with the enemy as every few steps we saw the forms of fallen comrades. Ahead of us could plainly be seen a glistening array of steel protruding over the breastwork[158] under the headlog,[159] while through the embrasures of the work could be seen the double shotted[160] guns awaiting our closer approach. Every man in the line with blanched face and determination stamped upon his features pressed steadily forward expecting every moment to see that volcano of lead and iron burst forth. Onward we pressed until within about seventy yards of the enemy's works, when we distinctly heard the word "Fire" given. To describe that moment requires an abler pen than mine. The very earth trembled while the roar of artillery, screeching of shells, and zipping of minie balls,[161] mingled with the sharp and heavy guns of the navy; the dense smoke that enveloped the field and the cries of the wounded and dying can better be imagined than described.

Down goes Old Glory dyed crimson by the blood of its defender, but only for a moment does its glistening folds trail in the dust. Again, willing hands and brave hearts raise it in defiance of the rebel hosts. Once more it is seen to drop as its gallant bearer's life goes out. The third time that emblem is raised in defiance of the enemy thicker and faster seemed to fly that storm of leaden hail. "Lay down and protect yourselves, and give it to them the best you can," came the order. No troops could stand that withering fire and live. Our Colonel [Milo Smith] had already been wounded by the bursting of a shell, and taken from the field, while our Adjutant [Thomas G. Ferreby] had received a terrible wound, part of his jaw being carried away and he was taken from the field. Lieutenant [William R.] Ward of Company F was also wounded. Lieutenant [James S.] Patterson of Company H had given up his young life, and the life blood of Lieutenant [Peter L.] Hyde of Company C was fast ebbing away.[162]

Still we kept up a terrible fire upon the enemy lying close to the ground, and directing our fire chiefly to the enemy's artillery, and the moment that an artillery man showed himself at the embrasures fifty shots would be fired at him. Our field artillery in the meantime had done good execution. One section of the 1st Missouri Light Artillery under the command of Lieutenant Fred Schinstten[163] did splendid execution making the rebels think the Dutch had taken Holland.

During the heat of the battle the writer was lying in a slight depression in the ground alongside of Sergeant Robert McClenahan [McLenahan],[164] and Corporal Charles Butler[165] of Company A, about fifty yards from the enemy's lines, and it seemed to us as though it were raining lead, but still we were untouched. Every time one of the enemy's artillery men showed himself we would greet him with a shower of lead. McLenahan was quite a large man, and the writer lay very close to him during the heat of the battle, not to protect himself, but in case anything should happen to him I could help him - You Know.

As we lay there during those scenes of carnages and the air filled with deadly missiles little did we know of the fearful loss our regiment had suffered. Nearly one-third of which, had been killed or wounded. The sharp and heavy reports of the guns of the ironclads that were engaged with the fort on the river bank became more frequent, as the navy and rebel fort were hotly engaged. Soon a lull in the enemy's fire was noticeable followed by the appearance of the white flag along the enemy's works. Could it be possible they were about to surrender. Soon our doubts and fears were ended as one of General Steele's aides rode between the lines, and ordered, "Cease firing."

The firing gradually ceased, and the remnants of the various commands, that had taken part in the battle, were ordered into line and to advance on the enemy's line of works, and standing on the breastworks with loaded arms we watched the enemy as they silently marched up in front of us as prisoners of war, and stacked their arms.

Their looks showed that the act was very humiliating to them, but they had no choice in the matter. Old Glory had won the day at a fearful cost.

Not until we had formed around the flag of our regiment after the battle did we fully realize our loss as we failed to recognize the forms of comrades who had that morning in the flush and vigor of early manhood, full of patriotism and love of country marched with us to battle. We need not ask, where are they, too well we knew for on either side could be seen their cold and stiffening forms.

When the enemy had stacked their arms, and details of soldiers had been made to guard the prisoners the 26th Iowa bivouac[k]ed on the battle field for the night. After stacking arms in company with a comrade I started to look over the bitterly contested field, where on every hand could be seen the forms of comrades cold in death.

James B. Ray[166] of Company K of the 26th with whom I was well acquainted fell with five bullets in his breast, and many others whose names will be appended to this work lay stiff and cold, silent witnesses of this hard fought battle.

After viewing our own side we followed the enemy's line of entrenchments. On every hand could be seen the fearful results of our fire. Directly in front of our line during the battle were two pieces of artillery,[167] and as we paused for a moment to look at the dead our attention was called to an artillery man who had been struck in the breast by shot from one of our guns, striking him in the breast, as it did at the moment of its explosion, the entire body had been blown away, while his entrails had been twisted into a rope connecting the lower part of the body with the upper part of the chest, and every particle of clothing had been burned leaving the remains in blackened and charred condition.

A few feet distant at the same battery lay the nude body of another unfortunate soldier, who had been struck by a shell that had carried away both legs below the knees, and the severed feet still in the shoes had been placed by some comrade near the mangled form. A short distance in the rear of this battery lay the mangled remains of all the horses belonging to this battery.[168] All of them, Iron Greys, still harnessed together and tangled in a manner beyond description.

Passing along the line to our left we soon approached the fort, which presented a sickening appearance, as the terrible effect of the heavy guns of the navy were seen on every side. Pieces of railroad rails, with which a portion of the fort had been covered, varying in length from one to ten feet were scattered all over the field by the force of the heavy missiles from the Navy's guns.[169] Occasionally a shell had dropped inside the fort, and exploding had hurled the body of some unfortunate over the ramparts hundreds of feet away. Thus could I continue to describe if space and time would allow. As before stated we bivouac[k]ed upon the battle field the night of the 11th, and the next day our time was occupied in burying the dead, the writer being one of a detail made for that purpose. Digging long trenches, one by one they were gently laid therein while all valuables taken from their bodies were carefully marked to be sent to their sorrowing friends at home.

The following is a list of killed and wounded of the 26th Iowa:[170]

Wounded:
Colonel Milo Smith*
Adjutant Thomas G. Ferreby [see note 35]

Co. A Wounded:
John Sinkey[171]

Co. B Wounded:
Sergeant Hugh Snodgrass[172]

(Privates)
William E. Whiteside[173]
[Corporal] George E. Fisher[174]
John Kilrain[175]
James Linn [Lynn][176]
Rudolph Herschie [Hiersche][177]

Co. C Killed:
First Lieutenant Peter L. Hyde [see note 55]
Corporal Henry L. [F.] Shaffer[178]
Private Michael Keal[179]

Co. C Wounded:
Second Lieutenant James McDill [see note 56]

(Privates)
Charles A. Thomas[180]
[Sergeant] Herbert D. Sage[181]
Absalom Lacock[182]
John C. Symonds [Symons][183]
Adolphus Cone[184]
George A. McDowell[185]
Jessie Hedges[186]
[Corporal] Joseph A. Savits[187]
Peter Cunningham[188]
August W. Schroder[189]
Milton Jackson[190]

Benjamin H. Greenlee[191]
Oliver T. Bowen[192]
John Dougherty[193]
Charles Johnston[194]
George N. Day[195]

Co. D Killed:
(Privates)
Joel Arthur [Austin][196]
Mathew Costello[197]

Co. D Wounded:
Captain N. A. Merrell [see note 57]
Corporal Burt [S.] Harrington[198]

(Privates)
Willam Maher[199]
John McDonnel[l][200]
William Stewart [Stuach][201]
Jacob D. Van Horn[202]
[James R. Van Horn][203]
Michael Cavanaugh[204]
Charles Corbin[205]
Job Walrod[206]

Co. E Killed:
Corporal Lewis Pankow[207]

(Privates)
Heinrich Krumwiede[208]
Wilhelm Nyrop[209]

Co. E Wounded:
Lieutenant Edward Svendsen [see note 61]
Sergeant Jurgen Urean [Unrau][210]

(**Privates**)
August T. Hoffman[211]
Paul S. Martensen[212]
Anton Meier[213]
Frederick Reisch[214]
Paul Schmutz[215]
Johann H. Schultz[216]
George Steinhilbert[217]
Detlef[f] Schnack[218]

Co. F Killed:
(**Privates**)
Daniel J. Campbell[219]
Christian Bollinger[220]
Omar H. Stanley[221]

Co. F Wounded:
Lieutenant William R. Ward [see note 64]
Sergeant Louis Rider[222]
Sergeant Sylvester Markland[223]
Corporal Alvira [Ahira] P. Stevens[224]

(**Privates**)
Alonzo D. Cady[225]
Daniel Correll[226]
Rufus M. Hudson[227]
David Mahar[228]
Edwin W. Preston[229]
John W. Loofborn[230]
Myron J. Mullett[231]

Co. G Killed:
Private William Farrel [Fanell][232]

Co. G Wounded:
Sergeant Cornelius Cahill[233]
Corporal John Gange[234]

(Privates)

Charles Beatty [Beaty][235]

Fletcher Cheney[236]

John Collins[237]

Samuel McCauley[238]

John McDonald[239]

John Owens[240]

John Welsh[241]

Co. H Killed:

Lieutenant James S. Patterson [see note 70]

Corporal John E. Stearns[242]

(Privates)

Sylvester Humeston[243]

Peter Bockholt[244]

John Henderson[245]

Sydenham W. Morgan[246]

William Marks[247]

Co. H Wounded:

Sergeant William H. Hall[248]

Corporal Job Trites[249]

Corporal Archibald McAlister[250]

(Privates)

Charles H. Bloom[251]

James Barnes[252]

Moses Jenkins[253]

Thomas Kyle[254]

George Kinney[255]

Marcus Yake[256]

Amos R. Tuttle[257]

Robert M. Howig[258]

Samuel N. English[259]

Byron Bunnell[260]

Alanson McLaughlin[261]

William H. Hyde [Hide][262]
Hollis Johnson[263]
Thomas J. Leeper[264]
Charles A. Ankeny[265]
Horace S. Humeston[266]
Edward P. Thomas[267]
Naman Barnes[268]

Co. I Wounded:
George E. Jenkins[269]
Levi Benedict[270]
James M. Riley[271]

Co. K Killed:
Private James B. Ray[272]

Co. K Wounded:
Corporal Henry J. Beck[273]
Sergeant C[onrad]. J. Henle[274]

(Privates)
James P. Douglas[s][275]
Richard Shields[276]
William [H.] Blakely[277]
James G. Moyses[278]
Benjamin T. Baker[279]
Francis Pomeroy[280]
Langdon Morse[281]
Ransom[e] [E.] Hulbert [Hurlburt][282]

CHAPTER NOTES:
Battle of Arkansas Post

❧ ──────────────── ❧

144. The infamous last battle of the Napoleonic Wars fought June 18, 1815, south of Waterloo on the central Belgium plain. The combined armies consisting of 156,660 allied soldiers, mainly English and Prussian, under the command of Sir Arthur Wellesley, the First Duke of Wellington, and Field Marshal Gebhard Leberecht von Blucher, decisively defeated the main force of the French Army, 71,947 men commanded by Napoleon Bonaparte. Oake references the great historic battle in comparison to his regiment's having faced its own supreme test of combat and resulting high casualties in assaulting the Confederate fortifications at the Post of Arkansas. David G. Chandler, *The Campaigns of Napoleon: The Mind and Method of History's Greatest Soldier* (New York: Macmillan Publishing Company, 1966), 1064–93.

145. The oldest permanent white settlement in the lower Mississippi, the river community of Arkansas Post was established by the French, roughly 25 miles upstream from the mouth of the Arkansas River, in 1686. From 1819 to 1820, the settlement had been the seat of the first Arkansas territorial government. For a brief period the largest town in the territory, the village was too inconveniently located, and, in 1820, the territorial assembly transferred the capital to Little Rock, 117 miles farther upstream on the Arkansas. Bearss, *The Vicksburg Campaign,* I: 349–50.

146. A full-bastioned fort, the Post of Arkansas resembled a four-pointed star, with four salient angles, whose exterior scarps (or sides of the defensive ditch excavated next to the parapet) were each 100 yards in length, as Oake describes. A bastion is a work that projects toward the field at a salient (junction of two faces whose apex projects outward) angle. The parapet's superior slope was 18 feet, the ditch 20 feet across on the ground level and 8 feet deep. There were three gun platforms in each bastion and one in the curtain (a segment of a wall that served to join two structures, such as bastions) facing north. Casement 18 by 15 feet in width and 6.5 feet high was constructed on the southern face of the northeast bastion. The walls of this casement were constructed of three thicknesses of oak timber 14 inches square, as was the roof, which was reinforced by sheets of flat iron 7/8 of an inch thick. One of the shorter sides of the casement was built into the parapet and was pierced by an embrasure 3 feet 8 inches on the inside and 4 feet 6 inches on the outside. The casement emplaced a 9-inch Columbiad mounted on a carriage made of railroad iron. A similar casement armed with an 8-inch Columbiad was constructed in the curtain facing the river. Mounted in the salient angle comprising the southeast bastion was another 9-inch Columbiad on a center-pintle barbette carriage. The three heavy cannon commanded the Arkansas River below (downstream from) the fort. Four 10-pounder Parrott rifles and four 6-pounder smoothbores were mounted on field carriages, located on artillery platforms in the bastions. Three frame buildings, a well, and two magazines were sheltered within the fort. Col. Thomas L. Stead, "The Conquest of Arkansas," Robert U. Johnson and Clarence C. Buel, eds., *Battles and Leaders of the Civil War,* 4 vols. (New York: *Century Magazine*, 1885–87), III: 453; *O.R.* I-17-I-705, 760–61; Bearss, *The Vicksburg Campaign,* I: 350–51; Garrison & Garrison, *Civil War Usage,* 22, 58, 218, 220.

147. The *Blue Wing No. 2* was a 170-ton sidewheel steamer that had been seized from Confederates on December 16, 1862, and delivered to Quartermaster service. On December 28, 1862, while transporting mail and supplies from Helena to Milliken's Bend, the unarmed vessel came under artillery fire from the Arkansas shore at Cypress Bend, eight miles below Napoleon. After its crew surrendered, the vessel was burned. At the time she was carrying army dispatches and ordnance stores as cargo, and towing two barges loaded with coal for the navy. The attack and destruction of the vessel became the strongest impetus for arming, with howitzers, army transports on the Arkansas River, White River, and lower Mississippi, and the policy was put into effect. After United States forces captured the Post of Arkansas, U.S. ammunition was discovered, "having come from the *Blue Wing*." Gibson & Gibson, *Dictionary of Transports and Combatant Vessels*, 38; Bearss, *The Vicksburg Campaign*, I: 354.

148. The Federal fleet bypassed the mouth of the Arkansas River to keep the Confederates in the dark as long as possible about the offensive's objective. The mouth of the White River was located perhaps fourteen miles farther upstream on the Mississippi. The natural cutoff provided access from the White to the Arkansas River, roughly 12 (air) miles below the Post of Arkansas. Alfred T. Mahan, *The Gulf and Inland Waters* (New York: Charles Scribner's Sons, 1883), 120.

149. The plantation belonged to a Col. Frederic Notrebe. Oake apparently secured his post-war spelling of the name from Sherman's published official report or from the general's own *Memoirs*, for he also cites the plantation name as "Notrib's." The Confederates had constructed a section of rifle-pits (known as the "lower pits") behind the levee immediately upstream from the plantation. The lower rifle pits were two miles below the Post, and extended inland from the river—terminating near Coines Hill. The line commanded the river road, followed the levee, and contained placements for ten cannon. Two additional lines of defense were located farther upstream. The second line was located 600 to 800 yards behind the lower pits, its right end anchored on the river, extending about 800 yards north, where the left anchored upon a large pond. The third line, 2,600 yards farther upstream, extended from the salient angle of the north-western bastion of the fort in a westerly direction for 720 yards, terminating roughly 200 yards short of the Post Bayou. Sherman, *Memoirs*, 325; *O.R.* I-17-I-754; Bearss, *The Vicksburg Campaign*, I: 362–64.

150. "A horse! a horse! My kingdom for a horse!" William Shakespeare, *The Life and Death of King Richard III* (1592-93?) Act 5, Scene 4, *The Complete Works of Shakespeare* (Stamford, Conn.: Longmeadow Press, 1990), 668.

151. Oake is mimicking Shakespearean prose in stating that on this horrendous night tramping around the swampy Arkansas floodplain, he would have gladly forfeited a seat in heaven for a little sleep.

152. Morpheus was the Greek god of dreams. *The New Lexicon Webster's Dictionary of the English Language* (New York: Lexicon Publications, Inc., 1990), 651. Hereafter cited as *Webster's Dictionary*.

153. This may well have been Maj. John H. Hammond, assistant adjutant general on Sherman's staff, employed by the corps commander to carry orders to Steele's division throughout the late morning.

154. The order of battle for the brigade, from left to right, consisted of the 26th Iowa, 34th Iowa, and 30th Iowa, with the 4th Iowa and 9th Iowa regiments held in reserve. A regiment was composed of ten companies, lettered A through K. When formed in order of battle—in line—the companies placed themselves in an official, strictly prescribed order according to the seniority of the company captains. The sequence thus maintained from right to left was: the 1st, 6th, 4th, 9th, 3rd, 8th, 5th, 10th, 7th, and 2nd companies. Prior to the resignation of Capt. Sherman Williams, on December 29, 1862, Company A had been 2nd Company, but now that Alanson D. Gaston had been promoted, January 1, 1863, becoming the regiment's junior captain, Company A, in regimental battle formation, would have occupied a position in the left center of the regiment in line. This practice could be traced back to 17th-century military procedure in Europe. The strict order of battle doctrine was designed to ensure the company commanded by the most senior (veteran or experienced) captain was posted on the right flank, the company with the next most experienced captain was posted on the left, while that of the third ranking captain was in the middle of the regiment. *O.R.* I-17-I-769–70; Silas Casey, *Infantry Tactics for the Instruction, Exercise, and Maneuvers of the Soldier, a Company, Line of Skirmishers, Battalion, Brigade, or Corps D'Armee*, 3 vols. (New York: D. Van Nostrand, 1862; reprinted by Morningside Press, Dayton, Ohio, 1985) 3; *O.R.* II-2-346; Brent Nosworthy, *The Bloody Crucible of Courage: Fighting Methods and Combat Experiences of the Civil War* (New York: Carroll & Graf, 2003), 138.

155. Oake is alluding to soldiers who habitually avoided combat. Garrison & Garrison, *Civil War Usage*, 230.

156. Thayer's brigade was posted on the right center of the attacking force. The Federal deployment from left to right consisted of the brigades of Lionel Sheldon, William Landram, Stephen Burbridge, Thomas Kilby Smith, Giles A. Smith, Thayer, and Alvin Hovey. Bearss, *The Vicksburg Campaign*, I: 384.

157. Common referred to as "buck and ball," it was a musket load made up of three buckshot and a one-ounce ball, the whole of which was wrapped in paper. Used primarily by Confederates at this stage in the war, the load was not effective beyond 200 yards. Garrison & Garrison, *Civil War Usage*, 37.

158. A hastily constructed defensive work of earth and wood, erected to protect defenders from artillery and rifle fire. In most instances its front was protected by a ditch—the excavated dirt from which the breastwork was made. The work could also be raised by ditching from the rear and throwing the dirt forward. Garrison & Garrison, *Civil War Usage*, 34.

159. Logs at either end of a simple defensive work, elevated so that weapons could be fired through a small aperture without permitting the enemy to view and aim at the heads of the riflemen or sharpshooters. Garrison & Garrison, *Civil War Usage*, 107.

160. Double shotting was placing two loads of ammunition into a cannon. Artillerists often double- and sometimes triple-shotted their field pieces if an enemy assault threatened to overwhelm or overrun the battery.

161. An elongated soft-lead projectile (bullet) with a hollow cone-shaped base used as ammunition for rifles (or more properly rifle-muskets, since it was designed for long-barreled shoulder weapons loaded by dropping the bullet or ball down the barrel of the weapon after inserting it base first in the muzzle), designed by French captains Henri-Gustave Delvigne and Claude-Etienne Minie in the 1840s. The bullet was easier to load, and the hollow base of the bullet expanded and forced the projectile into the rifled grooves of the barrel to gain improved accuracy and range. The bullet was adopted by the United States Army in 1855. Garrison & Garrison, *Civil War Usage*, 159, 213–14.

162. Colonel Smith and Adjutant Ferreby recover from their wounds and return to service. General Thayer reported, "Owing to the thick underbrush and want of space for a front of the brigade, I at first advanced in column of regiments, deploying them into line as fast as we could get a front. The Twenty-sixth Iowa, Colonel Smith, being on the left, gained an advanced position and did good execution. This regiment had two commissioned officers and sixteen men killed, and ninety-nine wounded, including Colonel Smith, who was compelled to leave the field." *Roster* 3: 1019–20, 1028; *O.R.* I-17-I-769. See note 170 for a different assessment of casualties.

163. The only Missouri battery present on the field was Capt. Clemenz Landgraeber's 1st Missouri Flying Battery or 1st Missouri Horse Artillery (officially cited as Co. F, 2nd Missouri Light Artillery in *O.R.*). The battery was assigned to Hovey's 2nd Brigade, which was deployed on the extreme right of the Federal line, immediately on Thayer's brigade right. The return of casualties for Union forces engaged at the Post of Arkansas, published in *O.R.*, cites the Missouri Battery was not engaged (as does General McClernand, who reported the battery held with the reserve), but this appears to be in error, for General Hovey reported he personally directed a section of the battery (with two 12-pounder howitzers) into action during the later stages of the assault. There is no officer by the name of Schinstten listed among battery personnel. However, a Lt. Louis Schneider and a Lt. John N. Siegel are identified on muster roll. The editor was unable to confirm whether the mistake in identification can be attributed to Oake or the unknown transcriber of Oake's now lost original manuscript. The battery assigned to Thayer's 3rd Brigade was the 1st Battery, Iowa Light Artillery, commanded by Capt. Henry H. Griffiths. *O.R.* I-17-I-704, 718, 765–66.

164. Robert J. McLenahan, born in Ohio, was 29 and a resident of Charlotte. He enlisted July 14, 1862 as seventh corporal, and subsequently advanced to fourth sergeant March 24, 1863; second sergeant, September 1, 1864; and finally first lieutenant (never officially mustered in at that grade) of Co. A., and mustered out June 6, 1865, at Washington D.C. *Roster* 3: 1075.

165. Twenty-one-year-old Charles M. Butler had been born in Illinois and was a resident of Charlotte when he enlisted on July 14, 1862, as fourth corporal of Co. A. He was promoted first corporal on March 24, 1863, and fifth sergeant on April 1, 1863. He was killed in action during the May 22, 1863, assault on Vicksburg, Mississippi. *Roster* 3: 1033.

166. Ray, age 21, was a native of Pennsylvania and resident of Clinton County when he enlisted on August 12, 1862. He was initially interred on the battlefield. After the war the bodies of the U.S. forces killed in action or died of mortal wounds at Arkansas Post were disinterred and transported to the National Cemetery in Little Rock, Arkansas. Ray is listed among the known dead. *Roster* 3: 1094.

167. Two 6-pounder guns, belonging to the right section of Capt. William Hart's Arkansas Battery, were positioned on the right flank of the 10th Texas Infantry, directly in front of the 26th Iowa. The right section of Hart's Battery was under the command of Lt. E. A. Du Bose. *O.R.* I-17-I-792; Bearss, *The Vicksburg Campaign*, I: 381–82.

168. Captain Hart's Battery, owing to its initial effectiveness in inflicting heavy casualties on the attacking U.S. forces, received considerable attention from Federal counter-battery fire and especially musketry from attacking Union infantry regiments that became pinned down in front of the Confederate rifle pits. As a result, the personnel and equipment assigned to the battery were severely shot up during the attack, losing 3 men killed, 13 wounded, and 22 men listed missing, for a total of 38 casualties, which was 17.8 percent of the entire Confederate loss for the day. Colonel James Deshler, whose infantry brigade was supported by four of Hart's six cannon during the assault, stated it had been impossible for any of the Arkansas artillerists "to show himself without being struck." Deshler added, confirming Royal Oake's field observations, that of the horses serving the four cannon and their caissons assigned to the battery in direct support of his brigade line, "only one or two of the battery horses escaped being either killed or wounded." The Confederate loss in killed and wounded is cited as 60 killed, 73 wounded, and 80 men missing, for 213 reported casualties. A total of 4,791 Confederates were listed as captured, along with seventeen cannons (seven of them destroyed during the bombardment). *O.R.* I-17-I-708, 785, 791–93.

169. Porter's gunboats silenced the guns defending the Post within three hours. The vessels participating were the City Class ironclads *Louisville, Baron De Kalb,* and *Cincinnati,* accompanied by the tinclad *Lexington.* Once the Post's heavy guns were silenced, Porter ordered the tinclads *Rattler* and *Glide,* supported by the ram *Monarch,* to pass the fort. Once this was accomplished, the three vessels proceeded upriver to sever the Confederate line of retreat. Naval casualties were six killed and twenty-five wounded. *O.R.* I-17-I-706; Bearss, *The Vicksburg Campaign,* I: 379–80, 402.

170. *O.R.* lists 18 killed and 99 men wounded; however, *Roster* 3: 1020, supports Oake's compilation of casualties, and cites the regiment went into action with an aggregate strength of 447 enlisted men and officers and lost 119 men (18 killed and 101 wounded), recording a significant loss of 26.6 percent of the men engaged—the highest numerical loss of any United States organization engaged in the battle. General Thayer's 3rd Brigade, in which the 26th Iowa served, suffered 24 killed and 156 wounded. The entire U.S. Army of the Mississippi recorded 134 killed, 898 wounded, and 29 missing, for a total of 1,061 casualties during three days of ground operations at the Post of Arkansas. The losses in the inexperienced 26th Iowa Infantry accounted for 11.2 percent of that total. *O.R.* I-17-I-716–19.

171. There were actually two men (father and son) named John Sinkey in Co. A, 26th Iowa. The wounded man was John Sinkey the junior, age 23, who had been born in Ohio. A resident of Canton, he enlisted along with his father on August 12, 1862. Sinkey did not recover from his wounds and died at a general hospital in Memphis, Tennessee, February 11, 1863. He is buried in the Mississippi River National Cemetery in Memphis. His father served another seven months before being discharged for disability, August 27, 1863, while the regiment was stationed at Walnut Hills, Mississippi, immediately north of Vicksburg. Significantly, Private Sinkey was the only casualty recorded in Royal's company. *Roster* 3: 1095.

172. Snodgrass, a native of Ohio and a resident of Maquoketa in Jackson County, was 30 when he enlisted as first corporal on August 10, 1862. He had been promoted to fifth sergeant on December 22. His wound was listed as slight, and he was subsequently promoted to third, then second sergeant, completing his term of service to muster out on June 6, 1865, in Washington, D.C. *Roster* 3: 1096.

173. A native of Pennsylvania and resident of Iron Hills, Whiteside was 21 when he enlisted July 8, 1862. He was listed among those severely wounded. His injury proved mortal and he died February 16, 1863, and is listed among those buried in the Mississippi River National Cemetery in Memphis. *Roster* 3: 1106.

174. A resident of Fulton, having been born in New Hampshire, Fisher was 30 when he enlisted August 10, 1862. Records cite his being promoted to fourth corporal, December 22, 1862. Listed among those severely wounded, he recovered to earn promotion to fifth sergeant, April 1, 1863. He was wounded again, August 15, 1864, outside Atlanta, Georgia, and sent home to convalesce. He never returned to field service, and was discharged for wounds, May 29, 1865, at Davenport, Iowa. *Roster* 3: 1054.

175. Born in Canada, Kilrain, age 19, was a resident of Maquoketa when he enlisted August 4, 1862. He recovered from being slightly wounded to complete his enlistment, mustering out June 6, 1865, at Washington, D.C. *Roster* 3: 1070.

176. Lynn, a native of Pennsylvania, was 21 and a resident of Otter Creek when he enlisted August 3, 1862. Listed as severely wounded, he recovered to complete his enlistment, mustering out June 6, 1865. *Roster* 3: 1072.

177. Hiersche, age 28, immigrated to America from Austria and was residing in Welton when he enlisted July 28, 1862. Cited among the severely wounded, he recovered and was promoted to second corporal. He mustered out June 6, 1865, in Washington, D.C. *Roster* 3: 1061.

178. Listed as Henry F. Shaffer in *Roster*, this native of Pennsylvania was 32 and living in Clinton when he enlisted as sixth corporal, August 15, 1862. Promoted to fifth corporal, November 1, 1862, he died in the assault and was buried on the field, being later moved to the National Cemetery in Little Rock, Arkansas. *Roster* 3: 1097.

179. Born in New York, Keal was 24 and a resident of Low Moor when he enlisted August 12,

1862. *Roster* reports he was wounded in the attack and died of wounds the following day, January 12, 1863. It is highly probable that Oake secured his information for this listing from *AGI*, 1863-I: 926, which lists Private Keal as "killed in battle" on January 11. *Roster* 3: 1070.

180. Private Thomas died aboard the hospital steamer *D. A. January* on January 13, 1863. A native of Iowa, the Clinton resident was 18 when he enlisted August 14, 1862. *Roster* 3: 1102.

181. Sage, who had been born in New York, was 26 and a resident of Clinton when he enlisted as third sergeant, August 9, 1862. Quickly recovering from his wounds, he was promoted second lieutenant of Co. C, February 27, 1863, and later to captain of Co. B; however, he was never mustered in at that rank. Sage mustered out June 6, 1865, at Washington, D.C. *AGI*, 1863-I: 925; *Roster* 3: 1095–96.

182. A former Hoosier, Lacock was 30 and a resident of Clinton when he enlisted August 15, 1862. Not able to completely mend from being wounded at Arkansas Post, he was transferred to the Invalid Corps (later renamed the Veteran Reserve Corps) on September 22, 1863, and reassigned to noncombat duty until July 8, 1865, when he mustered out while stationed in Philadelphia, Pennsylvania. The Invalid Corps was composed of men incapacitated by wounds or disease who performed garrison or hospital service. In the spring of 1864, this growing corps was re-designated the Veteran Reserve Corps, and Lacock joined an estimated 60,000 men in filling its ranks until it was disbanded at war's end. *Roster* 3: 1073; Garrison & Garrison, *Civil War Usage*, 121.

183. Listed as Symons in *Roster,* this native of England was 27 and residing in Clinton when he enlisted on August 15, 1862. He recovered from these wounds only to be wounded again at Resaca, Georgia, May 14, 1865. This time Symons's injury was severe enough that he was transferred to the Veteran Reserve Corps on March 18, 1865. He secured his discharge from service in July 1865, at Jefferson Barracks near St. Louis, Missouri. *Roster* 3: 1097.

184. Cone was a native of Germany who was residing in Clinton when, at the age of 44, he enlisted on August 14, 1862. Following his being wounded at Arkansas Post, he is cited as deserting from the service, January 13, 1864, while he was stationed (apparently in an invalid noncombat capacity) at Davenport, Iowa. *Roster* 3: 1042.

185. McDowell was 30, a native of Ohio, and living in Clinton when he enlisted August 15, 1862. In addition to being wounded at Arkansas Post, he was wounded outside of Atlanta, Georgia, August 11, 1864. He mustered out at Washington, D.C., June 6, 1865. *Roster* 3: 1075.

186. Born in Illinois and a resident of Camanche, Hedges was 20 when he enlisted August 14, 1862. After recovering from being wounded, he continued his service, being promoted to fifth corporal on May 1, 1865, before being mustered out in Washington, D.C., June 6, 1865. His older brother William, also from Camanche, having been born in Ohio and age 26 at enlistment, also served in Co. C, until a severe illness forced him to be transferred to the Invalid Corps, September 22, 1863, where he subsequently died, July 28, 1864, while stationed in Davenport. *Roster* 3: 1062.

187. A native of Pennsylvania, Savits, 27 and a resident of Camanche, enlisted August 15, 1862 as fourth corporal of Co. C. He never fully recovered from his injury at the Post and was discharged for wounds on June 14, 1865, while stationed in Keokuk, Iowa. *Roster* 3: 1096.

188. An immigrant from Ireland, Cunningham was living in Clinton when, on August 11, 1862, he enlisted for war service. Like several of his wounded comrades, he was unable to overcome his injury and was transferred to the Invalid Corps on December 27, 1863. He was mustered out in Washington, D.C., June 28, 1865. *Roster* 3: 1042.

189. Schroder, age 24, was an immigrant from Germany, living in Low Moor when he enlisted on August 15, 1862. He never recovered from being wounded and was discharged November 9, 1863, in St. Louis, Missouri. *Roster* 3: 1096.

190. Jackson, born in Ohio and a resident of Clinton, was 19 and a year older than his brother Mason when they both enlisted August 6, 1862. Unable to rebound from being wounded at Arkansas Post, Milton was discharged from the service at Memphis, Tennessee, on April 3, 1863. Mason continued to serve, being promoted third corporal, July 1, 1864, and completed his enlistment, being mustered out in Washington, D.C., June 6, 1865. *Roster* 3: 1068.

191. Greenlee recovered from being wounded only to die of disease, May 9, 1863, at Paw Paw Island, Louisiana. Born in Pennsylvania, he was 19 and a resident of Elvira when he and older brother William (age 21) enlisted August 15, 1862. William preceded Benjamin in death, dying of disease, February 10, 1863, while the regiment was encamped at Young's Point, Louisiana. *Roster* 3: 1058.

192. A native of New York, Bowen lived in Clinton and was 33 when he enlisted August 14, 1862. After being wounded in Arkansas, he was transferred to the Invalid Corps on August 1, 1863, and continued to serve in a noncombat role until discharged July 5, 1863, at Indianapolis, Indiana. *Roster* 3: 1034.

193. Born in Pennsylvania, Dougherty was 24 and living in Elvira when he enlisted August 15, 1862. After recovering from being wounded, he served until mustered out June 6, 1865, in Washington, D.C. *Roster* 3: 1048.

194. Johnston, age 21, was born in Iowa and was living in Camanche when he enlisted August 15, 1862. He recovered and completed his enlistment and was mustered out June 6, 1865, in Washington, D.C. *Roster* 3: 1068.

195. Listed as Nelson Day on the company muster role, this resident of Clinton (nativity: Iowa), enlisted August 15, 1862, at the age of 19. Day was promoted to fourth corporal, May 1, 1863; third corporal, February 1, 1864; and to fifth sergeant, July 1, 1864. He was mustered out July 23, 1865, at Albany, New York. *Roster* 3: 1048.

196. Austin was 22, a native of Illinois, and a resident of Grand Mount when he enlisted on August 14, 1862. His body was exhumed from burial at Arkansas Post and moved to the National Cemetery in Little Rock, Arkansas. *Roster* 3: 1031.

197. Costello, an immigrant from Canada, was 21 and residing in Charlotte when he enlisted August 14, 1862. He is buried in the National Cemetery in Little Rock, Arkansas. *Roster* 3: 1042.

198. One of three Harrington boys from Welton (nativity: New York) to serve in Co. D, Burt was 26 when he enlisted as eighth corporal, August 12, 1862. Wounded severely, he died three days after the assault on Arkansas Post, January 14, 1863, while aboard the hospital steamer *D. A. January*. He is buried in Mississippi River National Cemetery in Memphis. *Roster* 3: 1062.

199. Maher did not survive and died of his wounds, January 13, 1863. Born in Ireland, he was 21 and a resident of De Witt when he volunteered to enlist on August 11, 1862. *Roster* 3: 1080.

200. McDonell initially enlisted in Co. E, August 12, 1862, at the age of 18. A resident of De Witt (nativity: Ohio), he was transferred to Co. G and finally Co. D. Although he was listed as slightly wounded, complications set in and he died aboard the steamer *Von Phul* on January 27, 1863. *Roster* 3: 1076–77.

201. Stuach, 25, was an immigrant from Scotland, residing in Charlotte, when he enlisted in Co. G, August 20, 1862. Transferred to Co. D on December 11, 1862, he died of his wounds, January 19, 1863, aboard the hospital steamer *D. A. January*. He is buried in Mississippi River National Cemetery in Memphis. *Roster* 3: 1097, 1099.

202. A resident of Welton, having been born in Ohio, Van Horn was 19 when he enlisted August 7, 1862. He survived these wounds only to suffer the same fate at Lovejoy's Station, Georgia, September 2, 1864. He recovered, finished his enlistment, and was mustered out June 6, 1862, in Washington, D.C. *Roster* 3: 1104.

203. Royal Oake did not list James R. Van Horn among those wounded at Arkansas Post. James (nativity: Ohio) lived in Welton when he enlisted at the age of 25, on August 11, 1862. Although wounded severely, he recovered to earn promotion to third corporal, March 1, 1863; and second corporal, May 1, 1863; before being transferred to the Invalid Corps on September 22, 1863. He finished his service in Washington, D.C., being mustered out June 6, 1865. *Roster* 3: 1104.

204. Cavanaugh was 25 and a resident of De Witt (nativity: Ireland) when he enlisted August 13, 1862. Wounded slightly at Arkansas Post, he recovered only to die of disease, June 5, 1864, at Chattanooga, Tennessee, and is buried in the National Cemetery there. *Roster* 3: 1042.

205. Born in Massachusetts and a resident of Buena Vista, Corbin was 44 when he enlisted August 12, 1862. Only slightly wounded, he finished his enlistment, being mustered out June 6, 1865, at Washington, D.C. *Roster* 3: 1042.

206. Walrod was slightly wounded. He was 19, a native of Pennsylvania, and living in De Witt when he enlisted August 11, 1862. He was promoted eighth corporal, March 1, 1863; seventh corporal, May 1, 1863; sixth corporal; fifth corporal, September 1, 1863; and fourth corporal, February 19, 1864. He mustered out June 6, 1865, at Washington, D.C. *Roster* 3: 1107.

207. Pankow, 32, was an immigrant from Germany and residing in Lyons when he enlisted August 22, 1862. He is buried in the National Cemetery at Little Rock, Arkansas. *Roster* 3: 1087.

208. An immigrant from Germany, Krumwiede was 23 and living in Lyons when he enlisted August 22, 1862. He is buried in the National Cemetery at Little Rock, Arkansas. *Roster* 3: 1071.

209. Now buried in National Cemetery at Little Rock, Arkansas, Nyrop, age 23, was born in Denmark and residing in Lyons when he enlisted on August 18, 1862. *Roster* 3: 1084.

210. Unrau, an immigrant from Germany, was living in Lyons on August 25, 1862, when at the age of 22 he enlisted as first sergeant. He recovered from being wounded only to die of disease, June 27, 1863, at Walnut Hills, Mississippi. He is buried in Vicksburg National Cemetery. *Roster* 3: 1104.

211. Hoffman's wounding proved mortal and he died at St. Louis, Missouri, on June 3, 1863. An immigrant from Germany, the 44-year-old volunteer had been living in Lyons when he enlisted August 19, 1862. *Roster* 3: 1063.

212. A German immigrant, Martensen was 41 and residing in Lyons when he enlisted August 22, 1862. He earned promotion to fifth corporal, March 1, 1864, and was mustered out June 6, 1865, in Washington, D.C. *Roster* 3: 1080.

213. Meier was 27 and residing in Lyons when he enlisted August 22, 1862. Of German birth, he recovered from being wounded only to be reported missing (actually captured), October 12, 1864, at Kingston (or Cassville), Georgia. He was possibly held at Andersonville Prison (Georgia) for a brief time before being paroled at Camp Parole, Annapolis, Maryland, in December 1864, and mustered out of service, June 7, 1865, at Camp Chase, Ohio. Camps of parole were established to board prisoners who had been released from capture into parole status awaiting official exchange proceedings between the United States and Confederate governments. In this case, with exchanges having been ended by Lt. Gen. Ulysses S. Grant, the parolees—both in the North and South—like Anton Meier were held indefinitely in camps through the late winter and spring of 1865. *Roster* 3: 1081; "Andersonville Prisoner of War Records" cite an Anton Meyer, 26th Iowa, as a possible prisoner in the fall of 1864 (see http://www.itd.nps.gov/cwss/).

214. Born in Germany, Reisch was 25 and a resident of De Witt when he enlisted on August 12, 1862. He was again wounded in the summer of 1864 and died of his wounds, August 12, 1864, near Atlanta, Georgia. *Roster* 3: 1092.

215. A resident of Lyons and native of Germany, Schmutz was 34 when he enlisted on August 19, 1862. He never completely overcame these wounds, and transferred to the Invalid Corps, March 15, 1864, being mustered out June 6, 1865, at Washington, D.C. *Roster* 3: 1098.

216. Schultz recovered only to be killed in action on May 19, 1863, at Vicksburg, Mississippi. A native of Germany, he was 28 and residing in Lyons when he enlisted on August 15, 1862. *Roster* 3: 1098.

217. Born in Ohio and a resident of Calamus, 18-year-old Steinhilbert was a late enlistment when he joined ranks on October 7, 1862. His wounds proved mortal, and he died on board the hospital steamer *D. A. January* on January 20, 1863. He is buried at Memphis in the Mississippi River National Cemetery. *Roster* 3: 1098.

218. A native of Germany and a resident of Lyons, Schnack was 29 years old when he enlisted on August 19, 1862. He transferred to the Invalid Corps, March 15, 1864, being mustered out June 6, 1865, in Washington, D.C. *Roster* 3: 1098.

219. The 28-year-old Campbell had been born in Kentucky and was residing in De Witt when he enlisted on August 14, 1862. If later exhumed from his war grave, he is apparently classified among the "unknown" dead at Little Rock National Cemetery in Arkansas. *Roster* 3: 1043.

220. Like Daniel Campbell, Bollinger apparently lies among the unknown dead at Little Rock National Cemetery. He was a 34-year-old German immigrant living in Clinton County when he enlisted August 22, 1862. *Roster* 3: 1035.

221. When he enlisted on August 11, 1862, Stanley, a native of Vermont, was 30 and residing in De Witt. He is listed among the known dead at Little Rock National Cemetery, Arkansas. *Roster* 3: 1099.

222. Rider was 22, Ohio-born, and a resident of De Witt when he enlisted as first sergeant, August 15, 1862. He recovered from these wounds and earned a commission as second lieutenant, February 19, 1863; then first lieutenant, February 27, 1863. He was wounded on May 22, 1863, in an assault on Vicksburg and discharged for disability, July 27, 1864. *Roster* 3: 1092.

223. Markland, born in Indiana, was 35 and living in Welton when he enlisted on August 15, 1862, as fourth sergeant. He was promoted third sergeant, October 29, 1862, before being wounded at Arkansas Post. He recovered, was promoted first sergeant and wounded again, May 14, 1864, at Resaca, Georgia. Promoted captain, July 13, 1864 (not mustered), he was wounded for the third time, September 1, 1864, at Jonesborough, Georgia. He died of wounds on September 22, and is buried in the National Cemetery at Marietta, Georgia. *Roster* 3: 1081.

224. A resident of De Witt (nativity: New York), Ahira Stevens was 28 when he enlisted August 15, 1862. Promoted sixth corporal, December 14, 1862, he recovered and was promoted fourth corporal, April 30, 1863, but later transferred to the Invalid Corps on March 15, 1864, being discharged July 10, 1865, at Trenton, New Jersey. *Roster* 3: 1099.

225. Cady, born in Vermont, was 39 and a resident of De Witt when he enlisted August 6, 1862. He served out his enlistment term and mustered out June 6, 1865, in Washington, D.C. *Roster* 3: 1043.

226. Twenty-year-old Correll was discharged for disability on April 4, 1863. Born in Ohio, he was living in Welton when he enlisted on August 13, 1862. *Roster* 3: 1044.

227. Hudson was a native of Ohio, 28, and a resident of Burgess when he and his younger brother Josiah (age 26) enlisted on August 15, 1862. He served as eighth corporal until wounded. Transferred to the Invalid Corps, April 10, 1864, he was discharged for disability, April 29, 1864, and died of disease, March 20, 1864, in Davenport, Iowa. *Roster* 3: 1064.

228. A resident of Grand Mound (nativity: Ireland), Mahar was 38 when he enlisted August 14, 1862. Upon recovery from these wounds, he served another two years, being mustered out May 4, 1865. *Roster* 3: 1081.

229. Preston was 21, a native of New York, and living in De Witt when he enlisted as fourth corporal of Co. D on August 11, 1862. Transferred to Co. F, November 1, 1862, he is listed as dying of disease while a prisoner of war, January 24, 1864, in Richmond, Virginia, where he is buried in the National Cemetery. *Roster* 3: 1087–8.

230. Loofborn, born in Ohio, was 28 and living in De Witt when he enlisted on August 15, 1862. He recovered from these wounds but was wounded again, May 18, 1863, on the approach to Vicksburg, Mississippi. He was mustered out July 8, 1865, at Davenport, Iowa. *Roster* 3: 1073.

231. Mullett, age 27 and a native of New York, was living in De Witt when he enlisted on August 14, 1862. He served until May 31, 1865, when records cite him being mustered out at Memphis, Tennessee. *Roster* 3: 1082.

232. Listed as Farl in *AGI*, 1863-I: 939. Born in Vermont, Fanell was 21 and a resident of De Witt when he enlisted August 18, 1862. He is buried in the National Cemetery in Little Rock, Arkansas. *Roster* 3: 1056.

233. Born in Ireland, Cahill was 21 and living in Lyons when he enlisted as first corporal on August 8, 1862. Promoted fifth sergeant, October 24, 1862, he survived only to desert while recovering in St. Louis, June 8, 1863. War Department records cite: "Under the name of Con W. Clifford, he enlisted December 28, 1863, in Co. B, 10th United States Infantry and was discharged December 28, 1868, on expiration of term of service." *Roster* 3: 1044.

234. Gange was born in England, and was 22 and a resident of Clinton County when he enlisted August 14, 1862. Promoted sixth corporal he later, upon his own request, was reduced to ranks, February 22, 1863. He was mustered out of the service June 6, 1865, in Washington, D.C. *Roster* 3: 1059.

235. Beaty (spelled Beety in *AGI*, 1863-I: 938), age 18, enlisted on August 15, 1862. A resident of Clinton County and born in Illinois, he survived, but was discharged for disability, May 13, 1864, in Davenport, Iowa. *Roster* 3: 1036.

236. Cheney, born in New York, was 20 and living in Jackson County when he enlisted on August 15, 1862. He was promoted third corporal, July 1, 1864, and was slightly wounded again, October 16, 1864, at Ship's Gap, Georgia. Promoted second corporal, May 1, 1865, he was mustered out June 6, 1865, at Washington, D.C. *Roster* 3: 1045.

237. An Irish immigrant, Collins was 19 and living in Lyons when he enlisted August 9, 1862. He did not fully recover from being wounded and was discharged May 30, 1863, at St. Louis, Missouri. *Roster* 3: 1045.

238. McCauley did not survive the trials of campaign life and being wounded, and subsequently died April 1, 1863, at Young's Point, Louisiana. Born in Pennsylvania, he resided in Jackson County and was 25 when he and his younger brother William (age 23) enlisted August 19, 1862. William was also discharged for disability on May 7, 1863, at St. Louis, Missouri. *Roster* 3: 1076.

239. The 44-year-old McDonald was an Irish immigrant and a resident of Lyons when he enlisted August 22, 1862. He was discharged for wounds on July 16, 1863, at St. Louis, Missouri. *Roster* 3: 1077.

240. Born in Ireland, Owens was 25 and living in Lyons when he enlisted August 14, 1862. He never fully recovered from his wounds and was discharged January 11, 1864, at St. Louis, Missouri. *Roster* 3: 1085.

241. A native of Canada, Welsh was 26 and residing in Lyons when he enlisted August 9, 1862. He was discharged for disability, October 17, 1864, at Davenport, Iowa. *Roster* 3: 1110.

242. Born in Ohio and a resident of De Witt, Stearns, age 19, enlisted August 9, 1862, and was promoted second corporal on November 18, 1862. He is presumably buried as an unmarked grave in the Little Rock National Cemetery, Arkansas. *Roster* 3: 1100.

243. The oldest of three Humestons in Co. H, Sylvester was born in New York, 29, and a resident of De Witt when he enlisted on August 9, 1862. Both his brothers, Enos and Horace, survived the war and were mustered out June 6, 1865, at Washington, D.C. *Roster* 3: 1066.

244. A German immigrant, Bockholt was 26 and living in Clinton County when he enlisted on August 9, 1862. He is buried in the National Cemetery at Little Rock, Arkansas. *Roster* 3: 1037.

245. Of Scottish birth, Henderson was 33 and residing in De Witt when he enlisted on August 7, 1862. *Roster* 3: 1065.

246. Morgan, 19, was born in Indiana and resided in Davenport when he enlisted on August 14, 1862. *Roster* 3: 1083.

247. Prussian by birth, Marks was 26 and living in Camanche when he enlisted on August 9, 1862. It is presumed he lies within a grave marked "unknown" at Little Rock National Cemetery, Arkansas. *Roster* 3: 1082.

248. Hall was 28, a native of Pennsylvania, and living in Wheatland when he enlisted as a private on August 13, 1862. Promoted second sergeant, October 1, 1862, he survived being wounded and earned promotion to first sergeant on March 1, 1863. Wounded a second time, May 22, 1863, he earned a field promotion to first lieutenant, June 8, 1863, and then captain on September 2, 1863. He received a third wound at Resaca, Georgia, May 14, 1864, and was promoted major (not officially mustered), before being mustered out June 6, 1865, at Washington, D.C. *Roster* 3: 1065.

249. Trites, having been born in Nova Scotia, enlisted August 14, 1862, at the age of 33. He was a resident of De Witt. He had been promoted eighth corporal, December 1, 1862. His wounds proved mortal, and he died in a Memphis hospital on February 13, 1863. *Roster* 3: 1103.

250. McAlister, born in New York, was a resident of De Witt when, at age 35, he enlisted as fifth corporal on August 6, 1862. He had been promoted to third corporal. This wound proved mortal, and he died January 30, 1863, in a hospital at Memphis, where he is buried in the Mississippi River National Cemetery. *Roster* 3: 1077.

251. A German immigrant, 18-year-old Bloom resided in De Witt when he enlisted on August 9, 1862. He died from wounds on January 30, 1862, in a hospital at Memphis, and is buried in the National Cemetery there. *Roster* 3: 1137.

252. An Ohioan by birth, Barnes was 26 and living in De Witt when he enlisted on August 9, 1862 (a younger brother, Naman, enlisted on August 7, 1862—see note 268). James did not recover, dying of these wounds in a St. Louis hospital on February 3, 1863. He is buried in the National Cemetery at Jefferson Barracks. *Roster* 3: 1037.

253. Jenkins, 34, native of New Brunswick, was a De Witt resident upon enlistment, August 9, 1862. His wounds proved mortal, and he died in Memphis, February 14, 1863, and is buried in the National Cemetery there. *Roster* 3: 1069.

254. Kyle, 38, a native Ohioan, lived in De Witt when he enlisted on August 8, 1862. He died of disease in a St. Louis hospital, August 9, 1862, and is buried in the Jefferson Barracks National Cemetery. *Roster* 3: 1072.

255. Born in Ohio, 25 and a resident of De Witt, Kinney survived his wound but died of disease on the steamer *City of Memphis* on October 3, 1863. He is buried in the National Cemetery at Mound City, Illinois. *Roster* 3: 1072.

256. Yake, 21, survived being wounded. He and an older brother, Joseph (28), both De Witt residents, enlisted on August 9, 1862. Immigrants from Switzerland, they served together in Co. H until being mustered out in Washington, D.C., June 6, 1865. *Roster* 3: 1112.

257. Tuttle survived being wounded. Upon enlistment on August 6, 1862, this native of Pennsylvania was 32 and a resident of De Witt. He was mustered out June 6, 1865, in Washington, D.C. *Roster* 3: 1103.

258. A New Yorker by birth, Howig, 27 and a resident of De Witt, enlisted on August 8, 1862. Transferred to the Invalid Corps, September 1, 1863, he was mustered out June 6, 1865, in Washington, D.C. *Roster* 3: 1065.

259. Pennsylvanian by birth, English, who was 22 and a resident of De Witt, enlisted on August 9, 1862. Wounded severely, he subsequently died of disease, July 11, 1863, at Walnut Hills, Mississippi, and is buried in the National Cemetery at Vicksburg. He was survived by an older brother, William (33 at enlistment), who steadily rose through the noncommissioned ranks from corporal to sergeant; was promoted first lieutenant, October 24, 1864; and completed his service as captain (not mustered) on June 6, 1865, in Washington, D.C. *Roster* 3: 1053.

260. Born in Indiana, Bunnell was 22 and living in De Witt when he enlisted on August 8, 1862. He recovered and was mustered out on June 6, 1865, in Washington, D.C. *Roster* 3: 1038.

261. McLaughlin survived being wounded. Born in Pennsylvania, he was 32 and living in De Witt when he enlisted on August 9, 1862. He was promoted sixth corporal, September 1, 1863; third corporal, January 1, 1864; and fifth sergeant, September 1, 1864. He was mustered out June 6, 1865, in Washington, D.C. *Roster* 3: 1077.

262. One of three brothers to enlist on August 7, 1862, Hide was the youngest at 25 at the time. Thomas G. Hide was 33 and John A. Hide was 29, and all three were born in Ohio and living in De Witt in 1862. William's wounds were not severe, but perhaps served as a catalyst for an illness that claimed his life at Young's Point, Louisiana, on March 1, 1863. His older brother John had already died of disease aboard the steamer *Von Phul*, on January 30, 1863. Thomas himself was weakened by the hardships of field service and transferred to the Invalid Corps on September 12, 1863; he was mustered out July 8, 1865, at Clinton, Iowa. *Roster* 3: 1065.

263. Johnson was 34, a native of New York, and resident of De Witt when he enlisted on August 9, 1862. He completed his enlistment, being mustered out June 6, 1865, in Washington, D.C. *Roster* 3: 1069.

264. Leeper (21) and his younger brother John (18), born in Illinois and living in De Witt, enlisted August 28, 1862. Thomas survived being wounded to earn promotion to seventh corporal, March 1, 1863; sixth corporal, May 1, 1863; and fifth sergeant, September 1, 1863. He was killed in action, May 14, 1864, at Resaca, Georgia. John survived and mustered out with his comrades on June 6, 1865, at Washington, D.C. *Roster* 3: 1074.

265. Ankeny, 18, was from Illinois and a resident of De Witt when he enlisted in Co. E, August 9, 1862. Transferred to Co. H on October 12, 1862, he fell victim to illness following being wounded and was discharged for disability on November 28, 1863, at Paducah, Kentucky. *Roster* 3: 1032.

266. Horace Humeston, born in New York, was 22 and a resident of De Witt when he enlisted on August 8, 1862. He recovered and was later promoted to sixth corporal, April 1, 1865, and mustered out June 6, 1865, in Washington, D.C. His older brother Sylvester was killed at Arkansas Post. *Roster* 3: 1066.

267. Thomas, 33, was a son of Ohio residing in De Witt when he enlisted August 9, 1862. He survived to earn promotion to fourth corporal, January 1, 1864, being mustered out in Washington, D.C., June 6, 1865. *Roster* 3: 1103.

268. Naman Barnes, 25, born in Ohio and a resident of De Witt, enlisted on August 7, 1862. He survived being wounded (however, he lost his older brother James—see note 252) to earn promotion to eighth corporal, May 1, 1863; and fifth corporal, September 1, 1863, before he was transferred to the Invalid Corps, February 15, 1864, being mustered out on June 29, 1865, at Washington, D.C. *Roster* 3: 1037.

269. Jenkins, 19 and a Pennsylvanian, lived in Wheatland when he enlisted August 15, 1862. His wounds proved mortal, and he died January 20, 1863, at Memphis, where he is buried in the National Cemetery. *Roster* 3: 1069.

270. A native of New Jersey and resident of Wheatland, Benedict was 43 when he enlisted on August 9, 1862. Unable to recover from his wound, he was discharged September 14, 1863, at Davenport, Iowa. *Roster* 3: 1038.

271. Born in Pennsylvania and living in Wheatland, Riley was 25 when he enlisted on August 12, 1862. He was transferred to the Invalid Corps, September 30, 1863, and mustered out at Jefferson Barracks, St. Louis, Missouri, in July 1865. *Roster* 3: 1093.

272. Ray, 20, and his brother Oliver, 18, both born in Pennsylvania and residents of Clinton County, enlisted in Co. K (James, August 12, and Oliver, August 7, 1862). James is buried at the National Cemetery in Little Rock, Arkansas. Oliver was promoted first corporal and wounded slightly on May 21, 1863, at Vicksburg, Mississippi; was promoted fourth sergeant, May 15, 1865; and was mustered out June 6, 1865, in Washington, D.C. *Roster* 3: 1094.

273. Beck was 22, a German immigrant and resident of Lyons, when he enlisted as third corporal on August 14, 1862. Presumably he lies in an unmarked grave in the Little Rock National Cemetery, Arkansas. *Roster* 3: 1039.

274. Henle survived being wounded to complete his service. He was 24, a native of Ohio, and resident of Lyons upon enlistment as fifth sergeant on August 7, 1862. He was promoted fourth sergeant before Arkansas Post, and third sergeant, July 1, 1863; second sergeant, January 1, 1864; first sergeant, September 9, 1864; and first lieutenant for war service (not mustered), June 1, 1865. He was mustered out in Washington, D.C., five days later. His younger brother Joseph also served in Co. K and successfully completed his enlistment. *Roster* 3: 1067.

275. Douglass was 32, born in Ohio and living in Elvira when he enlisted on August 15, 1862. He died of wounds on February 7, 1863, in St. Louis, Missouri. *Roster* 3: 1052.

276. Shields, age 41, had been born in Indiana and lived in Lyons when he enlisted August 15, 1862. He died of wounds at Young's Point, Louisiana, on February 1, 1863. *Roster* 3: 1101.

277. Born in Connecticut, Blakely was 24 and living in Lyons when he enlisted August 15, 1862. He died of wounds on board the steamer *D. A. January* on January 20, 1863. *Roster* 3: 1039.

278. An immigrant from England, Moyses was 43 and living in Lyons when he enlisted August 15, 1862. Records cite his being accidentally wounded January 13, 1863. He was transferred to the Invalid Corps, September 30, 1863, and discharged at Jefferson Barracks, St. Louis, Missouri, in July 1865. *Roster* 3: 1083.

279. A Canadian by birth, Baker lived in Lyons and was 43 when he enlisted on August 12, 1862. He completed his term of service, being mustered out in Philadelphia, Pennsylvania, July 8, 1865. *Roster* 3: 1039.

280. Pomeroy, born in Ohio, was 27 and living in Lyons when he enlisted on August 15, 1862. Wounded slightly, he recovered to complete his enlistment, being mustered out on June 6, 1865, in Washington, D.C. *Roster* 3: 1089.

281. A son of Vermont, Morse was 18 and a Clinton County resident when he enlisted on August 15, 1862. He recovered from this wound and was promoted second corporal and later fifth sergeant, May 1, 1865, being mustered out in Washington, D.C., June 6, 1865. *Roster* 3: 1083.

282. Born in New York, Hurlburt was 18 and living in Lyons when he enlisted on August 15, 1862. He recovered, returned to service, and was taken prisoner on April 21, 1864. Exchanged and returned to Co. K, he was mustered out with his comrades, June 6, 1865, in Washington, D.C. *Roster* 3: 1067.

CHAPTER THREE

We Leave Arkansas Post and Return to Milliken's Bend for Winter Quarters[283]

✦ ——————————— ✦

After burying our dead on the 12th of January it commenced to rain, and towards morning of the 13th it turned into a snow. As we boarded the transports it was very disagreeable and cold; however we were soon under way, and after a short time again entered the old Mississippi River, and after going down it a short distance the boats landed at the little town of Napoleon, [Arkansas], where we again went on shore and we remained one day. When we embarked we continued our way down the river to Young's Point and Milliken's Bend, which was destined to be our camping place until the following May.[284] Our division[285] camped at Young's Point, a distance of about 6 miles from Vicksburg—[t]he higher part of the city being plainly visible from our camp.[286]

After establishing our camp the months of February and March were weary months for the troops—[t]he monotony of camp life being more irksome to the soldier than being on an active campaign. Besides drilling twice a day, details of soldiers were kept busy in working on Butler's famous canal.[287] This canal about one and a quarter miles in length was being built across a narrow neck of land opposite Vicksburg. As the river near Vicksburg forms almost a right angle this canal would cut off about 8 miles of the distance [traveling by way of the river] to get below the city, and as it was impossible to run the transports past the Rebel batteries that lined the east shore it had been decided to build this canal. The object of getting the transports below Vicksburg was to convey to the troops across the river below the city, and also as a means of getting supplies to the army while operating from below. As the first attempt to capture the city by way of Chickasaw Bayou had been a failure, it had been decided by General Grant to make the attempt from below and if possible to work around to the east cutting their only line of railroad and means of communication - thus compelling them to surrender.[288]

While lying encamped at this place there was a good deal of sickness amongst the troops, the soldiers dying by scores. On awakening in the morning and looking towards the regimental hospital we could generally see one or two cots outside in the rear with a blanket thrown over them covering the forms of soldiers that had died during the night. It was also the same in brigade, division, and corps hospital. I remember of being down to the steamboat landing one day just as a steamer from St. Louis was landing, besides her cargo of supplies for the army every available place on her was loaded with caskets, pine but stained to resemble walnut. It was not necessary to ask for whom they were intended as we well knew.[289]

While here George H. Peck and Henry Preffer spoken of earlier in this work as being two of the five in the tent at Helena were taken sick, Preffer with the measles and after a short time died. George H. Peck was also taken with chronic diarrhea, and after a time was sent to Memphis where he also died.[290]

Thus three of the original five were gone leaving Elijah H. Frank, and the writer. To properly understand the situation at our camp here I would state that the ground from Young's Point north was level and subject to overflow, and while part of it had been extensive cotton fields a good portion was covered with heavy timber, and swamps, all of it being protected from overflow of the Mississippi by a levee and embankment thrown up like a railroad. The height [of the levee] varying according to the ground. Now as most of the firm ground was occupied as camp and drilling grounds, we had to utilize the slopes of the aforesaid levee as a burying ground, and for miles its slopes were covered with little mounds denoting the last resting place of northern soldiers. During the high water of the following May a great portion of the levee was washed away scattering the remains of those that had been buried there all over the country, hundreds of whom I suppose were

We Leave Arkansas Post and Return to
Milliken's Bend for Winter Quarters

never recovered, and whose bones lie scattered over the adjacent territory.[291]

While here the writer was frequently detailed to work upon the afore mentioned canal, where also at work were hundreds of darkies.[292] From the canal to Vicksburg was a distance of about five miles, and while at work we would very frequently be shelled by the enemy, they having one gun in particular that could reach us, and from the peculiar whistle of its shot we called it "Whistling Dick."[293] As the darkies would be busily engaged in wheeling dirt from the canal singing their Negro melodies "Whistling Dick" would drop a shot nearby sometimes in the canal, throwing mud and water a hundred feet, and it was laughable to see the darkies, wheelbarrows and all roll into the mud, and water and after crawling out skin for some of the large cypress stumps. The officers in command of them would say, "Come back you black curs and go to work." The darkies would reply, "Lord God massa dye kill us all shuah."

While lying in camp here it was an interesting sight on a dark night to witness the mortar fleet, anchored near the river bank a short distance below our camp, as they threw their heavy missiles into Vicksburg elevating the guns at an angle of about 45 degrees. The course of the shells could be traced by the burning fuse as they in their course in the form of a rainbow were hurled into the City.[294] We also had, a half a mile below our camp, two thirty-two pound rifled [P]arrott siege guns that were constantly shelling the enemy to let the Rebs know that the Yanks were still alive.[295]

During the months of February and March large supplies were being accumulated, and reinforcements to the army were being received. It was rumored a forward movement of the army would soon take place, and the army would march across the country to New Carthage, [Louisiana] twenty-three miles below, while the transports would be run past the batteries or through the canal if the latter course proved feasible.[296]

Along about the latter part of March rumors were thick in camp that a portion of the army were to embark on steamers up the river, about 100 miles, and to march inland and down [the] Deer Creek Valley with orders to destroy the immense amount of corn and cotton that was known to be stored there.

We Leave Arkansas Post and Return to Milliken's Bend for Winter Quarters

283. Although the army established permanent bases of operations, or depots, in northeastern Louisiana during the winter of 1863, technically Maj. Gen. Ulysses S. Grant would keep three corps (XIII, XV, and XVII) of the Army of the Tennessee in the field and on campaign in the expedition against Vicksburg, and did not "stand down" or remain idle in quarters for the entire winter. Meanwhile, a fourth corps organized within Grant's department, the XVI Army Corps, headquartered in Memphis, garrisoned occupied western Tennessee and northern Mississippi.

284. The convoy departed Napoleon on January 18, 1863 and reached Young's Point on the afternoon of January 21. While at Napoleon, some XV Corps incendiaries had started fires, which left the buildings in one entire block as burned-out ruins. The troops disembarked from the steamboats at Young's Point on the 23rd. Bearss, *The Vicksburg Campaign*, I: 435–36.

285. As in the capture of the Post of Arkansas, Oake was assigned to the 1st Division, XV Army Corps, commanded by Maj. Gen. Frederick Steele; the corps was under the command of Maj. Gen. William T. Sherman. The 26th Iowa remained organized within the 3rd Brigade of the division, commanded by Brig. Gen. John M. Thayer. Dyer, *Compendium*, 498–99.

286. General Grant arrived on January 28, 1863, and assumed command of the Mississippi River expedition. Throughout the late winter, he would organize and direct a complicated series of canal and bayou operations meant to move major elements of the army (supported by Porter's Mississippi Squadron) onto high ground in Mississippi, either immediately north or south of fortress Vicksburg. From there the United States forces could effectively maneuver to either directly attack Vicksburg or isolate the enemy garrison, by permanently severing railroad and telegraph communications eastward with the rest of the Confederacy. Vicksburg rests on a high plateau, or chain of hills, on the eastern side of the Mississippi River, loess hills created by windblown Pleistocene deposits. The elevation of these bluffs varies from more than 250 feet above the surrounding delta plain north of Vicksburg to 150 feet elevation south of the city. (The delta extends from the west in Louisiana and extends north beyond the Yazoo River in Mississippi.) Vicksburg's prominent buildings—churches, factories, and especially the multi-storied Warren County Courthouse with its classic clock-faced cupola—were all visible from the Federal encampment at Young's Point. Sherman's corps camped downstream from Young's Point, closer to Vicksburg. The Federals established their camps on the natural levees and along the right-of-way of the Vicksburg, Shreveport & Texas Railroad. Bearss, *The Vicksburg Campaign*, I: 438.

287. Oake is making reference to Maj. Gen. Benjamin F. Butler, who commanded United States land forces during a joint operation with the deepwater naval squadron commanded by David Glasgow Farragut, which was conducted in the spring and summer months of 1862. The operation successfully opened the Mississippi from the Gulf to Vicksburg, capturing New Orleans and Baton Rouge. Under orders from Butler, Brig. Gen. Thomas Williams, whose 3,000-man infantry brigade accompanied the deepwater navy on the ascent to Vicksburg, started the canal on June 28. Williams's troops, reinforced by more than 1,200 blacks pressed into service from Madison and Tensas parish plantations, excavated a one-and-a-half-mile canal across De Soto Point (or Peninsula), opposite Vicksburg, attempting to divert the Mississippi and isolate the city. The project was hampered by drought, which lowered the river's level faster than the men could dig, and by sickness, which in less than a month slashed Williams's effective force by more than one-half. Williams abandoned the project on July 24, and his men, along with Farragut's fleet, ceased their efforts to capture Vicksburg, retiring downriver to Baton Rouge and New Orleans. The canal is more properly known as the Williams-Grant Canal. Warner, *Generals in Blue*, 60–61, 563–64; Bearss, *The Vicksburg Campaign*, I: 437.

288. Grant initially viewed the canal—to be sixty feet wide by six feet deep, and endorsed by army engineers, the War Department, and President Lincoln—as a feasible means for bypassing the dreaded batteries at Vicksburg, which commanded a three-mile stretch of the Mississippi. The canal would enable him to get below the city to more effectively employ his forces. Sherman's corps, to which Oake's regiment was attached, began work on the canal in January but was forced by high water to abandon it in March. Edwin C. Bearss, *Rebel Victory at Vicksburg* (Little Rock: Pioneer Press, 1963), 129–38; Bearss, *The Vicksburg Campaign*, I: 437; Boatner, *Civil War Dictionary*, 871.

289. The sick list of the regiment rapidly increased during this period, and the number of officers and men able for duty was less than one-half the number shown on rolls. *Roster* 3: 1021.

290. Over the course of the war, 208 members of the regiment, roughly 21.5 percent of the total enrollment of 965 officers and men, died of disease. *Roster* 3: 1027.

291. Hundreds of U.S. soldiers, weakened by exposure and disease while quartered in the Young's Point and Milliken's Bend encampments, died during the winter of 1863 and were buried within the artificial levees that bordered the river. The bodies located in war graves not destroyed by the spring flooding that Oake describes were exhumed after the war and re-interred in the Vicksburg National Cemetery. The vast majority of the remains could not be properly identified, and they represent a significant portion of the nearly 13,000 Federal soldiers buried at Vicksburg who are officially cited as "Unknown."

292. Like General Williams in 1862, Grant used contraband blacks to labor on the canal. On February 9, 1863, Capt. Frederick E. Prime, engineer in charge of the project, reported the lion's share of the work was being done by 550 contrabands, and by March 1, he reported more than 1,000 contrabands present and working on the canal. These men worked alongside Federal troops and the steam-driven dipper dredges *Hercules* and *Sampson*. Grant believed that the blacks were better acclimated to the region and exhibited more adaptability for working in mud and water than his soldiers. On February 24, he instructed Maj. Gen. Stephen A. Hurlbut to send to Young's Point as many "able-bodied negro laborers as can be had or spared from Memphis and other portions" of his command, for they were needed for work on the canal. *O.R.* I-24-I-119, 121; *O.R.* I-24-III-65; Bearss, *The Vicksburg Campaign*, I: 443–44.

293. "Whistling Dick" was a rifled, 18-pounder cannon. Initially, it appears this rifled gun was mounted in the Wyman's Hill Battery, immediately north of the city, above the mouth of Glass Bayou, where it was served by gunners from Capt. Paul T. Dismukes's battery. Later, the cannon was moved farther south to the "Railroad Battery," located roughly 100 feet above the river and just south of the railroad cut. It was mounted alongside a 20-pounder Parrott to form a two-gun battery manned by Co. E, 1st Louisiana Artillery. The gun was not, properly speaking, a piece of heavy artillery and was extremely light for its assigned purpose here, which was to use its high-muzzle velocity (penetrating power) against Federal gunboats. The light gun was effective only against unarmored transports and in duels with the Union guns emplaced on De Soto Point. Oake is not the only witness to remark on the unique sound made by the gun, with numerous war diaries and post-war publications describing the "screeching, whistling," almost "tortured" sound made by "Whistling Dick" when fired. Bearss, *The Vicksburg Campaign*, I: 460; Bearss, *The Vicksburg Campaign*, II: 63–64, 104; "A Woman's Diary," *The Century Magazine*, Vol. XXX, 768.

294. The mortar, among the oldest forms of artillery, was a large-caliber gun with an extremely short tube designed to fire shells at a high elevation (as much as forty-five degrees) using a relative small powder charge. Those used in the Civil War were made of iron and mounted on heavy wood and iron beds. The seacoast mortars—mentioned here by the author—being used by the U.S. Navy Mississippi River Squadron at Vicksburg were mounted on flat-bottomed barges and towed into position by steam-powered tugs, transports, and even gunboats. The seacoast mortars, thirteen-inch pieces (diameter of the bore), heaved a 220-pound explosive shell at ranges up to 4,325 yards (at full elevation) with a 20-pound powder charge. In theory, the projectile was to explode in midair, raining down fragments on the opponent's position. Garrison & Garrison, *Civil War Usage*, 162; Faust, ed., *Encyclopedia of the Civil War*, 512.

295. These Parrott guns were actually 30-pounders.

296. Oake's memory of events seems influenced by the "old soldier's disease," in citing camp rumors in February and early March about preparations for movement south to a new staging area. General Grant did not issue orders for the army to begin this specific movement until March 29, 1863. It is a safe bet, however, that daily rumors frequented the Federal camps about movements the army might next be engaged in. Grant ordered McClernand's XIII Corps to occupy nearby Richmond, Louisiana, and begin the task of opening a road to New Carthage. *O.R.* I-24-I-46; Warren E. Grabau, *Ninety-Eight Days: A Geographer's View of the Vicksburg Campaign* (Knoxville: University of Tennessee Press, 2000), 60. Hereafter cited as *Ninety-Eight Days.*

Major General Frederick Steele.
It was during his participation in Steele's Greenville Expedition in the Mississippi Delta in early April 1862 that William Royal Oake was captured, beginning a personal odyssey as a prisoner of war.
LIBRARY OF CONGRESS

CHAPTER FOUR

Expedition on Deer Creek and Capture by the Enemy

꙳ ———————————— ꙳

About the first of April 1863 orders[297] were given that our division, 1st of the 15th [A]rmy [C]orp[s], General Fred Steele in command, would embark on board steamers, and proceed about 100 miles up the river. There to land at a place called Greenville, [Mississippi] and to march east about 12 miles to Black Bayou on Deer Creek, and then to march down that valley as far as possible without bringing on a general engagement with the enemy. We were to destroy and capture the immeasurable amount of corn, cotton, and beef cattle that was known to exist there, thus preventing it being shipped to enemy at Vicksburg by the way of the Sun Flower and Yazoo Rivers. From Black Bayou to Rolling Fork on the Sun Flower River a distance of about 60 miles was, I think, the richest valley in the Mississippi.[298]

About April 3rd [*sic* 5th][299] we landed at the little town of Greenville, and marched to near Black Bayou where we encamped for the first night. Near our camp was a very fine plantation teeming with forage of all kinds— [the] said plantation being owned by General French of the rebel army.[300] I well remember that occasion for as soon as we had stacked our arms many of the boys started for the plantation to try to secure if possible a chicken or something equally as palatable for their supper. I remember in returning from the plantation we met General Steele resplendent in his general's uniform going towards the residence, I suppose to pay his respects to the Rebel general's wife. Some of the boys going later found guards placed over the premises. Early the next morning reveille sounded, and the troops were soon up; after partaking of breakfast were soon on their march down the valley on the west side of Deer Creek.

In the meantime the writer and the others, under command of Sergeant [*sic* Lieutenant] John W. Mason,[301] were detailed to cross the creek, and go to a large plantation about a mile distant. The creek here was about 50 yards wide, and quite deep. I remember that the surgeon of our regiment accompanied us, and as he was mounted we procured an old flat boat, and went over the creek, the surgeon leading his horse as he swam after the boat.

On reaching the plantation we found forage in abundance each man secured either a mule or horse, and after getting all we could pack in the way of turkeys, chickens, and hams, and having all the apple-jack[302] we could drink we started to retrace our steps to the creek crossing, and after some little trouble in getting our forage, horses, and mules over we started in pursuit of the division that had about three hours start of us. There being only six of us quite distance in the rear of the troops and in the enemy's country we did not know how soon we might run onto some scouting party of rebels. An incident of the crossing of the creek I well remember was as follows: One of us would stand in the hind end of the boat, and one at the oars, while others would get behind the animals forcing them into the water. I was standing in the rear of the boat leading a mule, when it made a plunge throwing the writer, and as I was encumbered, [with] cartridge box, haversack, and canteen, I was well loaded down, and it was with difficulty that I managed to get out. Of course I was wet through, and being in April the water was quite cold. After getting out, Major Hudson[303] suggested that I take a drink from a little flask that he carried in the holster of his saddle bag. Thinking of the suggestion I took his advice, and as I rode all day in wet clothes took not a particle of cold.

Following in the tracks of the troops we passed many fine plantations, and on every side smoke from burning buildings, cotton gins, and a large amount of corn, and other forage shared a common fate. All beef cattle, hogs, and poultry had been driven off or killed. As this valley was but a short distance from Vicksburg, and easily accessible with its vast amount of corn and other supplies of destruction.[304]

About four in the afternoon we overtook the troops that had already gone into camp, and as we rejoined our regiment, and passed our colonel's quarters we noticed quite a frown on his countenance, but after a short time we took over to him a fine young turkey, a smile lit up his face as he kindly thanked us.

We continued on our march of destruction down the valley until the 8th of the month when the cavalry encountered a stubborn resistance from the enemy, and it became evident to our commander that troops from Vicksburg were being sent to check our further progress of destruction.[305] As [General] Steele's orders from the commander in chief[306] was not to bring on a general engagement, he decided to encamp for the night, and the next day to leisurely retrace his steps to the Mississippi at Greenville.[307]

On our march down the valley we passed one fine plantation about 100 yards back from the road. In front of the place was a very fine lawn in the middle of which was placed a British Flag, while near it stood the owner dressed in his black broad cloth, while upon his head he wore a shining black tile. On this plantation was a great amount of corn in rail cribs, and the advance troops had set it on fire, and when we reached it the fire was under full headway. As the old gentleman stood by the flag from which he evidently claimed protection he looked very sour, but to his chagrin discovered the British Flag did not protect rebel corn.[308]

On the afternoon of April 8th, while the cavalry were skirmishing with the rebs we encamped on a plantation[309] that abounded with chickens, turkeys, ducks, and a few pea fowl. After stacking our arms the boys started for something for supper. The writer getting his eye on a very fine Muscovy drake,[310] it being in full feather with its fine top[k]not,[311] it was indeed a fine looking fowl, and I determined if possible to have it for supper.

Paying no attention to anything else I gave chase to the drake and captured it, returning to camp dressed it, and after stewing it about two hours took it off the fire, and in company of three other comrades with whom I was squad[ed][312] [with], sat down to partake of what we supposed would be a great feast. What was our surprise upon finding it the toughest thing we ever tackled. Talk about sole leather being tough, it was jelly as far as toughness was concerned, to that old drake, however not to be cheated out of our drake we concluded to again put it in the kettle and boil it until we turned in for the night, and to get up early in the morning and give it another two hours cooking which we did. When lo and behold it was tougher than ever,

Expedition on Deer Creek and
Capture by the Enemy

and we finally came to the conclusion that it was the original drake that was saved by father Noah at the time of the flood.

On the next morning April 9th the troops were early astir, and after partaking of our breakfast Lieutenant J. W. Mason[313] of Company A, with a detail of eight men was ordered to cross Deer Creek, and proceed to a certain plantation to capture a pair of very fine horses that were known to be there.[314] This information having been obtained from a Negro. To better understand the situation I would say that the road upon which the troops traveled, on their return march, ran parallel with Deer Creek, and some places for a long distance the road ran quite close to that stream, then again the stream would diverge off to the right making a big bend. At such places the road would be a mile or two from the river, leaving the troops to continue. Our detail crossed the creek in an old flat boat that we found nearby, and after about an hours march arrived at said plantation, where we found the horses together with other horses, and mules, so that our entire detail of eight secured a mount. The writer secured a fine gray mule. While at this plantation the lady of the place had the Negro servants prepare us a good meal of corn pone and ham, we furnishing the wherewith to make the coffee.

After finishing our breakfast we secured our mounts, and continued on our way. At this place the writer captured a very fine double barrel shot gun, which I decided to take along.

Along about noon we came to the creek on the opposite side of which the troops were halted for their dinner. As we halted on the bank of the stream opposite to them some of the boys in the 26th called over and wanted to know if we would let them ride our animals until night, if they would come over and swim them across. The lieutenant answered them that he would, when three of the boys swam over and rode the two fine horses spoken of, and one other across the creek, and as the balance of the animals seemed to object to going into the water he ordered Sergeant D. H. Denney [David H. Denny][315] to proceed with the rest of us to a bridge about four miles up the stream, while he the Lieutenant and the two dismounted men would cross the creek, and join their regiment. After the troops had eaten their dinner they resumed their march as we did also.

After marching a short distance the creek made a big bend to the east while the road upon which the troops were marching continued straight ahead. Upon arriving at the turn of the creek where we, for the time being were to part from the troops, we waved our hands at them and continued on our way around the big bend of the creek. Little did we at that time think that it was the last time we would see the regiment for six months, and before our return we would have traveled as prisoners of war through the entire Confederacy finally landing in Old Libby Prison.[316]

From the turn of the creek to the elbow bend of the stream was perhaps about one mile, from which point the stream gradually veered to the left and would again strike the road about four miles distant. The road upon which they were traveling ran close along the bank of the stream while on our right the bottom was covered in places with a heavy growth of cane-brake, which in places was twenty feet in height, and so dense it was almost impossible to penetrate it. After going about one mile we came to the ruins of an old bridge that had at one time spanned the creek, but had long since fallen into disuse, and fell down. Just about this time we began to realize that we were in the enemy's country and quite a distance from the troops, and the country around us desolate and wild. We did not know how soon some lurking body of the enemy with which the country was infested, might sur-prise and kill or capture us.

Upon reaching the ruins of the old bridge Horace Simpson,[317] one of our squad said, "Boys I don't like the looks of things, and am going to let my mule go, and make a raft of some of those old bridge timbers, and cross the creek and make for the troops, and I think it would be best if all of you did the same thing for I certainly believe that if we continue on our course we will all be captured by the rebs." Sergeant D. H. Denney, who was in com-mand of the squad, replied, "Simpson if you feel that way cross the creek and strike for the troops as I don't think they can be over two miles distant, but as for the rest of us we will continue on our way until we reach Black Bayou bridge, but however we will remain here until we see you safe over the stream." While one of the squad stood guard the rest assisted Simpson in making a raft with which he crossed the stream as he was about to disap-pear in the heavy timber bordering the stream he turned and said, "Boys I think you had better come along, if not Good bye," and he soon disappeared in the timber.

How many times before night did we wish we had taken Simpson's advice. There were now left in the squad five members as follows: Sergeant D. H. Denney, Privates, Leonidas Miller,[318] David W. Swihart,[319] W. R. Oake, the writer, of Company A, and John M. Leeper[320] of Company H, all of the 26th Iowa.

After taking leave of Simpson we mounted our animals, and continued on our way. The sergeant was riding a small black horse while the rest of us were mounted on mules. At this place I thru [threw] into the creek the fine double barreled gun which I had captured, not wishing to be encumbered with it, although I would have very much liked to have been able to have sent it home. About half an hour after we had resumed our journey, Sergeant Denney and the writer were riding in advance. On our right was a dense canebrake swamp, which at intervals was traversed by roads leading out into the country beyond. We had just passed one of those roads perhaps fifty yards when we heard one of the boys behind us say, "Boys the rebs are coming." Turning quickly we saw a squad of Rebel Cavalry emerging from one of those roads into the one we were traveling at a full gallop, and shouting, "Surrender you Yankees," and firing at the same time. Being on well trained horses they were rapidly gaining upon us. Just at that time my mule stumbled and fell. At the time I thought it was shot. Upon arising partly stunned from the fall I slipped into the creek that was close by intending to swim over, and if possible escape in the woods beyond, and reach the Division. Plunging into the creek I discovered that Miller also was there, but at that time a couple of the rebs discovered us, and standing on the bank of the stream with guns loaded and cocked politely invited us to come in out of the wet.

We were up to our necks in the water, and our legs had become entangled in the heavy growth of vines that grew along the banks, and in the water, the banks being over flowed in places by the spring rains. We concluded that discretion was the better part of valor, and informed our captors we would come out as soon as we could get our legs disentangled from the vines. After a short time we got out of the creek where we found the rest of our squad already rounded up by the rebels. It was a lucky job after all for us that not one of us was wounded or killed, although the clothes of two of the boys were cut by the bullets of the enemy, and when the fact is taken into consideration of having been fired upon at so short a range by twenty seven trained soldiers, that being the number of the enemy, our escape from death was miraculous. After relieving us of our hats and shoes which were comparatively new, and giving us their old ones in exchange, [they placed] us in charge of two guards with instructions to them to take us to the rear. The rebel officer in command of the balance of his cavalry started in the direction that our division [was] marching in the expectation of capturing other small bands of our soldiers that might become detailed from the main column.

The cavalry by whom we had been captured belonged to the command of the rebel [Lieutenant] Colonel [Samuel W.] Ferguson, and were a body of fine soldiers, formerly belonging to the Texas Rangers, and who upon the opening of the war had joined the Confederate army.[321] There was a peculiar incident in connection with our capture as we learned upon joining our regiment the following October. It seemed that the firing in connection with our capture had been heard by our troops and a troop of cavalry had been ordered to ascertain if possible the cause of the firing, and while on this mission surprised and captured the entire squad that had taken us with the exception of the two that were sent to the rear with us.

CHAPTER NOTES:
Expedition on Deer Creek and Capture by the Enemy

297. On March 31, 1863, Grant visited General Sherman's Young's Point headquarters, and there the two officers sketched plans for an expedition to Greenville, aimed at diverting the Confederates' attention from the movement of General McClernand's corps south to New Carthage on the Louisiana side of the Mississippi River. Bearss, *The Vicksburg Campaign*, II: 107.

298. This area is known as the Mississippi Delta, which was the richest agricultural region in the Mississippi Valley east of the river. It had no railroads, and wagon roads were primitive and discontinuous. Fodder and commissary supplies for Confederate forces flowed out of the region aboard small steamboats, barges, and even smaller oar- or pole-propelled bateaus designed to navigate the often shallow and restricted waters in the region's maze of navigable waterways. Grabau, *Ninety-Eight Days*, 36.

299. The expedition departed Young's Point on the afternoon of April 2. The river was at flood stage, and the vessels struggled to breast the powerful current. After a five-hour stop at Lake Providence, Louisiana, the convoy proceeded upstream at daybreak on April 3. General Steele placed the 5,600-man division ashore at 11 A.M., at Smith's Landing, roughly thirty-five miles south of Greenville. Finding that high water made the road inland toward Deer Creek impassable, the troops retired to the transports and spent the night. Early next morning, April 4, the convoy headed upstream to Washington Landing, about seventeen miles south of Greenville. The soldiers again thronged ashore while cavalry patrols probed eastward reconnoitering the road. The troopers returned to report the water level still too high to move overland to Deer Creek. Steele had the division embark again, and steamed on to Greenville, where the convoy tied up for the night. Bearss, *The Vicksburg Campaign*, II: 108–9, 127.

300. The plantation was owned by Samuel G. French, a major general in the Confederate army then serving in Virginia, who had acquired ownership through marriage. It was located roughly five miles east of Greenville on Fish Lake. General Steele's expedition disembarked at a landing a mile upriver from Greenville, and moved inland on the Deer Creek road. While Royal and his comrades took a break to forage for their supper, the Federal pioneers repaired the bridge across Fish Lake, located on the headwaters of Black Bayou. Bearss, *The Vicksburg Campaign*, II: 109–10; Grabau, *Ninety-Eight Days*, 63.

301. The only member of the regiment with the surname Mason was John W. Mason, a resident of Clinton. Born in New York, Mason was 34 when he enlisted as a private on June 6, 1862. Promoted fifth sergeant on January 14, 1863, he was commissioned second lieutenant of the company on February 27, 1863. He would be wounded in the initial assault Grant ordered against the Vicksburg fortifications, May 19, 1863. Mason resigned his commission three months later on August 21, 1863. It is probable that Oake simply made a contextual error in memory by referring to him as sergeant in this passage, for several paragraphs later he refers to him properly as lieutenant. *Roster* 3: 1078.

302. A form of brandy made from distilled apples. *Webster's Dictionary*, 44.

303. Abijah T. Hudson, the regimental surgeon.

304. Steele's instructions from his superior, General Sherman, stated, "If [the] planters remain at home and behave themselves, molest them as little as possible, but if the planters abandon their plantations you may infer they are hostile, and can take their cattle, hogs, corn, or anything you need. Cotton which is clearly private property should not be molested, but cotton marked

'C.S.A.' should be brought away or burned. Also all provisions which are needed by us or might be used by the army in Vicksburg, unless needed by the peaceful inhabitants, should be brought away, used by your men, or destroyed." *O.R.* I-24-III-158.

305. The Confederate force, or combat team, charged with guarding the Deer Creek approaches to Vicksburg was commanded by Lt. Col. Samuel W. Ferguson. Federal reports showed Ferguson's command as numbering between 600 and 1,000 men. Ferguson had alerted his superior in Vicksburg, Maj. Gen. Carter L. Stevenson, of the Federal raid, and Stevenson reacted promptly, issuing marching orders to Brig. Gen. Stephen D. Lee, whose command consisted of six infantry regiments and a battalion of artillery. Lee was to secure Rolling Fork and advance up the Bogue Phalia, in an attempt to take Steele's column in the rear. In addition, a small combat patrol commanded by Lt. Col. Edmund W. Pettus also participated in the defense of the delta. In total, around 4,300 Confederate troops assembled to combat Steele's expedition. Bearss, *The Vicksburg Campaign*, II: 110–11, 128.

306. Oake is referring to General Grant, who exercises delegated authority as commander, or head, of an armed force—the Army of the Tennessee—on a national level, not Abraham Lincoln, who as President of the United States exercises constitutional authority as commander in chief of all U.S. military forces. Scott, *Military Dictionary*, 168; *Webster's Dictionary*, 196.

307. Ferguson's combat team fought a delaying action against Steele's vanguard at Dr. Thomas's plantation, twenty-three miles southeast of Greenville (twenty-six miles north of Rolling Fork), on the afternoon of April 7, and then retreated five miles to the Willis plantation. Steele's column bivouacked at Thomas's plantation. The next day, Union cavalry patrols alerted Steele that Lee's Confederate brigade had entered Rolling Fork. The Union general, concerned about his vulnerable supply line, decided not to risk a major engagement and ordered a retrograde. In accordance with his instructions, Steele decided to destroy the economy of the Deer Creek area, and regimental commanders were ordered to burn all the cotton gins, corncribs, and bridges as the division retraced its route and evacuated. In addition, the troops were to remove all cattle, horses, and mules. The area serving the Vicksburg garrison as a granary would be stripped of the necessities of making war. *O.R.* I-24-I-502; Bearss, *The Vicksburg Campaign*, II: 114.

308. On the retrograde northward, down the valley of Deer Creek, Steele's men destroyed vast quantities of corn—estimated by some of his officers to total at least 100,000 bushels. The plantation cited here by the author might be that identified in Confederate correspondence as being owned by a Dr. Hill. *O.R.* I-24-I-502, 510.

309. The column bivouacked at Taylor's plantation (now the village of Wilmot), fifteen miles southeast of Greenville. The Union column, as it neared the plantation, was fired upon by Confederate guerrillas. The Southerners took to their heels once the Federals unlimbered two cannon and opened fire. Bearss, *The Vicksburg Campaign*, II: 110, 114.

310. A tropical American duck larger than a wild mallard, it was, and still is, widely domesticated. *Webster's Dictionary*, 658.

311. A small crest, generally glossy black in color, located on top of the drake's head. *Webster's Dictionary*, 658.

312. Scott states that a squad is "a small party of men" and that "a company should be divided into squads, each under a responsible officer or noncommissioned officer...." Routinely a squad was one-fourth of a company, which was anywhere from ten to twenty-five men. Scott, *Military Dictionary*, 565; Garrison & Garrison, *Civil War Usage*, 237.

313. See note 301.

314. The account of the April 9, 1863, incident on Deer Creek cited in *Roster* 3: 1021, states the detachment sent out to forage was commanded by Capt. Charles M. Nye of Co. H.

315. A resident of Lowden, former Ohioan David Denny was 25 when he enlisted July 9, 1862, as first corporal in Co. A. Recently promoted to third sergeant on March 24, 1863, he survived his war experiences and was mustered out June 6, 1865, in Washington, D.C. *Roster* 3: 1048.

316. In reputation, Libby Prison in Richmond, Virginia, was second only to Andersonville for Confederate prisons. While the vast majority of prison facilities operating in the capital of the Confederacy had been tobacco warehouses prior to the war, this building had been the warehouse of Libby & Sons, ship's chandlers and grocers, before being taken over by the government. The historical record routinely states that only Federal officers and high-ranking civilians were confined in the prison. Because the facility served as headquarters for all the Richmond prisons, many men, including enlisted personnel being transported elsewhere, were brought in to be registered. Thus the experience of Pvt. Royal Oake in being briefly confined there in late spring 1863 illustrates the post-war recollections of a large number of prisoners who claimed to have been held "in Libby." Boatner, *Civil War Dictionary*, 482; Garrison & Garrison, *Civil War Usage*, 143; Richard N. Current, ed., *Encyclopedia of the Confederacy*, 4 vols. (New York: Simon & Schuster, 1993), 2: 930–31.

317. Born in New York, Simpson was 23 and living in Clinton County when he enlisted in Co. H on August 9, 1862. Later promoted first corporal, he was mustered out June 6, 1865, in Washington, D.C. *Roster* 3: 1100.

318. Born in Indiana, Miller lived in Canton when he enlisted in Co. A at the age of 18, on August 12, 1862. He returned to the company on October 14, 1863, and was wounded at Kennesaw Mountain, Georgia, on June 16, 1864. He died of wounds, July 3, 1864, in a hospital at Boston Iron Works, Georgia. *Roster* 3: 1078.

319. Misspelled "Syhart" in *Roster* and *AGI*, Swihart was a native of Ohio and lived in Canton when he enlisted at the age of 23, on August 30, 1862. He returned to Co. A on October 24, 1863, and served through the remainder of the war, being mustered out June 6, 1865, in Washington, D.C. A resident of Sabula after the war, he is buried in the city cemetery, where his grave is located immediately to the west of his comrade in arms—William Royal Oake. In fact, their respective headstones actually face one another. *Roster* 3: 1095; *AGI*, 1863-I: 920.

320. Leeper, age 18, was born in Illinois and living in De Witt when he enlisted on August 6, 1862. He was mustered out in Washington, D.C., June 6, 1865. His older brother Thomas (age 21 at enlistment) also served in Co. H, being successively promoted corporal and then sergeant, before he was killed in action at Resaca, Georgia, on May 14, 1864. *Roster* 3: 1074.

321. The cavalry attached to Lt. Col. Samuel W. Ferguson's combat team, which was defending the Deer Creek approaches to Vicksburg, was a detached squadron from Col. Wirt Adam's Mississippi Cavalry Regiment, consisting of Co. C, commanded by Capt. Thomas B. Lewers, and Co. F, commanded by Capt. George Barnes. They were Mississippians, not Texas Rangers. Ferguson probably would have disagreed with Oake's assessment of the capabilities of this mounted force, for only two months earlier he cited Captain Lewers's company as the "poorest" he had ever seen, and stated of the entire force that "As cavalry they are not worth one day's support by the Confederate government." Bearss, *The Vicksburg Campaign*, II: 128; *O.R.* I-24-I-355; *O.R.* I-24-III-762.

CHAPTER FIVE

Headed for Vicksburg and Libby Prison

W̲e were soon retracing our steps under the guard of the two rebels, and as we reached the sight of the old bridge we thought: Oh if we had taken his advice we would not now be headed for Old Libby.

Our camp, the first night after our capture, was near the plantation of Major Lee of the Confederate army, and before whom we were taken, and closely questioned by that officer as to the command to which we belonged, the number of troops on this expedition, and various other questions, which of course we answered in a manner to suit ourselves, and from which he did not receive any important information.

The next day we continued our march, and in the afternoon again passed the plantation where the British Flag had been so conspicuously displayed as our troops had first marched down the valley. As we were marching past the planter hailed our guard, who halted us, and as the planter reached the road side he began calling us everything he could think of. When he was promptly told by our guards he must not do that as we were prisoners of war, and should not be abused. The old fellow was an English Jew, and not a naturalized citizen of U.S. As we looked over the old fellow's premises we could not much blame him for the way he felt. Everything alive on the premises had been driven away, and buildings burned while huge piles of corn that had been set on fire were still burning.

On the evening of the second day we came to a rebel encampment of about one brigade of infantry, the troops I think with which our troops skirmished at the termination of our march down the valley as they occupied the same position. The next morning we were placed in charge of the 35th [*sic* either the 41st or 56th Regiment] Georgia Infantry,[322] and our former guards returned to join their command.

Early the next morning reveille sounded in the rebel camp, and the troops were soon up and preparing their morning meal which consisted of corn pone and bacon with corn coffee to wash it down. I distinctly remember that night as it rained quite hard, and having no blankets we nestled up close to the side of an old log that sheltered us somewhat from the rain, but not enough to prevent us getting wet through, and I can assure my readers ours was anything but an enviable position. While the troops were preparing to march we could not but look at the position they had chosen to repel the advance of Steele's army, and at the time thought it was a good thing Steele did not attempt to advance farther down the valley as that brigade in their chosen position could easily have defeated an assaulting column of four times their number. While the rebels were forming in line I thought I never saw troops better drilled than the 35th [41st or 56th] Georgia. Every motion and move like clock work.

On the afternoon of that day we reached Rolling Fork landing on the Sun Flower River. At this place we were put on board a steamer on our way to Haines Bluff fourteen miles in the rear of Vicksburg. Following down the river we soon entered the Yazoo River, and on our way down to the bluffs passed near the place where the battle of Chickasaw Bayou which at the time seemed to be impregnable, and I at the time thought that had Sherman effected a landing across the swamp his troops would have been annihilated in their attempt to carry the enemy's lines of entrenchments.

Upon reaching Vicksburg we were placed in the city jail, an old two story brick building situated in the heart of the city near the Court House.[323] The building was enclosed by a brick wall about twelve feet in height, the enclosure containing about half an acre. In one corner of the yard was built a small brick cook house, used in cooking the food for the inmates of the jail. The cook was a great big buck Negro weighing about 250 pounds, and as important as a chef at Delmonicos in New York City, but I don't think it

Warren County Jail in Vicksburg *(1864 image taken from the courthouse).*
Within the walls of the Vicksburg jail, William Royal Oake and four of his comrades spent nearly four weeks of their incarceration as prisoners of war before being transferred by rail across the Confederacy to Richmond, Virginia. OLD COURTHOUSE MUSEUM

Warren County Courthouse.
This icon of the Vicksburg skyline was located across the street (southwest) from the jail in which William Royal Oake was kept while held prisoner in 1863. Today, the courthouse is now the Old Courthouse Museum, housing a wealth of artifacts, documents, and photos recording the remarkable history of the community and region. OLD COURTHOUSE MUSEUM

required as much skill to prepare a meal in the prison cook house as it would in the above named place, as about all he had to cook was corn meal, corn cob, and all ground together, and stirred up with water, which was our regular fare. At the time we entered the prison there were a few confederate soldiers confined therein, also nine Yankee soldiers besides our squad of five making in all fourteen Yankees. While we had free access to the jail yard in the day time at night we were locked in a cell of the jail. A room about 10 x 14 in which the fourteen Yankees were locked. One small window with a strong grating was all the light we had, as candles or lamps were not allowed in the jail. In one corner of the room was a large six gallon crock for the purpose of which can be imagined better than described, and as many of the boys were affected with the bowel complaint the stench at times in that cell was something fierce. No blankets or pillows - yes we had pillows. We could take off our old shoes, and laying them on our old hats or caps would manage to get along so far as pillows were concerned. We received two meals a day at this place, breakfast at 9 A.M., supper at 4 P.M., no change of diet which consisted of a chunk of the aforesaid corn bread, pieces about four inches square. It was laughable to see our old darkey cook after having prepared our corn bread. He would step outside of the cook house door and yell, "Hellow dar yo pore white trash, fall in two ranks and come and done git yoah grub." If one of the boys should happen to get a little out of line he would yell out, "You get back in line Sah imejately sah." After they had formed ranks to suit him and we would march past and receive our rations.

While confined in this old prison my four comrades were troubled quite badly with the bowel complaint, or as we in the army termed it the "Tennessee Quick Step," and were considerably under the weather and for a few days felt quite blue. They could not get anything in the way of medicine to help them, and the rations we were receiving did not in the least have a tendency to mitigate the complaint.[324]

One of my comrades David W. Swihart was the owner of a testament that his best girl had given him on his entering the army, and a confederate soldier in the prison offered him five dollars for it, and Swihart came to the writer for advice as to whether he had better sell it. He said if he had some money he could buy some pies, which he thought he could eat. The peddlers of the city came past the prison, and the inmates were allowed to buy of them if they had the means, and wished to, there being an iron grating in the door of the jail yard the openings of which a pie could be shoved through. Of course I told my comrade that I thought it would be the best thing he could do, and as I had a testament one would do for both of us. He accordingly sold his book, and bought five sweet potato pies the price being one dollar each. I had eaten pies prior to that and many since, but I think the crust of those pies took the cake. Swihart always claimed I ate all the pies.

J. M. Leeper, another one of our squad was quite a little under the weather, and being rather pious he would take from his pocket a little hymn book he carried and would sing that favorite old hymn, "There is a light in the window for thee brother, There's a light in the window for thee." I used to tell him, I don't see much light just at present Leeper.

In the jail yard there was quite a tall tree growing, and by getting up in the top of it we could see over the top of the wall and over the river see the camp of the Federal Army across the River at Young's Point, also the iron-clads and transports lying at anchor in the River opposite the camp. At such times how we wished we were there. Of course it was against the rules of the jail to get up the tree, and if caught in the act would be locked up for it, but we would watch our chance, and when we saw the jailer open the gate to go down in the city we would climb up the tree, and take a look at our friends so near, and yet so far away.

On the night of the 16th of April after being locked in our cell about two hours the boom of a cannon was heard, and in a very short time we thought every gun in the Vicksburg batteries were firing as well as the guns of the Federal fleet of gun boats, and as we lay in our cell we could occasionally see a streak of fire through the grating of our cell window, and which proved to be the burning fuse of Yankee shell thrown from the heavy guns of the navy. Again could be heard the screeching of the deadly shells as they were hurled on their death dealing mission. At times the very earth would tremble as some of the huge projectiles would drop nearby. One heavy shot carried away one corner of the jail cook house, and wall adjoining, although the nose of the screeching shell and heavy guns was something awful. There was a certain fascination about it, and as we lay locked in our cell, we wished one of the shots would strike the old jail, and knock it to pieces, thinking that by so doing it might give us a chance to escape if we could reach the river.

After about one hour of the terrific firing it ceased as suddenly as it began, and it was not until the next morning that we learned the cause of it. Early the next morning the jail yard gate was opened to admit some more Yankee prisoners, five soldiers and five civilians.[325] The soldiers were five men belonging to the 47th Ohio; the civilians were three newspaper correspondents, and the cabin boy and steward of the steamer [George Sturgess].[326] Upon entering the jail they were a sorrowful looking set. It seemed that General Grant had decided to run some transports past the batteries loaded with supplies, and hospital stores; the boats to be protected as much as possible by barges loaded with bailed hay on each side of them. Now to better understand the situation I would state that on the west shore of the river and opposite Vicksburg were quite a lot of empty buildings. The enemy also had a picket on that side of the river with instructions that in case the Yankees should attempt to run the fleet past the batteries they should set on fire some of the buildings thus enabling the enemy to better direct their fire.[327]

Grant having set the time upon which the attempt was to be made had called for volunteers from the army to man the transports. Of course the civilians manning the fleet could not be compelled to go if they did not want to. There was no lack of volunteers as hundreds volunteered where one was needed. General Grant's orders were for the boats to float quietly down the river, all lights to be extinguished as much as possible, until they were seen and fired upon by the enemy, then the transports were to put on full steam and try to pass the enemy's batteries, while the gunboats, that accompanied them should engage the rebel works. All of the transports with the exception of one succeeded in getting safely by.[328]

When the rebel pickets first discovered the passing steamers they set on fire some of the old buildings, thus lighting up the river, and enabling the enemy the better to direct their fire on the fleeing boats. One being hit below the water line soon sank, and as the crew of the doomed steamer managed to get upon the bales of hay by which the steamer had been protected the rebels put out from the Vicksburg shore with boats, and captured them, and they were placed in the jail with us.[329] Being wet through and many of them had lost their coats and hats they were indeed a hard looking set. The newspaper correspondents were writing for some New

York papers, and thought by making the run past the Vicksburg batteries they would be enabled to make a good write up for their respective papers.[330] They succeeded as far as having something to write about but how to send it was the question.

One of the correspondents, whose name was Albert Richardson,[331] was shot and killed in New York City a few years after the war by a quite prominent lawyer by the name of McFarland. The incident may be remembered by some who read this work. One of them escaped from prison during the following summer after lying in the swamp, and being chased by Blood Hounds, half starved and nearly naked succeeded in reaching the Union lines. He afterwards wrote a book entitled Four Years in Secessia[332] describing his capture and experiences while a prisoner in the hands of the Confederates.

While in the jail here we one day got hold of a copy of a paper published in Vicksburg at the time, which stated that the Yankees that were taken prisoners on the Deer Creek raid were to be turned over to the civil authorities and tried for the destruction of property that was destroyed there. Of course that meant us, and we thought that we could already feel the halter around our necks. We well knew that it would be in violation of all military law to do so, but at the same time we were aware that sometimes Might made right, and as we well knew that the rebels were terribly incensed at what they called wanton destruction of property we did not know to what extremity they would go, and I can assure my readers that after reading that article we were shaking in our shoes.[333]

While there I got acquainted with one of the confederates in the jail, at the time we took him to be a confederate. His name was Douglas.[334] At the breaking out of the war he belonged to the U.S. Texas Rangers and tried to escape north, but was arrested and put in prison, because he would not serve in the rebel army. He said that he would never fire on the Old Flag. At this time I think he told me he had been confined in prison for eleven months. He was a fine looking soldier about thirty years of age. He told me his folks lived in Springfield, Illinois, and he had one brother a Major in the Union Army then with General Grant near Vicksburg.

When we were sent east from Vicksburg we left him there still in jail. Along in the month of June following after we had been paroled and had reached our lines, and General Grant had invested the city of Vicksburg I read an account of his escape as published in a Northern Paper.[335]

It seems after the city had been completely surrounded by Grant's army for some little time the confederate army were getting short of percussion caps for their small arms and the rebel commander General Pemberton called for two men who would try and pass through Grant's lines, to General [Joseph E.] Johnston*, who was commanding the rebel forces [at] Jackson in Grants rear, and to get a supply of caps and return with them to the army in Vicksburg. It also seems that Douglas was one of the two men selected for the hazardous undertaking, but that after getting through Grants lines instead of reporting to Joe Johnston, Douglas went direct to General Grants headquarters stating the case to him, and telling him who he was and how long he had been in prison, and for what cause. After he had stated his case the General shook hands with him and furnished him free transportation to his home at Springfield, Illinois.

Early in May it was rumored that the Yankee prisoners at Vicksburg were to be sent east presumably to Libby Prison, and on the morning of May the 7th we were marched to the Depot boarded the cars, and started on our journey. Upon reaching Jackson a distance of forty miles we left the train and were put into an old building with a guard placed over us. We remained at Jackson over night, when we again took the train to continue our journey, sidetracking frequently to allow trains that were loaded with Confederate troops, going west to reinforce the rebel army at Vicksburg, to pass us. On our way through Alabama we were delayed a short time where occurred the incident I am going to relate. An incident that is deeply impressed upon my memory, and one that death alone can efface. Being as it were, one bright oasis in the desert of suffering, and starvation. One that showed that even in those dark and bloody times there were living south of the Mason Dixon Line those that did all they could to alleviate the sufferings of those that fortunes of war had placed in the hands of the enemy.

On the arrival of our train at Demopolis, [Alabama], we saw approaching a carriage driven by a colored man, the occupants of the carriage being an elderly man of about seventy years of age accompanied by his daughter who was perhaps aged about twenty years, and judging from their general appearance belonged to the aristocracy of the South. No sooner had they reached our car than they began to take from their carriage an abundant supply of the necessities of life, cooked and ready for the inner man. To say that we were astonished at the amount of delicacies that was placed before us would but faintly express our feelings, and we were informed it was for our particular benefit that princely repast had been prepared, and by those whom we had every reason to believe were bitter foes of anything that looked like a Yankee. As dish after dish were handed us by the old gentleman and his lovely daughter, to as quickly disappear in the expansive depositories of the half starved Yanks, expressions of the deepest gratitude were plainly visible on the countenance of every man of that little band of soldiers. Then did they tell us that day prior they had been informed that a band of Yankee soldiers would pass through the little town, and they had determined to give them at least one good meal.

At least for the time being the cravings of our stomachs were appeased, and as ringing of the bell warned us that the time for the continuation of our journey had arrived, and as we warmly pressed the hands of our kind friends who in return wished us good luck and a safe and speedy release from our imprisonment, and a safe return to loved ones at home. The train moved off, and with tearful eyes we gave them three hearty Yankee Cheers, and until we were half a mile from the depot could we see our kind friends waving their hands. Many a time after our arrival in old Libby when the acute pangs of hunger were upon us did our thoughts revert to that bright episode in our prison life. And when memories of the past rise before me like a dream I think if there is such a place as Paradise surely some day at the right hand of the throne of Grace will be seated the kind old gentleman and his lovely and accomplished daughter, who so kindly fed the half starved Yankee soldiers during the dark days of the Civil War.

From Demopolis our course of travel took us through the little city of Selma, Alabama, a place of some importance to the Confederates at that time, as a good deal of their munitions of war were manufactured there.[336] We arrived there on the eleventh of the month and soon after we left the cars, and marched through the streets to the steamboat landing, as being on the Alabama River, boats ran from there to Montgomery, the capital of the state. It was amusing as we passed through the streets to see the rebs gather to look upon a live Yankee. Up to that time they had never seen a Federal soldier, and looked upon as being some wild animal. I noticed in passing through the City there were quite a number of Home Guards dressed in their knobby new uniforms of gray, and made themselves quite conspicuous. One, a corporal, who when we were halted in the street, stated that he expected to be ordered to Vicksburg shortly to assist the Confederate army to whip General Grant, and in fact he was very anxious to go as he wished to secure a few Yankee scalps to bring home to his best girl.

In our squad of prisoners was a sergeant from an Illinois regiment by the name of James Miller[337] who upon hearing the reb make this assertion stepped close to him and said, "Johnnnie Reb do you think you would know me if you should see me again." The reb replied that he thought that he would be able to identify him, whereupon Miller said, "All right, I expect to be with Grants Army in short time and would be glad to meet you and nothing would give me greater pleasure than to give you an opportunity to take my scalp home as a memento to your best girl." The Johnnie turned red in the face and the bystanders all laughed as the Yankee had rather got in on the reb.

The gentler sex were very sarcastic towards us saying, my what nasty things. One of them made the remark that she supposed the nasty things had horns. "No the Yankees have but one horn," Miller replied. Our guards were confederate soldiers that had seen service and were fine fellows, and rather enjoyed the conversation between the Yanks and Rebs and would tell us, "Give them as good as they send boys."

The next morning we continued on our way arriving at Montgomery in the afternoon, and after a short stay continued our journey and May the 12th reached Atlanta, Georgia, and remained there one day. Little did we at the time think that in a little over a year's time we would again enter Atlanta not as prisoners of war but as conquerors. On May the 14th we reached Richmond, Virginia.

Headed for Vicksburg and Libby Prison

322. The 35th Georgia was not present in Mississippi, but instead was assigned to the Army of North Virginia, serving in Virginia. The 41st and 56th regiments of Georgia Infantry were serving in the delta, however, assigned to Brig. Gen. Stephen D. Lee's reinforced brigade, which in turn reinforced and supported Ferguson in the field against Steele's expedition. Stewart Sifakis, *Compendium of the Confederate Armies: South Carolina and Georgia* (New York: Facts on File, 1995), 244–45, 252–53, 270–71; Bearss, *The Vicksburg Campaign*, II: 128.

323. The wall-enclosed Warren County Jail was located on the corner of Grove and Cherry streets, immediately northeast of the Warren County Courthouse. *A Photographic Tour of Civil War Vicksburg*, http://www.oldcourthouse.org/.

324. Also known as the "Tennessee high step," in humorous reference to the distinctive high gait of a diarrhetic soldier—one suffering from diarrhea and dysentery. No laughing matter, chronic diarrhea and dysentery claimed 44,558 U.S. army lives during the Civil War. These were declared "the most important" causes of mortality from disease in the war for the armed forces of both sides. Garrison & Garrison, *Civil War Usage*, 247; *The Medical and Surgical History of the War of the Rebellion* (Washington, 1875), Medical Volume, Pt. I and Appendix, p. XLIII.

325. The "old soldier's disease" again affected Oake's memory, but only in regard to chronology. This specific group of Federal prisoners did not fall into Confederate hands on the night of April 16, 1863, when the transport *Henry Clay* was sunk by Confederate artillery fire, but rather were fished out of the water and seized by Confederates on the night of May 3, when another attempt to steam past the batteries was made. In the aftermath of Porter's successful runs past the batteries on April 16 and April 22, an army tug towing two barges loaded with supplies also ran past Vicksburg in the early morning of April 27. Encouraged by this success, Grant ordered two tugs, with four barges loaded with 400,000 rations and forage, to make a run past the batteries; however, only two barges and one tug, the *George Sturgess*, could be prepared in time to attempt what proved an unsuccessful run in the late evening of May 3, 1863. A shell from a ten-inch Columbiad, mounted in the Water Battery north of the city, hit the tug's engine room, exploding the boiler. After fifteen minutes under fire, taking more hits, the all-volunteer crew and passengers were forced to abandon the doomed vessel. *O.R.* I-24-I-687; Bearss, *The Vicksburg Campaign*, II: 438–39.

326. The regular crews of the two tugs refused to participate in the mission, so soldiers were called upon to volunteer for the desperate venture. Men from the 27th Missouri and 47th Ohio regiments answered the call, and Capt. William H. Ward of Co. B, 47th Ohio, was given command of the expedition. A total of twenty-four men was taken prisoner in the failed attempt to run the batteries the night of May 3. Along with the captured soldier volunteers, four war correspondents were taken. Nine of the volunteers, members of Co. B, 47th Ohio, were awarded the Medal of Honor for their service aboard the doomed army tug. Bearss, *The Vicksburg Campaign*, II: 438–38n, 439.

327. The small river port and railroad depot of De Soto lay opposite Vicksburg. Not only did the Confederate pickets burn the buildings, they rolled barrels of tar to the river's edge and set them on fire to aid in illuminating the scene.

328. Rear Admiral David Dixon Porter, commanding the Federal gunboat fleet, reported only "very light" loss, and stated that all ships (the seven gunboats, two remaining transports, a ram, and one tug) were ready for service within half an hour after the passage. As Oake accurately states, barges loaded with supplies, fodder, coal, and ammunition were lashed to the sides of the steam-driven vessels. On the night of April 22, Porter sent six additional transports and twelve lashed barges in another run past the Vicksburg batteries, losing one vessel sunk, another disabled, and a third badly damaged, while three others passed safely. The successful steaming of gunboats, transports, and barges past the heavy batteries contributed to the eventual fall of Vicksburg itself, and ultimately total Federal control of the Mississippi River. United States Navy Department, *Civil War Naval Chronology* (Washington, 1971), III-67.

329. As noted earlier, the capture of these prisoners occurred on the night of May 3–4, 1863, and not as Oake states in conjunction with Porter's first run of April 16. Twenty-four men were taken prisoner in the incident. Bearss, *The Vicksburg Campaign*, II: 439.

330. The reporters represented three papers, the *New York Tribune, New York World,* and *Cincinnati Times.* Ibid., 439.

331. Along with Richardson, who worked for the *New York Tribune,* Junius H. Browne of the *Tribune* and Richard T. Colburn of the *New York World* were among the captured correspondents. No record was found that provides the identity of the gentleman working for the *Cincinnati Times.* Ibid., 439.

332. Junius H. Brown, *Four Years in Secessia: Adventures Within and Beyond Union Lines...* (Hartford, 1865).

333. Immediately after their capture, questions arose among Confederate authorities of what should be done with the five Iowans, who had been caught mounted on stolen horses and holding property stolen from private residences. Adding to their embarrassment, the five Hawkeyes were identified as the party who set fire to corn stored on Dr. Hill's plantation. Only direct intervention by Colonel Ferguson prevented his troopers from lynching the prisoners. Ferguson forwarded the prisoners to Gen. Stephen D. Lee, along with correspondence summarizing his disgust with the looters, "Will not our Government make an example of them?" Luckily for Oake and his comrades, Confederate military authorities took no action against the prisoners and did not hand them over to civil authorities. *O.R.* I-24-I-510.

334. Could not identify or locate further information on this individual.—Ed.

335. Article not found.—Ed.

336. Access by water, railroad lines, stage routes, and nearby iron furnaces made Selma, founded in 1820 on a high bluff overlooking the Alabama River, an attractive manufacturing site for the Confederacy early in the war. Located far from active theaters of war, the city developed numerous war industries. As the industries grew, so did the population. By the end of the conflict, Selma factories and foundries employed at least 10,000 men who, as war industry employees, were exempt from conscription. It has been estimated that during the last two years of the war, roughly one-half of the cannon and two-thirds of the ammunition required by the Confederate army came from Selma. Current, ed., *Encyclopedia of the Confederacy*, 3: 1387-88.

337. No biographical data found.—Ed.

CHAPTER SIX

Libby Prison, Paroled, and Again in our Own Lines

On reaching Richmond we were marched to the famous old prison and upon entering it every man was searched, and all valuables taken from us, if we had any, but as we had none as all such had long before been taken from us it took but a short time to go through the Yanks. This famous old prison was a brick building three stories with basement dimensions of which were 100 x 120 [feet]. It had been an old warehouse, and in front of it hung the old sign, Libby and Son, Ship Chandlers [Groceries]. It was situated on the James River [and] on the north and east [of the building] were streets. The basement of the building was used principally as a storage room. The upper two rooms [*sic* floors] [had] two partitions running through each, dividing each floor into three compartments 40 x 100 [feet]. On the upper floor at the north end of the building [was] the room to which we had been assigned, and to which we had the honor of being escorted.[338] Upon entering the prison we were hailed with the usual greeting when fresh prisoners arrived, "Fresh Fish, Fresh Fish."[339]

Soon the boys began gathering around us to find out what part of the army we belonged to, and where and when captured, and many other questions, all of which we answered to the best of our ability. All of them being very anxious to know what was going on in the outside world, as they termed it. Just at this particular period of the war the prisons of the South were filled with Yankee prisoners, owing in part to a disagreement between the North and South in regard to status of the Negro soldier in being on the equality with the white troops.[340] In the room in which we were there were about three hundred prisoners,[341] and although the room was 40 x 100 feet I can assure my readers there was not much room for rent. In talking with the prisoners we found that many of them had been there six months, and some even as long as eleven months, and how they managed to exist for that length of time amidst such surroundings were beyond my comprehension. We had no blankets, the bare floor only, for pillows we could utilize our shoes, if we were lucky enough to have any, and by laying our old caps or hats on them we had a fair place to lay our heads.

At the side of the building next to James River a square wooden projection 10 x 12 [feet] at the end of the three rooms had been built, and as a floor had been laid level with the floors of the building this addition was used by the prisoners as a wash room and [water] closet. Troughs about twelve foot in length were built in both sides of it. One for washing purposes, and one to be used as a closet [sic toilet]. Pipes running from the river gave us our supply of water. We of course had an abundance of water but having no soap we did not as a general thing do a very good job in our laundry work, but still it would freshen up our old rags, and for a short time would feel quite comfortable until the heat of our bodies began to revive the greybacks[342] that had for a short time been put out of commission by being immersed in cold water. The rations, while we were here, consisted of three pounds of coarse bread a day, for twelve men. [These were provided] about 9 A.M. and 4 P.M., [with] no meat, no coffee. Once in a while a large kettle of liquid that meat, used for the rebel guards had been boiled in, would be brought in for us in which we could dip our bread making it slip down a little easier. After partaking of breakfast we would perform the only labor we had to do while in prison. Seating ourselves on the floor we would take off our old shirts turning them wrong side out, and going over them carefully would kill all of the varmints[343] we could find, and squeezing everything that we could find that would make more if let alone.[344] Afternoons [proceeded] the same way. Thus regularly twice a day we went through the same old routine, and yet they seemed to gain in numbers.

Out of the windows of the old prison we could see Castle Thunder

Libby Prison in Richmond, Virginia.
William Royal Oake was temporarily held in the infamous Confederate prison for ten days in May 1863. The building was a warehouse of Libby and Sons, ship chandlers, before the war. CHICAGO HISTORICAL SOCIETY

Interior of Libby Prison.
Primarily a prison for Union officers, Private William Royal Oake was one of the rare enlisted men to be held in Libby. Perhaps 125,000 prisoners stayed in the prison during the war, and of these, about 50,000 were held there for a prolonged time. CHICAGO HISTORICAL SOCIETY

another old brick building used by the confederates as prison for the Yankee soldiers.[345] One day as I was standing looking out of window in the direction of Castle Thunder I saw a rebel guard shoot one of the Yankee prisoners that had put his head out of the window. In Libby there was no glass in the windows, but three inch wooden bars were nailed across them both ways leaving openings large enough for a man to put his head through, but which was against orders, and good bye to anyone sticking his head through the opening, as the rebel guard on his beat would shoot without giving any warning. The writer came near being caught the same way, but was jerked from the opening by one of the older prisoners, who then told me rules of the prison, and I can assure my readers, I did not attempt it again. Belle Isle another place used as a place for Yankee prisoners was visible from old Libby, it being an enclosure in James River.[346] At this time all of there places were filled to their utmost capacity with Yankee prisoners. The question with us was how long were we to be kept there. Would there never be an exchange of prisoners made. As we had nothing to divert our minds the monotony of prison life became almost unbearable. Not anything to read nor anything to play games with. Of course some of the boys had the testaments given them by their best girls or other friends when they left home, and which the rebs had allowed us to retain as they did not seem to have much use for the word of God. The writer had one, and read it quite frequently, more than I ever have since. I attribute my present aversion to it, to the fact that in reading it so much at that time I became glutted and never recovered from its effects.

While here prisoners were daily dying.[347] Every day some poor fellow was being taken to his long home. Getting sick and not having proper food and medical attendance amidst such surroundings generally ended by being carried out on a stretcher. Others that had been wounded when taken and the wounds being not properly dressed, gangrene would set in and it would invariably end in death. To the soldier in good health it was bad enough, but to those that were inclined to be home sick and a little under the weather good bye. I will never forget one incident that occurred while I was in the old prison. The rebels had made a large new flag that was to be hoisted on top of the building and in order to get to the top of the prison they would have to enter the room in which we were confined as the stairs leading to the skylight went up from our room. One morning Dick Turner[348] the rebel sergeant having charge of the prison, with two soldiers carrying the flag came through the room on their way to hoist the old rag. As they passed through some of the Yanks hissed the flag, this making Turner hot under the collar. Upon returning from raising the flag he singled out a few of the prisoners whom he had noticed as being the prime movers in the hissing and ordered them bucked and gagged for twenty-four hours. Bucking is placing a person in a sitting position, and tying his wrists together below his knees and to place a stick under the hollow of his knees - over arms. While gagging in this instance consisted of placing a steel bayonet between the jaws and tying a string on each end of same, [then] fastening the strings behind the head, [there by] keeping it securely in the mouth of the victim.[349]

Along about the last of May rumors were circulated through the prison that some of the prisoners would soon be paroled, and return to the Union lines. I can assure my readers there was great rejoicing among the prisoners, and for about a week afterwards we heard no more of it, and the boys felt quite blue, and disappointed as we had again made up our minds that we were doomed to a long stay in that gloomy abode. We were destined for a pleasant surprise in the near future as early on the morning of June 8th [May 23rd] we were awakened quite early by the prison guards who informed us that we were to be taken by rail to City Point and paroled.[350] Before it was light we were ordered into line, and to descend from our quarters and march to the depot. As we passed out of the old jail we were counted - seven hundred was the number to be taken, leaving many a poor fellow behind, and while they waved a good bye to us as we left we could imagine their feelings at thus being left behind perhaps for months longer. After boarding the train we soon reached City Point which is situated on the James River about twenty miles distance, and as we came within sight of the steamship landing and saw lying at the dock, the Yankee steamer City of New York,[351] with old glory flying from the flagstaff in all of its splendor, we gave three rousing cheers. There were but a few dry eyes among that crowd of seven hundred men.

As the train came to a stop the boys were all anxious to rush for the ship but were kept in check until the preliminaries between the officers of both sides had been arranged and the ship ready to receive us. The steamer had brought from Annapolis, Maryland, nine hundred confederates, who were landing from the steamer. This steamer being used for the purpose of carrying prisoners from the two points. After the confederates had all left the boat and were counted as they passed through the lines of guards we were ordered into line and also counted as we passed through the lines. On this boat [was] a company of Hawkins' Zouaves[352] whose duty on the boat was to get and prepare grub for the prisoners as they were transferred and upon their arrival on the boat. On each side of the gang way as we went on board were large vats of steaming coffee, and stacks of bread and ham. As each man came aboard a new pint cup of coffee and a loaf of bread and a huge slice of ham were given to each man, and were told to come again when that was gone. Kind friends, no pen can describe our feelings on this occasion, after being so long without half the food that was necessary to properly sustain our bodies. Our clothes, a mass of rags and filth, we were again in the hands of friends and haven of plenty. Never will I forget that company of guards on the boat as they did all they could to appease our hunger.

What a difference there was between the Confederates and Yankee prisoners on being returned to their respective lines. When the rebels came off that ship every man carried a new blanket and a haversack full of grub that had been issued to them by Uncle Sam, while we were destitute of everything and half starved besides. It is true perhaps that the confederate government could not have treated the Yankee prisoners as well as we did there's, but there is no question but what they could have given us better treatment than what they did, and provided us means of keeping ourselves free from filth, and being eaten up by greybacks. It looked to us at the time that the confederate authorities were cognizant of the manner in which the prisoners were treated, and were determined to so treat the men, so that upon being exchanged they would for sometime after that be unable to return to duty owing that to their physical condition.[353]

About one hour after we boarded the boat it started on its journey to Annapolis, Maryland, and as we passed down the James to Fortress Monroe, [passing] the wreck of the Frigate Cumberland that had been sunk in that memorable engagement with the famous Merrimac.[354] As we steamed through the lines into Yankee waters the white flag that had floated over our vessel in company with the stars and stripes was hauled down and Old Glory was raised to the top of the flagstaff.

In a short time we reached Fort Monroe where we lay for a couple of hours, when we again resumed our journey up the waters of Chesapeake Bay. During the night on our trip up the Bay we encountered a severe storm, and in the intense darkness we were rammed by some other vessel, and for a short time everything was in confusion and a regular pandemonium reigned on the steamer. After matters had somewhat quieted down the officers of the vessel decided to anchor until morning.

Early in the morning the ship resumed its journey, and about nine in the morning we reached our destination, Annapolis. At the time of the collision with the craft on our journey most all of the soldiers were asleep in the lower deck of the ship, and being so suddenly awakened there was a great rush among them to reach the upper deck to find out what had happened. As the passage way was very narrow it was almost impossible to get out as every man wanted to go first and they pulled and crowded each other in their mad efforts to get out. They were all piled up in a bunch, and it was some little time before the officers of the ship could quiet them assuring them there was no danger, and advising them to remain in their places and sleep until morning.

At the time it was thought that we had been run into by a Blockade Runner,[355] but if such was the case we never learned. After leaving the ship we plainly saw the result of the collision, a hole about ten feet in length and about four feet in width, about six feet above the water line of the ship had been stove in, and as the sea was running quite high at the time it was almost miraculous that we had all not gone to the bottom of the bay.

The day after our arrival at Annapolis every man was given a new suit of clothes, and two months pay. It was always customary with the government before issuing clothing or paying the troops to first get their descriptive roll from the commands to which they belonged in order to see how they stood with the government, but after seeing our condition orders were at once given to issue us new clothing and two months pay. After receiving our new clothing the soldiers all started for the beach on an arm of the bay to bathe holding as we went our new clothing, at arms length, as we did not want the live stock by which we were invested to invade our new suits. After disrobing we plunged into the salt water of the bay and when the salt water came in contact with places that had been eaten raw by the to close acquaintance of the Confederate greybacks our feelings can be better imagined than described.

Libby Prison, Paroled, and
Again in our Own Lines

After bathing about half an hour and having put on our new clothes we felt like new men and throwing our old duds in the water, and for a few moments to watch the death struggles of the live stock we started for the city to get some of the delicacies we knew were obtainable for the inner man, and as we had two months pay in our pockets we got the best the city afforded in the eating line. The camp to which we had been temporarily assigned was about half a mile from the city, good frame buildings with three tiers of bunks on either side with mattresses and blankets and plenty of good grub, and men to prepare it for us. After being here a few days we were removed to a larger camp about two miles out of the city where we were supplied with tents but had to do our own cooking as we did when in the field, however we had an abundance of rations and lived like kings.

Upon our arrival at this place one of the first things we did was to write our friends in the North informing them of our location as we knew that they were very anxious to learn of our whereabouts. They of course knew that we had been taken prisoners, and were in the hands of the enemy and were in great suspense waiting to hear from us. After receiving two months pay some of the boys, the writer among them made a few purchases of mementos and such small articles as we thought we could use, and that were not furnished us by the government. We had our pictures taken, and bought small hand bags in which to carry them. One day after being away from my tent a short time I found upon returning that my hand bag with its contents had been stolen and many other of the boys were in the same boat. Upon discovering our loss we were terribly incensed at the miserable curs who would steal under such circumstances. Although the loss in dollars and cents was small we keenly felt the loss, and if we could have discovered the thieves they would have been roughly handled. After being in camp here a short time it became rumored that all paroled prisoners that belonged to the western army would soon be sent to the parole camp at Benton Barracks, St. Louis, Missouri.[356]

In a few days we received orders to march to the depot as a special train had been ordered to convey a portion of the troops to St. Louis. At that time paroled prisoners were constantly arriving from Richmond and as the camps at Annapolis[357] were crowded it was necessary to send some west in order to make room for the new arrivals.

On the morning of June the 20th [23rd] we boarded the train, and pulled out for our new camp at Benton Barracks, at St. Louis, where perhaps we would remain for sometime until a general exchange of prisoners took place. We would far rather be with our command engaged in an active campaign than to undergo the monotony of months in camp, but we could not return to our regiment until we were regularly exchanged, and it was useless to ask for a furlough, so as we were speeding west on the train the five of us belonging to the 26th Iowa made up our minds that when the train was passing through Illinois that when the train arrived at Pana[358] where it crossed the Illinois Central [Railroad], we would jump off and try to make our way home, taking what is termed a French furlough, simply going without permission.[359]

The train was in charge of a Federal Captain. Upon reaching the crossing the train came to a full stop, and as it again started on its way Leonidas Miller and twelve others got off the rear end of the train. Sergeant D. H. Denney, D. W. Swihart, and J. M. Leeper, the other three of the 26th Iowa being afraid to attempt it. As the train got under head way the officer in charge yelled at us to come on board, but we only waved our hands at him, and returned to the car, and I don't think he cared much as he himself was a paroled prisoner. After the train pulled out we began to count noses, and found that out of the 14 that left the train, eleven of them belonged to Illinois regiments whose homes were in different parts of the State. Some of the men being quite near there homes, [while] one belonged to the 13th Iowa and lived near Council Bluffs, Iowa. Consequently he had quite a distance to go. It was on Saturday about 4 P.M. when we left the train and upon inquiry there would be no trains North until morning we decided that we would walk along the rail road track North to the little town of Assumption about six [sic nine] miles North.

We arrived there a little before sundown and went to the only hotel the little town had and inquired if we could remain over night. We told the landlord that we were prisoners, having lately been paroled from Libby, and that we were on our way home for a short time, and had no funds to pay our way. The landlord proved to be a jolly old fellow and replied, "All right boys we will keep you all right, and by the way you look dry, take one on me." There being a bar in the hotel we accepted of his kind invitation. By that time there were several citizens gathered having learned of the arrival of the Union soldiers.

Libby Prison, Paroled, and
Again in our Own Lines

At supper time we were supplied with a fine meal again having the privilege of setting down to a table and partaking of our food. After supper as we sat out on the porch reciting our experiences in the rebel prisons to the intense gratification of our new friends the time passed quite pleasantly and it was near midnight when our friends began to disperse. Among the crowd was the Sheriff of the County who insisted upon my comrade Miller and myself on sharing his hospitality for the night which offer we gladly accepted, while several others of the boys were accommodated at the homes of other citizens. Next morning being Sunday we were informed by our friends that the passenger train going north did not stop there, so after having our dinner with our kind friends we decided that we would walk seven miles north to the little town of Moweaqua, as we were told that the express going at 6 A.M. would stop at that place. After bidding our friends good bye we started on our way reaching Moweaqua about 4 P.M., and went directly to the hotel where our reception was a repetition of what it was at Assumption. In the evening we were invited to attend services at the Baptist Church, and listened to a very good sermon. At the conclusion of the services the Minister explained to the congregation who we were, and where we had been, and that we were on our way to our homes and were not very well supplied with funds. They then took a collection and in a few moments raised seventy dollars, which was distributed as equally as it could be among us.

The next morning we were up and ate our breakfast bright and early and after shaking hands with our friends went to the depot. Upon inquiring what the fare was to Dixon[360] the agent told us it was $5.80. We told him we had but $5.00. He replied, "Boys I can't sell you a ticket for that so you had better get on the train and perhaps you can arrange it with the conductor of the train."

The train pulled in on time, and as it again started, and we were seated in the car the conductor came along, and said, "Tickets please." I replied, "We have no tickets but wish to go to Dixon." He replied, "The fare is $5.80." I replied, "We have but five dollars each." We told him how we happened to be there, where we had been and where we were going. He looked at us a moment, then said, "All right boys I will charge you but half fare."

We arrived at Dixon about 2 P.M. and found out that we would have to wait there until 9 P.M. the time the train west arrived from Chicago. We ate supper at the hotel paying only half price. Promptly on time the train pulled in, and after a short time reached Fulton, Illinois, on the Mississippi River. On our way from Dixon to the latter place the conductor charged us but half price. At this time, the railroad bridge had not been built across the Mississippi River at this point. Fulton, being the western terminus of the Chicago and Northwestern Railroad, and at night upon the arrival of the mails they were carried across the River in a small skiff, by the mail carrier with whom we also crossed upon reaching that point. We landed in Lyons, Iowa, which is directly opposite from Fulton. Upon landing in Lyons, I felt at home again as I was well acquainted there, and only twenty-four miles from my father's home. It was about midnight as Miller and I walked through the main street of the little city, and the citizens of the place were sound asleep. We continued on our way on the main road leading west, which I so well knew, and about sunrise had reached the Ten Mile Home.[361] The proprietor of whom I was well acquainted with, and when we approached the house he had just arisen and stepped out of the door. At seeing me he stopped quick and exclaimed, "My God Royal is that you?"

"I thought you were dead." It having been so reported at the time and he had heard no news to the contrary. After shaking hands with him I assured him we were much in evidence yet, and would like some breakfast if it was not too much trouble.

Soon we were partaking of a good meal and after thanking him, he would not take any pay, we continued on our journey to Charlotte, eight miles farther, the town which was credited with my enlistment. As we entered the little town and went into a little store and saloon kept by a man named Jackson Albright, who had a brother[362] in the same company and regiment to which we belonged, soon half of the citizens of the little town were there to see us tiring us out shaking our hands. Among them was a young man named John Varner[363] that had enlisted in the same company, but after a few months service had been discharged on account of sickness.

He kindly offered to harness up his team and take us a little way on our journey. Miller had about twenty-five miles to go, while I was within five miles of home. Hitching up he took me within half a mile of home, bidding him and Miller good bye I walked half a mile across the prairie to my home.

Libby Prison, Paroled, and Again in our Own Lines

338. Located on Cary Street with the James and Kanawha Canal and the James River located in the rear, the eight-room structure was about 300 feet long by 103 feet deep. Interior brick walls divided its upper two floors into thirds as described by Oake. Barred windows, many of them unglazed, provided ventilation. The prison was supplied with city water drawn from the James, used for drinking, bathing, and also flushing primitive water closets. Current, ed., *Encyclopedia of the Confederacy*, 2: 930.

339. The phrase has two uses, referring to new recruits and, in this instance, to newcomers in a prisoner-of-war camp or center. Longtime inmates often fell upon the new men, using force to relieve them of any valuables or food. Garrison & Garrison, *Civil War Usage*, 87.

340. The Emancipation Proclamation, issued by President Abraham Lincoln on September 22, 1862, which officially went into effect on January 1, 1863, significantly confused the prisoner-of-war exchange program once black men, the vast majority of whom were ex-slaves, were permitted to enlist as soldiers in the U.S. Army. Based on an agreement known as the Dix-Hill Cartel (negotiated July 22, 1862), the governments of the United States and Confederate States consented to exchange prisoners rather than confine them for any great length of time. The Confederate government, however, refused to officially recognize black soldiers as prisoners of war. The effective exchange of prisoners dramatically began to slow down and even stall out in 1863, and in 1864 Ulysses S. Grant suspended exchanges altogether. Mageret E. Wagner, Gary W. Gallagher, and Paul Finkelman, eds., *The Library of Congress Civil War Desk Reference* (New York: Simon & Schuster, 2002), 600–04. Hereafter cited as *Civil War Desk Reference*.

341. By the winter of 1863, records note more than 1,000 Federal officers were confined here. The prison was so crowded that men slept on their sides to take up as little space as possible. Throughout the war, perhaps as many as 125,000 prisoners actually passed through Libby, of whom more than 40,000 were incarcerated for a prolonged time. Ibid., 611; Current, ed., *Encyclopedia of the Confederacy*, 2: 931.

342. Although often used as an allusion to a Confederate soldier, in reference to the gray color of his jacket or coat, in this instance Oake uses the term to describe the parasite known as a louse (plural of which is "lice"), a wingless insect with mouthparts adapted for sucking or biting warm-blooded animals (including humans). *Webster's Dictionary*, 571, 588.

343. The varmints were lice and fleas.

344. A reference to the eggs of fleas and lice laid on the body or in the hair, or in this case in the clothes.

345. Another of the Richmond prisons, Castle Thunder comprised three buildings linked together by a highboard fence. The central structure was formerly Gleanor's tobacco factory, located at the corner of Cary and Eighteenth streets. The estimated capacity for the prison was around 1,400 hundred, with more than 3,000 men having been confined there during the war. Garrison & Garrison, *Civil War Usage*, 47.

346. Belle Isle was a small island in the James River. This prison facility was a stockade enclosure containing the overflow of enlisted prisoners from the city. Prisoners resided in tents and a few huts on one end of the eighty-acre island. While Oake was confined in Libby, several thousand men were being held on the island, with the total number of prisoners approaching 5,000 to 6,000 at any one time. Had Oake not been exchanged, it is highly likely he would have been moved to this facility. Wagner, et. al., *Civil War Desk Reference*, 611; Boatner, *Civil War Dictionary*, 57.

347. The mortality rate for Yankees confined in Southern prisons was 15.5 percent during the war. According to the U.S. Record and Pension Office, 211,411 United States soldiers were captured by Confederates during the war. Of this total, 30,218 died while confined in prison. E. B. Long, *Civil War Day by Day: An Almanac 1861-1865* (Garden City, New York: Doubleday & Co., 1971), 714.

348. Sergeant Richard R. Turner served as the jailor at the prison. A plantation overseer before the war, Turner was a large, often angry, and violent man whom most prisoners came to despise. In their recollections, just like Oake, they often confused him with his superior, Capt. (later Maj.) Thomas P. Turner, who served as commandant of the prison and supervised other Richmond prisons during most of the war. Current, ed., *Encyclopedia of the Confederacy*, 2: 930–31; *O.R.* II-5-684, confirms Thomas P. Turner's rank while Oake was confined at Libby.

349. This form of punishment was commonly used on soldiers during the war, whether they were prisoners or not. How long a soldier was bucked and gagged varied, depending upon the offense committed and the officer who prescribed the punishment. Garrison & Garrison, *Civil War Usage*, 37.

350. City Point, Virginia, was a common debarkation point for Richmond-based Federal prisoners of war being processed for parole and exchange. Oake's compiled military service record indicates he was paroled at City Point on May 23, 1863. *CMSR Wm. Royal Oake,* "Memorandum From Prisoner of War Records."

351. More commonly known as the *New York*, this steamer (listed at both 995 and 1,200 tons) spent most of her time at Fortress Monroe being utilized as a prisoner-of-war exchange ship and carrying mail on the James River. Gibson & Gibson, *Dictionary of Transports and Combatant Vessels*, 239.

352. There is a probability this was a veteran company of the 9th New York Infantry, organized at the start of the war in New York City as Hawkins' Zouaves under Col. Christopher Rush. The 9th New York had been mustered out of service, May 20, 1863; however, its three-year's-men (those enlisted for yet another year) were assigned to the 3rd New York, May 6, 1862. The 3rd New York was operating in the area at the time Oake was being paroled. Dyer, *Compendium*, 1406, 1408–09; Boatner, *Civil War Dictionary*, 387.

353. There is no documentation to support Oake's assessment that Confederate authorities mistreated Federal prisoners as official policy. Instead, the poor conditions and care provided in Confederate prisons is an example of the difficulties faced by the war-stressed Confederacy to adequately provide shelter, food, and medical treatment for the tens of thousands of Federal prisoners confined in Southern prisons from 1863 to 1865. The difficulties experienced by Confederate prisoners were just as severe in the worst of the Northern prisons. The emotion with which Oake writes appears to be common to virtually all Civil War soldiers who experienced the harshness of prolonged incarceration as prisoners of war. Oake's close friend and comrade in the 26th Iowa, Elijah H. Frank, wrote Katherine Varner on July 31, 1863, "I have just received a letter from Oake in which he gave me a detailed account of his *hardships & privations*. He saw some *pretty hard times* which by the tone of his letter makes him *hate the "rebs"* with a will and nothing would he like better than to have another chance at them [italics added by editor]." Long, *Civil War Day by Day*, 715–16; "E.H. Frank to Catherine Varner, Charlotte, Iowa, 1862-1863." *North Dakota Historical Quarterly* (Bismarck, 1930), 194. Hereafter cited as *NDHQ*. The proper spelling of Ms. Varner's name appears to be Katherine, based on Elijah Frank's consistent reference to "Dear Friend Kate" in the letters he wrote her in the field.—Ed.

Libby Prison, Paroled, and Again in our Own Lines

354. The U.S.S. *Cumberland*, a wooden sailing sloop, was rammed and sunk in Hampton Roads on March 8, 1862, by the ironclad C.S.S. *Virginia* (reconstructed by Confederates using the hull of the captured U.S.S. *Merrimac*). The next day, the *Virginia* fought her famous duel with the ironclad U.S.S. *Monitor*. Many war letters, diaries, and post-war memoirs refer to the *Virginia* using the older identity. U.S.N., *Civil War Naval Chronology*, II: 29–31.

355. A vessel whose sole purpose was to thwart the United States naval blockade of Southern ports, carrying out exports of cotton and other goods and transporting into the Confederacy vital war supplies and goods from foreign countries, namely those of Europe. Garrison & Garrison, *Civil War Usage*, 29.

356. Camps of parole were established to board prisoners who had been released from capture and confinement into parole status awaiting official exchange proceedings between the United States and Confederate governments. Benton Barracks, used throughout the war as a camp of instruction or staging area for Federal military organizations in the West, also served as a convenient location to detain returned prisoners of war who were forced to wait out official exchange. Faust, ed., *Encyclopedia of the Civil War*, 558.

357. See note 213 for citation on Camp Parole at Annapolis. The compiled service record for Royal Oake indicates that he reported to Camp Parole on May 24, 1863, and after spending a month there, was forwarded to St. Louis, by train, on June 23, 1863. *CMSR Wm. Royal Oake*, "Memorandum From Prisoner of War Records.

358. Pana is located roughly forty miles southeast of the state capital, Springfield, Illinois.

359. French leave meant being absent without leave (AWOL) but with the supposed intention of returning to service. In this case, Oake and his comrades collectively decided the normal procedure of requesting leave was not possible in their case, and being so close to their loved ones, they decided to jump train and make a brief visit home. Punishment upon return for those taking French leave was routinely not serious, and sentencing to a court-martial for being AWOL was rarely enforced. Garrison & Garrison, *Civil War Usage*, 87; Scott, *Military Dictionary*, 10.

360. The town of Dixon is roughly forty-three miles east of the city of Clinton, Iowa.

361. This business establishment was located ten miles northwest of Clinton. The small hamlet is still known as Ten Mile. The location of Ten Mile was confirmed by the editor while conducting research in Iowa in September 2003.

362. Jackson was the brother of Irving W. Albright, age 22 and a Pennsylvania native who enlisted July 11, 1862. Irving served his full enlistment, being mustered out June 6, 1865, in Washington, D.C. *Roster* 3: 1030.

363. John W. Varner was the brother of Katherine Varner, with whom Oake's close friend and comrade Elijah H. Frank corresponded during the war. Those letters, nine of which are known, were published in the *North Dakota Historical Quarterly* in 1930. Varner, age 19, enlisted August 13, 1862, in Co. A, 26th Iowa. According to Elijah Frank, Varner became extremely ill around November 26–28, 1862, while the regiment participated in a diversionary expedition from Helena, Arkansas, to the Tallahatchie River in Mississippi (described in Oake's memoir). Private Varner did not recover from the illness and was later removed from Helena to a general hospital at Jefferson Barracks in St. Louis, where he was discharged for disability on January 29, 1863. *NDHQ*, 189; *Roster* 3: 1054, 1104. (Dyer makes one of the rare oversights found in his masterfully researched *Compendium* by omitting the 26th Iowa Infantry from among those organizations cited as participating [engaged] in the expedition to the Tallahatchie in which Pvt. John Varner became ill.—Ed.)

CHAPTER SEVEN

At Home and Return to the Front

❧ ———————————— ☙

As I again tread the old familiar path my feelings can better be imagined than told and it was not until I stood on the doorstep did my dear old mother see me, too much overcome to speak or move. After regaining her composure, and she had embraced me she told me that it had been reported that we had been shot when captured, and it was not until father had written to the regiment and received an answer to his letter did they learn to the contrary, and they were overjoyed, upon receiving my letter from Annapolis telling of my return to the Union lines.

My father and only brother were working in the field, and did not know of my return until they returned from the field for their supper, and I walked out of the house to where they were. It was a happy meeting, one I long remembered after I again returned to the front. I remained at home about six weeks when hearing that a general exchange of prisoners would soon take place, I concluded to report at Davenport, Iowa.[364]

I will not attempt to describe the parting from my father, mother, and brother. Finally the last good bye was said, and once more I started to rejoin my regiment in the far South. I was well aware of the fact that my chances to again be home were slim, but so far I had been very lucky and who knew but my good luck might still attend me until my term of enlistment had expired.

After reporting at Davenport we remained there a short time when we were furnished transportation and sent to St. Louis. At Davenport we found another one of the five that was captured, and who did not leave the train with us at Pana, Illinois. D. W. Swihart who remained on the train until they reached St. Louis and from that point had taken a French furlough home.

Upon our arrival at St. Louis we were assigned to quarters in Benton Barracks they being situated on the old fair grounds. At this time there were several thousand prisoners [at the camp] waiting to be exchanged and return to their regiment. We remained here until about October 1st, [when] a general exchange of prisoners [was] affected between the North and South. Immediately after, all paroled soldiers were furnished transportation, and ordered to report to their respective commands. At that time our regiment was near Iuka, Mississippi, and we at once got on board of a steamer and proceeded to Memphis from which we boarded the cars to Iuka, and on the evening October 9th rejoined our regiment, having been absent six months.[365]

Upon our arrival there was a great shaking of hands as we were glad to meet once more, but several of one time familiar faces were missing who had either been wounded and discharged, or were lying under the sod in the vicinity of Vicksburg.[366] A few days after our return we marched to near Tuscumbia, [Alabama], and at that place had a sharp engagement with the rebels, defeating them.[367] We then retraced our steps and for a short time went into camp near Bridgeport [sic. Chickasaw, Alabama][368] on the Tennessee River.

About this time General Grant had assumed personal command[369] of the troops in the vicinity of Chattanooga, [Tennessee],[370] and troops from all points were being rushed to that point. After the disastrous battle of Chickamauga,[371] which had been fought about one month prior, the Union Army had fallen back to Chattanooga, and were closely invested by the Confederate army, who had control of the only rail road leading into that place from the north, thus compelling [Major] General [William S.] Rosecrans,[372] who was in command of the Union Army [of the Cumberland, then besieged at Chattanooga], to haul all supplies thirty-six miles by wagon over roads that were almost impossible.

It was towards this point that our corps, the 15th, was now headed. After remaining in the vicinity of Bridgeport [sic Chickasaw] some little time waiting for steamers to take us across the Tennessee River we began our march of nearly three hundred miles to Chattanooga, [on November 4, 1863] and after a weary and tiresome march on the evening of November 23rd we went into camp about six miles from Old Look Out Mountain.[373]

Union encampments sprawl across the hills of Chattanooga, Tennessee.
A key southern railroad and river hub, Chattanooga was located along an important line
of communication linking the western and eastern sections of the Confederacy.
MEDFORD HISTORICAL SOCIETY

At Home and Return to the Front

At Home and Return to the Front

364. Oake's service record indicates he was received at Camp Parole in Annapolis on May 24 and officially exchanged the following day, but cites him as absent without leave for July and August 1863. Thus, even if he did report of his own accord, as he states, he was officially declared a "straggler" and arrested on August 31, 1863, by J. P. Eaton, provost marshal for the 2nd District of Iowa. He was immediately sent to Camp McCellan, Davenport, Iowa, and subsequently forwarded to Benton Barracks, in St. Louis, arriving there on September 9. Government authorities exercised considerable patience and leniency concerning wayward soldiers like Oake and his comrades who left their posts and took short leaves without permission. On March 10, 1863, the U.S. War Department had issued General Order No. 58, announcing that President Lincoln would issue a proclamation "declaring that all soldiers now absent from their regiments without leave may return, within a time specified, to such place or places as he may indicate in his proclamation." Once reported, the wayward soldiers were to be restored to their respective regiments without punishment, except for forfeiture of pay and allowances during their absences. Davenport was selected as one of the eight rendezvous locations, being the only one designated in Iowa. Although the proclamation of pardon for those being absent without leave was in effect only until April 1, 1863, Davenport continued to serve as a point of rendezvous and incarceration for soldiers listed AWOL and residing in the region. *CMRS Wm. Royal Oake*, "Monthly Return Sept. 1863," "Descriptive List Deserters Arrested" [in this case the printed word "Deserter" has been scratched through and the word "Straggler" written above it by the War Department copyist]," and "Memorandum From Prisoner of War Records"; *O.R.* III-3-60–61.

365. After participating in the Greenville Expedition to Deer Creek, the regiment (while Oake was away) was actively engaged in Grant's campaign to capture Vicksburg. It participated in a demonstration on Haynes's and Synder's bluffs (April 28–May 2), then moved with the rest of Sherman's XV Corps to join the army in the rear of Vicksburg (May 2–14), entering Jackson, Mississippi, on May 14, and from there marched west, where it was engaged during the siege of Vicksburg (May 18–July 4), participating in two direct assaults on the Confederate fortress, May 19 and 22. Afterward, the regiment took part in Sherman's advance on Jackson, Mississippi, July 5–10, where it served during the siege of Jackson, July 10–17, and fought a minor action (no casualties) at Brandon Station, Mississippi, on July 19. The "Clinton" regiment was stationed on the Big Black River east of Vicksburg until September 22, at which time it was moved (by river transport) to Memphis (September 23–28) and thence eastward along the Memphis & Charleston Railroad to Iuka (arriving October 9), moving as part of the force being sent to relieve the Union Army of the Cumberland under siege at Chattanooga, Tennessee. On October 12, 1863, just days after Oake rejoined his outfit, the 26th Iowa was ordered to relocate to Burnsville, Mississippi, eleven miles east of Iuka. It remained there through October 19, guarding the railroad. Dyer, *Compendium*, 776–79, 1175; *O.R.* I-31-IV-306; *Roster* 3: 1022–23.

366. The regiment lost three men killed and eleven wounded in the May 19 assault on Vicksburg, and another four men killed and twenty-three wounded in the May 22 assault on the fortress city. Col. Milo Smith later stated that 1 man was killed and twelve wounded on the 19th, along with five men killed and twenty-nine wounded on May 22. Among those wounded were Colonel Smith, Captain A. D. Gaston, and Lieutenants John W. Mason, Louis Rider, Noble W. Wood, John Quinn, and William M. Magden. During the siege, another man was severely wounded on June 5, and one was killed on June 15, making the total casualties during the siege fifty-four (seven killed and forty-seven wounded) by Colonel Smith's count. This total accounted for 17 percent of the maximum number of the regiment present for duty on May 18, the day upon which the initial engagement of the siege of Vicksburg occurred. *O.R.* I-24-II-159, 162; *Roster* 3: 1022.

367. On October 20, the regiment marched from Burnsville to Cherokee, Alabama, and on the 21st continued to Tuscumbia. Between the 21st and 29th of October, in skirmishes with Confederate forces, the regiment lost one man killed and one severely wounded.

368. The move east to Bridgeport, Alabama, would not begin until November 4. After being engaged at Tuscumbia near Florence, Alabama, the regiment retraced its steps to Chickasaw, Alabama, east of Bear Creek where that stream enters the Tennessee River. Chickasaw was located opposite Waterloo, Alabama, on the river's north shore, and east of Eastport, Mississippi, which was on the west side of Bear Creek. *Roster* 3: 1023.

369. Appointed commander of the recently established Military Division of the Mississippi—which combined the departments of the Cumberland, Ohio, and Tennessee on October 16, 1863—Ulysses S. Grant arrived in Chattanooga to assume command just before nightfall, October 23. *O.R.* I-30-IV-404; Peter Cozzens, *The Shipwreck of Their Hopes: The Battles for Chattanooga* (Urbana: University of Illinois Press, 1994), 4, 45. Hereafter cited as *The Shipwreck of Their Hopes.*

370. A town of 2,500 people located in the rugged Appalachian Mountains, in the extreme southeastern corner of Tennessee, Chattanooga was of vital importance. Located on the Tennessee River, it enjoyed a national reputation as a transportation hub, and the popular label of "Gateway to the South." From Chattanooga, two important railroads (the Western & Atlantic and the Tennessee & Georgia) penetrated into the Confederacy. Holding the town was critical to the Confederacy's sustaining the war in the West. Its occupation was essential to any Union offensive targeting the South's interior, and to continued Federal control of Tennessee. There was no other viable base of operations for Grant's armies closer, other than Nashville, roughly 150 miles to the northwest. Cozzens, *The Shipwreck of Their Hopes*, 7.

371. Fought in northwestern Georgia, September 19–20, 1863, roughly seven miles southwest of Chattanooga, the massive battle of Chickamauga (named for a local creek) resulted in a decisive victory for the Confederate Army of Tennessee (with 18,454 casualties), commanded by Gen. Braxton Bragg, which defeated the Union Army of the Cumberland (16,170 casualties), under Maj. Gen. William S. Rosecrans. Wagner, et. al., *Civil War Desk Reference*, 289–91.

372. William Starke Rosecrans (1819–1898) was a West Point graduate and, later, an instructor there. Since the start of the war, he had held important Federal commands in West Virginia, Mississippi, and Tennessee, where he had commanded the Department of Western Virginia and, later, under Grant, the Army of the Mississippi and District of Corinth. Appointed commander of the Department (Army) of the Cumberland, October 30, 1862, he commanded the army during the battle of Stones River, the Tullahoma Campaign, and at Chickamauga, where his defeat cost him his command. He was relieved from duty by Grant, October 20, 1863, who replaced him with Maj. Gen. George H. Thomas. Ibid., 421; Boatner, *Civil War Dictionary*, 708.

373. After being transported across the Tennessee River to Waterloo, the regiment marched eastward via Florence, Alabama; Pulaski and Fayetteville, Tennessee; then Stevenson and Bridgeport in northeastern Alabama. During the difficult and tedious march, plagued by heavy rains and muddy roads, the regiment covered around 250 miles. It arrived, with its division, in the valley of Lookout Creek near Brown's Ferry, two miles west of Chattanooga and two and one-half miles north of the base of Lookout Mountain. The Oake manuscript consistently spells the mountain as Look Out Mountain—from here on corrected to Lookout Mountain. *Roster* 3: 1023; Cozzens, *The Shipwreck of Their Hopes*, 121–25; *O.R.* I-31-II-599.

Major General Peter J. Osterhaus.
This native of Prussia served as William Royal Oake's division
commander from Lookout Mountain to the capture of Atlanta,
and later as corps commander during the "March to the Sea."
U.S. ARMY MILITARY HISTORY INSTITUTE

CHAPTER EIGHT

The Battle Above the Clouds, at Lookout Mountain, and Missionary Ridge

✦ ———————— ✦

There perhaps was no more gloomy period of the Civil War than the fall of 1863, shortly after the contest at Chickamauga, where both armies claimed the victory, and where the gallant [Major] General [George H.] Thomas* won the name of the "Rock of Chickamauga." It is also true that which ever army won the victory that Rosecrans, the commander of the Union army, was compelled to fall back and fortify in the vicinity of Chattanooga, where for two months he lay, while the rebel army under [General Braxton] Bragg* held and fortified the lofty heights of Lookout Mountain and Missionary Ridge within cannon shot of his camp, and having complete control of the railroad six [two] miles north [southwest] of Chattanooga, thus compelling Rosecrans to haul all supplies by wagon from Bridgeport, Tennessee, a distance of thirty-five [actually 60] miles over a rough and mountainous country.[374]

It was at this particular time that General Grant was assigned to the troops of that department, then under the command of General Rosecrans.[375] Upon assuming command Grant at once took measures to organize, and strengthen his army by reinforcements from the Army of the Potomac[376] and a part of the victorious army from Vicksburg consisting of the 15th Army Corps.

On the evening of November 23rd, 1863, the First Division of the 15th

Corps, [commanded by Brig. Gen. Peter J. Osterhaus], to which the writer belonged, after a long march, of about three hundred [250] miles, went into camp about six [two] miles from Lookout Mountain.[377] On the morning of the 24th, at an early hour, the troops were awakened with orders to get breakfast as soon as possible, and to leave all extra baggage in charge of a guard, and with one hundred rounds of cartridges to hurry to the front to cooperate in the coming conflict at Lookout, which position was to be attacked by the Union forces under [Major] General [Joseph] Hooker*, early in the morning. Having finished our morning repast of hard tack and coffee we were ordered into line, and through a disagreeable rain pushed rapidly to the front. Soon we could distinctly hear the booming of cannon which told us that the battle had already been opened by Hooker's veterans.[378]

As we rapidly approached the field of action we could hear the rattle of musketry, which convinced us that infantry of the opposing forces were already engaged in a bloody conflict, At last we arrived near the field of action, and were halted in an open field within plain view, and one mile distant from the battle field, which position by the aid of a field glass we could distinctly see the stars and stripes carried by Hooker's men on the slope of the mountain as they floated above the clouds that settled in the valley below.[379] How steadily and with a fine alignment do the Potomac veterans face that storm of lead as they climb the rugged slopes of the mountain. For a moment they falter as the plunging shot and deadly grape, from the summit of the mountain, causes death and destruction in their fast thinning ranks. Again they press forward and above the roar of the artillery, and rattle of musketry could be faintly heard the Yankee Yell. Now is seen approaching our division at a rapid pace a mounted horseman, and as he draws near our division commander stops and salutes him.[380] Well do we know his errand. In an instant we hear the bugle call, "Fall In," only to be repeated by the brigade and regimental commanders.

We were soon in line when the command, "Right Face, Double Quick March," and were headed towards the frowning cliffs of the old mountain. Soon we reached its base while all around us was evidence of the bloody conflict. Again rang out the command: "On the right into line, Halt, Load Arms." Twenty men from the 26th, [were ordered forward to act as] skirmishers[381] for the regiment. The writer being one of that twenty. Once more rang out the order, "Forward," and soon were are climbing the rugged slopes of old Lookout.[382] At last we are in range of the deadly minie [balls] as with a sickening thug they pierce the form of some comrade while all around us were the ghastly forms of the dead and dying soldiers. At last we reach the advance line, and press steadily forward to be met with a shower of bullets at close range, while from the top of the mountain distant about 80 rods [440 yards] with guns depressed they poured into our ranks a withering fire of grape.[383] It was at this particular time that the writer received a gentle reminder that we were treading on dangerous ground as the spiteful minie came in contact with his shoulder and unceremoniously placed him in a sprawling position on the ground. My comrade Miller who was also on the skirmish line, and near me at the time seeing me fall, hastily approached, but before he had reached me I sprang to my feet. When I felt blood trickling down my arm I realized the fact that I had come in contact with rebel lead, and as I looked [at my shoulder], could plainly see the hole made in

Lookout Mountain, Tennessee.
The line of Union attack on November 24, 1863, carried the 26th Iowa Infantry across the rugged wooded base of mountain slope in the left of this photo. It was here that William Royal Oake was struck in the shoulder by a Confederate bullet. NATIONAL ARCHIVES

The Battle Above the Clouds, at Lookout Mountain, and Missionary Ridge

my clothing by the leaden messenger, but as I could move my arm without any inconvenience I felt somewhat easier and seated myself by the roots of a tree, a favorite position of mine in time of battle, not daring to unloosen my clothes to take an inventory of the damage fearing it might look worse than it felt.[384]

About this time our forces succeeded in flanking and taking prisoner several hundred of the enemy that were posted on the side of the mountain.[385] The main force of them being on top of the mountain, and still holding their position. Night coming on put an end to the operations for that day, and the troops bivouacked on the battle field during the night.[386] On the morning of the 25th the troops were early astir, and after partaking of coffee and hard tack anxiously awaited the coming of day. Soon the gray streaks of dawn became visible in the eastern sky and the skirmishers were again ordered forward, but what seemed to be the matter as they advanced they met with no opposition. Steadily they pressed forward, and [soon] are upon the loftiest peak of Lookout. The enemy had evacuated it during the night, and had fallen back during the night to Missionary Ridge,[387] about three miles [to the east], leaving us in possession of the contested field. As the sun in all its glory arose in the cloudless sky, the glorious old stars and stripes with three rousing cheers were flung to the breeze on the highest peak of old Lookout Mountain.[388] From our high position on the mountain, and spread [out] six miles to the east [north] in a beautiful valley bordering on the Tennessee River, [lay] nestled the little city of Chattanooga, while for miles to the eastward [north] could the eye follow the course of the river, as like some monster serpent through valley and mountain passes it wended its way until lost in the distance. Directly south [east] and about three miles distant was Missionary Ridge, which was strongly fortified by the confederate army under General Bragg, and at the particular place would a desperate battle for the key of Tennessee be fought. The rebel army had become very bold and defiant through success, and the falling back of the Union army from the field of Chickamauga. They had strongly fortified their position, and defended as it was by fifty thousand[389] men they considered their position impregnable. The results of the bloody conflict had proven to them that they had underestimated the fighting qualities of that army of veterans that were then and there marshaled under one of the greatest generals of modern times ably assisted by such men as Sherman, [Philip H.] Sheridan[390] and a host of others well known to everyone.

Early in the morning [November 25] did that grand army prepare for the coming storm as corps after corps led by able captains moved to their respective positions to await the signal gun that would in one instant set in motion that mighty army of about seventy five thousand men, as fine soldiers as the world ever saw. As the troops under Hooker consisting of parts of the 11th and 12th Army Corps with the 1st Division of the 15th Corps, crossed the valley[391] to get into position it was a sight once seen never to be forgotten. It was a beautiful clear day, and as the sun crossed the meridian it was slightly on the backs of the moving columns. Hooker's troops being on the extreme right of the Union army, and the 26th Iowa [Osterhaus' division] being posted on the [left] flank to prevent a possible surprise from the enemy's cavalry.[392] Soon after getting our position the signal gun from Fort

The Craven farm, Lookout Mountain, Chattanooga, Tennessee.
The famed "Battle Above the Clouds" of November 24, 1863, was actually fought along the rugged lower slope of the mountain, while a dense fog covered the scene. After a fight, Union forces seized the farm at noon. The Confederates defended their new line until midnight, before being ordered to withdraw. WESTERN RESERVE HISTORICAL SOCIETY

The Battle Above the Clouds, at Lookout Mountain, and Missionary Ridge

Wood[393] situated near Chattanooga sent its messenger of death over the head of the Union forces into the rebel lines, and instantly that mighty army moved forward upon its mission of death.

From our position we could plainly see for a distance of one mile the Federal army, as they moved rapidly towards the base of the ridge, while from the top held by the enemy all was silent. Soon the rebel batteries [on Missionary Ridge] open as a sheet of flame and smoke bursts forth from the mouth of the guns, and the death dealing missiles are sent on their errand of destruction. In an instant they are responded to by the Federal guns, and at one time did the writer count six shells bursting at one time over a rebel fort. Still the long lines of soldiers, clad in blue, move rapidly up the steep incline while their guns glistened like burnished silver in the bright afternoon sun. On they move until within fifty yards of the enemy's works, when they are met with a destructive fire of musketry at short range from the enemy entrenched position, still they falter not, but with a loud cheer they move forward with irresistible force and with one accord pour into the enemy a destructive fire. Now they scale the works and hand to hand fighting take place, but it is impossible for rebels to withstand the fierce onslaught of the Yankee forces, and they give way in every direction as the Union forces turn their own artillery on them, and literally sweep them from the field.[394] An orderly now approached our regiment with orders for it to move immediately, and to attack the enemy on their left flank. This order was promptly executed, and although we moved at double quick we were unable to intercept the fleeing enemy, who in a disorderly retreat left us in possession of the field.[395]

As night was fast approaching we went into camp, [occupying] a great many of the huts that had been erected by the enemy for their winter quarters, and from which they had so unceremoniously been driven, leaving in their haste the corn meal and bacon prepared for supper, but still uncooked, together with their camp equipage. This was conclusive evidence of the hurried manner in which they were driven from the field.[396]

"What next," was the question asked by the troops on awakening on the morning of the 26th, the day following the late battle. We were not long kept in suspense, as our scouts reported the enemy as having made a stand on the high ridge near the little town of Ringold [Ringgold], about twenty-five [twelve] miles south[east] on the Georgia Central [Western & Atlantic] Railroad.[397] General Grant at once gave orders to push forward, and the troops were soon in motion, following the tracks of the retreating enemy. As we advanced we found the roads strewn with broken wagons, guns, carriages, knapsacks, blankets, and everything that pertains to an army. This showed the demoralized condition of the defeated rebel army.

The march of our army was necessarily slow owing to the trees that had been felled by the rebels obstructing the road as well as by the resistance offered us by the enemy's cavalry,[398] which acted as their rear guard, thereby giving them more time to get their train beyond the reach of the victorious Yanks. On the evening of the 26th the troops camped within six [four] miles of the town of Ringgold, and at an early hour of the 27th, after eating our breakfast, we marched rapidly to the front. The boom of artillery told us that the advance were already engaged with the enemy, and soon we were within half a mile of the contested field, having lost about one third of our men from the ranks, owing to their inability to march at such a rapid rate. It was within about 80 rods [440 yards] of the little town that we lost one of the best men in the 26th Iowa. We were on the double quick, when we had to run the gauntlet of a six gun battery, and a solid shot struck Wm. McDonald, [spelled McDonnell in *Roster*][399] of Company G, taking off his right arm and tearing almost his entire breast away.

Soon we were in the center of the little town and found it filled with troops, who were anxiously awaiting orders to move into position, and who in the meantime were crowding beside the brick buildings to escape the storm of lead that was being rained upon them by the enemy.[400] In a short time our regiment received orders to move to the front, and as we left our regiment received orders to move to the front, and as we left our sheltered position in the little town to emerge into plain sight of the enemy we were met with a shower of lead. Our lines were soon formed, when the usual call for the skirmishes was heard, and as my old comrade Miller and the writer stepped to the front the line was ordered forward. Quickly the skirmishers climbed an old rail fence that ran parallel, and at the base of the ridge. As my comrade was climbing over about ten feet to my left a minie [*sic*] ball buried itself in the top rail between his hands. Well does the writer remember the remark he made. "The d——- fools might let a fellow get over the fence before

The Battle Above the Clouds, at Lookout Mountain, and Missionary Ridge

they shoot." Up the steep slope we went followed by the line of battle. Thick and fast fell the leaden hail, but as there was a good deal of standing timber on the side of the mountain I frequently managed to get a tree between myself and the rebel bullets. We were within one hundred yards of the top of the hill while the shots from our batteries that were posted in the valley below scattered death and destruction in the ranks of the rebels above us.

Soon we were within fifty yards of the rebel lines, and were met with a withering fire from the enemy. Just at this moment I heard some one in a loud voice call, "Company A 9th Iowa." Turning quickly I saw J. W. [A.] Davis,[401] a soldier of the 9th Iowa, and with whom I was well acquainted, in the act of falling. Being only about twenty feet from him I sprang to him and as he fell with his head down the steep incline I hastily pulled him around, his head up the hill thinking him dead. As the bullets were uncomfortably thick at that particular place I sprang to a position behind a rock where I was partially sheltered, and from which position I could do good execution. Beside a tree or rock, was a favorite position of mine when the bullets flew thick and fast. At this particular place did the 26th lose several

Battlefield at Ringgold, Georgia.
Grant's pursuit of Bragg's Confederate army retreating from Chattanooga was stopped by a stubborn "defense in depth" mounted by troops under Maj. Gen. Patrick R. Cleburne at Ringgold Gap. This rear guard action is also known as Taylor's or White Oak Ridge in reports. MEDFORD HISTORICAL SOCIETY

fine soldiers as at that short range the rebels a good many of whom were armed with squirrel rifles, and being good shorts, invariably sent the bullet to the object aimed at. Captain [John L.] Steele of Company I received his death wound. He was a fine officer and beloved by his men.[402] In another instant P. J. Potter[403] a fine soldier of Company A had a lock of his hair taken off as the deadly minie ploughed its way through his hat grazing the top of his head. The writer has often wondered how many times he might have been killed during that engagement had he not been a great admirer of trees and rocks. As I thought that a bullet struck that rock behind which I lay on an average of three times every second. Well do I remember one particular rebel that was a very conspicuous during the fight as he would step from behind his tree, and take deliberate aim causing more than one Yank to cross (over) the river. Many a good shot did the writer have at that Johnny as he stepped from behind his tree. On such occasions perhaps twenty shots would be fired at him. At last however, he no longer saw the familiar stepping from behind his tree.

As there was a lull in the battle our brigade commander General [James A.] Williamson* walked along the lines cautioning the men to hold their fire, and stand firm as the enemy were about to charge our lines. There was a death like stillness in the ranks as bayonets were fixed, and we awaited the coming storm. Still they came not. Could it have been possible it was a ruse on the part of the rebels to give such orders in order to mislead us into expecting an attack thereby giving them more time to retreat? The skirmishers were again ordered to advance, and Miller and the writer with the line move cautiously forward, still we were not fired upon. We grew bolder and were soon upon the top of the ridge. The enemy had evacuated leaving us in possession of the field, and as the line of battle moved to the top of the hill, and planted the Stars and Stripes we could plainly see the rear guard of the rebel army about half a mile distant as they were hurrying to escape the victorious Yanks. I suggested to Miller that we take an inventory of the damage we had done the rebels, more particularly did we want to see what had become of our rebel that had made himself so conspicuous in slipping from behind that tree. We soon found the tree, and beside it lay our rebel friend with five bullets through his breast, while the tree behind which he stood was literally riddled with bullets. He had stepped out once too often, but

The Battle Above the Clouds, at Lookout Mountain, and Missionary Ridge

although he was silent in death many of the deaths in our ranks that day could justly be attributed to him, and his unerring marksmanship. As he lay all doubled up at the roots of the tree with a newly filled haversack of corn bread and bacon my comrade suggested the idea of appropriating the same for our own use which we at once proceeded to do.

Another incident in connection with him I will remember. As he fell a pack of new cards fell out of his pocket, the Queen of Hearts lying face up and as my comrade saw them he remarked, "Injun, Hearts are Trumps."[404]

The Battle Above the Clouds, at Lookout Mountain, and Missionary Ridge

❧ ———————————————— ❧

374. Initially, the Confederates had controlled Lookout Valley, thereby severing the railroad and roads linking Chattanooga with Bridgeport and Stevenson, Alabama, and from there northward to Nashville. The route Rosecrans had been forced to use to haul supplies into Chattanooga was from Bridgeport northward up the Sequatchie Valley to a point northwest of Chattanooga, then across rugged Walden's Ridge southeastward to the Tennessee River crossing north of the city. The distance using this excruciating route of country roads was nearly sixty miles. Cozzens, *The Shipwreck of Their Hopes*, 17.

375. See note 372. Rosecrans had been relieved a month earlier. At this particular time, Ulysses S. Grant commanded the Military Division of the Mississippi, which included Rosecrans's old Department (Army) of the Cumberland, now commanded by Maj. Gen. George H. Thomas; the Department (Army) of the Tennessee, commanded by Maj. Gen. William T. Sherman (to which the 26th Iowa was assigned); and the Department (Army) of the Ohio, commanded by Maj. Gen. Ambrose Burnside. *O.R.* I-30-IV-404.

376. These reinforcements consisted of elements of the XI and XII Army Corps, Army of the Potomac, under the command of Maj. Gen. Joseph Hooker. In one of the most impressive transfers of men and material during the war, they had been ordered by the War Department west with all haste from Virginia. They traveled roughly 1,157 miles by rail to the relief of Chattanooga in late September–early October, following Rosecrans's disastrous defeat at Chickamauga. In three weeks, nearly 20,000 men and more than 3,000 horses and mules, plus supplies and equipment, artillery, and wagons, had completed the journey. Boatner, *Civil War Dictionary*, 142.

377. The 26th Iowa Infantry was organized within the 2nd Brigade, 1st Division, XV Army Corps, Army of the Tennessee. General Osterhaus commanded the division, within which Col. James A. Williamson commanded the 2nd Brigade. Brigaded with the 26th Iowa were the 4th, 9th, 25th, 30th, and 31st Iowa regiments. The 1st Brigade of the division was commanded by Brig. Gen. Charles R. Woods and consisted of the 13th Illinois, 3rd, 12th, 17th, 27th, 29th, 31st, and 32nd Missouri, and the 76th Ohio. Osterhaus had originally intended to cross the pontoon bridge over Lookout Creek at Brown's Ferry to join the rest of the XV Corps in Chattanooga; however, rising waters had torn a hole in the bridge too big to patch, stranding his two brigades and his division artillery in Lookout Valley. When it became evident the division would not be able to cross, in the early morning of November 24, Grant ordered Osterhaus to report to Hooker. *O.R.* I-31-II-598–99; Cozzens, *The Shipwreck of Their Hopes*, 143.

378. Hooker's previous mission had been protecting Federal lines of communication through Lookout Valley. Unable to cross the damaged bridge, Hooker was ordered on the morning of November 24 to attack and drive off the remaining Confederate forces on Lookout Mountain, then move to Rossville Gap and envelop the southern flank of the Confederate line on Missionary Ridge. Thus occurred one of the most curious actions of the war, and one romanticized as "the battle above the clouds" because a dense fog hugged the rugged mountain slopes during the day. Hooker, commanding the XI and XII Army Corps, had under his immediate command the 1st Division (Charles Cruft's), IV Corps, the 2nd Division (John Geary's), XII Corps, portions (William P. Carlin's brigade) of the XIV Corps, and the 1st Division (Peter Osterhaus's), XV Corps. Company K, 15th Illinois Cavalry, served as escort to General Hooker.

This provided an aggregate force, by Hooker's estimate, of 9,681 men. Eicher, *The Longest Night*, 606–07; Cozzens, *The Shipwreck of Their Hopes*, 401n; *O.R.* I-31-II-314–26.

379. General Osterhaus's division occupied the left flank of Hooker's battle formation, and was placed in a supporting role. This put Osterhaus's right on the Tennessee River, his troops fronting southwest and facing the extreme northern point of Lookout Mountain. Williamson's brigade, to which the 26th Iowa belonged, initially protected the artillery that Hooker was gathering on the hills near the mouth of Lookout Creek.

380. The mounted officer was General Hooker in person, who ordered Colonel Williamson to send the 26th Iowa down the railroad to support Federal forces engaged at the base of the northern end of the mountain. Col. Milo Smith reported that the 26th Iowa was "ordered by General Hooker to file to the left up the railroad to support the force stationed at the cut on the line of the road, where we remained until ordered by the brigade commander to rejoin the balance of the brigade, then advancing across the point of Lookout Mountain." *O.R.* I-31-II-614, 624.

381. A Civil War army on the march, making an attack, or on the defensive, protected itself with lines of "skirmishers." This loose formation, or body, of men—the composition of which varied according to circumstances—was thrown out in advance and/or on the flanks, to clear the way for, and to protect the advance of, the main force. These soldiers drew the enemy's fire, developed its position, and were in a position to be able to warn comrades of an imminent threat. The point at which groups of skirmishers contact the enemy is known as the "skirmish line." Casey, *Infantry Tactics*, 181–223; Faust, *Civil War Encyclopedia*, 691. In addition, using the jargon of Civil War prisoners of war, "skirmishing" meant to deal with body lice and other "varmints," as Oake earlier attested during his brief incarceration at Libby Prison. Garrison & Garrison, *Civil War Usage*, 230.

382. "After advancing to the crest of this hill," remarked Col. Milo Smith, the 26th Iowa was "placed in line of battle with the balance of the brigade…and while remaining in line of battle were ordered to advance a line of skirmishers for observation.…" *O.R.* I-31-II-624.

383. Grape, or grapeshot, was an artillery projectile assembled with iron plates and rings and holding a cluster of iron shot together. However, the field armies of the Civil War discontinued use of grapeshot in favor of canister—an antipersonnel projectile, consisting of a tin cylinder filled with metal balls and packed with sawdust. Grapeshot's effective range was less than 350 yards, being most lethal at one-third to one-half that distance. Garrison & Garrison, *Civil War Usage*, 44, 98.

384. Fortunately, the shoulder wound (possibly the right shoulder based on interpretation of a notation on the casualty sheet) Oake received was not serious. Although it appears to have broken the skin and inflicted slight damage to muscle tissue, the round did not penetrate far or break bones; thus he was able to remain in the field and continue his duty with the regiment. Colonel Smith reported that "while advancing the skirmishers to the necessary position, Lieutenant Colonel T. G. Ferreby was severely wounded in the left leg and carried from the field, two of the skirmishers [one of them Oake] were slightly wounded upon the evacuation of Lookout Mountain." *CMSR Wm. Royal Oake*; *O.R.* I-31-II-624.

385. Maj. Gen. Carter L. Stevenson commanded the Confederates posted in defense of Lookout Mountain. These troops consisted of parts of two divisions, Cheatham's (of Hardee's Corps), commanded by Brig. Gen. John K. Jackson (consisting of Jackson's, Moore's, Walthall's, and Wright's brigades), and Stevenson's own division (of Breckinridge's corps), commanded by Brig. Gen. John C. Brown (consisting of Brown's, Cumming's, Pettus's, and Vaughn's brigades). The majority of fighting on November 24 was conducted by Moore's, Walthall's, and Pettus's brigades until nightfall, when Clayton's brigade, from Stewart's division of Breckinridge's corps, relieved Walthall and part of Pettus. Most of the prisoners taken by the Federals came from Brig. Gen.

Edward C. Walthall's brigade, who lost 845 men captured on the mountain. The brigade of Brig. Gen. John C. Moore also cited a considerable number of men presumed captured on the mountain—a total of 199 missing for November 24, based on General Jackson's report. Moore lost 4 men killed and 48 wounded in the action, while Walthall reported 8 killed, 91 wounded. The big mountain had been lightly defended. Combined, both Moore and Walthall fielded only 1,205 and 1,489 men respectively. Hooker's nearly 9,700-man force was more than a match for the resistance they met on the rugged slopes. The heavy fog, drizzle, and difficult rocky terrain proved the greatest obstacles troubling the Federal offensive during the day, severely hampering communications, line of authority, and effective command and control over the mixture of organizations used to ascend the mountain. Cozzens, *Shipwreck of Their Hopes*, 187–88; *O.R.* I-31-II-684–738.

386. As night approached, "the fighting degenerated into a series of weak, half-blind punches and counterpunches in the foggy twilight." After repulsing what he reported to be a rebel charge conducted "with great vehemence" in an attempt "to regain the numerous intrenchments they had thrown up around the white house [Craven House]," Osterhaus bivouacked his division in and around the house "about two-thirds up the mountain," an area he believed was "the key to the whole Lookout." Ibid., 600; Cozzens, *Shipwreck of Their Hopes*, 189.

387. Throughout the day (November 24), General Stevenson had repeatedly requested reinforcements from General Bragg. The requests were not acknowledged, and at midafternoon, word came from Bragg that Stevenson was to withdraw all his troops to the extreme right of the Missionary Ridge line. Stevenson's division was to move to the support of Maj. Gen. Patrick R. Cleburne's division, then engaged against the advance of Gen. William T. Sherman's force at Tunnel Hill. To assist in making the complicated maneuver, Stevenson received aid from Maj. Gen. Benjamin F. Cheatham in supervising the withdrawal from the mountain. Confederates on the plateau (mountaintop) retired first, while the men fighting behind the Craven farm held the line. At 8 P.M., the last of the Confederate defenders were withdrawn under cover of fire from Clayton's brigade, commanded by Col. James T. Holtzclaw. It appears this lively firefight, conducted to provide cover for the last Confederate forces to slip away from the mountain, quite literally performed within the dark and foggy conditions of battle, was the action that General Osterhaus (see note 386) misinterpreted as the enemy conducting a charge "with great vehemence" in an effort to reclaim their lost entrenchments. Faust, ed., *Civil War Encyclopedia*, 447.

388. On the morning of November 25, Capt. John Wilson and five soldiers from the U.S. 8th Kentucky Infantry, Brig. Gen. Walter Whitaker's brigade, IV Army Corps, Army of the Cumberland, raced for the unoccupied summit of the mountain and near eight o'clock raised the U.S. national colors, signaling victory to Union troops deployed in the valley below. As Oake recounted, waves of resounding cheers immediately erupted through the Union lines. Richard A. Baumgartner and Larry M. Strayer, *Echoes of Battle: The Struggle for Chattanooga* (Huntington, WV: Blue Acorn Press, 1996), 264–65. Although the fighting on the slopes was chaotic, disjointed, and dispirited, inflicting relatively light losses, Hooker's three divisions succeeded in securing Grant's right flank and "cleared the final pathway for the main Federal thrust." Herman Hathaway and Archer Jones, *How the North Won the War: A Military History of the Civil War* (Urbana: University of Illinois Press, 1983), 461.

389. In the series of battles for Chattanooga, Bragg's Confederate Army of Tennessee numbered around 46,000 men present for duty and engaged. Eicher, *The Longest Night*, 613.

390. At Chattanooga, Maj. Gen. Philip H. Sheridan (1831–1888) commanded the 2nd Division, IV Army Corps, Army of the Cumberland. His performance in securing victory at Missionary Ridge caught the attention of Grant, who the following spring called him to Virginia and assigned him command of the Cavalry Corps, Army of the Potomac. Later that same year, Sheridan was given command of the Army of the Shenandoah, winning a string of victories that drove Confederate forces from the Shenandoah Valley that fall. He concluded the war in the spring of 1865, playing a leading part in operations that forced Robert E. Lee to abandon Richmond, and served a pivotal role in spearheading Grant's successful pursuit and capture of Lee's army to Appomattox Court House. He continued in military service after the war, being promoted to lieutenant general (1869), and, following the retirement of William T. Sherman (1884), he became commanding general of the U.S. Army, receiving promotion (1888) to the rank of full general a few months before his death. Warner, *Generals in Blue*, 437–39.

391. Hooker crossed the valley of Chattanooga Creek, advancing toward the extreme left flank of the Confederate line on Missionary Ridge, located at Rossville Gap. The gap is actually in extreme northern Georgia, and borders the Tennessee state line. Hooker's attacking force, in echelon from right to left, consisted of Osterhaus's 1st Division, XV Corps; the 1st Division, XIV Corps, under Brig. Gen. Charles Cruft; and finally, the 2nd Division, XII Corps, commanded by Brig. Gen. John W. Geary. Eicher, *The Longest Night*, 610–11.

392. While Thomas's army assaulted the Confederate center on Missionary Ridge, and Sherman struggled to overcome resistance at Tunnel Hill on the extreme left of the enemy position, Hooker advanced toward Rossville Gap, with Osterhaus's division in the lead. Upon arriving at Rossville Gap, Osterhaus ordered Colonel Williamson to take two regiments (4th and 31st Iowa) and ascend the hill in the left of the gap, while Charles Wood's brigade headed for high ground to the right of the gap. Meanwhile, the 25th and 26th Iowa regiments of Williamson's brigade were ordered by General Osterhaus to take a position on the western slope of the ridge (Missionary) to keep back any enemy flanking force that might come from the left. Colonel Smith stated the mission of the 25th and 26th Hawkeye regiments was "to prevent a flank movement for a regiment of the enemy's cavalry." The two regiments remained at their assigned position in reserve, watching left (or northward) for the possible Confederate flanking movement. The rest of the brigade (the 9th Iowa and 13th Illinois having joined Williamson on the ridge) moved forward into the valley east of the ridge, spearheading the advance of the entire division. *O.R.* I-31-II-601–02, 615, 624.

393. Fort Wood, a large entrenched lunette (or redoubt) constructed for artillery, was named in honor of division commander Brig. Gen. Thomas J. Wood. The fort was located on a salient angle in the center of the Union line, roughly one-half mile southeast of the city of Chattanooga and two miles west of Missionary Ridge. The Federals mounted 32-pounders and 4½-inch Rodman guns in the fort. It served as Grant's field headquarters until the morning of November 25, when he moved the headquarters one mile east to Orchard Knob, which had been captured on November 23 by Thomas's troops. Oake would have been roughly three and one-half miles south of the fort when his division moved forward to secure Rossville Gap. Baumgartner & Strayer, *Echoes of Battle*, 148, 150, 319; Cozzens, *Shipwreck of Their Hopes*, 126, 203.

394. From their position on the western slope of Missionary Ridge, looking north, Oake and his comrades had virtual stadium seating and a panoramic view of the massive frontal assault conducted against the Confederate center at Missionary Ridge. The attacking force consisted of four divisions of Maj. Gen. George H. Thomas's Army of the Cumberland, in order from left to right, the divisions of Absalom Baird, Thomas J. Wood, Phil Sheridan, and Richard W. Johnson.

395. Colonel Smith reported that the regiment "filed up through the defile in the ridge and took the position assigned us on the right [east] of the summit…and followed our advancing line until darkness put an end to the battle and the enemy had fled in confusion from the field." The regiment suffered no casualties. *O.R.* I-31-II-624.

396. The casualty total at Chattanooga was not heavy when compared with other titanic Civil War battles such as Shiloh, Stones River, or Chickamauga. Casualties suffered in the armies under Ulysses S. Grant totaled 5,815 men, with 752 killed, 4,713 wounded, and 350 missing or captured, out of 70,000 engaged. Confederate losses in Bragg's Army of Tennessee totaled 6,667 overall, with 361 killed, 2,160 wounded and 4,146 missing or captured, out of 46,000 engaged. The tactical and strategic results of the Union victory were significant. The principal western Confederate army had been defeated and thwarted from its attempt to recover the important transportation hub at Chattanooga. Morale in the Confederacy, which soared after the great victory at Chickamauga, plunged. Chattanooga was now firmly held by the Union army, and available for use as an important staging area to advance Federal military operations into Georgia and the Carolinas. Kennedy, ed., *Civil War Battlefield Guide*, Charles P. Roland, "Chattanooga-Ringgold Campaign: November 1863," 246.

397. Ringgold (Oake's spelling hereafter corrected by the editor) was located on the Western & Atlantic Railroad, fifteen miles southeast of Chattanooga, or twelve miles southeast of Rossville Gap. The Western & Atlantic linked Chattanooga with the important transportation and industrial hub located at Atlanta, Georgia, roughly 105 miles to the south.

398. Maj. Gen. Joseph Wheeler supervised the Cavalry Corps organized in the Confederate Army of Tennessee.

399. Born in Kentucky, McDonnell was 21 and a resident of Lyons when he enlisted August 15, 1862. Buried in the field, his body was later moved to the National Cemetery at Chattanooga. Also among those killed at Ringgold were Cornelius Beddon and John Phillips of Co. I. *Roster* 3: 1077; *AGI*, 1864, 484.

400. The 4,157 Confederate troops defending Ringgold Gap belonged to Maj. Gen. Patrick R. Cleburne's division of Maj. Gen. John C. Breckinridge's corps. The Federal force under Hooker, consisting of just Osterhaus's and Geary's divisions, numbered roughly 7,500 men. *O.R.* I-31-II-13, 757.

401. Born in New York, Joseph A. Davis was living in Boone Springs, Iowa, when he enlisted at the age of 21 in Co. A, 9th Iowa Infantry, August 10, 1861. He was wounded severely in the leg in the engagement at Ringgold, and took another leg wound at Dallas, Georgia, May 27, 1864. He was mustered out September 24, 1864, at East Point, Georgia, upon expiration of his three-year term of service. *Roster* 2: 41; *AGI*, 1863-I: 329, lists an enlistment date of August 8, 1861.

402. Captain Steele was mortally wounded and died December 1, 1863, and 1st Lt. Nathan D. Hubbard, Co. K, and 2nd Lt. William Nickel, Co. I, were also wounded. Six enlisted were wounded: Pvt. Charles H. Van Epps, Co. C; Pvt. Charles Hill, Co. D; Sgt. Fritz Horn, Co. E; Corp. James Farr, Co. F; Pvt. David J. Cranston, Co. H; and Pvt. Norman P. Russell, Co. I. The engagement at Ringgold Gap is also known as Taylor's and/or White Oak Ridge in reports. *Roster* 3: 1023, 1101; Byer, *Iowa in War Times*, 257–58; *AGI*, 1864, 484.

403. Peter J. Potter, having been born in Ohio, was 28 and a resident of Canton when he enlisted August 12, 1862. He was promoted to sixth corporal on August 1, 1863, and survived this narrow brush with death and also the war, being mustered out on June 6, 1865, at Washington, D.C. *Roster* 3: 1086.

404. Unknown to Oake, about noon, Ulysses S. Grant arrived in Ringgold and, after conferring with Hooker, ordered the attacks discontinued against the well-deployed Confederate rear guard at Ringgold Gap. These attacks Grant believed unnecessary and costly, labeling the entire incident an "unfortunate" affair. At a cost of 221 casualties, Cleburne saved the Confederate wagon trains and much of the artillery of the Army of Tennessee. The four-hour fight cost Hooker about 507 men, with 13 of those falling in the 26th Iowa, which listed only 16 casualties (1 captain and 2 lieutenants wounded, 3 privates killed and 7 wounded—one of these being Pvt. William Royal Oake) for the three days of fighting (November 24–25, 27, 1863). Francis H. Kennedy, ed., *The Civil War Battlefield Guide* (New York: Houghton Mifflin Co., 1998), Keith S. Bohannon, "Ringgold Gap, Georgia," 246–48; *Roster* 3: 1023; *O.R.* I-31-II-86, 625.

The Battle Above the Clouds, at Lookout
Mountain, and Missionary Ridge

Brigadier General James A. Williamson.
A prominent figure in the war experiences of William Royal Oake,
Williamson commanded the 4th Iowa Infantry, which was often brigaded
with and fought alongside the 26th Iowa from December 1862 to
December 1863. Williamson served intermittently as brigade commander
during this period. U.S. ARMY MILITARY HISTORY INSTITUTE

CHAPTER NINE

Taking a Rest in Winter Quarters at Woodville, Alabama

——✦————————✦——

After the successful termination of the series of battles, that had taken place around Chattanooga, in the fall of 1863, a portion of the army was ordered into camp along the lines of railroads entering the city from the north and west. The First Division of the 15th Corps was assigned to a position at Woodville, Alabama, about one hundred miles [forty-three from Bridgeport where the regiment was stationed] west and south, there to go into camp to recruit, and take a much needed rest to prepare for the next campaign.[405]

After a disagreeable march of several days in the midst of a cold rain we arrived at our destination. The little town of Woodville[406] consisted of an old dilapidated depot, and a few old cabins that had long since fallen to decay. Directly north of the station was situated one of the numerous heavily wooded mountains that are frequently met with in that part of the South. To the south and west, following the course of the Paint Rock Creek [River] to where that stream emptied into the Tennessee River, was an almost unbroken forest. Upon our arrival at Woodville, and after we had stacked our arms, we began to think of something to eat, it being about 2 P.M. Upon looking around we discovered a plantation about half a mile distant, and situated upon it quite a snug residence. I suggested to two of my comrades that we go to said place, and see if we could not prevail on the occupants to prepare us a good square meal. As it was Christmas Day we felt as if we would like a change of diet once more.

On arriving at the residence I rapped at the door, and stood awaiting further developments. Soon a lady appeared and upon seeing me, asked what was wanted. I politely informed her that after a long march we had just arrived at Woodville wet and hungry, and would be very thankful to her if she could prepare us something eat, which we were willing to pay liberally for. The lady said that their stock of provisions was somewhat low owing to the absence of the men folks, and to the frequent raids made upon them by scouting parties from both armies, but that if we would walk into the house herself and daughter would see what they could do for us. It might be well for me to mention here that before our arrival at the house we had agreed among ourselves to call each other by our military titles we had seen fit to give each other. I being honored with the appellation of "Major" [by] my comrades. Upon entering the house we were introduced to her two daughters, young ladies of about 18 and 20 years of age. They were as shown by their manners and conversation of the better class of Southerners. I then introduced myself and comrades as Captain so and so, Lieutenant so and so. After a few moments of pleasant conversation the young ladies asked to be excused in order to prepare our meal, stating that since the war began most of their servants had left them, consequently all culinary duties (had) evolved upon themselves.

In about half an hour the lady of the house informed us that our repast was ready, and we hastened to partake. To say that it surpassed our most sanguine expectations, but faintly expresses our surprise at the glorious repast that was spread before us. There was choice corn pone, ham, butter, sweet potatoes, and honey. A meal fit for a king.

Although before and since we may have been seated at tables that contained a great variety and richer food, never did the writer enjoy a Christmas dinner more than that at Woodville, Alabama, in 1863.

After finishing our repast we entered into a pleasant conversation with the ladies about, what at that time was the current topic, the war and its results. From their conversation we could plainly see that they had seen better times financially and deeply regretted their present condition, but it was easily to be seen that their sympathies were with the South. When comparing their present with the past circumstances it was with difficulty they could suppress their tears, as they told us that at the outbreak of the war they could count slaves and stock by the score. Whereas now they had been driven off by the soldiers, leaving them such means of subsistence as they could easily conceal where the prying eyes of foraging parties could not discover it, while all able bodied brothers, husband and father were in some distant part of the South battling, or perhaps dead.

That the above is no supposed condition, but a stern reality that could be testified by hundreds of soldiers now living and it is only one of thousands of such cases that existed in the South at that time. While it is true there were many homes in the North that mourned the loss of some loved one, little did they know of the horrors of actual warfare where the shot and shell of contending armies laid waste many once happy homes, and many that were once wealthy were reduced to beggary, not knowing where the next meal was coming from or where to lay their heads. We now, after liberally rewarding and thanking our benefactors for their kindness in procuring for us such an excellent meal, returned to our camp.

The first few days after our arrival at our new camp, at Woodville, the weather continued wet and cold, and during the night of 28th about four inches of snow fell. The next few days were intensely cold, and around the camp fires could be seen groups of soldiers endeavoring to keep warm and comfortable. As our camp was surrounded by an abundance of wood we managed to do so. It was at night, while in our little tents that we suffered the most from the cold, owing to the fact that most of our blankets had been thrown away during the hard and long marches of the last campaign.

January 1st, 1864 was a beautiful morning, but intensely cold necessitating that wearing of overcoats and gloves by all who were possessed of such desirable commodities. Well does the writer remember that bitter cold morning as being one of a detail of soldiers of the 26th that had orders to proceed to a point about one mile west of Woodville to prepare a camp ground for the regiment. As we walked up the railroad track, facing the cold wind, thinly clad, and the majority without gloves, it seemed to me colder than the winters in old Iowa.

For several succeeding days details of men were kept busy clearing away the brush and stones from the ground that was to be our camp. Having succeeded in putting the ground in good shape, the regiment was ordered to it, and for the next week they were busily engaged in building comfortable quarters, which after having been completed, so far as warmth was concerned, were comparable with huts of more recent date.

In erecting our huts we would in the first place cut small timber and build up a square pen about 7 x 7 and three feet in height leaving a projection at one end for a chimney, which we would build with sticks and mud. When the foundation was completed we would erect over the top our wedge tents[407] and by arranging two bunks, one above the other, and a fire place, we had quite comfortable quarters for four men.

After becoming comfortably settled in our new quarters, several of the boys of Company A received a Christmas box from friends in Iowa, and although it failed to reach us at the specified time it was very acceptable, more especially when it was found to contain one gallon of good rye whisky. My old comrade Miller being one of the stock holders it was only natural that the writer should come in for a small share. Right royally did we enjoy our gift and kindly remember our kind friends in old Iowa. At evenings our camp fire would be enlivened by the glorious and soul stirring army songs sung by comrades after partaking of a drink of the good old rye. We had in our Company a singular and eccentric character by the name of Patrick Murray [Murry],[408] who enlisted in the regiment at Clinton, Iowa, being a stranger to every man in the regiment, and a man of morose and uncommunicative disposition. No one knew anything of his history prior to his enlistment, but after being with us a short time it was plainly evident that at times he was a little off, and at such times dangerous. Squading [eating or taking his meals] all alone, never speaking except when spoken to, and then only in monosyllables, but it was the general impression that he had seen better days, and through adverse fortune had become slightly unbalanced. He was a fine and rapid penman. I remember once of our company forming in line when my comrade Miller spoke to Murray telling him to stand back a little to make a better alignment when quick as a flash, Murray brought his musket to a charge bayonet, and would have run Miller through with this bayonet had not Miller been a little too quick for him, knocking him down with the butt of his gun. While lying in camp here we would play all kinds of tricks on Murray and I will acknowledge that I was as bad as the rest of the boys. As he would be seated in his tent before his little ire in the evenings we would throw down the chimney a handful of cartridges[409] into the fire, and as they would explode scattering fire and ashes around the tent it would be fun to see Pat climb out, and call on the Virgin Mary and all the Saints in the calendar to protect him. Finally he would return and cautiously peering into see that everything was quiet, he would again enter and seat himself before the fire, when we would again approach and throw in a few more, and as they began to explode, out would come Pat and again invoke his patron saint to protect him. At last Pat was discharged and as he left the regiment he would not wait for the train, but said he would walk to Stevenson a distance of seventy miles although there was a train every half hour passing for that place.

That was the last we heard of Pat until about a month later, when our company commander received notice from the authorities at Annapolis, Maryland, that he had been arrested at that place as a deserter. Notice was at once sent them that he had been regularly discharged from the service, but presumably had lost his discharge papers. We never heard any more of Pat Murray.[410]

While at Woodville most of our time was occupied in drill, target practice, picket, and patrol duty. In our target practice from 200 to 600 yards some exceptionally good scores were made even at the longest range. About one mile west of our camp the railroad crossed the Paint Rock River a small stream of about seventy five feet in width, and beyond that about 80 rods [440 yards] were our pickets, and from the pickets west about six miles until we met patrols from the other direction did we have to patrol the railroad track once every night. The object in patrolling the track was to prevent the numerous bands of bushwhackers[411] from tearing up and placing torpedoes[412] on the track. The track for a distance of several miles skirted the base of heavily wooded range of hills on one side, while on the other side was a heavily timbered valley. Many cold and frosty nights, with two companions, has the writer taken that long and lonesome tramp: at times imagining that every stump he saw was some bushwhacker ready to open fire upon us. How glad we would be when we had reached the outward limit and start back on the home stretch. Many a time since the war in thinking of that long and lonesome tramp, have I thought how lucky we were in escaping the numerous bands of outlaws that were so thick in those parts. One incident of picket duty there I will relate.

*Taking a Rest in Winter Quarters
at Woodville, Alabama*

It was one cold and frosty moonlight night in the latter part of January that the writer was stationed on post, on the railroad west of camp. It was about 11 P.M. when I heard a hand car rapidly approaching from the west. Letting it approach to within about thirty yards of the post, with my musket to my shoulder I called "Halt." Instantly the brakes were applied, and as the sparks of fire flew from its wheels it came to a full stop within thirty feet of me. "Who comes there I demanded," "General Osterhaus," was the reply. "Advance and give the countersign," I replied. "We have not got the countersign," came the answer. "Then sir remain where you are," I answered. I then called the officer of the guard who upon approaching them and finding everything all right allowed them to proceed. This incident shows there are times when the private soldier outranks the major general.[413]

When in enemy's country the picket, when on post, is not supposed to know anyone or to allow any person to pass through the lines unless he can give the magic word. Although on that particular occasion I was confident that it was General Osterhaus and guard. If they had attempted to advance without at first giving the countersign, an ounce minie (ball) would have been their portion. In Company K of our regiment was a soldier by the name of Ranse Hulbert [Ransom E. Hurlburt],[414] and possessor of a very fine voice, and the songs that he knew and sang were unlimited, and many a night while on the reserve picket, has the stillness and monotony been broken as hour after hour Hurlburt would charm us by singing patriotic songs.

It was about this time, the last of February,[415] that our regiment received orders to break camp and go to the little town of Vienna, distant about 14 miles in a southwesterly direction, and we were to encamp until further orders. To say that we were thoroughly disgusted at the idea of leaving our comfortable quarters at Woodville, and moving to a new camp conveys but a faint idea of our feelings at that time. While at Woodville our colonel with a detail of two hundred men[416] was ordered to make a recognizance [reconnaissance] to Maysville [Claysville], a small town [to the south] about 18 miles distant, and about three miles [north] from the Tennessee River, the object of the expedition was, if possible, to capture some of the various bands of the enemy that frequently crossed the river at that point to harass any of our foragers that they could come upon. Accompanying us on this expedition were two scouts from division headquarters. They were civilians, both of them being Tennesseans, uncle and nephew, both being men over six feet in height, and well proportioned. They always were dressed in the regular butternut colored clothes of the South, and were familiar with the entire country in which we were now operating.

The first night after leaving our camp [January 21, 1864], we reached Claysville where we went into camp. The next morning we marched to the Tennessee River, about three miles, and formed in line along the river bank. The river at this point being about 80 rods [440 yards] in width. About half a mile back from the river bank on the opposite shore in the woods, could be seen the tops of some of the buildings in the little town of Guenthersville [Guntersville], and we had learned that a small company of the enemy were located there. On the opposite side of the river we could plainly see that breastworks had been built. When we first arrived and formed in line, not a soul was to be seen on the opposite shore, but in a few moments an officer mounted on a fine looking iron gray horse rode out of the woods down to the works that had been built near the river. Our colonel hailed him, and informed him that if they did not get out of there in half an hour, he would shell the town, we having two guns of the 4th Ohio Battery[417] with us. The officer hailed that he would give him an answer within twenty minutes. Twenty minutes went by and no answer. Soon we saw a small squad of the enemy emerge from the woods and run behind the works spoken of, and commenced to fire upon us, a good many of these bullets falling in the river, while a few reached our lines. Our colonel then ordered the battery to give them a few shots. After getting the range a few shells struck the works bursting directly over them and it was amusing to see the Johnnies getting out into the woods beyond. The colonel then ordered that a few shots be sent over the little town. After firing about a dozen shots the Colonel ordered the battery to cease firing as he did not wish to endanger the lives of women and children, for having given them a scare he was satisfied.[418] We then learned that on an island in the river about six miles below [west] there were lots of horses and mules that had been taken over from our side by the rebels, to keep them from falling into the hands of the Yankees. Upon learning this, our colonel determined if possible to capture them. Ordering one hundred men to return to camp, he proceeded to march down to the island spoken of, the writer being one of the remaining one hundred.

Taking a Rest in Winter Quarters
at Woodville, Alabama

Arriving opposite to the island a part of the command stacked arms, and proceeded to hunt for means of transportation to the island, and after a short time managed to secure several old boats to convey them to the island, the island being in the center of the river, the stream on both sides of the island about 40 rods [220 yards] in width. As our men were busily engaged in driving the animals into the water and heading them to our side of the river a company of reb cavalry were firing on them from the opposite shore, on which were located several old buildings, from which they would fire.

Colonel Smith seeing this, at once ordered the battery to give the rebs a few shots. The writer was standing close to the guns at the time and can distinctly remember those shots. The first few shots flew wild until they had range, then one shell struck the chimney of one of the buildings and burst, and for a few moments it was fun to see the Johnnies getting out from behind those buildings followed by a shell every few moments. After getting over quite a number of fine animals, one of which the writer secured for a mount, my comrade Miller also securing one, the colonel ordered the two scouts to proceed ahead on the road the troops would march, and at the first plantation they came to inform the owners to prepare a meal for twenty-five men, and at the next place the same, until the hundred men had been furnished with meals. At the last place the scouts were to remain until the troops should arrive.

My comrade and myself asked permission of the colonel to accompany the scouts which he readily gave, I distinctly remember that occasion, and I at the time thought it was tough on the planters. At the first place we arrived, the planter came out of the house when hailed, and the scouts told him to prepare meals for twenty-five who would arrive in a short time. The planter would reply, "My God, Mister I don't know where I can get the food." The scouts would reply, "We can't help it, you see that those meals are ready." Then we would ride on to the next place where the orders would be the same. At the fourth place we dismounted, and waited for the troops. The planter claiming his inability to secure food for so many, but they eventually did get the meal consisting of corn bread and bacon. At the time I did feel sorry for them for I well knew that in many instances they had a hard time to support their own families, and only by burying their food in some out of the way places, where it could not be found by the roving bands of both armies, could they manage to keep enough to maintain themselves. All their horses and mules (having been) driven off, as well as all hogs cattle and poultry. I often wondered how they did manage to subsist, but such is war. To have your friends all away to be shot and killed is bad enough, but when to that is added the fact that of those remaining at home being stripped of necessities of life it is indeed a sad condition, that can be realized only by those that have been placed in such a condition by the misfortunes of war.

The next morning [January 23], after partaking of breakfast and upon the arrival of the balance of the command, we returned to our camp at Woodville, losing not a man on the trip, and with quite a number of captured horses and mules.[419]

Taking a Rest in Winter Quarters at Woodville, Alabama

405. Grant's armies stood down during the winter to rest, consolidate their foothold in eastern Tennessee and northern Alabama, upgrade and repair railroad facilities, stockpile supplies, and refit the armies with men and equipment for the projected 1864 spring offensive. Shortly after the battle of Ringgold, the 26th Iowa with its brigade returned to Bridgeport, Alabama, where it arrived December 5. On December 14, Col. Milo Smith was assigned command of the 1st Brigade, 1st Division, XV Army Corps, and senior Capt. Nelson C. Roe assumed command of the regiment. The brigade moved to Woodville, December 21–26, 1863, where it established winter quarters. Adjutant J. D. Fegan reported that there were 31 officers and 471 men on the rolls for the 26th Iowa Infantry on December 31, 1863. At Woodville, the regiment received orders to turn in their old arms, and on January 11, 1864, new U.S. (Springfield) rifle-muskets, with complete accouterments, were issued. *Roster* 3: 1023; S. H. M. Byers, *Iowa in War Times* (Des Moines: W.D. Condit & Co., 1888), 533; *AGI*, 1865-II: 1165.

406. The town, in Jackson County, was located in northeastern Alabama, on the Memphis & Charleston Railroad, 65 miles southwest of Chattanooga.

407. Commonly known as "A" tents because from the end they looked like a capital A without the bar, wedge tents were pieces of canvas stretched over horizontal ridgepoles, staked at the ground on both sides, and closed at the ends. The seven square feet of floor space accommodated four sleeping men with reasonable comfort; however, there was very little head room, and soldiers could not stand erect in the shelter. Bell Irving Wiley and Hirst D. Milhollen, *They Who Fought Here* (New York: Bonanza Books, 1959), 84.

408. A native of Ireland, Murry (spelling of name found in *Roster* and *AGI*) lived in Clinton and was 30 when he enlisted August 4, 1862. *Roster* 3: 1078.

409. The cartridges Oake refers to were prepared ammunition charges used to load the rifle-muskets issued to the soldiers. They were cylinders made of butcher's paper, sometimes linen, in which were placed 60 grains of black powder and the lead projectile.

410. In *Roster* 3: 1078, Murry is listed as having died August 30, 1864, and being buried in the National Cemetery at Marietta, Georgia.

411. The usage alludes to Confederate partisan rangers or guerillas. Drawn from the civilian population, guerillas were loosely organized clusters of men who harassed the enemy behind the lines. They were not members of the Regular Army. Partisan rangers, however, were authorized by the government to infiltrate and raid behind Federal lines. They wore uniforms and were paid for arms and munitions captured and turned over to the government. Confederate regulars routinely resented the freedom afforded the irregular rangers, especially concerning the money they received from capturing Union supplies. Garrison & Garrison, *Civil War Usage*, 39, 101, 187.

412. The earliest land mines (later employed in the water as well) were called torpedoes in the 19th century. Ibid., 249.

413. Picket duty was, and still is, one of the most important duties assigned to a soldier. Whether he is on guard alone or with others, the soldier's most urgent duty is to remain vigilant and give warning of an approaching enemy to prevent surprise attack.

414. Born in New York and a resident of Lyons, Hurlburt was 18 when he enlisted August 15, 1864. He was taken prisoner, along with seven other members of the regiment, during an action with Confederate partisans at Harrison's Gap on April 21, 1864, and after being paroled and exchanged, returned to his company. He was mustered out on June 6, 1865, in Washington, D.C. *Roster* 3: 1067.

415. The regiment moved to Vienna, Alabama on March 9, 1864. *Roster* 3: 1023.

416. One hundred men and four officers of the 26th Iowa participated on this expedition to Claysville, Alabama. Ibid.

417. The 4th Ohio Battery, commanded by Lt. Louis Zimmerer, was assigned to the artillery battalion attached to Osterhaus's division. *O.R.* I-32-II-298.

418. Guntersville, located south of the Tennessee River, was more than once shelled by Federal forces, and a Mrs. Rayburn was killed by a shell during one such action. W. Brewer, *Alabama: Her History, Resources, War Record, and Public Men From 1540–1872* (Montgomery, AL: Barrett & Brown, 1872), 383.

419. This expedition occurred January 21–23, 1864, and sustained no losses. Oake's account is the only detailed record of this event known to exist. *Supplement to the Official Records of the Union and Confederate Armies* (Wilmington, NC: Broadfoot Publishing, 1995), Pt. II, Vol. 20, 578. Hereafter cited as *Supplement to the O.R. Roster* 3: 1023; *AGI*, 1865-II: 1165.

CHAPTER TEN

Camp Life at Vienna

❧ ———————————— ❦

On the 9th day of March, the 26th Iowa left its comfortable camp at Woodville, and went to the little town of Vienna, Alabama.[420] The little town is situated about 14 miles from Woodville in a Southwest direction, Vienna being about 9 miles from the Tennessee River. It contained about 75 buildings among them two churches. All the store buildings had long since been vacated, while all of the able-bodied male population were (serving) in the Confederate army, leaving as residents only a portion of the women and children and men that were incapable of bearing arms. The town was beautifully situated in a picturesque and heavily wooded valley, while adjoining the town were several partially cleared and cultivated fields. About 9 miles in a southwest direction, following the course of the Paint Rock through a heavily wooded valley, was the Tennessee River on the opposite side of which were encamped quite a force of the enemy, who were in the habit of crossing the river at that particular point, and surprising small parties of our foragers. As it was supposed they were kept posted as to the movements of our troops by the inhabitants of Vienna and surrounding country, it was deemed advisable to occupy that point by a regiment as an outpost, and to keep mounts for fifty men who should be ready at all times to scour the country in search of the numerous bands of bushwhackers that infested that section of country.

We arrived at our new quarters about 5 P.M. of the 9th, in the midst of a cold rain. Upon our arrival pickets were at once detailed to guard the camp. The town was entered by four roads from different directions, the writer being one of four pickets that was posted on the road half a mile out in a Northwest direction. Upon reaching our post the writer was the first vidette[421] posted, and stood for two hours when I was relieved. After being off four hours, would again take my place as vidette.

Right well does the writer remember the first two hours I stood as vidette on that post. The dark and somber shadows of night were fast falling when I took my position on that post, at the end of a lane that led to the town. At this point the road forked, one (branch) running north while one ran in a westerly direction, and both running through heavily wooded bottoms. As I seated myself at the corner of a fence, with my gum poncho around me to protect myself from the fast falling rain, my position was not an enviable one. I had been on post about half an hour when the darkness of the night had settled so thick it was almost impossible to discern an object ten foot distant, when my attention was called to a noise in the brush that lined the fence where I was sitting. In an instant with my musket at a ready, I arose to my feet, when whatever it was sprang from the top of the fence over my head alighting on the ground about ten feet from me where it instantly disappeared in the darkness, and what it was I never knew.

From that time until I was relieved the least stir I heard in the brush I imagined a bushwhacker was after my scalp. At last the relief picket appeared, where upon I returned to the reserve post about one hundred yards in the rear, and after partaking of a cup of coffee and hard tack, wrapped myself in my poncho and was soon fast asleep, again at 4 A.M. I was aroused to take my place on post standing guard until 6 o'clock, when as the silver steaks of the early dawn appeared in the eastern sky, I was again relieved. Observing a house distant about 40 rods I took my canteen and a coffee pot and went there to procure water for breakfast. On arriving at the house I was met in the door yard by the lady of the house and her daughter, a young lady of perhaps 20 years of age, both of whom seemed greatly surprised upon seeing a live Yankee in the neighborhood. Explaining to them the object of my visit, and also informing them that our entire regiment were encamped in their little town where undoubtedly we should remain for sometime, I succeeded in buying from them some corn bread and honey. After filling my canteen and coffee pot with water from their well I returned to my comrades, fully equipped with the grand essentials for a good square meal.

Along towards evening we were relieved by a new detail, and we returned to the regiment which we found quartered in the various empty buildings in the town. The colonel of the regiment selected as headquarters a fine unoccupied residence situated on a slight eminence part, and overlooking the entire town.

The next few days the entire regiment was busily engaged in building a fort around headquarters, which was to be occupied by Company A, but large enough to hold the entire regiment in case we should by attacked by superior numbers. After we had completed the earth works of our fort it was completely surrounded by a heavy and almost impenetrable chevaux-de-frise:[422] whereby we could have held our own against five times our number. After the completion of our fort, Company A erected therein, with small pine logs, a comfortable barracks, which, by arranging bunks around the sides, afforded ample accommodations for the entire company. After getting our new quarters nicely arranged we were very much pleased with our new camp. After becoming acquainted with the citizens of the town, a good many of the boys made arrangements with the ladies of the town to cook our grub, each man paying them so much a week, and giving them all the surplus grub, of which there was always plenty when we were in camp, and drew full rations. It was a God send to them to be once more enabled to have plenty of old Government Java Coffee.

Five of Company A, besides the writer, had our cooking done at a place about 40 rods from our quarters, and a good cook the lady proved to be. The following are the names of the squad: W. R. Oake, L. Miller, D. S. Swihart, P. J. Potter, T. J. Houston,[423] and W. P. Rhodes.[424] Many a little delicacy that we were almost strangers to did the lady prepare for us, and as we could seat ourselves at a table and partake of our food in a civilized manner it seemed more like home than army life.

We were fast becoming acquainted with the inhabitants of the little town, especially the bonnie southern lassies of which there were quite a number, who seemed not at all averse to become acquainted with the Yankee Soldiers. During the long evenings many a social game of cards did we enjoy with them. In quite a spacious residence in the central part of the town lived a war widow of about 25 years of age, and with her lived an unmarried sister of about 30 years. The husband of the first lady was a lieutenant in the Confederate army. Many a long evening with Lieutenant Frank of Company A has the writer spent playing social games of cards with the two ladies, and I sometimes thought that the lieutenant was somewhat mashed on the younger one.[425]

Although they were very sociable and invariably invited us to call again, whenever any allusion to the war was made it was plainly to be seen that they fervently wished for the time when they would again be united with their loved ones, and the mantle of peace and prosperity again float over an undivided country. Not being satisfied with spending our evenings in social games we arranged to hold a series of dances, the building selected being the M. E. Church,[426] and as it was seated with the old fashioned moveable seats, it was no great job to clear the floor. As the regiment could boast of several good violins, as well as musicians we spent many an enjoyable time. As the musicians and callers took their seats in the pulpit with our fair partners, who seemed to enjoy it as well as we did we would dance until the small hours of the morning. It may shock some of my readers to think that we should be so sacrilegious as to desecrate so holy a building as a church by dancing, but my friends must remember that in a great many cases there are extenuating circumstances. A good many of our army chaplains advocated and preached the doctrine: That if a soldier fell while battling for his country it mattered not what his views were he would surely enter the gates of Paradise, and as most of us had accepted that doctrine as gospel truth we thought there could be no harm in any amusement that made the majority happy without making anyone unhappy.[427]

As has been stated the regiment kept fifty horses and most of the time a detail of mounted men were scouring the country in quest of bushwhackers. One day near the last of March [April 21, 1864] news reached our camp that a forage detail of our men had been captured by the enemy, who had the night before crossed the Tennessee near Claysville.[428] A special detail of mounted men were at once dispatched to intercept the rebels before they had succeeded in re-crossing the river with their prisoners, one of whom we learned had been severely wounded before he was captured. Although it was but a very short time after the news reached camp of their capture, and troops were hurriedly sent to their relief, the rebels succeeded in re-crossing the river with their prisoners.[429]

It was about the first of April [March 22, 1864], it had been raining all day and the troops in camp had retired for the night when the adjutant[430] of the regiment entered our quarters and inquired of the orderly sergeant, where Oake and Miller bunked. Not being asleep we answered for ourselves, when the adjutant stated that he wanted a detail of men to take a night ride of about thirty miles to arrest two rebels that were home on furlough. We at once signified our willingness to go, the adjutant telling us to report at the stables as soon as possible. In about twenty minutes, fully equipped with our arms we reported at the stables, where we found the adjutant and the rest of the detail of three men. The adjutant then informed us as to the cause of our night's journey. It appeared that information had reached headquarters that distant about 12 to 15 miles in a northwest direction two Confederate soldiers who were home on furlough were staying with friends. One (was) a private soldier who had on his return been married and was staying at the home of his brother, about 12 miles from our camp. The other was a major [lieutenant] in the rebel army and was at the home of his father about three miles further than the first one. Having saddled our horses they were led from the stable when again carefully examined the girths, we mounted and started on our long ride of thirty miles in the enemy's country.

As we headed for the picket post, distant about half a mile we realized that our task was anything but a pleasant one. The night was intensely dark, and the rain was fast falling, water being ankle deep in the roads. At last we reached the picket line when, "Halt who goes there," greeted our ears, "Friends," "responded the adjutant, "Advance friends and give the countersign." The adjutant then advanced and gave the talisman, at the same time informing the pickets that as our duty would require our absence most of the night that they should, on discovering a body of men approaching their front during the night, not fire on them, but first to ascertain who they were. Just prior to this time as some of our pickets had been fired upon by bushwhackers the orders had been to halt no one coming from the front at night, but to fire upon them; hence the adjutants orders not to fire.

As we threw our ponchos around us to protect ourselves as much as possible from the fast falling rain, we bade good night to the pickets, and started on our long and disagreeable ride. After a ride of about ten miles we arrived at quite a large residence, the first one we had seen during one ride. Part of our squad dismounted and approached the house, and after some loud knocking succeeded in arousing the inmates. We then informed the owner a man of perhaps 50 years of age, the object of our visit requesting him to guide us to the residence of one of the parties we were in search of. At first he showed a reluctance to comply with our request, when he was given to understand that force would be used in case he declined to pilot us, and any treachery on his part would be met with instant death. Having procured one of his own horses to ride we again resumed our journey, which from the place was in a southwest direction about 2 miles by an unfrequented road, through a low swampy country where at times our horses would for rods have to wade through water two feet deep. At last we emerged from the heavy timber into a clearing of perhaps twenty acres, and near quite a large log house, which our guide told us was the residence we were in search of. Arriving at the house we dismounted leaving the horses and guide in charge of one man, while three of us approached the rear and two the front door. As it was about 11 P.M. the house was shrouded in darkness, and everything was quiet. Upon rapping on the door, a voice demanded who was there. The adjutant replied, "United States soldiers," and ordered him to at once strike a light and to unlock the door. We then heard the parties inside unlocking the door without at first lighting up the house. He was at once peremptorily ordered to at once light the house before unlocking the door which he proceeded to do.

Upon entering the house, which was quite large, we inquired of the owner, a man of middle age, if his brother a soldier in the Confederate army and now on furlough was stopping there. We were answered in the affirmative by both the owner of the house and the solider himself, who was sleeping in an adjoining room, and in plain view, the door to the room being open. He was then informed as to our business ordering him to at once dress and get ready to accompany us to camp. It was there that one of the stern features of martial law was visible. The soldier had during his brief visit home been married and at the time of our arrival was in bed with his young bride, who also hastily arose and piteously implored us to let her husband remain at home. We explained to her that military laws were inexorable and our duty as soldiers. We to some extent consoled her by telling her that we thought her husband would soon be paroled when he could soon return to his home. Upon asking the owner of the house if there were any fire arms in the house we were informed there were none on the premises. Thinking him to be telling a falsehood one of the boys, Wm. Gardner[431] of Company I and the writer lit a light and proceeded up stairs where we found two army muskets and three colt revolvers, all being loaded and ready for immediate use. On descending and confronting the man with the direct evidence of his falsehood he was deathly pale, as we in language more forcible than eloquent explained to him the punishment he so richly merited, but after taking everything into consideration we would for once respect his gray hairs, but cautioned him never to repeat it as he might come in contact with those that were not as lenient as we were, and who would hang him to the first tree they came to.

I have often thought, how if they had been notified of our coming and had possessed the necessary grit, armed as they were could have made it warm for us. As it was, we considered ourselves very lucky in escaping as we did. After securing a mount for our prisoner from his brother's stables and amidst the lamentations of the prisoner's young bride, we started on our journey for the major, three miles distant. When we arrived in due time, and found our man sound asleep at his fathers house, but greatly surprised to think that the Yankees had learned of his whereabouts. He proved to be a very intelligent young man of about 25 years of age holding the rank of major [lieutenant] in the Confederate service, and while deeply regretting his capture took it very philosophically, and as a true soldier should do. Having procured a horse of the major's [lieutenant's] father for his son to ride informing him by calling at our camp at Vienna the animal would be returned to him, we started on our return to camp. Upon arriving at the home of our old guide and thanking him for his assistance we bade him good bye, and continued on our journey arriving at our pickets just at the break of day. Upon reaching our quarters, and disposing of our prisoners, hungry and tired from our long ride, we proceeded to prepare our breakfast.

The next day our prisoners were sent to division headquarters at Woodville, and what disposition (was ever) made of them we never learned.[432]

In Company A of the 26th Iowa was a soldier by the name of H____ S____ [William H. Swift][433] who was very witty and full of fun, and who could at almost any time have the Company in a roar of laughter. He was naturally timid, and the report of a musket, or the ring of the deadly minie (ball) would cause him to turn deathly pale, and he would have no more strength than a child. About one mile from our camp on the main road as it crossed the Paint Rock Creek [River], the mode of crossing being an old fashioned flat boat, large enough to accommodate one team at a time in crossing. The boat was propelled by the hand. During our stay in Vienna we always kept a guard of four men to watch it to prevent its falling into the hands of the enemy as we frequently used it when foraging.

One day in the latter part of March the writer was one of the four on guard one night at the crossing. It was about 6 P.M. when we relieved the old guard. Upon relieving the guard the writer was the first one of the four on duty as vidette for the first two hours. The vidette standing on the bank of the stream near the boat, while the reserve pickets, those off duty, were in the woods about 80 yards in the rear, where they could build a fire. Promptly at 8 P. M the Sergeant relieved me by putting my friend S____ on vidette. Upon being relieved I returned to the reserve post, and leaning my gun against a tree I took my coffee pot and returned to the stream to get some water to make a cup of coffee, before I lay down to sleep. I had placed the water on the fire and was in the act of cutting a piece of sow belly to fry, when the crack of S____'s musket was heard, and in came S____ jumping over the fire and lay down behind a large tree. Instantly we grasped our arms and inquired of our bold picket why he had left his post. All the answer he gave us was, "There's a thing out there." By this time we could distinctly hear the cracking of brush in our right front. The sergeant at once ordered the other picket George Waggoner [Wagoner][434] and the writer to take our arms and discover if possible the cause of S____'s alarm, and of the noise we could hear. With guns at ready we advanced in the direction from whence the noise came. Straining our eyes, and expecting every moment to see about a dozen bushwhackers. The nearer we approached whatever it was the more distinctly could be heard the cracking of the bushes. Making up our minds that whatever it was, it was no rebel we boldly advanced and just at that moment the moon shone brightly through a rift in the clouds, and revealed to our visions the sorrowful countenance of an old mule, one that had perhaps broken loose and had gone on a foraging expedition of his own.

As we returned to report it was with difficulty we restrained ourselves from laughter, thinking of S____'s narrow escape. The sergeant again ordered our bold picket to his post, but it was of no avail as he could not get him to move from behind his tree. So the balance of the night the sergeant took turns with Waggoner and the writer in standing guard.

The next day on being relieved and returning to camp, we refrained from mentioning or laughing at him about it, fully realizing his mental condition on such occasions and knowing it was impossible for him to do otherwise. Poor fellow, in less than two months he received his death wound at the hands of the rebels, the particulars of which will be given later.

About this time the officers of the regiment decided that they would have a dance which they intended should be the event of the season. No one, but invited guests and commissioned officers, being allowed to participate. It was then that some of the fun loving spirits of the regiment began to lay their plans, hoping to be able to frustrate their schemes, and at the same time take a part in the dance themselves. One of the churches of which the town boasted was situated in the outskirts of the town, and just outside of the picket line, and was selected by them wherein to hold their dance, making it obligatory on all attending to have the countersign in order to be able to get through the picket line.

At last the eve of the dance approached and during the day great preparations had been made by the officers who anticipated a grand time. It was a beautiful moonlit night, and the church was already brilliantly lighted, while the sweet notes of the violin were being wafted to our ears by the gentle southern breeze. The question with us was how to get hold of the countersign, and be enabled to attend, as we did not like the idea of the officers monopolized the fair southern damsels with whom we were so well acquainted. It was suggested that we take in inventory of the picket line, and if possible find its weak spot. After a careful survey of the pickets the writer made the discovery that on one post stood a Company A man with whom he was well acquainted, and quite intimate. Thinking that faint heart never won (a) fair lady the writer approached said soldier and was met with the customary, "Halt, who goes there," I answered, "A friend." "Advance friend and give the countersign." Approaching the sentry who stood with arms at a ready, "Levi[435] I have forgotten the countersign, what will I do." He replied, "You will have to get it, or you can't pass." "Say Levi," I replied, "You know me, know that I would lose my arm rather than give you away." He replied, "Injun, if you will swear that you won't give me away I will give you it," I replied, "Levi you know I will swear to anything in order to get out to that dance." "All right," he said, and then he gave me the word "Claysville."[436] I thanked him and returned to my quarters. It took only about 10 minutes to give the countersign to about a dozen of the boys, and in about half an hour quite a squad of the boys were fully prepared to take part in the dance, and one at a time at short intervals approached the picket and upon giving the pass word were allowed to pass out, when after going a short distance they would halt until all had passed out, when in a body we marched to the church. To say the officers were surprised would not express their astonishment on finding so many outside of the line, and at first they showed a disposition to resent the intrusion, but finally very wisely looked upon it as a sharp gainer in which they were fairly beaten, and good naturedly invited us to take in the festivities of the occasion. The Southern lassies seemed to enjoy the discomfort of the officers as much as we did.

For several days after the dance did our commissioned friends try to find out how we obtained the countersign, but finally gave it up, and to this day I don't believe anyone knows how I obtained the pass word, except the party that gave me it, and who is now living in Jackson County Iowa, and who if this article should reach his eye will distinctly remember the occasion. For fear that my comrade's memory should be a little treacherous I will after a lapse of so many years give him the magic word that was used on that occasion. It was, "Claysville."

Camp Life at Vienna

CHAPTER NOTES:
Camp Life at Vienna

➜ ──────────────────── ◀

420. This is not the Vienna, Alabama, located 35 miles southwest of Tuscaloosa, near the Mississippi state line on the Little Tombigbee River. Rather it is a now extinct community in the Paint Rock Valley, northwest of Claysville. The regiment was ordered to the community to establish an outpost. It occupied vacant houses as barracks, performed picket and camp duties, and conducted patrols along the Tennessee River between the mouth of the Flint and Paint Rock rivers. Maj. John Lubbers was in command of the regiment, since Colonel Smith was commanding the brigade and Lt. Col. Ferreby had not recovered from his wound received at Lookout Mountain. Lubbers, previously captain of Co. E, had received promotion to major on February 6, 1864 (see note 60). Ferreby returned to duty and assumed command before March 23, 1864. Ibid.; *Roster* 3: 1023, 1072.

421. Also spelled "vedette." The term routinely applies to a mounted sentinel on picket, or guard duty.

422. The principal uses of *chevaux-de-frise* are to obstruct a passage, stop a breach, or form an impediment to an attacking enemy force, when placed in front of a fortification. The obstructions were formed of stout squares of hexagonal beams, with iron spikes or sword blades or, as was more common in the field, stout pointed stakes inserted into and standing perpendicularly from the faces; or made of stout palisades, pointed and laid together side by side, furnished with legs for support, with the points facing toward the enemy. The fort, if constructed to standard practice for the time, was most likely a large earthen redoubt, ditched on all sides, with a sally port (covered entryway) located in the rear of the work. Often a palisade of logs was erected on the parapet, creating a stockade fort. The regiment named the fortified installation Fort Osterhaus in honor of their division commander. Scott, *Military Dictionary*, 160, 431–32; *O.R.* I-32-I-677.

423. Thomas J. Houston, born in Ohio, was a resident of Canton and 22 when he enlisted August 12, 1862. He had recently been promoted to fifth corporal, February 19, 1863, and later would become fourth corporal, April 1, 1863. He was mustered out with the regiment on June 6, 1865, at Washington, D.C. *Roster* 3: 1060.

424. William P. Rhodes, born in Virginia, was 22 and living in Canton when he enlisted August 12, 1862. He was promoted second corporal, August 1, 1863, and fifth sergeant, September 1, 1864. He was mustered out at Madison, Indiana, June 7, 1865. *Roster* 3: 1090.

425. Unfortunately, the series of letters Lt. Elijah Frank wrote to Katherine Varner stop in December 1863, and thus his impression of these matters are unknown.

426. Methodist Episcopal Church.

427. As historian James M. McPherson notes, being actively exposed to combat offers the extreme challenge to the belief that any soldier can control his own fate. Bullets and shrapnel can strike the just and unjust alike. Faced with this reality, most soldiers rapidly develop fatalistic attitudes. The Christian fatalism displayed by Civil War soldiers contained both pessimistic and optimistic overtones. The differences were subtle, but both helped soldiers overcome the fear of death and thereby strengthen their will to fight. In this case, while Oake exhibits that he has accepted the possibility of being killed, he displays a playful optimism about death on the battlefield, and that such service for one's country will be rewarded by God, who naturally would overlook the necessity of the faithful and good soldier to enjoy life to its fullest—just in case. James M. McPherson, *For Cause & Comrades: Why Men Fought in the Civil War* (New York: Oxford University Press, 1987), 62–67.

428. At attack was made on a Federal outpost camp at Claysville, Alabama, on March 14, 1864, by a partisan, Capt. H. F. Smith, with about 65 men (Federal report lists 150 dismounted men). It involved, however, capture of about 30 members of the 32nd Missouri Infantry, commanded by Capt. William T. House, and not the 26th Iowa. The incident involving a detail of the 26th Iowa occurred on April 21, 1864. *O.R.* I-32-I-497–98.

429. On April 21, 1864, at Harrison's Gap, a force of Confederate partisans (about 30 to 40 men) led by a "Parson" Johnston, formerly a Methodist preacher, ambushed and captured a detail of eight enlisted men from the 26th Iowa returning from duty patrols on the Tennessee River. Reported to be captured April 21 were Sgt. John Whelan, Co. D; Corp. Hazen Chase, Co. G; John L. Baird, Co. H; Henry Clausen, Co. E; Samuel P. Driskell (wounded), Co. F; Ransome E. Hurlburt, Co. K; and Johann Peterson, Co. E. Pvt. Richard O'Conner, of Co. I, is listed as captured on April 25, 1864. However, the eighth man captured on April 21 could not be identified. No documentation exists of an incident occurring on April 25 in which a member of the regiment was captured. Therefore, the probability is that the eighth man taken on the 21st could have been O'Conner. Both Corporal Chase and Private Hurlburt were paroled, exchanged, and returned to company; however, the other six men, incarcerated as prisoners of war at Andersonville, Georgia, all perished in prison within five months of capture, the last of them dying on September 4, 1864. In conjunction with the affair at Harrison's Gap, Major Lubbers received a communication left on the bank of the river and addressed "To the Officer Commanding Post at Vienna, Alabama," which was apparently from Parson Johnston, stating, "If any citizen or any house is injured or destroyed for what we have done over here, we will retaliate by putting these prisoners to death. We have 8, but will treat them as prisoners of war. We are not bushwhackers, and you must not hold citizens responsible for what we do." *O.R.* I-32-I-676–78. *Roster* 3: 1023–24, 1037, 1043, 1045, 1050, 1067, 1088, 1108.

430. The new regimental adjutant was Dennis G. Butterfield, promoted December 12, 1863, replacing Joseph D. Fegan, who had been promoted captain of Co. B, June 12, 1863, but continued to perform the role of adjutant into December 1863. *Roster* 3: 1038, 1054, 1056.

431. William H. F. Gardner, a native of Pennsylvania, was 22 and living in Wheatland when he enlisted on August 12, 1862. He was killed in action, March 21, 1865, at Mill Creek, North Carolina, and is buried at the National Cemetery at Raleigh. *Roster* 3: 1059.

432. The two men captured by Oake and his comrades on March 22 appear to have been Lt. and Adj. R. T. Daniel, from Lt. Col. Lemuel G. Mead's Alabama Rangers, or Mead's Guerillas, as the Federals referred to them, and a soldier named Anderson. Daniel provided intelligence information to the Federals and, as reported by General Osterhaus, was released by direction of Maj. Gen. John A. Logan, commanding the XV Army Corps, on his (Daniel's) taking the oath [of his allegiance to the Union] and giving bond. Records indicate that Anderson was still in confinement at Woodville, having been brought before a military commission, as of April 21, 1864. *O.R.* I-32-I-677; *O.R.* I-32-III-124, 213–14.

433. The witty soldier was William H. Swift. Born in Ohio, he was 26 and a resident of Canton when he enlisted August 12, 1862. He died from wounds on August 24, 1864, in a hospital in Nashville, Tennessee. *Roster* 3: 1095.

434. George Wagoner (spelling in *Roster* and *AGI*), born in Virginia, was living in Davenport and age 27 when he enlisted on July 1, 1862. He was mustered out with the regiment on June 6, 1865, in Washington, D.C. *Roster* 3: 1105.

435. The man on picket was Pvt. Levi Strong from Canton. Born in Ohio, Strong enlisted July 7, 1862, at age 21. He was wounded slightly at Ship's Gap, Georgia, October 16, 1864, but finished his service, being mustered out at Washington, D.C., on June 6, 1865. *Roster* 3: 1095.

436. The transcribed manuscript states the password as "Maysville"; however, given the proximity of Claysville to Vienna, and the fact that Oake earlier mistakenly cited Maysville (instead of Claysville) as the town located immediately across the river from Guntersville, the password was changed by the editor to reflect the greater probability that it indeed was "Claysville." There is a Maysville, Alabama, located fifteen miles northwest of Woodville, making it 25 miles north of Vienna.

Brigadier General Charles R. Woods.
The relationship of Woods with the war experi-
ences of William Royal Oake dates to November
1862, when their respective regiments participated
in operations in the Mississippi Valley. Later,
beginning in February 1864 until the close of the
war, Woods served almost constantly as either
Oake's brigade or division commander.
ROBERT M. COCH COLLECTION

CHAPTER ELEVEN

We Leave Vienna and Start for the Front

❧ ———————————————— ❧

It was near the latter part of April [orders issued on April 28, 1864] that we began to hear rumors of an early move to take part in one of the greatest campaigns of the war. A campaign made memorable by the great achievement of that gallant army of one hundred thousand men. That in the face of almost insurmountable natural obstacles, and resisted by an army of sixty thousand, the flower of the Southern army. We succeeded in penetrating 130 miles into the enemy's country and capturing the Gate City of the South, Atlanta; thereby severing the last line of communication between the eastern and western parts of the fast dying Confederacy.

Soon we received orders for a general inspection, a sure indication of an early move, to say that the leaving of our comfortable quarters, where for about two months we had been so comfortably situated, was repugnant to the feelings of the majority would but faintly express our feelings. Not only did we dislike to leave our pleasant situation, but during our stay there our acquaintance with the citizens of the little town had been of the most pleasant character, and I am afraid that some of the boys, omitting the writer, had been smitten by the charms of the many dark eyed southern lassies, that resided in the town. We realized the fact that as long as there was an armed rebel in the field duty called us to the front, and that again must we forgo the pleasant scenes of camp life, and once more take part in the turmoil and carnage of inevitable battles.

We soon became reconciled to the fact of our approaching move, and began overhauling our personal effects, discarding all surplus and unnecessary clothing, and retaining only such as was actually necessary for our personal comfort.

At last we received orders to move on the following day. At an early hour [on April 30th] the reveille sounded and the troops were soon astir and busily engaged in getting what was to be their last meal in Vienna. After eating our breakfast the familiar call, "Fall In," was heard, and as the soldiers fall into line our Southern friends, who had been apprised of the move, gathered around to shake our hands, and bid us good bye. How indelibly is that scene at Vienna on that April morning, impressed upon the memory of the writer. After a lapse of fifty years he again can see the old 26th Iowa, standing in line surrounded by our southern friends. Conspicuous among that throng was the wife of the rebel officer, and her sister spoken of earlier, with whom Lieutenant Frank and the writer had played so many friendly games of cards during our stay in the little town. Any one viewing the countenances of our Southern friends at that time would hardly believe they were the friends and representatives of the party with whom we were at that time engaged in the most desperate civil struggle of modern times. At last

Battlefield of Resaca, Georgia.
This George Barnard image of Confederate entrenchments at Resaca shows the combat environment that confronted Sherman's troops in May 1864. The fieldworks pictured here have survived the ravages of time and are preserved on the battlefield today. LIBRARY OF CONGRESS

the order is given, "Forward March," and as the band played the "Girl I Left Behind Me"[437] with the bright folds of old glory thrown to the breeze, and with kind wishes to our friends we bid good bye to the little town of Vienna. Upon reaching our former camp at Woodville where we found the rest of the division we camped for the night, and on the following morning [May 1st] the division started on its march to Chattanooga, the point of concentration of the grand army of invasion that was destined to make Georgia howl.[438] After several days we arrived at Chattanooga. On May 5th, that grand army of ninety-eight thousand men with 250 pieces of artillery was put in motion led by one of our ablest generals, W. T. Sherman.[439]

At this time the enemy numbering about sixty thousand men, and under the command of the Confederate General, Joe Johnston*, held a very strong position in the mountains on the Georgia Central [Western & Atlantic] Railroad[440] in the vicinity of the town of Dalton.[441] Their position was a strong one, and the task that Sherman had before him, of dislodging them from that position was indeed Herculean in its character, to penetrate one hundred and thirty miles into an enemy's country in the face of sixty thousand men. A country that was naturally strongly fortified, and traversed by several distinct range of mountain ranges the country beyond being accessible only by roads running through the narrow passes which were heavily fortified by the enemy, positions where five hundred men could successfully defy ten times their number.[442]

While part of the army moved directly South against the enemy at Dalton the Army of the Tennessee consisting of the Fifteenth,[443] Sixteenth and Seventeenth Army Corps, commanded by (Major) General (James) McPherson, moved by the right flank with the intention of penetrating the mountains by the way of Snake Creek Gap, thus striking the railroad at the town of Resacca [Resaca], about 10 [13] miles south of Dalton, and in the rear of the main body of the rebel army.[444]

On the morning of May 9th the advance of our army encountered the enemy in force in Snake Creek Gap, which by the way was a long and narrow valley through the mountains, varying in width from one to a quarter of a mile, the distance through the pass being about six miles. Although the enemy (was) in considerable force they were easily driven by our cavalry, which was rapidly followed by our infantry.[445]

As we marched through the narrow valley, evidences of the sharp skirmishing were visible on every hand as at short intervals the rigid form of some comrade could be seen lying at the roadside while the shattered trees showed plainly the work of the deadly shell.

As we approached the south entrance to the gap [on the east side of the mountain range] we could distinctly hear the rattle of the cavalry's carbines, soon the roar of artillery was heard, which indicated the enemy to be in force and stubbornly resisting the further advance of the cavalry. Soon we discovered the cavalry drawn up in line about 80 rods [440 yards] in advance and hotly engaged with the enemy (forces) that were posted in the woods in their front. As we reached the lines of the cavalry we were hurriedly formed in line with orders to move forward. Just at this time the gallant Kilpatrick,[446] in command of the cavalry, received a severe wound and was taken to the rear. Steadily we pressed forward through the dense growth of underbrush, while the sharp ping of the deadly minie (ball) is heard on every side, and occasionally the thug of a bullet told us plainly that it had found a resting place in the form of some comrade. Gradually but surely they give way, and are forced back to their lines on the main body at Resaca, which is distant about one mile. We were now ordered to halt where we remained until the evening when we were moved back to a strong position at the mouth of the gap a distance of about two miles.[447] It was while making this move to the rear, that the 26th Iowa had a narrow escape from capture or being cut to pieces by the enemy. Our regiment was lying in a piece of young timber, and when ordered to move it was quite dark, the balance of the brigade having preceded us some little distance. Upon receiving our orders we were promptly in line when the command, Forward, was given, and we hurriedly, but silently marched as we supposed to the rear. After marching about five minutes, an officer rode rapidly past to the head of the regiment, which at once came to an abrupt halt, when the officer, above mentioned, accompanied by the commander of the regiment rode quickly to the rear giving as they passed along orders to, "About Face." It was then that we discovered that instead of marching as we supposed to the rear, we had taken the wrong road, and were marching towards the enemy's lines. Had not the absence of the regiment been discovered by our brigade commander we would have marched directly into the lines of the rebels.

A tempting breastwork.
This illustration highlights many of the skirmish line combat experiences of William Royal Oake, who, like so many of his comrades, when given the opportunity, often sought out natural features to provide personal shelter, cover, and concealment on many a battlefield during the war. BATTLES AND LEADERS OF THE CIVIL WAR

After about facing we marched rapidly to the rear, but did not overtake the balance of the troops until we arrived at the chosen position at the mouth of the gap. The next few days the troops were busily engaged in building a line of works, and felling the heavy timber in our front.[448] On the morning of the 14th [13th] we were again ordered to advance approaching within half a mile of the enemy's line of entrenchments, where we camped for the night.[449] On the 15th [14th] the troops were early astir preparing for the inevitable battle. Soon we heard the guns on our extreme left, which told us that Hooker and Thomas were already attacking the almost impregnable position of the enemy at Buzzards Roost and Rocky Face (Ridge) near Dalton.[450]

Our breakfast having been eaten we were ordered into line, when the usual call for skirmishers was made. At this time occurred an incident that goes to show what is to be, will be, in spite of all we may do to avoid it. Among the skirmishers detailed from Company A 26th was comrade S___ of Vienna Ferry fame, who upon being detailed (for this duty), piteously begged of the company commander to excuse him (from it), as it was an impossibility for him to go. Taking pity on him L. Miller, my bunk mate, volunteered in his place leaving him to go with the line of battle, or get excused if he could. How distinctly I remember that scene on the hill side near Resaca on the 15th [14th] of May 1864, poor S___ lay close beside the writer apparently out of all danger, when the fatal shot from the enemy gave him his death wound. Poor fellow after my comrade had so kindly taken his place on the skirmish line, leaving him in a place of comparative safety, to thus meet with a fatal wound was indeed a sad ending. The poor fellow was taken to the rear and finally sent to Nashville, Tennessee, where he died from his wounds August 24th, 1864, and was buried at Nashville, Tennessee.[451]

Our skirmishers were soon in line when a general advance was ordered, the line of battle following. As we reached the top of the hill upon which we had been lying, and came within view of the enemy we received a withering fire of both artillery and musketry.

Still we moved steadily down the slope towards the enemy on the double quick, and as we reached the base of the hill, along which ran quite a large creek, we did not wait for ceremony, but plunged into the mud and water, and were soon scrambling up the opposite bank to face the leaden storm. We were then on a comparatively level piece of ground, about 400 yards from the enemy, who were lying behind works, and plainly visible from our position. Now for the first time we returned their fire, moving steadily to the front, while many a poor fellow received his death wound, and crossed the dark river.

About this time Sergeant Jeff Leeper[452] of Company H fell with a ball through the brain, and in the next instant poor Tom Wilson[453] of Company D met with the same fate, Wilson was a good soldier, and the life of the company as he was quite an entertainer, and full of fun, and what made his fall sadder was the fact that at the time he received the fatal ball he was standing beside his only brother, who was in the same company. Poor Jeff Leeper, just before going into the battle that morning took his personal effects out of his pocket and handed them to Horace Humeston[454] of the same company, and requested him to send them to his folks in Iowa in case he should not survive the battle. He said that he had a premonition that he would be killed in the coming action. How true the premonition came. He was an only brother of J. M. Leeper that was captured and in prison with the writer in 1863.

We had now approached quite close to the enemy, and were ordered to lay down and protect ourselves, in the meantime to keep up an incessant fire on the enemy. While we were thus hotly engaged with the enemy in our front, the thunder of Hooker's artillery on the left, told us plainly that the enemy were hotly pressed at that point. The writer was very fortunate in getting a good position behind a large tree, a favorite position of his in such warm times, and I think can truthfully say that to that tree I owe my present existence as it was literally riddled with bullets. As I would peer out around its friendly trunk to aim at some rebel the bullets would rattle like hail against it. At last the shadows of night approached and after establishing our pickets, the main body of the (National) troops, were withdrawn to the position held in the morning prior to the attack.[455]

After falling back, the troops began to prepare there evening meal to satisfy the cravings of hunger, and to retire and take a much needed rest, for the decisive contest that we thought would be inevitable on the morrow. After partaking of something to eat, in company with a comrade, the writer paid a visit to our field hospital, which was in a sheltered position a short distance in the rear of our lines.

Upon arriving at the hospital we found the wounded that had been carried from the field lying in rows on the ground while the surgeons, like phantoms, were moving among them. The cries and groans of the unfortunates would melt a heart of stone. Now a surgeon would stop a moment and examine one of the unfortunates, who perhaps at that moment was delirious, and as the surgeon with a shake of his head withdrew, and passed on to the next, told plainly that the poor fellow was beyond all earthly help. Well does the writer remember one instance of a fine stalwart young soldier of about 25 years of age, who had received a terrible wound in the shoulder, the ball lodging in some vital spot. As the surgeon raised the blanket that had been placed over him, and laid bare the gaping wound into which he ran a steel probe, and which he soon withdrew with a shake of his head, and again replaced the blanket over the soldier, told us that he was beyond all mortal aid, and at that time was oblivious to the scenes of carnage by which he was surrounded. As I watched the poor fellow, the cold clammy hand of death was plainly visible on that noble brow. As I stood before him and raised the blanket from his face and watched the flickering spark expire, I though of his many friends in the far north per-haps a mother who at that very moment was thinking of her boy in a far off land, and praying for his safe return. Dear readers the scenes that I have portrayed are not imaginary ones, but are of an every day occurrence, and while to us they were considered of little moment at that time, after the lapse of nearly half a century, as I sit in the quiet of my home, and recall those familiar scenes of some comrade writhing in the agonies of death without one loving hand to administer to his dying wants, in spite of all I can do, feelings of sadness force themselves upon me. Returning to the reg-iment we lay upon the ground, and wrapping our ponchos around us we were soon fast asleep.[456]

About 2 A.M., [3:30 A.M., May 16] the troops were aroused by the cry of fire, when springing to our feet we discovered that the railroad bridge across the Ostenaula [Oostanaula] River, about half a mile west of Resaca, was on fire. In an instant we took in the situation. The enemy, were evacuating their position and had set fire to the railroad bridge to delay us if possible, in fol-lowing them. At the break of day, the pickets, upon advancing, discovered that the enemy had evacuated their works, and were in full retreat, (moving) south following the line of railroad.[457]

The Army of the Tennessee was at once ordered to move rapidly to the right to cross the river at Lays Ferry, a distance of about six miles and if pos-sible to strike the enemy while in motion. Upon arriving at the Ferry we dis-covered that the enemy had already escaped and were in full retreat towards the little town of Kingston. After marching a few miles we encamped, and we remained there until the next morning. At an early hour the troops were again in motion, our brigade being in the advance. An incident of that morning march I well remember. After marching about half an hour we dis-covered, lying by the road side in a nude condition with a bayonet sticking in his throat, the body of one of our soldiers. The supposition was that he had been taken prisoner by some band of bushwhackers, who had thus bru-tally mutilated and murdered him. On arriving in the vicinity of Kingston [May 19, 1864] it was discovered that the enemy were still retreating, when we went into camp in quite a large wheat field that at the time was nearly ripe, and I don't think I ever saw a field of grain harvested as quick as that was. On stacking our arms the troops at once broke ranks and every man pulled up an armful to sleep upon the coming night, and I believe that in a half hours time that field of wheat was harvested.[458]

On the 21st [20th], the 26th Iowa received orders to board a train and proceed to the town of Rome, Georgia, a distance of about 20 [14] miles [to the west of Kingston]. For a good part of the way the railroad[459] ran parallel with and close to the Coosa River, a stream of perhaps 80 yards in width. The cars of the train had been made up of common box cars, and a good many of the boys were riding on top of them. We had proceeded about half way, the train running perhaps about 20 miles an hour, when we were fired upon by some of the enemy's cavalry that were concealed in the heavy timber on the other side of the river. As the bullets rattled like hail against the cars the commander of the regiment at once ordered the train to stop, and us to get quickly off and into line, and give the Johnnies a few rounds to let them know that we were not asleep. It was fun to see them getting out of that timber. While on top of the cars, and the bullets were rattling around it was fun to see those riding on top of the cars fall flat and see how close they could lie to the cars. The writer was one of them, and I think I rolled into a crack of the boards so the rebels could not see me, and my comrade D. W. Swihart, with eyes bulging out about the size of a hen egg told me that he could smell the bullets. Luckily no one was hit, but our escape was miraculous. After the enemy ceased firing, the colonel ordered Company A to remain there as guard, while the balance of the regiment were to proceed to Rome.[460] In the afternoon the train with the balance of the regiment returned, where Company A boarded it and we returned to our camp at Kingston. On the 22nd [21st] the regiment was drawn up in line when its commander in a brief but appropriate speech presented the regiment with a beautiful new silk flag that had been made expressly for the 26th Iowa by the patriotic ladies of Clinton County, Iowa. As the beautiful emblem was unfurled and swung to the breeze disclosing in letters of gold the names of the hard fought fields the regiment had taken part in, three times three rousing cheers were given in honor of our patriotic and fair friends in old Iowa.

We Leave Vienna and Start for the Front

437. A popular song among soldiers on both sides during the war.

438. The reference to "make Georgia howl" quotes a statement written by Maj. Gen. William T. Sherman in correspondence with his superior Lt. Gen. Ulysses S. Grant, on October 9, 1864. In this correspondence, Sherman was soliciting Grant's approval for his (Sherman's) projected march from Atlanta to the sea. "I can make the march," Sherman boldly proclaimed, "and make Georgia howl." Oake uses it somewhat out of context, but since many of the Union soldiers who participated in both the Atlanta campaign and later the March to the Sea viewed the separate events as simply the first and second phases of the same offensive, Oake's use of the phrase strikes the mood he wished to produce in this portion of the narrative. Sherman to Grant, October 9, 1864, *O.R.* I-39-III-162.

439. Osterhaus's, Morgan L. Smith's, and William Harrow's divisions of the Army of the Tennessee marched from their winter camps along the line of the Memphis & Charleston Railroad, in northern Alabama, via Stevenson and Bridgeport to Chattanooga, arriving there during the night of the May 5 and morning of May 6. The grand aggregate present in the three armies concentrated under Sherman in northern Georgia was 98,797 troops and 254 guns. Initially the army group consisted of all or parts of six infantry corps and a cavalry corps. The Army of the Cumberland, Maj. Gen. George H. Thomas commanding, consisted of the following corps: Oliver O. Howard's IV, John M. Palmer's XIV, Joseph Hooker's XX (consisting of what had been the XI and XII Corps, Army of the Potomac), and Washington L. Elliott's Cavalry Corps. The Army of the Tennessee, commanded by Maj. Gen. James B. McPherson, consisted of John A. Logan's XV, Grenville M. Dodge's XVI, and Frank P. Blair's XVII Corps, which joined the army group on June 8, making a total of seven infantry corps. Maj. Gen. John M. Schofield commanded the Army of the Ohio, consisting of his XXIII Corps and Stoneman's Cavalry (division). John E. Smith's 3rd Division, XV Corps, and initially Blair's XVII Corps, plus three additional cavalry brigades, were designated to guard the lines of communications. *O.R.* I-38-I-62–63, 89–117.

440. The Western & Atlantic Railroad linked Chattanooga southward roughly 110 miles to the important Deep South transportation hub at Atlanta, Georgia. It passed through Rocky Face Ridge at Buzzard's Roost or Mill Creek Gap.

441. The small town of Dalton, Georgia, lay three miles southeast of Mill Creek Gap at Rocky Face Ridge. The Tennessee & Georgia Railroad linked with the Western & Atlantic Railroad just north of the town. Two corps of the Confederate Army of Tennessee spent the winter of 1863–1864 quartered in and around Dalton, following the decisive defeat and withdrawal from Missionary Ridge in the previous November. *O.R.* I-38-III-612–15.

442. The heavily entrenched position was located north and west of Dalton, stretching for ten miles along the rugged slopes and plateaus of Rocky Face Ridge. It was centered at Buzzard's Roost, and ran west-east astride Crow Valley four miles north of the town. The prominent ridge sheltered the railroad and town from direct attack from the northwest and west. Cavalry outposts were deployed ten miles north beyond Varnell's Station, and picketed a line stretching twelve miles west from the southern tip of Rocky Face Ridge to Lafayette, Georgia. The Confederate Army of Tennessee was commanded by Gen. Joseph E. Johnston, who replaced Bragg when he asked to be relieved after the retreat from Chattanooga. Johnston's effective command numbered 49,911 troops and 144 guns. The army was divided into two infantry corps commanded by Lt. Gen. William J. Hardee and Lt. Gen. John Bell Hood, and a cavalry corps commanded by Maj. Gen. Joseph Wheeler. *O.R.* I-38-III-612–15, 676–77.

443. The 26th Iowa was now assigned to the 1st Brigade, Osterhaus's 1st Division, John A. Logan's XV Army Corps, Army of the Tennessee. Commanding the brigade was Brig. Gen. Charles Robert Woods, an experienced army officer from Ohio and graduate of West Point (1852). He was the younger brother of Col. William B. Woods, who commanded the 76th Ohio Infantry, now brigaded with the 26th Iowa, along with the 30th Iowa and 27th Missouri. Col. Milo Smith had resumed command of the regiment. At times during the next three months, Smith would be called upon to command the brigade in Woods's absence. In those instances, Lt. Col. Thomas G. Ferreby commanded the regiment. On August 22, 1864, Woods would assume command of the 3rd Division, XVII Corps, and Smith resumed supervision of the brigade. At the start of the campaign, the aggregate combat strength of the 1st Division was 4,410 men and 10 cannon; 1st Brigade, 1,428 troops; and 26th Iowa, 292 officers and men. *O.R.* I-38-I-103; *O.R.* I-38-III-124; Boatner, *Civil War Dictionary*, 947–48.

444. In an attempt to turn Johnston's left, the Army of the Tennessee, numbering roughly 24,500 troops, moved south on May 7, 1864, from Lee & Gordon's Mill, using Taylor's Ridge to screen the flank movement to Snake Creek Gap (or, more accurately, Pass), via Villanow. Meanwhile, Thomas's army demonstrated against Confederate positions at Tunnel Hill and Rocky Face, while Schofield probed Confederate outposts at Varnell's Station. The XVII Army Corps did not join the army until it was at Acworth on June 8, 1864. Long, *Civil War: Day by Day*, 495.

445. Sherman's orders to McPherson were to "move rapidly" and make a "bold attack" on the enemy's line of communications. McPherson was to drive through the gap, smash the railroad at Resaca, then retire on the gap. When Johnston retreated from Dalton to repair his broken communications, McPherson was to hammer him with his entire force, while Sherman advanced south with the main force and pounced on the retreating Confederates from the north. The Confederate force occupying the gap consisted of a single cavalry brigade. *O.R.* I-38-I-63.

446. A experienced cavalry officer with previous service in the East, Brig. Gen. Hugh Judson Kilpatrick (1836–1881), nicknamed "Kil-Cavalry," commanded the 3rd Division of Elliott's Cavalry Corps. He was a native of New Jersey and a graduate of the West Point class of 1861. He recovered from being wounded and returned to duty on July 23, 1864. He supervised Sherman's cavalry during the March to the Sea and the Carolinas. Ibid., 102; Warner, *Generals in Blue*, 266–67.

447. McPherson decided that the Confederate defenses fronting Camp Creek west of Resaca were too strong, and he pulled back west to Sugar Valley, at the south mouth of the gap, without having accomplished his critical objective of smashing the railroad. There were roughly 4,000 Confederate troops at Resaca. Besides the brigade of cavalry, an infantry brigade under Brig. Gen. James Cantey and advance elements of Lt. Gen. Leonidas Polk's corps (which was joining Johnston from Alabama) manned the entrenchments to protect the railroad bridge over the Oostanaula River south of town. Sherman was greatly disappointed in McPherson's failure to cut in behind Johnston, and it has been a source of historical dispute ever since. Long, *Civil War: Day by Day*, 497.

448. 1st Brigade commander Gen. Charles Woods reported that from May 9 into the afternoon of the 14th, "Our skirmishers were…constantly engaged with those of the enemy." *O.R.* I-38-III-142.

449. This advance forced Thomas Scott's Confederate brigade to abandon its exposed fortified outpost and retire on the main rebel line east of Camp Creek. The 26th Iowa lost one man killed and two wounded. *AGI*, 1865-II: 1165.

450. Oake is in error as to the location of the rest of Sherman's army group. On May 10, Hooker had been ordered to reinforce McPherson, followed by Thomas (minus Howard's corps left at Buzzard's Roost to defend the railroad) on May 11. On the 13th, Schofield's army also moved into the gap. Howard's IV Corps moved later, following Johnston's retreating force southward down the railroad. Thus, on the morning of the 14th, Thomas's, Hooker's, and Schofield's forces were on line at Resaca to battle the entrenched Confederate army. Johnston used the valuable time provided him by the cautious McPherson to concentrate his forces at Resaca and to prepare the battlefield. The fresh corps (also known as the Army of the Mississippi)—19,245 men and fifty guns, under Lt. Gen. Leonidas Polk, which had arrived from Alabama—occupied the Confederate left, their flank anchored on the river; Hardee's corps held the center; and Hood's corps deployed on the right, his line extending east to a hill near the Conasauga River. As Oake describes, Sherman advanced his armies against Johnston's defenses on May 14. Kennedy, ed., *Civil War Battlefield Guide*, Jay Luvaas, "Resaca Georgia," 329; *O.R.* I-38-IV-704.

451. This unfortunate comrade was William H. Swift. See note 433.

452. A native of Illinois and resident of De Witt, Thomas Jefferson Leeper was 21 when he enlisted August 7, 1862. He had been successively promoted seventh corporal, March 1, 1863; sixth corporal, May 1, 1863; and fifth sergeant, September 1, 1863. *Roster* 3: 1074.

453. Thomas J. G. Wilson was the youngest (age 22 upon enlistment) of three brothers in Co. D, the others being Daniel L. (age 35) and Enoch (age 27). Born in New York, Thomas enlisted in the 26th Iowa with his brothers on August 9, 1862. Thomas had earlier enlisted in Co. F, 4th Iowa Cavalry, October 17, 1861, but had been discharged for disability, February 21, 1862. Enoch was no longer serving in the regiment, having been discharged for disability, January 20, 1863, at St. Louis. Daniel, the oldest, was mustered out as third corporal of Co. D, June 6, 1865, at Washington, D.C. *Roster* 3: 1108; *AGI*, 1863-II: 537.

454. Horace S. Humeston was the younger brother of Sylvester Humeston (see note 266), who was killed in action at Arkansas Post. A native of New York, he was 22 and living in De Witt when he enlisted on August 8, 1862. He earned promotion to sixth corporal, April 1, 1865, and was mustered out in Washington, D.C., on June 6, 1865. *Roster* 3: 1066.

455. The XV Corps occupied the extreme right of Sherman's forces, on high ground overlooking the confluence of Camp Creek with the Oostanaula River. The attack, made at 5:30 P.M. on May 14 by Woods's and Smith's brigades of Osterhaus's division, advanced to within a half mile of Resaca and the all-important railroad bridge. The 26th Iowa was in the advance as skirmishers for Woods's brigade. Encouraged by thousands of "hurrahs" from their comrades in the corps, the two brigades crossed the creek under heavy fire and ascended the slope, establishing a lodgment before nightfall. By dawn, Logan's troops had secured the position, while Polk reformed the Confederate right overnight, taking position in the very outskirts of Resaca. *O.R.* I-38-III-141–43.

456. Oake's narrative mistakes the fighting on May 14 with that of May 15. Therefore, he does not relate any of the actual events of May 15, where the majority of the more active large-scale fighting occurred in front of Thomas and Hooker, against Hardee's and Hood's corps. McPherson, under orders from Sherman, held the position he had gained on the extreme right near the mouth of Camp Creek, and sent Thomas Sweeny's 2nd Division, Dodge's XVI Corps, supported by Kilpatrick's cavalry, to attempt again to lay a pontoon bridge across the river, downstream at Lay's Ferry, and establish a lodgment with his division south of Resaca. Sweeny had crossed the river on the previous afternoon, actually getting a portion of his command onto the south bank, but withdrew these men, based on fears they would be cut off by an advancing Confederate division. With Thomas and Hooker making attacks to the north on May 15,

Sweeny's troops, under intense fire from pickets posted across the river, successfully forced a crossing using a flat-boat. This vanguard drove back the Confederate pickets, and while the pontoon bridge was being laid, more men crossed to join the fight, pushing the Confederates back, and a strong bridgehead was established south of the river. *O.R.* I-38-III-395, 419, 447.

457. Since McPherson's artillery, having advanced to the high ground captured on May 14, easily commanded the railroad bridge over the Oostanaula, General Johnston ordered a pontoon bridge erected a mile upstream. Now that Sherman had forces across the river at Lay's Ferry, after dark on May 15 Johnston stole away, leaving only skirmishers in the trenches around Resaca. Polk's and Hardee's corps crossed on the rail- and wagon-road bridges, marching to Calhoun, while Hood crossed on the pontoon bridge and headed for Adairsville. The railroad bridge was torched, and the rear guard crossed the pontoon bridge, removed it, and continued south. Sherman followed, advancing on a broad front. The loss sustained by the 26th Iowa at Resaca was two killed and twenty-one wounded, four of whom died a few days later. *O.R.* I-38-III-761, 812; *Roster* 3: 1024.

458. Not finding favorable defensive ground at either Calhoun or Adairsville, Johnston continued his retrograde to Cassville. There he attempted to strike a counterblow on Sherman's separated corps. While the Confederates left under Hardee checked the advance of McPherson and Thomas from the west and north, Hood on the right (east) was to attack Schofield on May 19 as he moved his corps (Army of the Ohio) to attack Polk in the center. The effort failed, however, when Hood discovered a Union cavalry division on his own right. Hood moved east, instead of making the planned ambush on Schofield to the west, and engaged the Federal cavalry. Although the resulting combat involved a relatively small number of men, "it caused Hood to redeploy his corps so that the ambush of Schofield became impracticable." This misjudgment spoiled the opportunity, and the Confederates retreated roughly eleven miles, crossing the Etowah River on May 20, and continuing to the rugged Allatoona Mountains, south of the river, where they fortified a strong defensive position at Allatoona Pass, at the point where the Western & Atlantic Railroad penetrated the mountain range through a deep cut in the rock. William R. Scaife, *The Campaign for Atlanta* (Cartersville, GA: Civil War Publications, 1993), 39–48. Hereafter cited as the *Campaign For Atlanta*.

459. A spur line of the Western & Atlantic Railroad, linking the industrial community of Rome with Kingston.

460. The mission of the 26th Iowa, May 20–21, 1864, was to guard a railroad construction train to Rome. *AGI*, 1865-II: 1165; *Roster* 3: 1024.

Major General William T. Sherman.
With the formation of the Yazoo Expeditionary Force in December
1862 through the momentous maneuvers and battles fought by the
Army of the Tennessee over the next two and one-half years of war,
Sherman commanded—in succession—the corps, the army, and
the army group in which William Royal Oake and the 26th Iowa
was assigned. A BOY'S SERVICE WITH THE 76TH OHIO, BLUE ACORN PRESS

CHAPTER TWELVE

Following Hood and Battle of Dallas

＊ ———————————— ＊

On the morning of [May] 23rd, the right wing of the army were again pushed rapidly to the front, having been preceded by the left wing under General Hooker, who had met the enemy at Pumpkin Vine Creek [May 25], and after a short and bloody engagement had forced them to retire to a strong position in the mountains, near Altoona [Allatoona] their right resting on the railroad near that place, their left extending west about six [16] miles, a little beyond the little town of Dallas.[461]

To the latter point our army under General McPherson was being moved rapidly to the front. On the 26th the enemy's skirmishers were encountered but were easily driven back on their main line near Dallas.[462] When near that point we were halted in an open field, and ordered to lay down, the better to evade the fire of the enemy's guns. At this particular time quite a laughable incident occurred, at least laughable to parties not directly interested. As we lay in line a shot from one of the rebel guns struck the knapsack of one of our boys, as it was strapped upon his back, and strange to say although it scattered his blankets and personal effects promiscuously over the ground and rolled him quite a distance he was not seriously injured, but a more scared man I never saw.

We were again ordered to the front [on May 27th], and as we marched through the little town of Dallas, which consisted of about a dozen houses, I witnessed a scene that at the time made a deep impression on the minds of the troops, and it was another proof of the horrors of war. As we passed through the little town, while the balls were flying thick and occasionally a shell or solid shot would come screeching through the air, we halted near a private residence, when our attention was called to the peculiar actions of the lady of the house who was standing in the door yard near the entrance to the house, and who seemed perfectly oblivious to the turmoil and scenes of carnage that surrounded her. It took but a glance at those finely chiseled features, and the strange and wild look in her eyes for us to realize that the poor unfortunate was insane driven so, no doubt by the fearful scenes that surrounded her usually quiet home. At times she would throw her arms wildly about, while her beautiful black hair, reaching far below her waist, flew wildly about, then she would throw herself upon her knees in fervent prayer invoking the divine blessing to rest upon us. It was a pitiable sight, and one not easily forgotten, and it was quite a relief when we again moved forward.

As we moved hurriedly to the front, we formed our lines on a ridge in the heavy timber about 40 rods [220 yards] south [east] of the little town, the enemy occupying another ridge about 80 rods [440 yards] distant, but their exact position being hid from us by the dense underbrush. Midway between the enemy and us ran a deep ravine parallel with our lines. The ravine was quite deep, and on the enemy's side of the ravine our pickets had been posted for the night. [Throughout the next day, the regiment was held in reserve, 75 yards behind the main line which skirmished heavily with the enemy until the forenoon, and until 4 P.M., when the rebels advanced in force and attacked along the entire front, but were repulsed. Toward dark the 26th Iowa was sent forward to relieve the 12th Missouri, of the 3rd Brigade. The enemy did not attack again that night. The next morning, the regiment was relieved from the front line and assumed a position in reserve second line. That evening, the 26th Iowa again advanced to the front and entered the trenches, with part of the regiment thrown forward as skirmishers.] The writer being one that occupied a position on the picket line, on that long-to-be remembered night [of May 29. 1864]. With the exception of the pickets the troops had laid themselves down to sleep with cartridge boxes on, and guns where they could lay their hands upon them in a minutes notice.[463]

It was a beautiful, still May night. Not even breeze enough to stir the leaves, which hung listlessly upon the thick underbrush. Not a thing to indicate the coming battle, which the midnight hour was destined to burst forth in awful grandeur that would defy description by mortal agency.

Near the midnight hour a single shot was fired on our right. At that moment the ear of every picket was strained to if possible discover the cause of the shot. Soon the second shot was fired, and in an instant the firing continued along the line until it reached our front, when we could distinctly hear commands given by the enemy. In an instant we realized the fact that the enemy was making a midnight[464] attack upon us, with the intention of surprising us, but through the vigilance of the pickets they had been detected in time to give the main line ample time to prepare for the struggle.

Firing at the rapidly advancing lines of the enemy, we hastily started back towards (our comrades holding) our main lines, who by this time had been aroused and were already in line, and ready to receive rapidly advancing columns of the enemy. As we neared the ravine we could hear our officers cautioning the men to hold their fire until the pickets got safely within the lines, but the troops having been hurriedly awakened from their sound slumber, and hardly realizing their position, commenced to fire upon the advancing foe who by this time had already opened fire upon us. Thus the pickets were caught between the fire of both parties. The firing by this time was one continuous roll of musketry, while the sheet of flame that burst forth from our batteries lit up the heavens with a lurid glow, the light of which enabled us as we lay in the ravine to see the struggling mass of slowly advancing enemy, as with the demoniac yells they frantically attempted to face the storm of lead, and iron that was being hurled into their fast thinning ranks.

As we lay in our partially sheltered position in the ravine within a few rods of the advancing enemy our lot was an unenviable one. To attempt to gain our lines between the two lines of fire was sure death. To remain in our position seemed like inevitable capture, which to one that had already been in the Hell Holes of the South death was preferable. Now the enemy waiver, as with lightening like rapidity the double charges of grape pierce their decimated ranks. Our infantry seeing them waver pour into them a murderous fire. Again they waiver, and finally their bleeding ranks gave way, leaving us in possession of the field. Thus ended the rebel General Pat Cleburne's*

[William B. Bate's] famous midnight charge on the 15th Army Corps at Dallas, May 27th [29th], 1864. The battle was over, and the rattle of musketry and roar of artillery was followed by a stillness that was oppressive, broken only by the groans of the wounded and dying enemy, while the dense clouds of smoke settled like a funeral pall over the hard fought field.[465]

It was then that another picket and the writer arose and started to go into our own lines. Our comrades supposing that all the pickets that did not succeed in returning to the lines before the battle were surely dead or captured by the enemy. After walking a few yards we halted, and called 26th Iowa, and received a response, when we told them not to fire, as we were some of the pickets. We then hurriedly entered our lines, and were heartily received by our comrades, who had given us up as dead, thinking it impossible for troops to live between the fire of both lines of battle.

One incident in connection with this battle I well remember Wm. Jackson [Otis Parks][466] a member of Company H was one of the pickets on that memorable night, and when we were attacked [he] endeavored to reach our lines, and the next morning his dead body was found a short distance in front of our lines. He had bravely striven to reach our lines, and when so near had fallen undoubtedly killed by our own men.[467] Jackson [Parks] was a fine soldier and was liked by the entire regiment. As we tenderly raised his cold and lifeless form and carried it inside our lines the tearful eyes and stern features of that armed band of veterans spoke plainer than words their feelings. To thus lose a beloved comrade, one with whom we had touched elbows with in many a hard fought field, to be thus cut off in the flush and vigor of early manhood, and undoubtedly by our own guns made it doubly sad.

Following Hood and Battle of Dallas

461. Sherman had decided not to attack the Allatoona fortifications, and instead moved to turn Johnston's left again, by leaving the railroad and moving south, west of the mountain range, hoping to reach Marietta or the Chattahoochee River in Johnston's rear. Joe Wheeler's cavalry quickly detected the Federal movement, and, before the end of the day (May 23), Johnston began a countermove. Hood remained at Allatoona, while Hardee moved eight miles west toward Dallas, and Polk tramped to the vicinity of Lost Mountain east of Dallas, midway between the other corps and from where he could rapidly move forward to support either. The hard-fought action on May 25, which resulted in heavy casualties but ended with both forces digging in, became known as the battle of New Hope Church. It pitted Hooker's XX Corps against Hood, who had been shifted southwest from Allatoona. Scaife, *The Campaign for Atlanta*, 49–51.

462. McPherson approached Dallas from the west, moving southeast from Van Wert. The Confederates entrenched on a line roughly one mile east of Dallas, their left extending one and one-half miles southeast of the town. The troops initially confronting McPherson were Maj. Gen. William B. Bate's division of Gen. William J. Hardee's corps, supported later on their right by Maj. Gen. W. H. T. Walker's division, and then Maj. Gen. Benjamin F. Cheatham's division. The irregular Confederate front extended southwest to northeast. Beyond Cheatham's left, Hood's corps held their two-mile front, which extended from Elsberry Mountain past New Hope Church. One mile east of the church, Maj. Gen. Patrick R. Cleburne's division (Hardee's corps) anchored the right flank of this front at Pickett's Mill, roughly six miles northeast of Dallas. His division, supported by Maj. Gen. Thomas C. Hindman (left), thwarted an attack by Maj. Gen. Oliver O. Howard's IV Corps, Thomas's Army of the Cumberland, at Pickett's Mill on May 27. Scaife, *The Campaign for Atlanta*, 49–55.

463. New material has been added to create the proper context for the narrative. Oake mistakenly cited the night action as having occurred on May 27, instead of May 29, and his chronology for these events does not agree with reports written by superiors closer to the fighting in 1864. *O.R.* I-38-III-129–31,145–46; *Roster 3*: 1024.

464. Night assaults during the Civil War were rare, and when attempted, routinely hazardous and chaotic. However, on the evening of May 29, Johnston decided to press Sherman to prevent or delay his slipping away to the east. Johnston correctly suspected Sherman was attempting to redeploy and shift his army back to the railroad, but he needed better intelligence on the disposition of the Federal forces. Thus, he had ordered Hardee to make the May 28 combat reconnaissance in force, the movement that McPherson and his men interpreted as a vigorous attack at Dallas, and again hit the Federal center (Thomas) and right (McPherson) in a series of furious night attacks throughout the evening on May 29 and early morning of the 30th. Some Union organizations reported as many as seven or eight separate assaults. These attacks, although not inflicting great harm on the Federals, did effectively block all attempts to execute Sherman's instructions for an orderly withdrawal. McPherson was not able to pull free until June 1. *O.R.* I-38-I-145; *O.R.* I-38-III-131; Scaife, *The Campaign for Atlanta*, 56–59.

465. The combat waged within the impenetrable jungle located around New Hope Church, Pickett's Mill, and Dallas involved more than 85,000 Federals and 70,000 Confederates. Losses sustained for the period May 25–31 are difficult to ascertain, primarily because no one was keeping a daily tally and reports filed at later dates tended to total the casualty figures over extended periods of time. However, it appears that the U.S. forces suffered roughly 2,645 casualties for the week, while the Confederate States forces lost perhaps 1,800 to 2,300 men killed, wounded, and captured. The 26th Iowa entered the fighting on May 26 with a reported 200 men present for duty. Records indicate the regiment lost only 3 men, 1 killed by friendly fire, 1 slightly wounded in the leg (see note 401), and another reported missing, presumed killed but later listed as a prisoner of war. Woods's 1st Brigade, with roughly 1,200 men present, sustained only 11 casualties during the same period: 1 man killed, 1 officer and 8 men wounded, and 1 man missing. The terrain and heavy vegetation appear to have provided sufficient cover for the men. The low casualty rate serves as testimony that the regiment, when deployed on the front line, manned the hastily constructed field fortifications, unless they were deployed as skirmishers on night picket duty. Even then, the pickets probably prepared squad pits to provide suitable protection. *Roster* 3: 1024; *O.R.* I-38-III-144, 146; Kennedy, ed., *Civil War Battlefield Guide*, Jay Luvaas, "New Hope Church, Pickett's Mill, and Dallas Georgia," 335.

466. The editor is not sure why Oake makes this mistake in identification, for no record of a William Jackson exists among the muster roll of the 26th Iowa. An investigation of *Roster* located only three members of the regiment being reported as casualties during this period, specifically, "On the 23d the regiment with its brigade again advanced and arrived in front of the enemy's works at Dallas, Ga., on the 26th. On the night of May 29th, the regiment lost one man mortally wounded and one missing, supposed to have been killed in repulsing an attack of the enemy." In his report of the fighting at Dallas, Brig. Gen. Charles R. Woods, commanding the brigade to which the 26th Iowa was assigned, wrote that during the night action of May 29, "One man of the pickets of the Twenty-sixth Iowa Volunteers was wounded—mortally, I fear—*by our own fire* [italics added], and 1 man of the Seventy-sixth Ohio Volunteers pickets was missing." The soldier mortally wounded by fratricide (friendly fire) on May 29 was Pvt. Otis Parks of Co. H. Parks, who had been born in New York, was residing in De Witt and 19 when he enlisted on August 9, 1862. He died from his wound the day after the night action (May 30). In addition to Parks, Pvt. Christe Granshoff (alternate spelling is Graushoff), Co. I, was captured May 29, 1864, at Dallas, Georgia. Granshoff, born in Germany, lived in Wheatland when he enlisted on August 14, 1862, at the age of 18. Confined to Andersonville Prison, in Georgia, he died there July 21, 1864, and is buried in the National Cemetery. *O.R.* I-38-III-146; *Roster* 3: 1024, 1059, 1088.

467. Common to virtually every tactical combat situation is the problem of fratricide, or friendly fire—mistakenly firing upon fellow military personnel. Thousands of soldiers—National and Confederate—experienced some of the most tragic incidences of "fire in the rear" carnage in American military history. At times, entire regiments and brigades were victimized by the inherent chaos and confusion of close-order battle, when their organizations came under direct fire delivered by fellow army units. As a result of one such large-scale incident in Tennessee, on the morning of April 6, 1862, and during the first day of the battle at Shiloh, elements of five Confederate brigades unknowingly became embroiled in deadly serious fratricidal combat, killing or wounding perhaps as many as 200 of their own soldiers in a matter of a few minutes. David W. Reed, *The Battle of Shiloh and the Organizations Engaged* (Washington, 1902), 81; *O.R.* I-10-I-430, 489.

CHAPTER THIRTEEN

Burying the Dead and a Brief Rest

The 28th was spent in burying the dead, and caring for the wounded. Now that it was light we could see the effects of the night's conflict, as from our position we could plainly see the position of the enemy where they were first met by that storm of lead. The heavy growth of underbrush had been cut down as grass before the sickle, while among the tangled debris could be found scores of the brave fellows that had so vainly striven to face the cyclone of lead. Now we would find a poor unfortunate that had been struck with the deadly grape or shell, and bore no resemblance to a human being. Others with pallid upturned faces, eyeballs almost starting from their sockets, and terribly distorted features, told plainly of their awful suffering as the last spark of life went out. As we would recognize the form of some loved comrade, who but a few hours before had been in the flush of early manhood we would carefully consign him to his last resting place, while sad thoughts would force themselves upon us as with tearful eyes we would look back upon the pleasant past, and wonder if such would be our fate.

On the 29th [June 1st], we were ordered to the left about three miles, and while lying in that position, occurred the following incident. I was detailed, while there, as a picket. Our picket lines were about seventy-five yards from the enemies, and about forty rods in advance of our main line. The country was heavily wooded making it difficult to determine the exact

On the skirmish line.
Throughout three years of military service, many of William Royal Oake's combat experiences included duty on the skirmish line, as he found himself and his regiment routinely deployed in dispersed skirmish order either in front, or on the flanks, of the general line of advance on numerous battlefields. BATTLES AND LEADERS OF THE CIVIL WAR

position of the rebel lines, but we were convinced we were not far in the rear of their picket line. I had been on post about half an hour, sitting down, my back resting against an old dead tree, listening attentively, and straining every nerve to detect if possible the ever alert Johnnies. Now every one that has been in the south are aware that in some sections the swifts[468] are very numerous. They are the lizard family, but unlike that sluggish reptile in one particular, (to wit) whereas the lizard is very slow in its motion, the swift moves with lightening like rapidity, and while in motion in the sunlight assumes the various colors of the rainbow. As I sat by the tree I detected in the leaves something coming directly toward me, now they are a great thing to frequent old hollow trees and will run up a standing tree like a flash. In a moment I discovered the object approaching to be a swift, but before I could regain a standing position it ran up the leg of my pantaloons, undoubtedly taking them for a hollow log. In an instant I was on my feet, and unbuttoning my suspenders was outside of my unmentionables in the twinkling of an eye. The swift also vacated them, and ran up the tree by which I had been sitting. While this drama had been taking place I paid no attention to the rebels who luckily for me failed to see me, while in the midst of my performance, else I might have received a gentle reminder in the shape of a minie ball. Kind readers if there are any that envied me that position I ask them to place themselves in a similar position on the ground, and let a swift toad or snake invade the sacred precincts of their pantaloons, and then to report as to the peculiar sensations they might experience.

Upon being relieved from picket, and returning to camp I placed my musket against a tree, and taking my coffee pot procured some water to make coffee, and on returning to the company was in the act of placing it on the fire with my back towards the enemy, while behind me and not three feet distant stood a small tree not over six inches in diameter. As I stooped to place the coffee pot on the fire a minie ball fired by the enemy buried itself in the tree at my back. Had it deviated an inch or so from its course I perhaps would not have penned this article. I mention this incident to show how small a thing sometimes may change the destiny of mankind.

After remaining in this position a few days we discovered that the enemy had fallen back to a strong position on Kenesaw [Kennesaw] Mountain, about 12 miles south of our present position.[469] On June 5th, we moved about 6 [10] miles to the left to the little town of Ackworth [Acworth], situated on the railroad about 12 [8] miles north of Kennesaw Mountain. We remained here during the 6th, the time being spent by the boys in washing their clothes, and writing letters to friends at home, who although so far away were undoubtedly anxious to hear from their friends at the front.

Well does the writer remember what a clamor there would be when the mail arrived in camp, how we would crowd around the orderly as he called the names of those for whom there were letters. Those not receiving any would have a face as long as a church deacon.

On June 7th we again headed toward the enemy who were strongly fortified on the lofty heights of Kennesaw, which was bristling with fortifications, and armed men towering hundreds of feet above the surrounding plain.[470] On arriving at Big Shanty, within six [three] miles of Kennesaw, we were halted while the advance [forces] were busily engaged with the enemy that were strongly entrenched in the timbered valley about one mile in our front. How distinctly I remember one incident of that brief halt. Just to the right, and a little in advance of our regiment the ambulance corps of the division had halted, while the employees had erected quite a long table to be used by the surgeons in performing operations upon the wounded. In the

Burying the Dead and a Brief Rest

meantime the hospital stewards were busily engaged in getting ready the surgical instruments used on such occasions, while the surgeons were standing with sleeves rolled up ready to perform their unpleasant duty. It was indeed a sight that would blanch the cheek and unnerve the strongest heart. Soon mounted aids, and orderlies are seen riding in every direction, and the familiar, "Fall In," call of the bugle is heard. We are soon in line, and the call for skirmishers is heard, and we are soon picking our way through the dense growth of young timber, and the deadly shells warn us that we are treading on dangerous ground. We press steadily forward until we reach the edge of an open field, when we were ordered to halt and reform our lines. Directly in front of us and extending on either side for quite a distance, was an open field, varying in width from 80 rods to half a mile, being skirted on the south by a dense growth of young timber, in which the enemy were posted while their skirmishers occupied a line of pits in the open field about 100 yards in their front.[471]

After reforming our lines we had orders to remain in that position for the present. We remained in that position for three days sharp skirmishing taking place between the opposing lines. On the 14th, our batteries kept up a sharp fire on the enemy that were plainly visible on Pine Mountain, about 600 yards distant, and the next day we learned from prisoners, that during the cannonading the day previous the rebel General (Leonidas) Polk had been killed a cannon ball striking him squarely in the breast.[472]

On the morning of the 15th a general advance of the skirmish line was ordered. Our batteries some little time before the advance of the line had opened a brisk fire upon the enemy's skirmish pits compelling the occupants to lay low. Promptly at the command our lines moved forward to cross the open field, and succeeded in getting half way over before we were discovered by the enemy who now opened upon us a sharp fire of musketry, which only tended to increase our speed, and in spite of the shower of bullets we advanced upon the enemy who hastily left their rifle pits, and fell back into the dense growth of young timber, about seventy-five yards in their rear leaving us in possession of their line of skirmish pits, one of which a 30th Iowa man, my comrade D. W. Swihart, and the writer took possession of. The pit was simply a pile of rails laid up about three feet in height with dirt thrown in front of it.[473] The end of the rails on the right, [were] resting against an old dead tree about fourteen inches in diameter. While Swihart and the other soldier lay down behind the tree peering over the top of the pit watching to get a shot at some Johnnies, the writer stood up behind the tree. Soon I saw a rebel step out from behind a tree within about seventy-five yards and within plain view. He was looking off to my left, and had not seen me. Taking deliberate aim along side of the tree I pulled the trigger, but to my chagrin the gun missed fire. I quickly reached for my cap box and was in the act of putting on a fresh cap, when the rebel, having heard my cap snap, on discovering me, fired, the ball striking the tree about breast high, fortunately missing me. Had I taken the precaution to step behind the tree when my gun missed fire, he would not have seen me, but being a little excited I remained in plain view taking eyes off the rebel at the same time. It was a close call and one I never forgot.[474]

Burying the Dead and a Brief Rest

468. A genus of fast-running lizards. *Webster's Dictionary, 1000.*

469. The regiment, with its brigade, division, and army, encamped at New Hope Church. *O.R.* I-38-III-131, 146.

470. On June 4, Johnston pulled his troops back from the New Hope Church–to–Dallas line, retiring farther east to another line of prepared fortifications. These new works extended roughly ten miles from Lost Mountain through Pine Mountain to Brushy Mountain (one mile north of Kennesaw Mountain), and shielded Marietta and the railroad. McPherson's army now occupied the left of Sherman's front, with Thomas, supported by Hooker, in the center, and Schofield on the left. Scaife, *The Campaign for Atlanta*, 59–62.

471. McPherson advanced south, parallel with the railroad, through Big Shanty toward Marietta. Osterhaus's division was posted to the right of the Marietta road, north of Brushy Mountain. Dennis Kelly, *Kennesaw Mountain and the Atlanta Campaign* (Atlanta: Kennesaw Mountain Historical Assoc., Inc., 1990), 21. Hereafter cited as *Kennesaw Mountain.*

472. Sherman made a personal reconnaissance of the Pine Mountain area that day, to determine how best to dislodge Johnston without directly attacking the fortifications on the mountain, which was located one mile in advance, or salient, of the main Confederate line. When Sherman spotted a group of Confederate officers on the mountain he commented, "How saucy they are." He then ordered artillery volleys fired at the group, which included Generals Johnston, Hardee, and Polk. A shell from the second salvo crashed through Polk's chest, killing him instantly. That night Johnston abandoned Pine Mountain. One embittered Confederate, from William Bate's division, before departing the mountain left a personal message: "You damned Yankee sons of bitches has killed our old Gen. Polk." Kelly, *Kennesaw Mountain*, 22.

473. A squad or skirmish pit, as Oake calls it, was more commonly referred to as a rifle pit: a short, shallow trench large enough to provide protection for a single soldier or upwards to a squad (ten to twenty-five men).

474. McPherson's men encountered Confederate outposts a mile beyond Big Shanty, and drove them from successive positions to the base of Brushy Mountain, where Brig. Gen. William Harrow's 4th Division of XV Corps swept around their flank and captured 150 prisoners. Kelly, *Kennesaw Mountain*, 23.

CHAPTER FOURTEEN

A Warm Place on the Skirmish Line and the Wounding of an Esteemed Comrade

few moments after my narrow escape, as my old comrade Swihart was in
the act of firing at the enemy a bullet pierced the top of his hat cutting off
a lock of his hair. As he rolled over, and rubbed the top of his head he
exclaimed, "Injun, I could smell that bullet." Just to our right and a little in
advance and about fifty yards from our pit was another rebel pit that had
not been occupied by our men when the enemy fell back. It was about forty
feet in advance of our pit, and the one on its right.

Shortly after Swihart's narrow escape, five of the enemy were seen by us
to emerge from the timber in our front and with their muskets ran rapidly
to the aforesaid pit, on our right, which from its peculiar position gave them
complete control of our pit. I then suggested to my comrades the importance of keeping a sharp watch on our new neighbors, and while they were
giving their attention to the enemy in front I would keep a sharp lookout on
the five rebs in the pit on our right. There being five of them, and only three
of us the advantage was decidedly in their favor. If they should look over the
top of their pit we would be in plain view of them. In order to get a shot at
us they would have to raise their heads above the pit, and at that short range,
woe be to the head that showed itself above the pit. For a short time the
enemy in the timber directly in our front made it quite lively for us, but saw
no move from our five neighbors in the pit on our right. I then told my

comrades that under no consideration must we all fire at once, because if we did the rebels could kill us with impunity. Knowing as they did how many there were of us in the pit, if our guns were all empty at one time it would be all up with us.

Still there was no move from our five rebels on the right. I then told my two comrades to keep their guns loaded as I would see if I could wake them up by cutting the dirt from the top of their pit. Taking deliberate aim I fired and the dust flew from the top of their pit. In a few seconds I loaded my gun, but no reply came in answer to my shot. In an instant we understood the situation: they wanted to surrender. We at once called to them, "Come in." At that all five jumped up, and in a stooping position ran within our lines amidst a shower of bullets fired at them, by their one-time friends, on seeing them desert.

Now we fully understood why they had been so quiet. They came to that pit with the intention of deserting at the first opportunity. That accounted for them not firing on us. Having gotten rid of what at the time we considered dangerous neighbors, we now paid closer attention to the enemy in our front, who at the same time, made it uncomfortably warm for us. While in this position I am afraid my mind reverted back to my boyhood days. Thinking what a bad boy I had been at times, when instead of being at Sunday School, I with a lot of other boys equally as bad had been robbing some man's melon patch. Soon the shadows of night began to settle over the valley, and we anxiously looked for a respite from the strain that had been upon us for several hours, and get a cup of good coffee. As the evening shades settle in inky darkness we could look along the lines, and see the bright flashes of hundreds of muskets, which in the gloom resembled the myriads of lightening bugs that are so common in our northern country.

In short time the firing had ceased with the exception of an occasional shot, and as the main line of our troops had moved up we were soon busy in preparing something for the inner man. After satisfying our hunger we were soon busily engaged in building a line of rifle pits, and upon completing the same we wrapped ourselves in our ponchos and lay down on Mother Earth to take a needed rest.

On the next morning, (June 16th), at the first sign of coming day the troops were up, engaged in getting breakfast, and when at last the light appeared as the sun arose in a cloudless sky, more beautiful a June morning could not be wished for. Thus far not a shot had been fired, and not a thing to indicate that one hundred thousand men lay in that beautiful valley armed with the most improved weapons of that time, and that at any moment a storm might break upon us that would deluge that lovely valley in blood and cause mourning in the homes of thousands throughout our fair land. An incident of that June morning I will relate. It is so deeply impressed upon my memory that death only can efface it. L. Miller one of

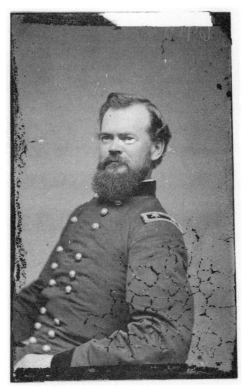

Major General James B. McPherson.
Favored by his seniors, Grant and Sherman,
McPherson commanded the Army of the
Tennessee during the spring/summer 1864 offen-
sive in north Georgia. He was killed in action on
July 22, 1864, by Confederate skirmishers during
the battle of Atlanta. NATIONAL ARCHIVES

A Warm Place on the Skirmish Line and
the Wounding of an Esteemed Comrade

the comrades in Libby with the writer, and with whom I was at the time bunking, Peter J. Potter,[475] and the writer were standing outside of the ditch behind the breast works, not thinking about the proximity of the rebels. We had been standing there a few moments, when directly in front of us the crack of a musket was heard, and at the same moment I heard the dull thug of the deadly missile, which told me as plainly as words that it had found a resting place in the body of one of my comrades. Turning quickly I saw comrade Miller clasp his right breast, and at the same time saw a piece of his blouse drop from his back, with a look upon his face, that I shall never forget he exclaimed, "Oake and Potter, I am shot help me." In an instant we were at his side, and gently assisted him to an ambulance standing a little in the rear, which conveyed him to the division hospital. Poor fellow although the ball had struck him squarely in the right breast and passed clear through him it did not knock him down. As the ambulance drove away we could not suppress the tears knowing that to him death was inevitable in a short time. It was with saddened hearts we returned to our command, having been with him on many a hard fought field, and confined with him in the prisons of the South, there existed between us an attachment that only but those placed in like circumstances could appreciate.

When the writer was hit by a bullet at Lookout Mountain in 1863, Miller forgetful of all danger to himself, and amidst a shower of lead, sprang to my assistance, his looks told as plainly as words his solicitance [sic] for my welfare.

Twice during our stay in this position did I apply to the colonel of the regiment for permission to go to the division hospital to see my wounded comrade only to be refused. The colonel said that the orders were that no man should be absent from his command, as we did not know what moment an engagement might take place, and owing to the depleted condition of the army through sickness, and those killed and wounded in battle it was imperative that every able bodied soldier be present for duty.

The third time I applied I again met with the same argument. I looked the colonel in the eye, and replied, "Colonel ever since my connection with the regiment I have always been present for duty, except when I was a prisoner in the hands of the enemy. As you are well aware, Miller and I have been very intimate, (since) we were captured and confined together in rebel prisons in the South, and for the third time (you) deny me a pass to see the poor fellow before he dies. Pass or no Pass, Colonel. I will go back and see Miller today." The colonel replied, "Sir, did I understand you to say that you would defy my authority and absent yourself from your command without my permission." I replied, "That is what I said Colonel." "Then sir," he said as his eyes twinkled with good humor, "I guess I had better give you a pass," and he forthwith wrote the desired pass. The hospital was at Big Shanty about three miles in the rear and quite a number of the wounded, Miller among the rest, were occupying some old empty buildings that were at that place. On arriving at the hospital about the first one I saw on entering was Miller, lying on a cot facing the door. As he recognized me with a smile he extended his hand to shake hands with me, and made inquiries about the boys of Company A. Although he was in good spirits and felt confident that he would pull through, I could plainly see that death would soon claim him. I stayed with him until near sunset, and telling him I would have to leave him, he grasped my hand and said, "Royal, I believe I shall get well, and if I do the rebs shall pay for this." Then with a strong voice he said, "Take good care of yourself, and give my love to all the boys, I am so glad you came to see me, good bye." Turning hastily away to conceal the falling tears I returned to camp. Poor fellow he lingered along until the morning of July the 3rd, when realizing that death was near bid his attendants good bye, and sending his love to Company A, peacefully as a child passed away, and tender hands consigned him to his resting place in the lonely pass of Allatoona.[476]

The following October, while Sherman's army was following back in pursuit of [General John Bell] Hood's army,[477] we marched near the place my comrade was buried, knowing the spot, which was distant from the road about 100 yards, in the stillness of the night it being about 8 P.M. I quietly left the ranks, and was soon alongside of the little mound that marked his resting place, where I spent several minutes, and in spite of all I could do the tears came to my eyes as visions of the happy past forced themselves upon me. Taking a last fond look at the little mound I quietly left what was to me a sacred spot.[478]

A Warm Place on the Skirmish Line and
the Wounding of an Esteemed Comrade

A Warm Place on the Skirmish Line and the Wounding of an Esteemed Comrade

❖ ———————————————— ❖

475. Peter J. Potter. See note 403.

476. See note 318. Soon after their farewell meeting, Miller was relocated to Boston Iron Works, north of Allatoona Pass, then being utilized as a Union medical station, and, as Oake accurately states, died there on July 3, 1864.

477. Hood attempted to cut Sherman's supply and communication line, the Western & Atlantic Railroad, by attacking the Federal garrison stationed at Allatoona Pass, on October 5, 1864. After an artillery bombardment, the Confederates asked for surrender. The Union commander, Brig. Gen. John M. Corse, refused. The Confederates, commanded by Maj. Gen. Samuel French, attacked and gained some ground, but failed to seize the pass. The casualties were high. Corse suffered 706 men killed, wounded, and missing out of 2,000; while the Confederates lost 799 men. Long, *Civil War Day by Day*, 579.

478. Oake would have visited the grave on the night of October 10, 1864, while the XV Corps bivouacked at Allatoona. *AGI*, 1865-II: 1167.

CHAPTER FIFTEEN

Incident of Picket Duty, Retreat of the Enemy, and a Grand Electrical Storm

Shortly after the wounding of comrade, Miller, the rebel skirmishers were forced back a short distance and our pickets were posted in the thick young timber in advance of our main line.[479] On the night of June 20th [probably the 21st], the writer was one of the picket detail and as the shadows of twilight were falling we relieved the pickets then on duty. During the day it had rained quite hard, and at night had settled into a drizzling rain, making it very uncomfortable lying on the wet ground beneath the wet foliage of the dense growth of young timber.[480]

Our picket line consisted of a continuous line of men about twenty feet apart, who as a rule would stand on post two hours, and off four hours. Our reserve pickets were posted in the rear of the outposts, about thirty yards where the relieved pickets could sleep until called to take their turn on post. Upon relieving the old pickets, the writer was one of the first to be placed as vidette, and upon taking my position with my gum poncho[481] around me I seated myself by a small tree, and tried to make myself as comfortable as possible while I would strain my eyes trying to penetrate the inky darkness of that gloomy night. I had been on post about one hour, when, in the oppressive stillness, I thought I heard a slight noise in front of me. Not wishing to make any noise I did not mention the fact to the pickets on the right and left of me who were distant only about twenty feet.

I redoubled my vigilance, and again heard the cracking of brush, and a moment later heard voices directly in front of me, which from the sound seemed to be advancing. Knowing that the pickets of the enemy were at least fifty feet in advance of us, I could not account for the voices, except on the grounds that they were again trying to post their pickets further in advance, not knowing our exact position. As I lay in suspense waiting further developments, I thought the beatings of my heart could surely be heard by the enemy. Again I heard the voices, which I was not convinced could not be distant over fifty feet in front of me, but owing to the darkness, and heavy growth of underbrush it was impossible for the eyes to penetrate the gloom.

Once more the voices were heard, and shots in rapid succession were fired from our reserve picket post, and the bullets whistled uncomfortably close as they passed over my head. For an instant retreating footsteps were heard, then all was quiet. To say that our pickets were thoroughly disgusted at the actions of the reserve pickets in firing over us at their fancied danger, but faintly expresses our feelings, and disgust, at such a gross violation of all military discipline, and it certainly showed timid ness or cowardice on the part of the officer in command of the reserve pickets. The safety of an army when in an enemy's country depends altogether on the vigilance of its pickets, and under no circumstances should those in reserve fire, until the videttes have first given the alarm. The only excuse offered by our bold officer of the reserve picket was that he thought the pickets were asleep on their posts. Had the reserve held their fire they would have advanced directly on our line, and would have been killed or captured without a doubt. For lying as we were, perfectly still, and motionless, they could not see us, whereas they being in motion we could easily have seen them when they had gotten within the length of a gun from us. I will leave it to my readers to judge what the result would have been.

After our little scare everything was quiet until we were relieved the next day. We occupied our position here for several days, part of the time the skirmishing between the opposing forces assuming the proportions of a battle. One morning we discovered that during the night the enemy had fallen back to their main position on the lofty heights of Kennesaw Mountain, whose summit towered hundreds of feet above the surrounding heavily wooded plain, while its crests and slopes teemed with armed hosts.[482]

In a few days [night of June 26] we moved to the right about four miles,[483] and on the morning of June 27th was fought the bloody battle of Kennesaw, in which the part of our army [Sherman's army group] that fought the battle were repulsed, losing in killed and wounded 2000 men,[484] among the killed was [Brigadier] General [Charles G.] Harker.[485] The attack on that strongly fortified position showed conclusively that to carry that strong position by storm would cost an enormous sacrifice of life, and General Sherman wisely concluded to accomplish by strategy what so far he had failed to accomplish by a direct assault. Having an advantage in number of men we gradually extended our lines until July the 3rd when the Confederate commander saw that his left flank and line of communication was threatened wisely decided to evacuate his position.[486]

I will here give an incident or two of the battle of Kennesaw of June 27th, 1864. Our division, the 1st of the 15th Corp, was occupying a strong line of works on the right facing Kennesaw. About half a mile from the base of the mountain, and between our lines and the base of the mountain, was a small creek, and a strip of woods about 50 rods [275 yards] in width, and from which to the base of the mountain was an open piece of ground about thirty rods [165 yards] wide. In the rear of our lines of works was an open field about forty rods [220 yards] wide. As we sat in the trenches that beautiful June morning, we all at once heard the enemy's artillery, all along the top of the mountain, open fire and the screeching of the shells over our heads, and hastily looking up saw a line of battle of our men coming over the open field in our rear, and were going right over our works to attack the rebels on the mountain. I will never forget that grand sight as with a fine alignment and Old Glory they sprang over our works, and went to the front. Just as they went over our works one fine looking soldier fell upon the writer's blanket, and upon which, with a few others, the writer had been playing cards, when we first saw them coming. Going to the poor fellow we raised him up, and as he asked for water we held a canteen to his lips, but the poor fellow could not drink and with the word "Mother" on his lips he gave a shudder, and all was over. The fatal bullet had struck him right in the throat. In the meantime those brave fellows had charged across the strip of timber in our front, and nearly to the base of the mountain, only to be cut to pieces, as no troops in the world could face that storm of lead, and live.

At intervals, during the day the wounded kept coming back to our works. Some alone others were helped by those only slightly wounded. I remember one fine looking lieutenant came in, and the writer helped him over the works. He had lost his hat and sword, and one of his thumbs was shot off, and he was badly wounded in the thigh. As I helped him into the pits, and unbuckled his belt a piece of thumb dropped from between his belt and his body, where it had been driven by the bullet. As I showed it to him he smiled and said he guessed he had no use for it. The stretcher bearers then took him to the rear, and as he moved I could hear the blood squash in his high military boots from the wound in his thigh.

That night the writer was again on picket post on the edge of the woods about 40 rods [220 yards] from the base of Kennesaw, and on ground that had been fought over during the day, the dead and some of the wounded were still lying as they fell. Between our picket post, and the enemy was an open field, and as it was a beautiful moonlight night and one could see almost as well as in the day time objects a hundred yards away we had dug pits for the pickets, a hole about ten foot in length and about three feet in width, and depth, throwing the dirt out in front, and at the ends making a good shelter as we kept a sharp lookout over the top. There were four others in one pit with the writer: Swihart of Company A, J. Durney[487] of D, and Michael [actually Dennis] Kelly[488] of D, the other's name I have forgotten. We had been on duty perhaps one hour. The writer and my comrade were lying out on the back side of the pit on our sides. Everything was quiet. The other three were in the pit. As we lay there our eyes closed, we heard a single shot fired off to our right, perhaps a mile away. Then another shot was fired, and then quite a volley. Still we lay in our position, and the firing on the right seemed to increase. All at once Durney of Company D fired off his gun, and yelled, "Swihart and Oake, wake up d—m your souls. Here they come ten thousand of them." In an instant we slid into the pit, and were glancing over the top of it. There were no rebels in sight, everything was quiet, and soon the firing on the right ceased, and all was again quiet along the lines. After giving Durney a piece of our minds we again lay down. The firing on the right was undoubtedly caused by some picket half scared firing off his gun at some imaginary object, thus causing false alarm.

Our main line [of] works at Kennesaw were across an open field, and in a very much exposed position, not only being exposed from the enemy directly in our front on Kennesaw, but from a flank fire on our right, and about every hundred feet of our lines we had built and barricaded about twenty feet in length running at right angles from the main line. This was done to protect us from the enemy's flank fire.[489] We had dug the ditch behind our works about ten feet wide, and about two and a half foot deep, using the dirt taken there from in building our lines. In cooking our meals here we would build a little fire on the bank at the back part of the wide ditch, behind the works, and stand in the ditch. Our heads and shoulders could then be seen by the enemy who were posted on the mountain.

One day I was frying a little sowbelly[490] for dinner, when a shell from Kennesaw struck on the outside of our works, and bounded over, and dropped in the ditch in the midst of our Company, every man dropped flat in an instant thinking every moment it would explode. Not exploding, Michael Galvin[491] chief fifer of the regiment jumped up, and threw it out of the works, exclaiming, "Keep your d—d old shells, faith an we have no use for them here," it was a daring thing to do as even at that time it was liable to explode, but it shows how little fear some men have of death. Mike was a good soldier, and lived to return after the war, but was sun struck and died from its effects the summer of his return, near Lyons, Iowa.

One day while in this position the boys were sitting in the shade of the works, it being intensely hot we would also stick the bayonets of our muskets in the ground, and on the butts of them we would fasten our dog tents making an awning to protect ourselves from the heat. Four of us were playing cards, when we saw a soldier of Company F in the act of fixing his gun to make a shade, and we spoke to him, and said, "Look out Dunham[492] the rebs can see you from there, you will get hit." He replied, "I guess not I am not afraid." A minute later a crack of a gun was heard, and we heard something, like striking a rock with a hammer. Looking up we saw Dunham all huddled up on the ground. One of the boys spoke up, "I guess you will keep down now won't you," not thinking he was dead. As he did not move we went to him; poor fellow he was dead, shot through the brain, died without a struggle, and never knew what hurt him.

While here we had to get our water from a little creek on our right, and rear, about fifty rods [275 yards] distant, and in going after it for half the distance we were in plain view of the enemy. We would generally get what we could during the night when dark, but as the weather was extremely hot we would often go in the day time to get fresh water. At such times we would take turns in getting it. One of us would take as many canteens as he could carry, and the next time some one else would go, and when we got to where the Johnnies could see us, we would in our best licks, while scores of bullets would whistle around us, as the rebs were on the watch all the time. On such occasions it was fun for the boys in the works to see us run, but not much fun for the one carrying the canteens of water.[493]

As before stated, on the evening of July the 3rd General Johnston withdrew his army and had fallen back to a strong position, just north of the Chattahoochee River.[494] While marching over a portion of the battle ground on the right of Kennesaw we camped for a short time on what had been one of the hardest contested positions of the battle field, and where the batteries of both armies had so hotly contested for the mastery of the field. It was heavily wooded and level plain, and at that point the lines were about fifty rods [275 yards] apart. Huge trees that had withstood the storms of centuries were shattered and torn beyond description, and the ground was covered with fallen debris. I remember one tall stately old chestnut tree, that I at the time took the dimensions of it being thirty three inches in diameter three feet from the ground, at that point had been perforated by a solid shot. Before viewing the work of that shot I should have considered myself safe lying behind a tree of such dimensions especially so far as a ten pound was considered, but after viewing that stately old tree I concluded that a hole in the ground was preferable.[495]

On continuing our pursuit of the retreating enemy we found that they had evacuated their strong position north of the Chattahoochee, and had crossed to its south side.[496] At the time it was beyond our comprehension why they should vacate so strong a position without making a show of defense, but their fear of Sherman crossing the river on either flank putting his army between them and Atlanta hastened their departure. Right here perhaps a brief description of those formidable works might interest my readers that had not the pleasure of seeing them.

They had been erected under the skillful direction of a military engineer,[497] and occupied weeks of time in their construction, and consisted of a continuous line of young trees from eight to ten inches in diameter, placed close together in the ground, and projecting above the ground about twelve feet. For miles that impassable barrier extended, broken only at intervals by gate ways that were in turn protected by a heavy cheveaux de friese. Formidable as were those works they had not benefited the enemy one iota as by a master stroke of strategy Sherman had compelled them to evacuate them without striking a blow.[498]

Finding that they had successfully crossed the river, our portion of the army were ordered to move to the left, and cross the river at a ford near the Roswell cotton factories.[499] The day was intensely hot, and the heavy clouds of dust that arose made it almost unendurable, while the rumbling of distant thunder gave warning of an approaching storm. About 6 o'clock in the evening [July 14] we reached the crossing of the river which at this point was about 150 yards in width, but quite shallow, and as we reached the opposite bank there broke upon us one of the severest rain and electrical storms I ever witnessed. Although quite early in the evening the darkness of midnight broken only by the vivid flashes of the lightening, and as we went into camp, and stacked our arms a continual stream of the electrical current in a thousand fantastic shapes, seemed to play along that glittering array of steel while the terrific peals of heavens artillery made the earth tremble and which seemed to mock the efforts of mankind in attempting to imitate its awful grandeur.

Incident of Picket Duty, Retreat of the Enemy, and a Grand Electrical Storm

479. The position of the regiment changed extremely slightly over the course of two weeks; however, the regiment was engaged nearly every day until June 26. The 26th Iowa lost, during this period, one officer and seven men killed and wounded. Intermittent strong rain affected the campaign, interfering with the Federal offensive. General Osterhaus reported, "The heavy rains which set in at this time considerably retarded operations, and no material changes were made in the respective positions of the troops between June 11 and June 13." On the latter day, Osterhaus's division conducted a feint at noon to dislodge some Confederate infantry entrenched in front of the 3rd Brigade (on the left). That brigade advanced and carried the enemy rifle pits, which the men set about reversing for their use. The 2nd and 1st Brigades followed on the right, and thus the entire line advanced about 400 yards. Rain again affected the campaign and, "This episode was succeeded by a period of monotony, lasting till June 19." *O.R.* I-38-III-132; *Supplement to the O.R.* 20-II-579.

480. On the night of June 18, the pickets posted in front of the division reported indications of a retrograde movement on the enemy's part. This proved correct, for the Confederates had retired a mile from a strong line at the foot of Big Kennesaw into a second line of works running along the crest of the mountain. The 2nd Division of McPherson's army advanced into the abandoned line on June 19, and, on June 20, the 2nd Brigade of Osterhaus's 1st Division advanced and assumed position on the right of the 2nd Division; however, the remainder of Osterhaus's division remained in reserve. Then, on June 21, Woods's 1st Brigade occupied an interval between the right of Williamson's 2nd Brigade and the cut of the Western & Atlantic Railroad, and entrenched. This position was directly in front of the Confederate batteries deployed on the summit of Big Kennesaw, and exposed to plunging fire. The probability is that the event described here occurred on the night of June 21 or immediately thereafter. *O.R.* I-38-III-132.

481. A capelike outer garment made of waterproof material with an opening in the center for the soldier's head. Usually, it was made of cotton muslin coated with India rubber. Garrison & Garrison, *Civil War Usage,* 194.

482. Big Kennesaw rises nearly 700 feet above the surrounding terrain and forms a natural citadel. The mountain is a bumped ridge extending over two miles long, consisting of twin peaks—Big Kennesaw and Little Kennesaw—and a spur on the south end, today called Pigeon Hill. The northern and western slopes, which faced the Union army, are steep and rocky. From the mountain, located in the center of Johnston's line, the Confederate defenses ran off to the right and left in a six-mile arc to the northeast and south, covering the railroad and dirt roads into Marietta. The Confederate force opposing McPherson's army was Polk's Corps, now commanded by Maj. Gen. William W. Loring. Kelly, *Kennesaw Mountain,* 23–24.

483. On the night of June 26, Osterhaus's division was moved about two (air) miles, and relieved Baird's division, XIV Corps, Army of the Cumberland, which slid farther south. This placed the left center of Osterhaus's division astride the Burnt Hickory road, nearly a mile west of Pigeon Hill. Woods's brigade (with the 26th Iowa) manned trenches to the right of Williamson's brigade (its left on the road), and occupied the extreme right of the division line roughly 1,000 yards south of the road. Woods's position overlooked a headwater branch of Noye's Creek. Ibid., 31–34; *O.R.* I-38-III-98–99, 133.

484. The main attack carried out by Sherman was made by elements of Thomas's Army of the

Cumberland (against the Confederate left on the Dallas road), while a secondary thrust was attempted by McPherson's Army of the Tennessee (against the Confederate center at Little Kennesaw on the Burnt Hickory road). Feints and demonstrations were carried out on the extreme left and right flanks of the line. At Little Kennesaw, Osterhaus's division, held in reserve, played no significant role in the fighting except to provide some skirmishers who preceded the attacking column. The division suffered only 26 casualties for the day. The XV Corps sustained a loss of 629 total casualties in the failed attempt to break through the Confederate line along the Burnt Hickory road at Little Kennesaw and Pigeon Hill. The total loss for Sherman was roughly 2,980 men killed, wounded, and missing. Relatively safe in their well-entrenched positions, the Confederates suffered possibly 700 killed, wounded, and missing. Ibid., 85; Albert Castel, *Decision in the West: The Atlanta Campaign of 1864* (Lawrence: University Press of Kansas, 1992), 319. Hereafter cited as *Decision in the West*.

485. Harker (1837–1864), born in New Jersey, graduated from West Point in 1858. An experienced officer, having fought at Shiloh, the siege of Corinth, Stones River and Chickamauga, Missionary Ridge, Knoxville, Dalton, Resaca, and Dallas, he had been promoted to brigadier general, September 20, 1863. At Kennesaw Mountain, he commanded the 3rd Brigade, 2nd Division, IV Army Corps, Army of the Cumberland. Boatner, *Civil War Dictionary*, 375.

486. Johnston evacuated his entrenchments on Kennesaw Mountain during the night of July 2, moving to avoid Sherman's shifting armies, which had reverted to flanking maneuvers. Kelly, *Kennesaw Mountain*, 45.

487. Durney, born in New York, lived in De Witt and was 21 when he enlisted August 14, 1862. Wounded on September 3, 1864, at Lovejoy's Station, Georgia, he was mustered out May 16, 1865, at Davenport, Iowa. *Roster* 3: 1049.

488. Dennis Kelly lived in De Witt and was 26 when he enlisted on August 12, 1862. Promoted fifth sergeant, October 31, 1862, he was mustered out on June 6, 1865, in Washington, D.C. Oake's memory is faulty. Michael Kelly, born in Maryland, lived in De Witt and was 39 when he enlisted August 11, 1862. He was discharged for disability while the regiment was in winter quarters at Woodville on January 22, 1864. *Roster* 3: 1070.

489. The features were traverses, constructed as Oake describes for protection along a line of field works that is vulnerable to enfilade or flank fire. Scott, *Military Dictionary*, 625.

490. A common slang term for pork—one Federal soldier noted it was served "with the tits on" and frequently was tainted or infested by maggots. Wiley & Milhollen, *They Who Fought Here*, 54.

491. A native of Ireland, Galvin was 21 and living in Lyons when he enlisted as fifer on August 15, 1862. Promoted principal musician on April 1, 1865, he was mustered out in Washington, D.C., on June 6, 1865. *Roster* 3: 1058.

492. This was William Dunham. Born in New Jersey, he was 32 and lived in De Witt upon enlisting on August 15, 1864. Records have him killed in action on June 27, 1864. Thus, this incident may have occurred sometime in the afternoon following the morning attacks made by Sherman's forces. The regiment appears to have sustained a total loss of two men killed and three wounded on June 27. *Roster* 3: 1050; *Supplement to the O.R.* II-20-579.

493. For this period of the campaign, following the June 27 morning assaults, General Woods reported, "All subsequent operations in our front were limited to artillery practice and sharpshooting from June 27 to the morning of July 3." The 26th Iowa assumed "a position in front about 100 rods [550 yards] from the enemy's works and were constantly exposed to their fire." They lost a total of three men killed and four wounded from June 27 through July 2. *O.R.* I-38-III-133; *Supplement to the O.R.* II-20-579–80.

494. The Confederates retired to prepared field works four miles southeast of Marietta, laid out along a ridge extending from the railroad station at Smyrna. Farther to the south, an even stronger crescent-shaped line was being constructed to guard the Chattahoochee River crossings. Johnston maintained his line at Smyrna until the night of July 4, when he retired to the stronger river line. Kelly, *Kennesaw Mountain*, 45.

495. On the night of July 2, the 26th Iowa, with its brigade and division, was relieved by elements of the XVI Corps and marched—throughout the night—back around (moving north then east) Big Kennesaw Mountain (which had been evacuated by Johnston), and then on south to Marietta, arriving there at noon, July 3. *Roster* 3: 1024.

496. On July 4, the regiment marched nine miles and camped for the night. The next day it moved toward Howell's Ferry on the Chattahoochee, engaged in some skirmishing during the march, and bivouacked two miles from the river. The division front entrenched on high ground north of Nickajack Creek. It remained in that vicinity until July 11, when the Confederates evacuated their fortifications north of the river and fell back across the Chattahoochee. The 26th Iowa, with its brigade and division, moved to the vacated works as supports for the pickets. On July 12, the regiment fell back in the evening toward Marietta, 7 miles, and camped at midnight. On July 13, it marched at 5 A.M., arriving at Marietta at noon. After a five-hour rest, it again moved forward in the direction of Roswell, 10 miles, bivouacking at midnight. *Supplement to the O.R.* II-20-580.

497. The skillful military architect was Brig. Gen. Francis Asbury Shoup, chief of artillery for the Confederate Army of Tennessee. Construction began June 19 using gangs of slaves. Oake is describing what he apparently viewed from the opposing Federal field works, as well as learned about later: the special series of earthen forts, or redoubts, with connecting stockades designed by Shoup, which were built above grade—on top of the ground instead of digging into it. Each fort was diamond shaped, with its two outer faces pointing in the direction of the enemy like an arrowhead. The parapets were made using double walls of logs filled with compacted earth. Exterior walls were ten to twelve feet thick at the base and extended ten to twelve feet above grade, surmounted by an infantry parapet or banquette for sharpshooters, for a total height of sixteen feet. These Shoupades were built at intervals of 60 to 175 yards and connected by stockades of vertical logs firmly embedded in the ground and extending eight feet high with sharpened points. Midway between each fort, the stockades formed a re-entrant angle and were broken by an emplacement or redan for two artillery pieces. Thus, the artillery could provide enfilading fire at point blank range across the faces of each Shoupade, which was designed to be manned by a company of eighty riflemen. Sherman was astounded by the formidable line, stating, "I confess I had not learned of beforehand of the existence of this strong place.…During the night Johnston drew back his army and trains inside the 'tete-du-pont' at the Chattahoochee, which proved one of the strongest pieces of field fortifications I ever saw." Scaife, *The Campaign for Atlanta*, 76; F. A. Shoup, "Works at the Chattahoochee River," *Confederate Veteran Magazine* III (1895), 262–65; Sherman, *Memoirs*, II: 65; *O.R.* I-38-I-69.

498. As the main body of Union forces approached the front of Shoup's *tete-du-pont,* Sherman sent forces downstream to scout for crossing points. Schofield's army and a cavalry division under Kenner Garrard moved upstream to do the same. On July 8, Schofield brushed aside Confederate pickets at Soap Creek and secured a ford. The next morning, farther upstream, Garrard's troopers, stripped naked but for weapons and cartridge boxes, secured a crossing under fire at Roswell. Johnston's river line, located downstream, was rendered untenable. The Confederates evacuated and retired south of the river. Castel, *Decision in the West*, 336–40.

499. The 26th Iowa marched, with its division, at 3 A.M., July 14, crossing the river just downstream from Roswell, and bivouacked one-half mile south of the river. The regiment built and manned field works until July 17, then moved, with its division, at 6 A.M., crossing Nancy Creek (6 miles south of the river). *Supplement to the O.R.* II-20-580.

CHAPTER SIXTEEN

Arrested for Running the Picket Lines

❧ ———————— ❧

For two hours the storm continued, the rain falling in torrents, the troops in the meantime being busily engaged in trying to build fires in order to get our supper. At last the strength of the storm was spent and after partaking of a cup of coffee, and our usual allowance of sow belly and hard tack, having previously put up our dog tents although wet through, we wrapped ourselves in our ponchos, and retired for the night. The next morning the old adage of a storm being followed by a calm was again verified, as the sun arose in a cloudless sky while the rain drops hanging from the foliage of the trees glistened like millions of diamonds in the bright sunlight, and the troops were early astir, and busily engaged in getting breakfast. It was then we learned that during the storm of the evening before, that four soldiers of a battery camped near us had been killed by lightening. Having reached camp before us they had erected their tent, and retired, when without warning the fatal bolt descended and blotted out their young lives.

During the next two days we remained in camp at this place. The day after the storm the members of the battery consigned to their last resting place the bodies of their four comrades that had been killed by that fatal bolt of lightening, and as the four rough boxes were placed on the caissons and drawn by six horses it was an impressive sight as they were tenderly lowered into their narrow homes on the banks of the Chattahoochee River.

It was with sorrowful hearts that we turned away wondering if kind friends in the far North were not anxiously, at that moment, wishing for their safe return. No more would they respond to the bugles call. The bloody scenes of carnage that were so soon to follow would make no difference to them. Their part in the great drama had been played, and they had joined the hosts of comrades that had preceded them. The day being very warm the soldiers took advantage of the nearness of the river, and for the first time in a long while concluded to take a bath in its cooling waters and for the greater part of the day thousands of them could be seen swimming in its placid waters. I have often times thought that the natives living along its banks below us, seeing its muddy condition did not attribute it to a severe storm up the stream. Just at this season of the year the blackberries were ripe, and in this section of the country there was an abundance of them, but in order to get them in any quantity it was a necessary to go beyond the picket lines, and there was very strict orders not to pass the lines without a pass, because to the proximity of the enemy. As we lay in camp we could occasionally hear shots exchanged between our outposts, and the enemy.

About a quarter of a mile in our front was an old field, where, we had reasons to believe the delicious fruit could be found in abundance, but the question was, how were we to get past the picket line, as there was very strict orders against running the pickets. On the opposite side of the field in the heavy timber adjoining it we had every reason to believe the enemy were watching us. On the morning of the 15th I approached Sergeant D. H. Denny, who had been in Libby with me, and John M. Huge [Hague],[500] and John Simpson[501] all of Company A. To them I suggested the idea of running the pickets, and getting some berries. I think my reasons for not approaching my old friend Swihart was that he was rather of a pious disposition, and generally opposed to so gross violation of military rules, unless he was sure of getting larger game. Having made all necessary arrangements for utensils for holding the fruit, we left camp, and started for the front, picking our way through the dense underbrush a little to the left of the main road, where we knew was posted a strong picket post.

As we neared the line we stealthily picked our way, unobserved, through the lines, and after going about 20 rods [110 yards] decided to go to the road as it was better walking, and as there was a slight bend in the road we thought we would not be seen by the pickets. We were in high glee walking rapidly to the front contemplating the pailfulls of the delicious fruit that we thought now was surely within our grasp, when hearing the clatter of horses feet in our rear we turned our heads, and the familiar "Halt" greets our ears. In an instant we realized our position. We had been discovered by the patrol guard.

In a moment our blackberry castles fell to the ground, and as the guard ordered us to about face, and marched us back inside of the lines we real-

Milo Smith, Colonel of the 26th Iowa Infantry.
Smith commanded the 26th Iowa from August 1862 until August 1864, when he assumed command of the brigade. After directing the brigade through the capture of Atlanta and the "March to the Sea," he resigned from service in January 1865. Wounded twice in battle, at Arkansas Post and Vicksburg, Smith was repeatedly commended for gallantry on the field of battle.
STATE HISTORICAL SOCIETY OF IOWA–DES MOINES

ized our position, and we felt in no pleasant mood at being so easily entrapped; however we were in for it now, and would have to suffer the consequences. At that time Colonel Smith of the 26th Iowa was in the command of the brigade, and we knew we would be taken to his headquarters.[502] Right well I remembered that occasion. The colonel was sitting in front of his tent when our guard marched up with us and after saluting the colonel said, "Colonel here are four men I arrested outside the lines without passes." The colonel said not a word, but looked at us quite sharp, and I wish to say right here, that if a man could ever look sour at times it was Colonel Milo Smith. At last the colonel turned to the guard and said "You can return to your duty I will attend to these men." In the meantime I was closely watching the colonel's countenance, which at the time I thought bodied no love to us. Raising his head and looking squarely at me he said, "Oake, how did you get through the pickets." I replied, "I walked out colonel." He dropped his head in an instant, and could hardly keep from smiling, while I thought I had scored one point surely. He again spoke up, "That is not what I mean (I knew what he meant) "I mean did you have a pass." "No Sir," I replied. He replied, "Have you not heard the orders about being outside of the lines without a pass." "Yes Sir I have." "Then why did you run the picket line?" "Well colonel to tell the truth (I never told a bigger lie in my life,) we were out in the woods picking berries not thinking about the picket line when the first thing we knew the patrol arrested us. In fact colonel we did not think we were outside of the lines." The colonel replied, "Oake and Denny, both of you were once taken prisoners, and I should think it would be a warning to you to be more cautious in the future, and I will have to punish you for this. All of you can report to your command, and I will attend to your cases in the morning." So far as our punishment was concerned, morning never came. Several times since the close of the war in speaking with the colonel I have mentioned that instance, which he distinctly remembered, and he would smile.

A little over a year before this time in company with several others I was returning from a foraging trip with plenty of plunder we passed the colonel's tent. The colonel upon seeing us looked unusually severe, but upon being presented with a fine young turkey well dressed, and a few eggs, it was amusing to see how quick his stern features relaxed, and a big smile stole over his face. A fat chicken or something equally as good seemed to be the requisite panacea for all such complaints, and its effects were instantaneous, and rarely failed to cure. If this article should reach the eyes of the Colonel I think he would corroborate my statements, especially so far as the chicken and eggs were concerned. The next day after our arrest the army again moved a short distance to the front, and halted for dinner in a large clearing, where there was an abundance of ripe berries, and while the advance were busily engaged with the enemy we were picking the fruit by the handful, and although not quite as delicious as cream and strawberries, by putting a little sugar with them we made a fine dinner, quite a change from sowbelly and hardtack.[503]

Arrested for Running the Picket Lines

500. Hague, born in Pennsylvania, was 18 and a resident of Mechanicsville when he enlisted on July 9, 1862. He completed his service, being mustered out on June 6, 1865, in Washington, D.C. *AGI* 1863-I: 919 incorrectly lists him as John W. Hane. There was no soldier named Huge in the regiment. *Roster* 3: 1060.

501. A native of New York, Simpson lived in Charlotte and was 18 when he enlisted on July 11, 1862. Promoted seventh corporal, March 24, 1863, and sixth corporal, April 1, 1863, he was mustered out on June 6, 1865, in Washington, D.C. *Roster* 3: 1094.

502. General Osterhaus, taken ill, was granted sick leave, which he formally took on July 17. Brig. Gen. Charles Woods temporarily commanded the division. Colonel Smith assumed command of the brigade on July 14. Lt. Col. Thomas Ferreby assumed supervision of the regiment. The temporary chain of command continued until Osterhaus returned and assumed command on August 15, 1864. *O.R.* I-38-III-133–34; *Supplement to the O.R.* II-20-580.

503. The most familiar bread ration provided to United States soldiers during the war. Also known as a seabiscuit, hardtack was a rectangular cracker $3^{1}/_{2}$ inches wide, $2^{7}/_{8}$ inches high, $^{3}/_{8}$ inch thick, and weighing about $1^{1}/_{2}$ ounces. It came packed in barrels or wooden boxes. Wiley & Milhollen, *They Who Fought Here*, 56.

CHAPTER SEVENTEEN

Battle of Atlanta

→ ———————————— ←

We were now distant from Atlanta about 15 miles, and were steadily driving the enemy until we had reached a position about three miles from Atlanta where we found the strong lines of the enemy had been evacuated during the 21st.[504] Here we encamped for the night, part of our army occupying the deserted works of the enemy. The Army of the Tennessee comprised of the following troops: 15th, 17th, and three divisions of the 16th Army Corps, and was the left wing of Sherman's Army, the 4th, 14th, 20th and 23rd Corps being the right wing. The army of the Tennessee was commanded by General [James B.] McPherson.* Our corps, the 15th, being on the right of that army.[505]

On the morning of July 22nd the sun arose in a cloudless sky, the troops were all up, and had eaten their morning meal, as the sun rose higher in the heavens and the dew drops glistened in the morning sun. It was an ideal Sunday [Friday] morning, and as it was so quiet it reminded us of a beautiful Sunday morning in far away Iowa. Not a leaf stirred on the trees, but the feathered songsters could be seen hopping from limb to limb upon the trees, chirping merrily to their mates, and bespoke a day of peace, and quiet. Not a thing to denote the coming storm, which by night would blot out the lives of thousands of the bravest in the land.

About 8 o'clock a few shots were heard on the left, and within a short time the bloody contest began.[506] Aids and orderlies were seen galloping along the lines with orders to the different brigade and division command-ers to at once form their lines and prepare for the approaching conflict. Our division the first of the 15th Corps were on the extreme right of the Army of the Tennessee, our right resting on the 23rd Corps, while part of the 2nd Division of the 15th Corps was on our right, and occupied a portion of the deserted works of the enemy, supporting De Grees [De Gress'] Battery[507] of four 20-pound[er] Parrott guns, while our division was lying about fifty rods [275 yards] to the right of it, and slightly in the rear.

Soon the battle was in full swing along the entire front of our army of three corps, and as we lay on the ground as noncombatants we could see the enemy charging across an open field, on the 2nd Division, and the four Parrott guns with a battery[508] of six [four] Napoleon guns [and two 10-pounder Parrott rifles] a little farther to the left. As the enemy charged across that open field, in the face of those ten guns supported by a line of infantry,[509] they were cut down as grass before the sickle, but still they closed ranks, and again moved forward. In the meantime the firing about one mile to the left had increased in severity, and it was rumored that the left of our army were being driven back by the enemy. It was then that the third brigade of our division received orders to hasten to the left to the support of the left wing. At this time our corps commander [Major] General [John A.] Logan* was sitting on his horse near our regiment, when a staff officer rode up to him and reported that General McPherson was killed.[510] By this time the enemy had succeeded in driving back the second division, and cap-turing the two batteries in our left front, but not until some of the guns had been spiked, and the cannoneers had dropped by their guns.[511] It was then that General Sherman who stood near a battery of the 23rd Corps, a short distance on our right,[512] ordered our division commander C.R. Woods to form his division in echelon, and to recapture the batteries.

General Wood replied, "General, my division is light, I don't think I will be able to do it." General Sherman replied, "General, if it costs the lives of every man in the division those guns must be recaptured." At once the bugle called, "Fall in," and we were quickly formed in three lines of battle, the 76th Ohio the first line, 26th Iowa the second, and the 27th Missouri the third.[513] At once we were ordered forward. Meanwhile General Sherman had given orders to the captain of the battery of the 23rd Corps, to turn his guns on the horses of the captured batteries, and kill them to prevent the enemy from taking the guns from the field, as they were then in the act of doing.[514]

At the same time our three lines of infantry were advancing on the enemy, who failed to see us until we emerged from the woods about 100 yards from them, as they were so confused from the terrific fire from the guns of the 23rd Corps battery. As they saw us they jumped behind the works, and began to pour a deadly fire into our ranks, but still we did not fire a shot, but pushed rapidly to the front, the three lines all being mixed up in the fallen brush in our efforts to get to the enemy's works.

About fifty yards from the works, the writer was stepping over a fallen log with two of the 76th Ohio boys, when in an instant both of them were shot. Still we pressed to the front, and the enemy seeing that they could not hold the works started to fall back, and as we reached the works they were falling back over the open field, over which they had charged when they had taken the guns. As they were falling back over the open ground quite near us and we crawled up to the works with loaded guns, and poured a deadly

Confederate fortifications at Atlanta.
Stoutly prepared fortifications around the city initially thwarted Sherman's direct attempt to seize the important transportation center. However, they could not halt him from maneuvering around the city to sever all the railroads supplying Hood's entrenched army.

Battle of Atlanta

fire into them at short range, the scene can be better imagined than described.[515]

We had retaken the battery but at a fearful cost, and most all of the horses were dead, killed mostly by the guns of the battery of the 23rd Corp. I well remember Captain De Gress, whose battery, of four twenty-pound[er] Parrott guns, we recaptured that day. Bare headed with revolver in hand he followed the line of battle in that desperate charge, and upon being in possession of his guns once more and seeing his men lie around them dead the tears ran down his cheeks, and he had nothing but words of praise for the first division of the 15th Corps.[516]

After we had been in possession of the works a short time the enemy opened on us with their heavy guns from Atlanta, and for a time we hugged the works quite closely. Just to the left of the battery was quite a large empty house, that had been used as a hospital by the second division, and upon our recapture of the works several of the enemy were taken prisoners there while in the act of robbing our wounded, and I can assure my readers they were not handled with gloves.[517]

One incident in connection with this battle is still fresh in my memory. Sergeant R. J. McClenahan of Company A and Sergeant M. Davis[518] of Company F were on the picket line in a piece of dense brush, and the lines were in a very confused state when McClenhan, on looking behind him, saw some rebels coming, and turning around as if to speak to his own men said, "Close up boys." The rebels thinking he had a company of men dropped their guns, and he ordered them to about face, and started them back towards our lines. It was then that Davis came to his assistance, and it was not until they had nearly reached our lines that the rebels discovered that nine of them had been captured by two Yankees. This story seems almost incredible, but is an absolute fact, and goes to show what confusion there sometimes is in time of battle.[519]

When the enemy were [was] driven back, they made no further attempt on us, as they had been badly beaten at every point leaving us in possession of the hardly contested field. That night the writer was detailed as one to guard the prisoners we had taken during the fight. Thus ended the Battle of Atlanta, July 22nd, 1864.[520]

CHAPTER NOTES:
Battle of Atlanta

504. On July 18, the 26th marched with its army southeastward to within three miles of Stone Mountain, east of Decatur, protecting Gen. Kenner Garrard's cavalry, while the dismounted troopers "played smash with" (destroyed) the Georgia Railroad, which linked Atlanta with Charleston, South Carolina. The regiment bivouacked at Henderson's Mill, eleven miles northeast of Atlanta. The next day it moved five miles, to within one mile of Decatur, and camped all night. On the 20th, it moved through Decatur in the direction of Atlanta. It again advanced on July 21 and threw up field works. The only significant fighting occurred on the extreme left of McPherson's army, where Mortimer Leggett's division of Frank Blair's XVII Army Corps fought a sanguinary and bitter engagement with Cleburne's division of Hardee's Corps, driving the Confederates from their hasty entrenchments and securing a lodgment on Bald Hill. McPherson's entire front was strengthened overnight by earthworks, headlogs, and other improvements. *Supplement to the O.R.* II-20-580; *O.R.* I-38-III-102; James Lee McDonough & James Pickett Jones, *War So Terrible: Sherman and Atlanta* (New York: W.W. Norton & Co., 1987), 219. Hereafter cited as *War So Terrible*.

505. Sherman's army group advanced toward fortified Atlanta in a wide arc from the north and east. The Army of the Tennessee occupied the left wing, moving westward from Decatur. The Army of the Ohio under Schofield advanced in the center, on McPherson's right, while Thomas's Army of the Cumberland, fresh from its battle with the Confederate army at Peachtree Creek (July 20), formed the right wing, approaching Atlanta from the north. McPherson's and Schofield's troops fronted west and Thomas's fronted south. On the night of July 21, the XVII Corps held the left front and the XV Corps (astride the Georgia Railroad) occupied the right front, while the XVI Corps was in reserve, behind the XVII Corps. McDonough & Jones, *War So Terrible*, 220–22.

506. Informed that the left flank of McPherson's army was "in the air" and vulnerable to a turning movement, Gen. John Bell Hood, who had been ordered to replace Joseph Johnston as commander of the Confederate Army of Tennessee on July 17, moved to attack the Army of the Tennessee. Throughout the night of July 21–22, Hardee led his corps on a fifteen-mile circuitous march around McPherson's left to strike the unprotected enemy in the rear. Wheeler's cavalry moved to attack the Union supply wagons parked farther to the east in Decatur. With these forces behind the Union left, Benjamin F. Cheatham, temporarily in command of Hood's old corps, would in turn assault McPherson's front, which was one mile east of the Confederate fortifications, two miles from Atlanta. Castel, *Decision in the West*, 222; Kelly, *Kennesaw Mountain*, 48.

507. This was Battery H, 1st Illinois Light Artillery, commanded by Capt. Francis De Gress, who also served as chief of artillery for M. L. Smith's 2nd Division, XV Corps. On July 20, as Logan's XV Corps advanced west along the railroad and Decatur road, De Gress's battery reached a point two and one-half miles from downtown Atlanta. The location was within the effective range of the Parrott rifles assigned to the battery, providing an opportunity to fire shells into the city. At 1 P.M., De Gress unlimbered his cannon and fired three shells into Atlanta—"the first ones of the war." The battery advanced again on July 21 and 22, and on the latter day occupied the works evacuated by the Confederates on July 21. Its position was roughly 300 yards north of the Georgia Railroad cut, immediately north of the Troup Hurt house. *O.R.* I-38-III-265.

508. This was Battery A, 1st Illinois Light Artillery, Lt. Samuel S. Smyth commanding, consisting of four 12-pounder Napoleon guns and two 10-pounder Parrott rifles. The battery was deployed on the railroad cut south of the Troup Hurt house. *O.R.* I-38-III-262.

509. The infantry belonged to M. L. Smith's division, reinforced at 4:30 P.M. by August Mersy's brigade from Dodge's XVI Corps. The Confederate attack along this sector of the front began at 4 P.M., four hours after Hardee struck the Union left, and was delivered by the left flank of Cheatham's corps. On the left, Hardee's men, instead of hitting McPherson's left "in the air" and from the rear, slammed into Dodge's XVI Corps, which McPherson had earlier been ordered to move forward to support Blair's XVII Corps on Bald Hill. Although he was not moved there for the purpose of blocking Hardee's strike against the rear of the Army of the Tennessee, Dodge's presence inadvertently had positioned four brigades squarely in the path of Hardee's surprise flank attack. Two of Hardee's divisions were consequently repulsed, nullifying any threat to the Union rear, but his other two divisions crushed the flank of the XVII Corps, rolling it up. For a while, Blair's veterans took a severe pounding. Throughout the afternoon, the Confederate assaults were delivered from three directions, but uncoordinated, and Hood was tardy in committing Cheatham to the battle. The Army of the Tennessee, through a determined and tenacious defense, managed to hold out. McDonough & Jones, *War So Terrible*, 225–36.

510. Corp. Robert Coleman, 5th Confederate Infantry, assigned to Cleburne's division, shot and killed McPherson as he, his orderly, and a signal officer rode forward to investigate the attack on the XVII Corps, a half mile southeast of Bald Hill. The party mistakenly rode into the advancing Confederate skirmishers, and the Union commander was cut down around 2 P.M. as he attempted to evade capture. Also among the dead was Maj. Gen. William H. T. Walker, commanding a division in Hardee's corps, killed during the initial attack on Dodge's troops. Castel, *Decision in the West*, 398; Eicher, *The Longest Night*, 708.

511. Smyth's battery lost heavily in men, equipment, and horses. The casualties were thirty-two men killed, wounded, and missing, including Lieutenant Smyth captured, and fifty-five horses killed and captured. Two of the six guns were retaken when the Federals counterattacked and recovered their original works. De Gress's battery suffered fourteen men killed, wounded, and captured, and thirty-nine horses lost. *O.R.* I-38-III-262, 265.

512. Sherman observed Cheatham's breakthrough from his headquarters at the Augustus Hurt house, three-quarters of a mile to the northwest. The Confederate forces were men assigned to Henry Clayton's and John C. Brown's divisions. Scaife, *The Campaign for Atlanta*, 98–99.

513. When the Confederates broke through and overran the Union entrenchments, driving Smith's 2nd Division before them, Woods discovered the position of his division untenable. "I threw back my left," he recalled, "forming a new line, facing the enemy's flank, my right resting at the Howard [Augustus Hurt] house." Later, he received a verbal order from M. L. Smith, now temporarily commanding the XV Corps, to attack the Confederates in flank and rear. *O.R.* I-38-III-139.

514. Sherman directed Schofield to mass all the artillery he had (five batteries) and open on the Confederates. "The shells tore through the lines or exploded in the faces of the men with unerring regularity," remembered Confederate Brig. Gen. Arthur M. Manigault, whose brigade of Brown's division spearheaded the attack and breakthrough at the railroad cut. The use of Schofield's artillery was virtually all the assistance the Army of the Tennessee received from the other Federal forces under Sherman's command. The fact that Sherman did not order Thomas's and Schofield's infantry forces to attack the Atlanta defenses, or at least strike Cheatham's left flank as it engaged McPherson/Logan's forces, has been a subject of debate and controversy ever since. Arthur M. Manigault, *A Carolinian Goes to War: The Civil War Narrative of Arthur Middleton Manigault*, Edited by R. Lockwood Tower (Columbia: University of South Carolina Press, 1983), 223; Castel, *Decision in the West*, 414.

515. Milo Smith, commanding the 1st Brigade, reported his troops "moved rapidly forward across the swamp now appearing in my front, at once attacking the enemy on their flank, and so vigorously that they were soon obliged to abandon the works they had temporarily occupied, together with De Gress' battery…" Woods's division had not acted alone. John A. Logan had assumed command of the Army of the Tennessee after the death of McPherson. Upon learning of the Confederate breakthrough, he had ordered up reserves from Dodge's corps, and rallied the units of Smith's 2nd and William Harrow's 4th divisions, recently flushed from their entrenchments by the massive Confederate onslaught. In all, Logan pieced together a formidable mass of eight brigades that steadily pressed forward to restore the line. This counterattack became the subject so prominently presented in the famous Cyclorama of the Battle of Atlanta. *O.R.* I-38-III-147; Scaife, *The Campaign for Atlanta*, 99.

516. Exposed to combat and the elements, horses and mules died in great numbers throughout the conflict. This attrition placed great logistical strain on the combatant armies when coordinating and implementing military maneuvers. The purposeful killing of De Gress's horses to save the cannon from being removed was not unique. There were similar instances throughout the war when troops were called upon to kill their own animals harnessed to the artillery, caissons, and wagons. In the four years of carnage, an estimated 1.8 million horses and mules perished.

517. The empty residence was the severely damaged Troup Hurt house.

518. Martin D. Davis, age 20, was born in Michigan and living in De Witt when he enlisted on October 10, 1862. Promoted fourth sergeant, September 1, 1864, then first sergeant, he transferred to Co. A, 6th Iowa Infantry. *Roster* 3: 1050.

519. General Logan reported that 481 prisoners were captured by the XV Corps on July 22, with 1,017 walking prisoners and another 1,000 wounded Confederates recovered from the field. *O.R.* I-38-III-28–29.

520. Milo Smith reported that his brigade lost 32 men killed and wounded during the afternoon. Four of those wounds were sustained by the 26th Iowa (including Lt. Enoch F. Byng of Co. B), which had 182 men present for duty that day. Woods's division lost 10 killed, 64 wounded, and 3 missing. John A. Logan, temporarily in command of the fallen McPherson's army, attributed Hood's failure on July 22 to "the lateness of the hour at which the attack was made, a lack of concert in his movements, the opportune presence of a portion of the Sixteenth Corps in the rear of the left of our line, but more than all of these to the splendid bravery and tenacity of the men and the ability and skill of the officers of the Army of the Tennessee." The general reported that the Army of the Tennessee, with 30,000 men engaged, sustained 3,722 killed, wounded, and missing, whereas the Confederate loss was "at least 10,000" of the estimated 40,000 engaged. However, historian Albert Castel places Hood's losses at around 5,500 out of perhaps no more than 35,000—and suggests that the number of Confederates engaged was even fewer. *O.R.* I-38-III-27–28, 139, 141, 148, 150; *Supplement to the O.R.* II-20-581; Castel, *Decision in the West*, 412.

Major General John A. Logan.
In December 1863, Logan assumed command of the XV Corps,
Army of the Tennessee, in which William Royal Oake and his
"Clinton County Regiment" served. Logan commanded the corps
during Sherman's offensive against Atlanta and the invasion of
the Carolinas. ILLINOIS STATE HISTORICAL LIBRARY

CHAPTER EIGHTEEN

Move to the Right and Battle of Ezras [Ezra] Church

W e remained in this position until the night of July 27th when we made a night move to the extreme right of our lines.[521] About midnight we went into camp, and at an early hour were up, and after eating our breakfast the line was in motion, skirmishers in advance feeling for the enemy through a heavily wooded and extremely rough and hilly country. After advancing in line of battle about a mile we crossed quite a large open field onto a heavily wooded ridge just in the rear of an old frame building, called Ezra Church.[522] There we were halted to reform our lines as they were in a bad formation having marched so far in line of battle, through the heavily wooded and rough country. We hardly began our formation, when orders came to build works at once as the enemy were about to attack.[523] Soon, up drove the pioneer wagons[524] loaded with picks, shovels, and axes, and the troops at once began cutting down the young timber, and building a line of works. Soon our pickets were attacked by the enemy and were driven in to the main line, and in a short time the enemy were [was] seen coming, in line of battle, while part of our men met them with a destructive fire of musketry. The balance [of which], were busily engaged in strengthening our line of works.[525]

Again, with the well known rebel yell, they advance to the attack, and with a deafening Yankee cheer we pounded into their faces a murderous fire of musketry. Soon our men ceased work on lines of entrenchments, and every man in the ranks was giving their attention to the enemy, who in desperation seemed determined to carry our line of works. The dense growth of young timber in front of our lines, through which they came, seemed to melt as snow before a hot sun, as it was mowed down by that cyclone of lead. There would be a lull in the battle as they would fall back to reform their depleted ranks, when they would again hurl themselves upon us, only to be again hurled back in disorder. For a short time it seemed as if they would be a successful on our right, but fresh troops were rushed to our assistance, and General Logan himself could be seen carrying cartridges to the front, while just in our rear General Sherman's horse was killed. About 40 rods [220 yards] in our rear was an open field in which lay a heavy reserve of our men for use in case the enemy should carry the front line of works. They could then be hurled upon them. As the position of our reserve was very much exposed the troops suffered severely from the fire of the enemy as the bullets passing over our line of works would drop among them.

Thus the battle continued until about 4 P.M. when the bleeding and shattered ranks of the rebels withdrew from the field.[526] After the enemy had withdrawn I suggested to Comrade P. J. Potter that we go in front of the works and take a look over the contested ground. At one place on a piece of ground, about twenty feet square, lay twenty of the enemy's dead, among them three colonels,[527] showing that three different regiments had been there. Another place, behind an upturned stump of a tree lay, five of their dead and seven muskets. At another place I saw a dead rebel in a crouching position his shoulder resting against a small tree, his eyes wide open, but stiff in death. From the formation of our lines it was impossible for the enemy to avoid our front and flank fire. As I passed over that field and saw those sights I realized that war was indeed "Hell." Old grey-haired men and boys in their teens lie on every side while gaping wounds and bloated forms with blood and froth oozing from mouth and nose which were covered by thousands of flies was a sight that time can never efface.[528]

The next day we were busily engaged in burying the dead—600 being buried in front of the 15th Corps.[529] Being [assigned to] one of the burial details, the writer helped put seventy-five of the enemy in one pit and thirty-six in another. About 40 rods [220 yards] to the right of the position held by our regiment during the battle, and one of the most hotly contested parts of the field was a head of a steep ravine, and in passing over that after the battle I saw tracks that had been made by cattle, and horses in the ground while wet, which left quite a depression and I noticed that they were filled with human blood.

In front of our position at this point was a small clearing, and on the enemy's side of it was a rail fence, where they halted to reform their lines, and along it they lay in rows. Perhaps my reader will think that I am exaggerating when I say that in places on the field one could sit at one place and pick up a handful of bullets. During my three years of service I don't think I ever saw a field where the timber and underbrush were cut down by bullets as it was at the battle of Ezra's Church.

521. Sherman had reached as far around the eastern side of Atlanta as he believed practical without risking his own line of supply—the Western & Atlantic Railroad. Therefore, he shifted the Army of the Tennessee, now commanded by Maj. Gen. Oliver O. Howard, from his left all the way to the right, west of Atlanta, in an attempt to sever the last two railroads serving the city—the Macon & Western Central Railroad to Macon, and the Atlanta & West Point Railroad, which split off from the former at Eastport (five miles south of Atlanta) and ran southeast to Montgomery. Russell F. Weigley, *A Great Civil War: A Military and Political History, 1861–1865* (Bloomington: Indiana University Press, 2000), 364–65. Hereafter cited as *A Great Civil War.*

522. On July 23, the 26th Iowa had moved one mile to the rear along the Georgia Railroad. From July 24 to July 25, the regiment was engaged all day in destroying the railroad, and lay in camp until the afternoon of July 26. They camped that night in old field works. The next morning the regiment moved early, with the army, and throughout the day marched north then west, passing to the extreme right of the Federal armies. At 3 A.M., July 28, the unit advanced with the corps southward. Ezra Church, a Methodist meeting house, was about two and one-half miles west of the center of Atlanta, one and one-quarter miles west of the Confederate defenses and Whitehall Fort. It rested one mile north of the intersection of the east-west Lick Skillet road with Green's Ferry road. *Supplement to the O.R.* II-20-581; Scaife, *The Campaign for Atlanta,* 104.

523. Colonel Smith formed his brigade of the XV Corps in two lines, placing the 27th Missouri and 26th Iowa (left to right) in advance. Skirmishers were thrown forward, but met little opposition. About 8 A.M., the Federal line moved slowly southward, continuing to meet slight resistance from enemy pickets. At noon, the line was halted on a wooded ridge, in front of which was a gentle, open valley, rising to another timbered ridge a half mile away. As the opposing skirmishers dueled away, the Confederates opened with artillery, and "the two regiments in the front line were at once ordered," by Milo Smith, "to throw up works with such tools as could be obtained." The Federal line resembled a horseshoe. The XVII Corps deployed to the left (north) of Smith's brigade, fronting east. Williamson's 2nd Brigade and Wanglelin's 3rd Brigade, of Woods's 1st Division, XV Corps, dug in on the right of Smith, fronting southeast. To the right (west) of the 1st Division was M. L. Smith's 2nd Division, fronting southwest. The primary fighting occurred in front of Logan's XV Army Corps. *O.R.* I-38-III-148; Scaife, *The Campaign for Atlanta,* 111.

524. Wagons carrying tools for entrenching and construction work. Pioneers were skilled soldiers who were given detached duty to clear roads, construct bridges, and excavate and erect fortifications. Initially the Union army had no formal organization for pioneer companies, but later some units were created. As the war continued, pioneers were often drawn from the veteran reserve corps or the United States Colored Troops. Army commanders routinely formed pioneer companies by assigning a handful of men from each company in the regiment. Realistically, virtually every soldier became his own pioneer or engineer while on campaign, as changing battlefield conditions called for every man to perform such duty. Garrison & Garrison, *Civil War Usage,* 192.

525. General Hood responded to the threat posed by Howard's Army of the Tennessee by dispatching two of his three corps, those of Lt. Gen. Stephen D. Lee (who had assumed command of Hood's old corps on July 27) and Maj. Gen. Alexander P. Stewart (who had assumed command of Polk's corps on July 7), on another tactical offensive. The initial attack, conducted by

Lee's corps, struck at around 12:30 P.M. Stewart's corps followed on the Lick Skillet road and was not committed to the attack until 2:00 P.M. Scaife, *The Campaign for Atlanta*, 104–7, 178, 181; Weigley, *A Great Civil War*, 365.

526. The Confederates began to break off the poorly coordinated and wasteful frontal attacks at 5 P.M., when Lee withdrew the two battered corps. Well protected behind their hasty fortifications, Howard's troops easily repulsed the exposed Confederate formations, inflicting costly casualties that Hood could ill afford. Kelly, *Kennesaw Mountain*, 51.

527. Given the narrow frontage (one mile) that the Confederates attacked, it was probable that three field officers could fall in such close proximity. Records list the following Confederate field officers as killed at Ezra Church: Lt. Col. Thomas Shields and Maj. Charles J. Bell, 30th Louisiana (both in Gibson's brigade); Lt. Col. J. D. Wilson, 46th Tennessee, and Col. John R. White, 53rd Tennessee (both from Quarles's brigade); Lt. Col. James T. Smith, 2nd Arkansas, and Lt. Col. Eli Hufstedler, 25th Arkansas (both from Reynolds's brigade); and Col. Benjamin R. Hart, 22nd Alabama (Deas's brigade). The probability is that the dead field officers witnessed by Oake and his companions were from William A. Quarles's brigade, Walthall's division, of Stewart's corps. The line of attack for Gibson's, Reynolds', and Quarles's brigade would have placed them to the left front in and around Ezra Church, in close proximity to the position of the 26th Iowa and Colonel Smith's brigade, which was located roughly 200 yards northeast of the church. *O.R.* I-38-III-777, 857, 932, 940.

528. The 26th Iowa suffered only 1 officer and 1 man wounded, both severely. Brigade losses were 12 men wounded, with Woods's entire division sustaining 1 killed, 63 wounded, and 1 missing. Total Federal casualties were 489 killed and wounded, 73 missing; aggregate 562. The Confederates probably lost upwards of 3,000 killed, wounded, and missing in the lopsided battle. *Roster* 3: 1023; *O.R.* I-38-III-105, 141, 148; Castel, *Decision in the West*, 434.

529. *O.R.* I-38-III-42, 105.

CHAPTER NINETEEN

Death of a Fine Officer, a Scared Comrade, and a Warm Place on Skirmish Line

✦ ———————————— ✦

After the battle of the 28th the rebels showed no further disposition to assault the Union lines, but contenting themselves with holding their strong line of defenses that loomed in front of the Federal army.[530]

General Sherman seeing the futility of further attempts on the enemy's works by direct assault contented himself with strengthening his works, and extending his lines hoping to accomplish by strategy what would cost an enormous sacrifice of life to accomplish by assaulting their lines, although no general engagement took place between the main lines of the two armies until the last of August, the skirmishing at times assumed the proportions of a battle.[531]

The part of the lines that we occupied[532] were about 60 rods [330 yards] from the main line of the enemy while their skirmishers were strongly entrenched in rifle pits about 100 yards in front of our line of works. At this time occurred a sad accident whereby the 26th lost two fine soldiers, and cast a gloom over the whole regiment. About thirty rods [165 yards] in the rear of the 26th on a slight eminence, was posted the 4th Ohio Battery[533] of six guns, which at times would open on the rebel picket lines compelling them to lay low.

About noon on the 15th [12th][534] of August the writer was frying sow belly for dinner, when the above mentioned battery opened with their six guns on the rebel picket lines throwing their shells directly over our regiment. One of them burst directly over the regiment, one large piece of shell cutting off the leg of Lieutenant E. H. Frank of our company, another piece tore off the top of the head of the colonel's cook,[535] while a third piece fell directly in the fire where the writer was cooking his sow belly, filling the frying pan with ashes and demoralizing the cook. Poor Frank lived several days after the sad accident, but the shock was too much for his naturally strong constitution, and his brave young spirit took its departure, and he was tenderly laid to rest under the Georgia pines, which sighed a mournful requiem over his lonely resting place. The death of Frank following so soon after the death of my Comrade Miller made a deep impression on my mind at the time. It was through Frank that I had enlisted, and although at the time of his death he was in command of the company and a commissioned officer, I was on the most intimate terms with him, and while in camp was in his tent almost as much as in my own. It was with him I spent so many pleasant evenings in playing cards with the ladies during our sojourn in Vienna, the winter prior. On Frank's death four out of the five spoken of earlier in this work as occupying the same tent at Helena in 1862 were gone, the writer alone being left.[536]

A day after the above accident [August 13, [there] occurred a laughable incident in which Swihart my old comrade was principal. Sergeant A. Fassett,[537] Swihart, and the writer were messing together at the time. We had made a little table to eat from at meal times by driving small pine saplings in the ground, and placing a board thereon, that we had procured from some old buildings a short distance in the rear. We also in the same manner made three seats to sit on while eating. The only difference between the table and the seats was, that while the table had four legs the seats had but three. The legs of the seats being little pine sticks about the size of a chair leg, being driven in the ground and a small board placed on top to sit on.

Our table was about 60 feet in the rear of our line of works, which made it possible for the enemy to drop in a shot once in a while. It was about noon and Fassett and the writer had taken our seats at the table waiting for our Comrade Swihart, who was cook that day, and who had the meal about prepared, and which he soon brought and placed upon the table. He had comfortably seated himself when a shot from the enemy knocked off one of

Death of a Fine Officer, a Scared Comrade,
and a Warm Place on Skirmish Line

Swihart's chair legs letting my old Comrade fall on his back while his eyes bulged out like two hen eggs. He quickly picked himself up, and as he started for the works with his hands full of hard tack and sow belly, he exclaimed in language more forcible than eloquent, "D—m the rebels they won't give a fellow time to eat." If living and should read this article I think my old comrade would verify this statement.

Owing to the proximity of the rebel pickets at this place, it was quite dangerous to move outside of the ditch behind our works, and it soon became rumored that a general advance of our lines were soon to be made, and force the enemy to fall back nearer their main lines. All the necessary arrangements had been made, it being ordered that our batteries all along the line should open fire on the rebel picket line for half an hour; whereupon they would cease firing for a few moments, when a signal gun would be fired, and the entire detail of our skirmishers would jump the works and go for the Johnnies. One hundred and fifty men had been detailed from our brigade, and about the same number from each brigade along the entire line.[538]

The writer had the honor of being one of the detail [selected] from the 26th Iowa. Promptly at the designated hour we were in line behind the works, and ready at the signal to scale the works, and go for the enemy. Soon the batteries along the line cease firing, and for a few moments all was quiet. At once the signal gun was fired, and over the works to the front we go for the enemy. In a few minutes we were at the rebel pits taking the enemy completely by surprise as they lay close to the bottom of the pits expecting every moment that our batteries would again open a terrific fire upon them. Seeing us on both sides of them, loaded guns pointed directly at them in their pits, the entire line dropped their arms and surrendered and were sent to the rear as prisoners. Thus had our brigade skirmishers, one hundred and fifty strong, captured the entire line of the enemy's pickets in our front, numbering ninety men, without the loss so far of a single man.[539]

As soon as the main line of the enemy saw that their entire line of pickets had been captured by us, they opened on us a terrific fire from their guns, and for a short time the air was filled with the flying missiles, while our main line stood behind their works ready to support us in case the enemy should attempt to drive us from our position, which we expected they would.

In a short time Captain James Crosier [Crozer][540] of Company C of the 26th, who was in charge of the 26th skirmishers, came to me and asked if I would go back to the main line, and get a supply of cartridges, as our ammunition was about exhausted. It being a dangerous task he did not want to detail a man if he could possibly get some one to volunteer for the undertaking. I told him I would go, although I would have given any amount of money, if possessed with it, if I could have honorably avoided it.

In order to reach our lines I would have to go diagonally across a ravine of about fifty yards in width, which was in a direct line of fire of the enemy's guns. Giving my gun to Mike Galvin, our chief fifer, who was on the line acting as a stretcher bearer, and handing my canteen filled with water to Wm. Johnson[541] of Company D, I was ready for undertaking.

I walked leisurely back until I reached the edge of the ravine, and I could plainly see the men in our main line of battle behind the works as with loaded arms they stood awaiting, as they supposed, the inevitable storm. As I reached the ravine I put in my best licks and at the time thought I was going about three miles a minute while every moment the shells were bursting on every side. When within about twenty feet of the works a shell passed my left side, and burst near and directly in front of me, and completely enveloped me in smoke, while the fragments of the shell filled the air with their deadly minnie. Still I was unharmed, and as I emerged from the smoke I heard the colonel say, "Oake is gone," but in an instant he found out his mistake as I jumped upon the works and stood for a moment entirely out of breath. When the colonel said, "Get down Oake or you will be shot in an instant." "What is wanted." asked the colonel. I replied "Ammunition, our supply is about exhausted." "All right," he replied, "I will have a man detailed to help you carry it back." Filling a haversack[542] nearly full he called a certain party by name and ordered him to assist me in carrying back the cartridges. The party that he detailed was a good fellow, and although an enlisted man did not carry a musket. Being well acquainted with him and considering myself much more active than he was I thought he would retard my progress on my return trip, but the sequel will show that I was greatly mistaken.

All being in readiness each of us caught hold of the haversack, when I said, "Bill, now you will have to put in your best licks." Over the works we sprang, and started on the return trip, while the air was filled with bursting shells. Talk about being more active than my partner, I wasn't in it. He dragged me, cartridges and all, until we reached the line, when being completely exhausted by the efforts he had made he lay down behind a tree as helpless as a child, while his face was deathly pale. I then approached Mike Galvin and took possession of my gun, and being thirsty I went to a large tree to get my canteen I had given Johnson. I got it but poor Johnson was dead, shot through the brain,[543] and I tenderly raised his head in order to get the canteen strap from around his neck. After removing my canteen from around the neck of poor Johnson I took a position behind a friendly tree which afforded good shelter, and by lying close to the ground, and peering around its friendly trunk I managed to get a few good shots at the enemy.

The skirmishing continued quite sharp until quite dark, when we were relieved by a new detail of pickets, and upon returning to the main line found that our bunk mates had prepared for us the usual allowance of sow belly, and hardtack. After partaking of the same we wrapped ourselves in our ponchos and lay down to take a much needed rest.

The troops had, while lying in this position, erected their dog tents,[544] and under the same we had made bunks about one foot high, by driving in the ground four crotched sticks, and putting a cross bar at both ends, we would then lie lengthwise small saplings upon which we covered with green pine boughs, which not only made our bed comparatively soft, but protected us from the wet ground.

About one week prior to the skirmish just mentioned, D. H. Denny of Company A, and the writer went a little in the rear of the line one night to cut a fine sapling for the purpose above mentioned. To have gone in the day time would have been almost sure death as it was in plain view of the enemy. While busily engaged in cutting the desired sticks, Denny, who was about fifteen feet to my right, said "Oake there is a dead man near here, don't you smell it?" In fact I had already and was about to speak of it when he interrupted me. As I started towards him he stumbled and fell over the putrid remains lying in the thick brush. In advancing to our present position, we had sharp skirmishing with the enemy, and more than one poor fellow had lost his life, and in gathering up the dead, this poor fellow had not been found. Perhaps at that time he was marked on the rolls as missing. Gathering up what sticks we had cut we returned, to our company and

Battlefield of Atlanta, Georgia.
This image shows the stark trench warfare conditions that characterized William Royal
Oake's experiences while fighting in and around Atlanta. LIBRARY OF CONGRESS

reported the finding of the body when a detail was made to bury it.

We lay at this position until the night of August 27th [26th], and most of the time brisk skirmishing daily occurred between the lines, although for a few days the opposing skirmishers agreed not to keep up an annoying fire at each other except when ordered to do so, and on such occasions we would meet midway between the lines and exchange with them coffee for tobacco. We would frequently give them a Yankee Newspaper, but the coffee would please them the most, and we would often times get a pound of tobacco for a sufficient amount of coffee to make three or four cupfuls of the delicious beverage.[545]

On the 27th [26th], in the evening, the writer was detailed on picket duty. And during the early part of the evening, the lines were unusually quiet, but as darkness settled over the earth the various bands of the enemy played several of the patriotic airs of the South, the sweet strains of which were wafted to our ears by the gentle evening breeze. After playing for about an hour, they suddenly ceased playing, when their batteries all along the lines opened up a terrific fire for over two hours the air was filled with

Death of a Fine Officer, a Scared Comrade,
and a Warm Place on Skirmish Line

bursting shell, and shot. As we lay in our pits watching the course of the deadly missiles as they sped on their errand of destruction, they could plainly be seen by the fire of the burning fuse, and while the air resounded with the rapid explosions and screeching of the missiles of destruction, it was a grand, but awful sight. One calculated to make the bravest heart quail, and strike terror into the hearts of the more timid. What meant such terrific firing was the question we asked ourselves at the same time we thought we could hear a commotion in the main lines of our army. Was it possible that the bloody scenes of Pat Cleburne's [William B. Bate's] midnight charge of May 27th [29th] at Dallas was to be repeated? Would it be possible for us to pass through another such conflict? To a person that knows nothing of such scenes it would be impossible to describe the peculiar sensations experienced by troops on such occasions. As we lay there under that terrific fire, with nerves strung to the highest tension, our hearts beating and as we thought, audible to a person a rod away, while visions of similar bloody scenes floated before our eyes. It was a scene well calculated to induce us to form good resolutions for the future, and I thought if I should succeed in getting safely out of that I would never go fishing on Sunday in the future.

For two hours the enemy kept up that terrific fire then suddenly ceased. Soon we heard footsteps approaching on our lines. What could it mean, was it friend or foe? Firmly we grasped our guns and waited further developments. Soon they were close to us, a little in our rear, and we discovered them to be our own men. The officer in charge of the guard was removing the picket line, and upon falling into line we quickly but silently marched to the rear to find that our main line had evacuated their works three hours prior, and during that time the picket line only confronted the rebel army, which had it been known by them they could have either killed or captured the entire line of pickets. To make it more plain to the reader, I will try and give the cause for the retrograde movement on the part of the Union Army.

During the last month it had been plainly demonstrated to General Sherman, by several attempts made on the enemies lines, that to carry their lines by assault would cause an enormous sacrifice of life, and he wisely decided to make what proved to be the grandest strategical [strategic] move of the campaign, and which gave to us without a great sacrifice of life the goal for which we sought, Atlanta. Ordering the 20th Army Corps, commanded by [Major] General [Henry] Slocum,* to fall back to a strongly fortified position on the north side of the Chattahoochee River, General Sherman with the remaining five [six infantry] corps decided to withdraw from the front, and by a rapid march to the right cut the enemy's last line of communication, by placing his army astride the railroad at Jonesboro, thirty miles in their rear. This would compel them to evacuate their present strong position at Atlanta.[546] The pickets upon being informed of the contemplated move of the army were soon following in the wake of the troops being guided by the fires that had been built along the road by the marching columns to serve as a guide for those in the rear, and although marching at a rapid pace we did not overtake the troops until the break of day, and shortly after we halted for a short time to partake of our breakfast, when we again resumed our march until we reached the railroad, running west from Atlanta, where the troops were again halted and were soon engaged in tearing up and destroying the road.[547]

Once more we resumed our march towards Jonesboro, which was about 12 miles distant. Soon we heard the guns in front that told us that our advance had met the enemy who were stubbornly resisting our further advance on their only remaining line of railroad at the little town of Jonesboro. As we drew near we could hear the rattle of musketry, a sure indication that quite a force of the enemy had been encountered, and were determined to resist our further advance. They were gradually driven back, however until we were within about one mile of the railroad, when night coming on we were compelled to cease hostilities for the day.[548] During the greater part of the night could be heard the rumbling of cars, and whistling of engines which told us that the enemy [was] being strongly reinforced by troops from Atlanta.[549]

At an early hour in the morning [August 31st],[550] our breakfast was eaten and we began to prepare for the conflict. The natural surface of the country was quite rolling, and to a great extent covered with young timber, although directly in front of our division the ground was partially cleared, while in front of our regiment on a slightly elevated position was posted the 4th Ohio Battery. Soon our skirmishers were fired upon by the enemy whose columns could plainly be seen about half a mile in front of us. Soon they were seen to advance directly toward our lines, and in an instant our

Death of a Fine Officer, a Scared Comrade,
and a Warm Place on Skirmish Line

artillery opened upon them with shot and shell. Still they moved steadily forward to be met with the more destructive fire of canister. As the death dealing messengers tear gaps in their ranks they were seen to waver and fall back. During the firing our regiment had been lying within supporting distance of the aforesaid battery, and as the enemy for the time being fell back, in front of us heavy firing was heard from a battery about 40 rods [220 yards] on our right. We at once receive orders to move to its support, and under a burning midsummer sun, at a double quick, we moved to its support leaving along our line of march more than one comrade that had succumbed to the excessive heat.

All day did the enemy attempt to carry different parts of the Union lines, only to have their shattered columns hurled back in disorder. Welcome night came at last, and the tired troops again took a much needed rest to prepare for the morrow.[551]

On the morning of August 31st [1st] the enemy again moved to attack, but our lines stood firm and defied their redoubled efforts to dislodge [our men from] them. Thus did the battle rage until about 2 P.M., when General Sherman realizing their exhausted condition after such desperate and continued efforts to dislodge us, ordered an advance of our entire line of battle on the left, and soon the veterans of the 4th [14th] Corps on the extreme left were seen to advance, and gain possession of the railroad. At last their only remaining line of communication was cut and the flanks of the Union Army were gradually encircling them within its deadly embrace, and right appropriately could the rebel commander, at that time, used the language of the Duke of Wellington at Waterloo, "Night or Reinforcements."[552]

Surely all that could possibly save the enemy was night which at this time was fast approaching, and as the sun sank in the lurid western sky the enemy [was] subjected to a terrific cross fire from the artillery of the Union Army. Night at last settled upon the two armies, after two days of incessant and bloody warfare, and the soldiers again rested.

About 3 A.M., September 1st [2nd], several successive explosions were heard in our rear, in the direction of Atlanta, which could be distinctly heard, and which seemed to jar the ground. What could it mean, was the question we asked each other. At an early hour in the morning our curiosity was gratified when a mounted carrier arrived with the information that

Atlanta had been evacuated by the enemy during the night, and that our troops, on the north side of the Chattahoochee under General Slocum had marched in and taken possession of the city. The explosions we heard were caused by the enemy, who blew up eighty car-loads of ammunition to prevent it falling into our hands, and which was impossible for them to save.[553]

At the first break of day our skirmishers on the advance found that, during the night, the thoroughly beaten rebels had retreated, leaving us in possession of the field, and a short time afterwards our scouts brought the information, that they had fallen back to a strong position at Lovejoy Station nine miles south.

Thus after four months of incessant fighting, that invincible army of 100,000 men had, in the face of 60,000 [70,000] of the enemy posted in a rough and mountainous country, succeeded in driving them 100 miles and wresting from them the goal we sought, Atlanta. Yes Atlanta was ours, and fairly won[554] although our loss in killed and wounded during the campaign was 34,000 men.[555]

Death of a Fine Officer, a Scared Comrade,
and a Warm Place on Skirmish Line

Death of a Fine Officer, a Scared Comrade, and a Warm Place on Skirmish Line

✦ ———————————————— ✦

530. In the aftermath of his third costly defeat, at the battle of Ezra Church, Hood was advised by President Jefferson Davis, "The loss consequent upon attacking him [the enemy] in his entrenchments requires you to avoid that if practicable…" Thus cautioned, Hood posted his army within the fortifications of Atlanta. Located an average distance of one-half mile outside the edge of the city, a siege line of forts and artillery redoubts, with connecting rifle pits and entrenchments, encircled the entire community for a distance of nine miles. The siege line was designed by Col. Lemuel P. Grant, chief engineer of the Department of Georgia, and built using slaves provided by their owners for $25 per month. *O.R.* I-38-V-946; Scaife, *The Campaign for Atlanta*, 127–31.

531. Sherman, *Memoirs*, II: 96.

532. Howard's Army of the Tennessee occupied the right of the Union siege line. Thomas held the center and Schofield was on the extreme left. On August 15, Maj. Gen. Peter J. Osterhaus returned to resume command of the 1st Division, which was "intrenched in three lines, some hundred yards to the right and in front of Ezra Chapel…. The opposing lines had been pushed so close together that operations had come to a stand-still…." The *Record of Events* for the regiment documents that, on July 30, the troops of the 26th Iowa "were worn out and exhausted from continual exposure and excessive fatigue, being almost constantly on duty and kept under arms day and night." Held in reserve, on August 9, the regiment was thrown into the advance line, losing one man killed. Ibid.; *O.R.* I-38-III-134; *Supplement to the O.R.* II-20-581.

533. The battery consisted of two 20-pounder Parrott rifles and four 12-pounder Napoleons, commanded by Capt. George Froehlich. On July 30, the battery had moved forward to a new position on the right, where it was "reported engaged against the enemy until the 26th of August…." *O.R.* I-38-III-124, 141, 175–76.

534. Records cite this incident as occurring August 12, 1864. *Roster* 3: 1054.

535. Identity not found.—Ed.

536. Elijah H. Frank's leg was amputated on August 12, and he died on August 14, 1864. *Roster* 3: 1054.

537. Almond Fassett, born in New York, was 29 and residing in Canton when he enlisted on June 30, 1862, as third corporal. He was promoted second corporal, April 1, 1863; fifth sergeant, August 1, 1863; and fourth sergeant, September 1, 1864. Fassett was mustered out on June 6, 1865, in Washington, D.C. *Roster* 3: 1054.

538. This assault on the enemy's entrenched skirmish line occurred in the dark, after midnight, on the morning of August 13, 1864. *O.R.* I-38-III-158.

539. Col. John A. Williamson, commanding the 2nd Brigade, reported that the assault carried out by the combat team was "a complete success, capturing nearly the entire force in the pits." On August 13, General Howard sent word to Sherman that "General Woods advanced and took the enemy's rifle pits, capturing sixty-five prisoners—four commissioned officers and sixty-one enlisted men. This in front of the extreme right of my line." Ibid.; *O.R.* I-38-III-485.

540. James G. Crozer, a native of Ohio, was 23 and living in Clinton when he enlisted on August

6, 1862, as first sergeant. Promoted captain, February 27, 1863, he was wounded slightly on September 1, 1864, but was mustered out with the regiment on June 6, 1865, in Washington, D.C. *Roster* 3:1042.

541. William J. Johnson was a resident of De Witt, having been born in Ohio. He enlisted on August 14, 1862, at the age of 19. *Roster* 3: 1068.

542. A carryall bag, usually worn slung over the right shoulder to hang over the soldier's left hip and not interfere with his loading a musket when he took cartridges from the cartridge box worn on the right hip. There was no standard shape, size, or material for the haversack, although most were made from cotton cloth. The U.S. Army regulation cloth haversack was painted with black enamel, had a round or pointed top flap, and had a removable unpainted cotton bag held by three buttons. Infantrymen used the sack to carry personal items and rations. Frederick P. Todd, *American Military Equipage, 1851–1872* (New York: Charles Scribner's Sons, 1980), 212.

543. Either Oake's memory is faulty or he honestly believed that Bill Johnson was killed outright, given the head wound. Most likely Johnson was quickly removed to the rear. He was mortally wounded on August 13, 1864, and died eleven days later on August 24. He is buried in the National Cemetery at Marietta, Georgia. *Roster* 3: 1068.

544. The standard summer shelter of the rank and file Federal soldier was the canvas tent, widely known as the dog tent. The common version was a two-man shelter made by buttoning together the half-shelters (one issued to each soldier) and stretching them over a horizontal pole supported at each end by a pronged stick or even a musket stuck in the ground with the bayonet fixed. If a soldier wished to sleep alone, he simply tied the corners to the tops of four upright sticks and crawled inside. Often three or four men would combine their half-shelters to make a larger habitation. As Oake alludes, they were designed only for sleeping. Wiley & Milhollen, *They Who Fought Here*, 84.

545. Although it was usually forbidden, or at least not authorized, by their superiors, there is considerable documented evidence that fraternization between enlisted combatants on picket duty was common whenever two opposing armies spent extended periods in close proximity, particularly during siege operations. As described by Oake, these informal truces on the picket line most often occurred at night and involved bartering food, beverages, tobacco, newspapers, lies, and "whatever would vary the monotony of picket life." B. A. Botkin, *A Civil War Treasury of Tales, Legends and Folklore* (New York: Promontory Press, 1960), 269.

546. Sherman had tried to break the Macon Railroad with cavalry raids, but two converging strikes ended in failure. Sherman, *Memoirs*, II: 103–5.

547. The Atlanta & West Point Railroad, extending from East Point to Red Oak Station and Fairburn, southwest of Atlanta. Sherman remembered that Howard's troops spent August 28–29 "in breaking it up thoroughly." Osterhaus's division struck the railroad at noon, near Shadna Church, two miles north of Fairburn. Brushing aside a light picket, they built entrenchments before getting to the task of smashing the railroad. Ibid., 105; *O.R.* I-38-III-134.

548. After assisting in destroying the railroad, Sherman's forces marched on August 30 for Jonesboro, nearly sixteen miles south of Atlanta on the Macon & Western Railroad. The order of march placed Osterhaus's division in the rear of the XV Corps, and it consequently took no part in the skirmishes with Confederate troops resisting the advance. Therefore, Oake writes this without actually having participated in the skirmishes. The army crossed the Flint River, advanced in force to a point two miles from the railroad, and bivouacked behind field works. The next morning Howard advanced, only to find an entrenched enemy at Jonesboro, "and his men began at once to dig their accustomed rifle-pits." Farther to the north, Thomas on Howard's left, and Schofield to Thomas's north, moved toward the railroad at Rough and Ready,

Death of a Fine Officer, a Scared Comrade, and a Warm Place on Skirmish Line

and also between there and Jonesboro. Sherman, *Memoirs*, II: 106–7. The 26th Iowa was briefly engaged, losing one officer and four men wounded. The regiment lay north of the Confederate lines, within one mile of Jonesboro. *Supplement to the O.R.* II-20-581.

549. Initially confused by the absence of Sherman's forces west of the city, Hood was now alerted to the Federal designs to break his communications, and on the evening of August 30, he sent the two corps commanded by Hardee and Lee down the railroad to Jonesboro. Weigley, *A Great Civil War*, 366.

550. Pursuant to an order from Osterhaus, Milo Smith detached two regiments, the 76th Ohio and 26th Iowa, to report to Brig. Gen. William B. Hazen, commanding 2nd Division, XV Corps. The 26th Iowa was temporarily under the command of Capt. James G. Crozer of Co. C, and Col. William B. Woods, 76th Ohio, commanded the two-regiment detachment. Hazen's division was entrenched three-quarters of a mile west by north of the Jonesboro railroad depot, with the divisions of William Harrow and John M. Corse deployed on the line to its right. *O.R.* I-38-III-149, 151, 183.

551. General Hazen stated that he posted Woods's detachment where most needed. At 2 P.M., the enemy commenced a vigorous artillery fire and sent infantry forward. "We had good works, and the attack was met with the most perfect confidence." After nearly an hour, the Confederates were repulsed and driven back to their line. The attacks were poorly coordinated, and, by the end of the day, Thomas and Schofield stood astride the Macon Railroad at Rough and Ready, and between there and Jonesboro at Morrow's Station. These three corps turned south and pushed down the railroad toward Jonesboro from the north, hoping to trap the Confederate forces. Ibid., 183; Weigley, *A Great Civil War*, 366.

552. Lee's corps had been recalled to Atlanta by Hood. Thus, Hardee faced the entire Federal force alone on September 1, and Sherman had an excellent opportunity to isolate and destroy the Confederate corps. Oake describes the arrival of the XVI Army Corps, part of Thomas's Army of the Cumberland, commanded by Brig. Gen. Jefferson C. Davis, which attacked the Confederate works north of town. Meanwhile, Sherman had Howard advance the XVII Corps to cut the railroad south of town, while Maj. Gen. David S. Stanley, commanding the XIV Corps, was to advance left and eastward of town to enclose the whole ground occupied by Hardee's corps. The Confederate general was alert to his peril, however, and when Stanley failed to seal off an eastward avenue of escape by nightfall, Hardee withdrew his beleaguered corps southeastward. On August 31, the Federals lost 179 men out of nearly 14,200 engaged. The Confederates lost about 1,725 out of the 23,800 engaged in the two corps. The next day, Union losses totaled 1,274 out of 20,460 engaged. Hardee had 12,660 engaged; Cleburne lost 911, but numbers for the other divisions are not known. It appears, however, that as many as 3,100 rank and file Confederates may have been killed, wounded, and captured at Jonesboro. In the two days of fighting there, William B. Woods's detachment lost 4 men killed and 8 wounded, and, of these, the 26th Iowa reported 1 officer and 4 men wounded on August 31, and 1 officer and 3 men severely wounded on September 1. Woods stated that the two regiments "rendered valuable assistance in repulsing the attack" on August 31 and, on September 1, "pressed the flanks of the enemy with a strong line of skirmishers" while being attacked in front by the XIV Corps. Sherman, *Memoirs*, II: 107–8; Boatner, *Civil War Dictionary*, 445; *Supplement to the O.R.* II-20:581; *Roster* 3: 1025; *O.R.* I-38-III: 151.

553. Hood realized that Sherman's force astride the Macon Railroad was too strong to dislodge with further wasteful attacks. Atlanta no longer had a dependable line of supply, now that the three railroads east, west, and south of the city were destroyed, and the northern line was under Union control. Therefore, Hood was forced to evacuate. He halted the return of Lee's corps, and ordered Lee to cover the withdrawal of Cheatham's corps (Maj. Gen. Benjamin H. Cheatham, who had assumed command of the corps when A. P. Stewart was wounded at Ezra Church) the night of September 1–2, which moved southeastward down the McDonough road. The tremendous explosions Oake and his comrades heard after midnight were the partially successful attempt of the Confederate rear guard to destroy the ordnance stores and locomotives in the city. Ibid., 108; Castel, *Decision in the West*, 521–25.

554. At 6 A.M. on September 3, having received confirmation from Slocum that the XX Corps had assumed possession of the city, Sherman, near Lovejoy Station, telegraphed Maj. Gen. Henry W. Halleck at the War Department in Washington, "So Atlanta is ours, and fairly won." *O.R.* I-38-V-777.

555. It is difficult to assess the loss sustained by the combatants in this campaign, for the records vary; however, a solid compilation of the casualties sustained by the United States forces is 4,423 killed, 22,822 wounded, and 4,422 missing/captured, equaling 31,687 troops. So many Confederate records were destroyed that only estimates can be made. It seems likely that Johnston and Hood suffered at least a combined total of 3,044 killed, 18,952 wounded, and 12,913 captured, equaling 34,909 total troops. The 26th Iowa, with a maximum effective strength of 292 the first week in May, lost during the campaign 7 killed, 59 wounded, and 1 captured, for 67 total casualties; whereas its brigade suffered 51 killed, 267 wounded, and 3 missing/captured, totaling 321; and its division 130 killed, 725 wounded, and 37 missing, 892 total. David S. Heidler & Jeanne T. Heidler, eds., *Encyclopedia of the American Civil War: A Political, Social, and Military History* (New York: W.W. Norton & Co., 2000), John McKay, "Atlanta Campaign: May–September 1864," 128–46; *O.R.* I-38-III-113–14.

Death of a Fine Officer, a Scared Comrade,
and a Warm Place on Skirmish Line

Major General Oliver O. Howard.
A graduate of West Point, Howard became the fifth commanding
general of the Army of the Tennessee under which William Royal
Oake and his regiment would serve, directing the veteran army
during the "March to the Sea" and the invasion of the Carolinas.
LIBRARY OF CONGRESS

CHAPTER TWENTY

In Pursuit of Hood's Army

The troops were soon in line following Hood's Army, whom we found strongly entrenched at Lovejoy Station, and here we remained a few days skirmishing with them.[556] As the campaign was virtually over, and the army in need of clothes and rest, we were moved back to East Point about 12 miles west of Atlanta, and went into camp for a short time.

While lying here, an armistice was held by the commanders of the opposing forces pending a correspondence between the two commanders concerning the removal from Atlanta of noncombatants,[557] and at the same time a number of prisoners were exchanged by the two armies. It was a sad contrast to witness the physical difference of the prisoners. While the rebels were returned to their commands well fed, and with their well filled haversacks a great many of our men that had been in their hands had to be helped or carried from the train, while their garments hung in rags, and teemed with vermin, and the stench arising from their bodies was almost unendurable, with quite a few, from the idiotic grin that overspread their countenance it was plain to be seen that reason was dethroned by the treatment they received while in the hands of the enemy. Kind readers some of you may think I am coloring the case, but they are statements that could be verified by hundreds of living witnesses on that occasion, and it will to the end of time remain a lasting disgrace and blot on the record of the leaders of the lost cause.[558]

After being in camp about ten days it was learned that the rebel commander, General Hood, had dispatched his cavalry to prey upon Sherman's line of communication, and to break up the railroad in the rear of the army, and by which means we received our supplies. In a few days the entire rebel army was on the move north in support of their cavalry. The move was for the ostensible purpose of drawing Sherman out of Georgia. At Allatoona, about thirty-six miles in the rear, was stored an immense amount of stores for the army, a grand prize for the rebels if they could but capture it, while the loss to our army would be irreparable. At Allatoona Pass at that time there was a garrison of about 900 men under the command of Colonel [John E.] Tourlelotte [Tourtellotte],[559] while at Rome [Brigadier] General [John M.] Corse[560] was stationed with about the same number of men. General Sherman had upon discovering what he supposed to be the object of General Hood, telegraphed General Corse at Rome to hasten with all available troops to Allatoona, and to assume command and hold the place as long as a man lived. Our portion of the army that had already been put in motion would hasten to his assistance.[561]

General Hood not deeming it necessary to take his whole army to capture a small garrison of 900 [860] men dispatched [Major] General [Samuel] French's division, of about 7,000 [3,276] men, to capture Allatoona, while he with his main army would continue northward. On the morning of October 5th, having invested the place, General French sent General Corse a note demanding the unconditional surrender of Allatoona with its garrison, stating that he had the place completely invested, and that its surrender would save the needless effusion of blood. He little knew the metal of General Corse who in his reply stated that he was ready for that needless effusion of blood, and if he wanted Allatoona he would have to take it by force of arms.[562]

Then for a short time (for the numbers engaged), raged one of the most desperate conflicts of the war. How vividly are the scenes of that bright October morning impressed upon the memory of the writer while near Kennesaw, 18 miles distant, we could hear the thunder of the guns at Allatoona engaged in the deadly conflict.

General Sherman who was on Kennesaw anxiously endeavoring by the aid of the signal flags[563] to discover if General Corse had reached and assumed command of the forces at Allatoona. At last the tell tale flag informs him that Corse was there. Upon receiving the glad news the general said he would hold the fort, "For I know the man.' Shortly afterwards General Corse was wounded in the cheek and ear when he sent the following dispatch to General Sherman, "I am short one ear and a cheek bone, but can whip all hell yet."[564]

For several hours the enemy continued to assault the Union position, but the garrison stood firm, while their batteries mowed down the rebel hordes in great swarms, and the rebel general fearing the approach of Sherman's army, and realizing the futility of any further attempts to carry the Union position, hastily withdrew leaving their dead and wounded in the hands of the Federal troops. Some idea of the terrible conflict can be gained from the fact that nearly one-half [one-third] of the Union forces were killed and wounded during the brief but sanguinary struggle.[565]

While the battle was in progress, we were marching rapidly to the assistance of the gallant little band following the line of railroad which for miles had been torn up and destroyed by the rebel forces. About two miles north of the little town of Acworth, and about eight miles south of Allatoona the enemy had intercepted a number of car loads of cattle en-route to our army, which they had not even unloaded, but had set the train on fire burning the poor brutes to death in the cars, and when we marched past the wreck the air was filled with the stench of the burning flesh.[566]

On the next morning we passed through the hard fought field of the previous [week] and evidences of the deadly conflict [were] visible on every hand while scores of the dead were still unburied. We were fast gaining upon the enemy, who upon reaching the vicinity of Resaca, left the railroad taking a northwest course through Snake Creek Gap.[567] About noon on the 16th day of October we struck the rear guard of the enemy about 200 strong that were strongly posted behind a stone wall at Ship's Gap on Taylor's Ridge. The ridge was merely a branch of the [many] mountain ranges that are so common in that part of Georgia. Our brigade was in the advance when the enemy [was] encountered, and we quickly placed in line of battle while the 26th Iowa was detailed as skirmishes to cover the front of the brigade.[568]

We were soon forcing our way through the thick underbrush that covered the side of the mountain, while once more the ping of the minie was heard on every side. Henry [actually George W.] Birch[569] of Company A fell a victim to the flying bullets, and as Robert J. McLenahan, Henry O'Farrell,[570] and the writer were advancing within about 60 feet of the enemy's outpost, consisting of about thirty men, who were posted behind piles of stone, and completely hidden from our view, we received a deadly volley, and poor O'Farrell fell dead with a bullet through his heart. McLenahan and the writer jumped behind a tree which was hardly large enough to conceal our bodies, and which was soon filled with bullets. As I generally try to confine myself to facts in this work I will admit the facts in this instance. McLenahan was a much larger man than I, and as the tree was hardly large enough to cover one, and he was the first behind it I had, by getting behind him, double protection. Bob was behind the tree, and I was behind Bob. A cooler or braver man, than Bob McLenahan, never faced the guns of an enemy. He was a physical giant, and always present for duty, but the hardships of the service was too much for even his strong constitution, and a few years ago at Spirit Lake, Iowa, for him, the last roll call sounded. He joined the hosts that had preceded him, and today rests in the cemetery at Clinton, Iowa.

After being behind the tree a few moments, and finding that some of the rebel bullets came from the flank I thought it would be advisable to change my position. About twenty feet to my right I noticed Peter J. Potter, and T. J. Houston of Company A, lying behind a log. Taking a few hasty steps I threw myself down beside them. When Potter said, "Oake give me your gun quick," I handed him my gun, and as he quickly pointed it over the log, I could by looking under the brush see what he wanted it for: about fifty feet in front I plainly saw a rebel at whom Potter took aim and fired. Just at that time our main line advanced and poured into the rebels a volley, when the rebels raised the white flag, and the outpost surrendered. Then the skirmishers again advanced, and as we passed the spot where the rebel had stood, who Potter had shot at, we found him lying beside the tree in the last struggle of death, and I remarked to Potter, "You got your man." He replied, "I did not kill him." Potter passed on, and I stopped for a moment to look at the poor fellow who was shot directly through the breast, and at that moment was about to expire. Potters denial could not change the facts, and after the lapse of many years I often times think of that poor fellow lying on the slope of Taylor's Ridge. Methinks I can yet see Potter on that occasion as he passed by him without looking at him, and claiming he did not kill him.[571]

In Pursuit of Hood's Army

❖ ———————————— ❖

556. Hood, having linked up with Hardee, dug in a mile north of Lovejoy, five miles south of Jonesboro, and saw some minor action over several days while Sherman pulled back to Atlanta to reorganize, rest the men, and plan. "Since May 5," Sherman wired Washington, "we have been in one constant battle or skirmish, and need rest." The 26th Iowa lost, on September 3 in fighting at Lovejoy, four men severely wounded, and on September 6 had one man wounded while on the march north to East Point, where they arrived on September 8, 1864. *O.R.* I-38-V: 777; *Roster* 3: 1025.

557. Sherman ordered the evacuation of Atlanta on September 7. "I have deemed it to the interest of the United States that the citizens now residing in Atlanta should remove, those who prefer it to go South and the rest North," Sherman advised Hood. Between September 12 and 21, the people left, roughly 446 families, 709 adults (mostly women), 867 children, and 79 "servants" proceeding with their belongings to Rough and Ready, where they and their property were transferred to Confederate wagons and forwarded to Lovejoy Station. The decision created indignation and angry protest. Sherman, however, felt he had difficulties enough in securing food and medicine for his own troops, and he had written, "If the people raise a howl against my barbarity and cruelty, I will answer that war is war and not popularity-seeking. If they want peace they and their relatives must stop the war." Hood was appalled, and a lengthy heated exchange of correspondence with Sherman followed—but to no avail. "I am not willing to have Atlanta encumbered by the families of our enemies," a determined Sherman wired Halleck in Washington. "I want it a pure Gibralta, and will have it so by the 1st of October." Ibid., 822; Weigley, *Decision in the West*, 548–49; *O.R.* I-39-II: 414–22; *O.R.* II-7: 791.

558. The exchange was 2,000 prisoners, the last taken in the campaign, from each army, and Sherman reported on September 29 that it had been accomplished. In addition to rank and file volunteers, the Federals received back Maj. Gen. George Stoneman, captured July 30 during a cavalry raid to break Hood's supply lines and attempt to liberate Union prisoners at Andersonville. Oake's outrage and impression of how the Union prisoners had been treated is understandable but mistaken. Thousands of Confederates held in several Northern prisons suffered the same harsh, disease-ridden conditions. In fact, although slightly more than 30,000 Union soldiers (15.5 percent of those imprisoned) died in Confederate camps, nearly 26,000 Confederates (12 percent) died in Federal prison camps. After the war, many Northerners ignored stories of brutality and mistreatment in Union prisons. In addition, Oake would have observed only recently captured Confederates, most of them taken at Jonesboro, while many of the Federal prisoners being exchanged had spent several weeks, even months, in prison. In addition, the Confederacy frequently suffered from serious food shortages throughout the war, not so much from lack of food, but from its inability to distribute rations to its armies—the first priority—and to the prison camps, the last priority. Inflation, incompetence on behalf of the Confederate Subsistence Department, and an increasing lack of sufficient transportation combined to diminish the amount of food reaching the front and prisons. Ibid., 784, 791–92, 797, 808, 817–18, 822, 846–47, 851–52; *O.R.* 39-II-517; Michael Fellman, Lesley J. Gordon, & Daniel E. Sutherland, *This Terrible War: The Civil War and its Aftermath* (New York: Longman, 2003), 190–91, 293–94.

559. John Eaton Tourtellotte, from Connecticut, began the war as a private in Co. H, 4th Minnesota Infantry, on September 12, 1861, and was promoted captain, December 13, 1861;

lieutenant colonel, September 1, 1862; and colonel, October 5, 1864. Wounded at Allatoona, he later commanded the 2nd Brigade, 3rd Division, XV Corps, Army of the Tennessee, and was promoted to brigadier general of volunteers for war service at the conclusion of hostilities. Boatner, *Civil War Dictionary*, 844.

560. John Murry Corse (1835–1893), from Pennsylvania, graduated from West Point (1857) and was a lawyer and politician when commissioned major of the 6th Iowa on July 13, 1861. He rose steadily through the ranks and was appointed brigadier general of volunteers on August 11, 1863. His active war service included New Madrid/Island No. 10, Corinth, Vicksburg, and Missionary Ridge (where he was severely wounded), and he commanded the 2nd Division, XVI Corps during the Atlanta campaign. At the time Hood struck Sherman's supply lines at Allatoona, Corse commanded the 4th Division, XV Corps. Ibid., 203.

561. Unable to engage Sherman's much larger force in open battle and thus reclaim Atlanta, Hood took up the campaign against Sherman's supply line in hopes of drawing small Federal forces out of Atlanta to defend their rear, and then defeat them in detail. On September 29, Hood forded the Chattahoochee northwest of Atlanta and continued northward, dispatching A. P. Stewart's corps to strike the Western & Atlantic Railroad north of Marietta. Stewart overran small garrisons at Big Shanty, Moon's Station, and Acworth, and by the night of October 4, had destroyed about eight miles of track and captured 600 prisoners. Hood then asked Stewart to send one division (Stewart dispatched French) to destroy the railroad cut at Allatoona Pass, by filling it with dirt, rocks, and debris, then march north to the railroad bridge over the Etowah River and burn it. Corse's arrival raised the number of men defending Allatoona to 2,025 rank and file troops. Stored at Allatoona were roughly a million rations for Sherman's forces. Heidler & Heidler, *Encyclopedia of the American Civil War*, James Meredith, "Allatoona, Battle of, 5 October, 1864," 33–34; *O.R.* I-39-I: 581, 763.

562. For the 26th Iowa, the pursuit of Hood began on October 4, 1864, when it marched with its corps from East Point, Georgia, where the regiment had been encamped since returning from Lovejoy on September 8. *Roster* 3: 1025.

563. Signal flags were made of cotton, linen, or some other light but closely woven fabric. The flags were mounted on hickory staffs, which came in four joints or pieces, and were fitted together for use. From the beginning of the war, the signal corps had used a wigwag system of flags and torches but soon included rockets and signal flares. On a clear day, wigwag signals could be distinguished at up to twenty miles. The morning of October 5, 1864, was extremely foggy, making it impossible to see wigwags between Allatoona and Kennesaw Mountain. J. Willard Brown, *The Signal Corps in the War of the Rebellion* (Boston: U.S. Veteran Signal Corps Association, 1896), 116, 543–48.

564. Oake has this message out of context. It was sent at 2 P.M. on October 6, 1864, a day after the failed Confederate attempt to destroy the pass. The actual message sent to Capt. L. M. Dayton, Sherman's aide-de-camp, reads, "I am short a cheek bone and one ear, but am able to whip all hell yet." While the engagement was going on, Sherman attempted to communicate with signal flags from Kennesaw Mountain. Several messages were sent, but were not answered. The telegraph north of Marietta had been cut by the Confederates, and since his original message to Corse in Rome had been sent by signal flag, Sherman did not know whether Corse had actually reinforced Tourtellotte. Corse had great difficulty in sending signals from Allatoona while engaged, and Sherman and the signal officer managed to catch a glimpse of only one coded wigwag sequence, "C.R.S.E.H.E.R." The signal was interpreted as "Corse is here." *O.R.* I-39-III-113; Boatner, *Civil War Dictionary*, 8.

565. French's troops carried the outer works and appeared on the verge of capturing the garrison occupying the primary fortification—Star Fort—but French received reports (later proved false) that a large Union force was moving to cut his retreat. He broke off the attacks, and retired without having accomplished the desired objective. Corse suffered 142 men killed, 352 wounded, and 212 missing/captured, for 706 casualties. French sustained 134 soldiers killed, 474 wounded, and 289 missing/captured, for 897 casualties. *O.R.* I-39-I: 766, 802, 813, 820.

566. It appears that the regiment moved through Acworth on October 9. It had reached a point four miles south of Marietta on October 5, camping there in old fortifications until the 8th, when it advanced with the corps up the railroad via Big Shanty and Acworth, arriving at Allatoona in the late afternoon of October 10. General Osterhaus was in temporary command of the corps. *AGI*, 1865-II: 1167; *O.R.* I-39-I: 740–41.

567. With its division, the 26th Iowa crossed the Etowah at Cartersville on October 11, marching eighteen miles in the afternoon, when several men of the regiment, being completely worn out from the rapid forced march, fell out by the side of the road. These men "were either butchered, or taken prisoners by the guerrillas who were hovering in our rear." The 26th then moved to Rome, bivouacking four miles from town, and, on October 14, it marched north through Calhoun to Resaca. *AGI*, "History of the Regiment" 1865-II:1167.

568. The 1st Brigade was in the advance on October 16, moving early through Villanow, then moving west four miles to Ship's Gap. Upon making contact with the Confederate forces, the 26th Iowa was moved to the left of the assaulting line to assist in dislodging the enemy force. Ibid.; *O.R.* I-39-I: 742.

569. Birch had been with the regiment only ten months. A native of New York, he was 40 and living in Sac City when he enlisted on January 4, 1864. His severely wounded arm had to be amputated, and he was discharged for disability January 4, 1865, in St. Louis, Missouri. *Roster* 3: 1032.

570. Born in New York, O'Farrell was 17 and living in Fort Dodge when he enlisted on January 4, 1864. *Roster* 3: 1085.

571. General Osterhaus stated in his report that when he ordered Gen. Charles Woods to send a demonstrating detachment on the enemy's left flank at Ship's Gap, the commanding officer of the 26th Iowa "executed his instructions so well that when the order to attack was given most of the rebel infantry fell into our hands; those on the farther ridge retired suddenly." The 26th lost one man killed and four wounded, and captured about thirty prisoners. *O.R.* I-39-I: 742; *AGI*, 1865-II: 1167.

CHAPTER TWENTY-ONE

Still in Pursuit of Hood and Abundance of Forage

❦ ——————————— ❧

Steadily the skirmishers moved forward, and were given a warm reception by the enemy on the top of the ridge. Returning the compliment, and backed by the [main] line of battle we succeeded in compelling the rebels to beat a hasty retreat, and mounting their horses they disappeared down the opposite side of the ridge, and when we reached its top we discovered them about 100 rods [550 yards] distant in the valley, riding rapidly in the direction taken by Hood's army. Raising our guns we gave them a parting shot, and in line followed down the slope of the mountain to the valley below.

At the foot of the mountain we came upon quite a large plantation, which was teeming with an abundance of chickens, sheep, hogs, and other forage. In company with a comrade I entered a log outhouse, and was agreeably surprised to find a fine assortment of apples, that were arranged and partitioned off in old fashioned log troughs, that rested against the walls of the building.

Hastily removing our gum ponchos, which we spread on the floor, we were soon busily engaged in filling them with choice apples, which I secured by tying the corners of the blanket and placing them in charge of our company's cook, Bill Wallace, a negro, who had followed us over the ridge.

Taking a few of the finest I started out to find other forage. On leaving the building, what was my surprise to run against General Osterhaus our division commander, who with some of his staff, had followed the line of skirmishers over the mountain. Approaching the General, I asked him if he would like a fine apple, which he readily accepted, kindly thanking me for the same. Just at that moment the General was approached by the owner of the premises who imploringly asked him to stop his soldiers from taking everything he had. The General with a twinkle in his eyes turned to the soldiers, and with a rich German brogue said, "Boys, I don't want you to take nottings you cannot carry." Highly gratifying as his answer was to the soldiers the sorrowful look that overspread the countenance of the planter told more plainly than words his feelings at thus seeing the accumulations of years swept away in an instant. Had we persisted in the course practiced in the early part of the war, to wit; of taking nothing from the enemy, but placing guards over it, simply guarding it for the use of the rebel army, it might have been the means of the war continuing for years.

Leaving the locality, where I got the apples, I was soon busily engaged in procuring a lot of fine sweet potatoes that I discovered in a patch a short distance from the house. At the same time my comrades were making it warm for the chickens, and other forage. By this time the brigade had reached the plantation, and ordered into camp, the rest of the army remaining on the other side of the mountain. Taking our forage to camp we were soon engaged in getting ready our evening meal, such a meal as I had not partaken of since leaving Vienna. We remained in camp until the afternoon of the next day. A good portion of the time being spent by the boys in gathering the ripe and delicious chestnuts the trees of which covered the slopes of the mountain, and although an abundance could be had by knocking them from the tree with poles, the plan was not expeditious enough to suit a good many who soon procured axes and felled the trees, that the delicious nuts could be more readily obtained.[572]

On the afternoon of the 17th the troops were again following Hoods army, and for several days while marching down the rich valley we had an abundance of forage. Upon reaching the little town of La Fayette [actually vicinity of Blue Pond, Alabama, on the Little River] we encamped for a few days, when Sherman seeing it was impossible to overtake or force Hood to battle, and believing that Nashville, Tennessee was the objective point of the rebel army, determined to send General Thomas there with a force sufficient to hold the enemy in check, and if possible whip him if a battle should occur. While Sherman with the main army would retrace its steps to the vicinity of Atlanta, to rest and prepare for what he had already contemplated, the March to the Sea.[573]

We reached our camp at Vinings [Vining] Station, about 16 miles north of Atlanta, the first [fifth] of November where we remained until we started on our long march to the sea. While lying at Vining Station, occurred the Presidential Election and the writer had the honor of casting his maiden vote for the great emancipator, A. Lincoln.[574]

While at this place the only duty we had to perform was picket duty. One incident that occurred here while on picket is too good to omit. In company with Sergeant Robert J. McLenahan, Private George Waggoner, and George M. Lynch [Linch][575] all of Company A, the writer was one day on picket. Now the orders were very strict against pickets firing their guns while on duty, unless it was at the enemy. We were on duty in the woods about a mile from camp. I had just been relieved as vidette, my place being taken by Waggoner. On returning to the rear about 100 yards, where McLenahan and Lynch were on reserve post I leaned my gun against a tree, when Lynch called my attention to a large black squirrel in a small tree just over our heads. Now kind readers before going any farther with the squirrel it is perhaps necessary that I should inform you of what all soldiers know to be a fact, that is customary to give all the boys nicknames. As a general thing the name would be suggested by some peculiarity of the soldier in way of speech, action or dress. Now there was no word in the English vocabulary drawn upon more frequently by Lynch than the word "Christ," hence he was named Christ. He was very fond of squirrels, and as an order obeying soldier was above reproach. He would look at me then the slick fat squirrel, not daring to fire at it for fear of extra duty in case he should be discovered by the picket officer, and who might appear at any moment. I at last told him I would kill it for him. Drawing the charge from my musket, I removed half the charge of powder and putting in the rest with a fresh bullet. I raised my gun and taking aim fired, and the squirrel fell at our feet. It had no sooner touched the ground than Christ had hold of it, and hastily placed it under cover. I then quickly reloaded my gun, and we resumed our loafing attitudes, when in about ten minutes the division picket officer appeared.

Halting at our post, we saluted him, when he inquired of Sergeant McLenahan if he had not heard a gun fired along the line (I then thought Injun you are in for a weeks extra picket duty.) The Sergeant replied, "I think it was farther down the line major." I thought I discovered a twinkle in the major's eye as he replied, "I will find out," and rode in the direction indicated. I never learned if the major found out who fired the shot, but we saw no more of him, and as a sequel to my story we had a fine fry for our dinners. If this story should meet the eyes of my old comrade Christ, I am certain he would corroborate every word of this story.[576]

CHAPTER NOTES:
Still in Pursuit of Hood and Abundance of Forage

✦ —————————————— ✦

572. The possession of Ship's Gap, reported Osterhaus, "secured the road to La Fayette and the rich country of the Chickamauga Valley, which furnished us the most needed means of subsistence to both men and animals." *O.R.* I-39-I-742.

573. From La Fayette, five miles west of Ship's Gap, the Army of the Tennessee followed Hood's retreating army southwest through Summerville and Gaylesville, Alabama, reaching the Little River on October 21. Bridges were built across the river, along with a *tete-de-pont* fortification network "capable of holding a full brigade." There the 26th Iowa lay for a short time waiting for Hood's army to form up. While there, the regiment participated in a reconnaissance in force to Leesburg. After deciding it was fruitless to try to run Hood down, Sherman recalled Howard's army to Atlanta. On October 29, the 26th Iowa again took up the march, re-crossed the Little River and the Chatooga River, moving eastward into Georgia, passing over the Coosa River through Cedartown, and arrived at Cave Springs on October 30. There the regiment bivouacked for a few days to muster and rest. Ibid.; *AGI*, 1865-II: 1167.

574. Sherman's triumph at Atlanta in effect reelected Lincoln, electrifying Northern opinion behind continuing the war. In addition, other Federal victories at Mobile Bay and Shenandoah Valley helped rescue Lincoln from what that summer had loomed as a smashing defeat. Lincoln received a major electoral victory over the Democratic presidential candidate, Gen. George B. McClellan, on November 8, 1864. Lincoln won by 400,000 popular votes—winning 55 percent of the ballots. He carried thirty-two states, all but three. Many soldiers had been furloughed to go home to vote, and in other states Republican administrations sent ballot boxes to the front. Lincoln won 78 percent of the soldier vote, demonstrating the army's—and not only William Royal Oake's—deep commitment to the war effort. Fellman, Gordon, & Daniel, *This Terrible War*, 271, 282.

575. Linch, from Ohio, was 26 and lived in Charlotte when he enlisted on August 13, 1862. He was mustered out on June 6, 1865, in Washington, D.C. *Roster* 3: 1072.

576. The major was John Lubbers.

CHAPTER TWENTY-TWO

Colors Point to the South and Trip to Savannah

While lying in camp at this place, great preparations were being made in accumulating supplies for the army to subsist upon while on its great march to the sea.[577] Some idea of the vast amount of stores necessary for an army of 65,000 men, for thirty days, can be formed when it is known that it would require 3,000 car loads of 20,000 pounds to the car to furnish an army of 65,000 men, half rations only for thirty days. Of course we would to a certain extent have to depend on the country through which we passed for forage for the animals, hauling trains, and the artillery. Rumors reached our ears that in a few days we would start on our long trip. All the sick and convalescent were being sent to the rear, and the troops were informed that if they wished to send any word home to their friends in the North, they had but a few days to do it. For the next few days the soldiers were busily engaged in writing letters to friends at home, and [for] many [it] proved to be their last letter home. Well does the writer remember the last train that left for the North with a full head of steam and a whistle almost deafening, which seemed to say Good Bye, it sped with lightening like rapidity to the rear.[578]

The last train had left; the telegraph wires were cut; no means of communicating with friends until we reached the coast. We were indeed a lost army. I well remember my feelings at that time, and I have no doubt, but similar feelings were experienced by my many comrades. As we stood there in central Georgia, one hundred and thirty miles from the nearest military post, surrounded on all sides by a hostile enemy, our position was certainly not an enviable one. However we had unbounded faith in our leader, General Sherman, whom we were satisfied could with an army of 65,000 men, as good soldiers as ever were marshaled in battle, cut his way thru to the coast.

On the 14th day of November my old comrade and the writer were engaged in a little game of Daw [Draw or Maw],[579] when I felt a hand upon my shoulder. Turning around, to see who it was, what was my astonishment at beholding George Sims[580] and Edwin Coon [Koons],[581] two old friends and neighbors from Iowa, standing beside me. I instantly arose and grasped their hands eagerly inquiring of them about friends at home. They then informed me that they had lately been drafted,[582] and had been hurried to

Union army wagons in Atlanta, Georgia.
To make the great "March to the Sea," William T. Sherman had to amass tons of ammunition and rations for his invasion force in occupied Atlanta. Army wagon trains could only carry the essential military supplies required to conduct a vigorous overland campaign across Georgia. CHICAGO HISTORICAL SOCIETY

the front, and had been assigned to the 10th Iowa[583] which at that time belonged to the 2nd Division of the 15th Army Corps, and at that time were camped about one mile from ours, the 1st Division of the same Corps. For about one hour I kept them busy in answering questions about my many friends and acquaintances at home, when bidding me good bye they returned to their command at the same time requesting me to come over to their camp in the evening.

After supper, according to my promise, I started to pay them a visit, and I found them in a peck of trouble. One thing that was bothering was, they had not got forty rounds[584] of cartridges that the regulations required them to have (having lost some.) As there was to be an inspection in the morning, and they being recruits and not being acquainted with the tricks of the old soldier, they were afraid they would be severely reprimanded for their carelessness in losing their cartridges. I told them I would fix that all right. Upon examining their cartridges I found they were fifteen short of the requisite number. Taking out fifteen from the lower box I filled the upper one, and told them when the inspection officer came around to tell him the lower part was full also, and he would not take the trouble to look at it. At first they did not seem inclined to favor my plan, but I insisted upon it, assuring them that every good soldier lied once in a while, and that my plan would work all right. I learned subsequently that it worked to a charm. One thing more troubled them. Being new recruits they had drawn about a mule load of clothing, blankets and so forth, and were wondering how to carry them; after looking their plunder over I said, "Boys you want to throw all that plunder away with the exception of the dog tent and ponchos, and an extra shirt and stockings."

After bidding them good night I returned to my regiment. I saw no more of my friends until we reached Savannah, [Georgia], when they kindly thanked me for the advice I had given them assuring me it would have been impossible for them to have carried that load of plunder on that long march.

The morning of November 15th was a beautiful morning, and the troops were soon busily engaged in getting ready for the march to the sea, and with the bands playing, flags unfurled, and the colors pointed to the South we started on what proved to be one of the most memorable marches of modern times. Whatever point might be our destination our path the greater part of the way led through a pine wilderness. For the first part of the way we found plenty of forage, and at a small place called Winston, where we encamped for the night, the country literally teemed with sweet potatoes. When we broke camp in the morning they were lying in heaps like small haycocks around our camp ground.[585]

At this place our adjutant that fine young soldier D. G. Butterfield[586] secured a fine Arabian horse which he rode until the close of the war, and upon returning to his home at De Witt, Iowa, after the war he took it with him, where for several years it did him good service.

Upon leaving our camp at this place quite a large rebel mail was captured by the advance of the army, and it was amusing to read some of the loving epistles it contained. Now we would find a letter written by some Southern lass to her Dear John Henry who was in the rebel army. It would be couched in the most endearing terms and hoping they would succeed in driving those horrid Yankees away and speedily return to her loving arms. Then we would find one written by some soldier to his fair Imorata in which he would respect his deeds of valor, and mighty prowess, telling her how many Yankees would soon all be done gone, and that he would then hurry home to his dearly beloved. It was amusing also to read the rebel newspapers containing as they did flaming head lines to the editorials. The editor claiming they had the Butcher Sherman just where they wanted him, and urging upon the citizens to turn out en masse to burn bridges, fell trees, and obstruct the highways in every conceivable manner, and to waylay and shoot them at every opportunity, and thus drive them from the sacred soil of Georgia. Perhaps at that moment the Editor was getting out of our way as fast as horse flesh or steam could carry him. In fact we hardly ever saw a rebel on account of the clouds of dust they raised in trying to escape from us.[587]

On the morning of the 24th we continued our march, and as we proceeded the country became more level, and was one vast wilderness of pine, the ground being covered with a growth of wire grass. At times we would march a day without seeing a living habitation, and from the swampy nature of the ground it was evident we were rapidly nearing the coast in the vicinity of Savannah. Small bodies of the enemy were rapidly driven before us, and the morning of December 12th found us within nine miles of the city, while confronting us, and about one mile distant the enemy [defenders] were strongly entrenched. The intervening distance being old rice fields covered with water and the only way of crossing the same being a turnpike commanded by the rebel artillery.[588] We lay in this position for several days during which the weather was extremely cold. Our rations were now getting low, and for about three days we subsisted principally upon parched corn, and rice in the sheaf, that we would have to thrash out, and hull the best we could. If any of my readers ever undertook to hull oats with the end of an iron rod they can form some idea of the task we had in hulling rice with the end of our bayonets. We would manage to get about half of the hull off, and then getting tired of the job we would cook, and eat it, hull and all. Great preparations had been made by those in authority to have supplies on hand at the time we reached the coast, and at this time an abundance were awaiting us on board of the fleet then lying in Ossabane [Ossabaw] Sound at the mouth of the Ogeechee River about seventy miles distant.[589]

Riverfront at Savannah, Georgia.
The prize awaiting Sherman on the Atlantic coast was the commercially important, cosmopolitan city of Savannah, the population of which totaled 23,000 inhabitants in 1860. Confederate engineers had constructed an excellent system of fortifications around the city, and Fort McAllister, located on the south bank of the Ogeechee River, blocked Sherman's route from being supplied by the U.S. Navy from the sea. LIBRARY OF CONGRESS

Colors Point to the South and Trip to Savannah

❖ ————————————— ❖

577. Sherman had proposed the march to his superior, Lt. Gen. Ulysses S. Grant, in September, after the fall of Atlanta. Sherman's plan was to strike across Georgia to Savannah, destroying what he could of military value and emerging on the seacoast to turn north into the Carolinas. There he would rely on the navy and logistical supply by water to support his movement north. Grant's primary concern was Hood's elusive army. Therefore, Sherman had detached Thomas and the Army of the Cumberland, plus additional reinforcements, to Tennessee, where they could thwart any possible aggressive movement by the Confederate Army of Tennessee. Satisfied that Sherman had made the necessary arrangements to counter any threat from Hood, Grant gave his permission for the march. Eicher, *The Longest Night*, 737–39; Sherman, *Memoirs*, II: 164–66.

578. Sherman's force for the "big raid" consisted of the Army of the Tennessee, with the XV and XVII Corps, commanded by Oliver O. Howard, and the newly christened Army of Georgia, with the XIV and XX Corps, commanded by Henry W. Slocum. The entire force numbered nearly 62,000 men (55,000 infantry, 5,000 cavalry, and 2,000 artillerymen serving sixty-four guns). The force carried twenty days' rations. The troops, Sherman's "bummers," as they came to be called, would subsist from the farms and plantations encountered along the march as they played havoc with the railroads linking the coast with Atlanta, and destroyed industry of value to the Confederate war effort. Ibid., 159, 171–77.

579. If Oake was playing "Draw," then it was a form of poker wherein the players are dealt a number of cards, wager, then draw to replace all but one undesired card, then wager again before showing their hand. "Maw" was a card game of Gaelic origin. The earliest record comes from Ireland in 1551. Players (from two to ten) wager an even amount to enter. The object of the game is to win three or five tricks or prevent the other player(s) from doing so. Five cards are dealt (from a fifty-two-card deck), with the top card of the remaining turned up to determine trump. The players play their hands a card at a time, with trump suit cards ranked: five, then jack, then ace of hearts regardless of trump suit, ace of trump (if not hearts), king, and queen.

580. George W. Sims, born in Pennsylvania, was 28 and a resident of Clinton County when he enlisted as a substitute for one year's service in Co. C on September 23, 1864. He was mustered out May 28, 1865, in Washington, D.C. *Roster* 2: 247; *AGI*, 1865-II: 630.

581. Edwin (cited as Edward in *Roster*) E. Koons, born in Pennsylvania, was 28 and living in Clinton County when he was drafted into Co. C on September 23, 1864. He was mustered out May 28, 1865, in Washington, D.C. *AGI*, 1865-II: 629; *Roster* 2: 209.

582. The Federal Conscription Act was passed by Congress in February 1863, and signed by President Lincoln on March 3, 1863. The first effective Federal draft, it imposed liability on all male citizens between ages 20 and 45 with exceptions for the mentally or physically unfit, men with certain types of dependents, felons, and various high federal or state officials. Quotas were set by the president based on population and the number of men already in service from each district. A drafted man could hire another as a substitute or purchase his way out for $300. The measure actually increased volunteering, and for the entire war only 162,535 men, or about 6 percent of all Union soldiers, were raised by the draft. Of these, 46,347 actually served, and 116,188 hired substitutes, while 86,724 paid for exemptions. Long, *Civil War Day by Day*, 325.

583. Initially formed in September 1861, the 10th Iowa saw service at New Madrid/Island No. 10, Siege of Corinth, Iuka, Battle of Corinth, Vicksburg, and Chattanooga, and guarded railroads in Alabama and Georgia during the Atlanta campaign. In November 1864, it was assigned to the 3rd Division, XV

Army Corps, commanded by Col. Paris P. Henderson. *Roster* 2: 145–52.

584. The standard allotment of cartridges supplied and carried in the rifleman's leather cartridge box, carried in two removable metal tins, twenty cartridges in each tin, ten in the top compartment and ten in the bottom.

585. The regiment moved with the 1st Brigade, 1st Division, XV Army Corps, Brig. Gen. Charles R. Woods in command of the division, from Vining Station to Atlanta on November 13, where it bivouacked until the morning of November 15. That day, the entire army moved south, the regiment passing through Rough and Ready, McDonough, Indian Springs, Monticello, Hillsboro, and Clinton, striking the Georgia Railroad near Griswoldville on November 21, where it lay in the reserve lines. Sherman's two armies advanced on a sixty-mile front, with the Army of the Tennessee (Howard) on the right and the Army of Georgia (Slocum) on the left. The XV Army Corps, under Maj. Gen. Peter J. Osterhaus, occupied the extreme right flank of Howard's army during the advance. *AGI*, 1865-II: 1168.

586. Butterfield, born in New Hampshire, was 19 and a resident of De Witt when he enlisted on August 6, 1862, as sixth corporal of Co. H. He was promoted fourth corporal, December 1, 1862; second corporal (date not found); fifth sergeant, March 1, 1863; sergeant major, May 1, 1863; and adjutant December 12, 1863. He was wounded May 14, 1864, at Resaca, and was mustered out on June 6, 1865, in Washington, D.C. *Roster* 3: 1038.

587. On November 21–22, the 2nd Brigade and part of the 1st Brigade, 1st Division, XV Army Corps, engaged the Georgia militia at Griswoldville and Joseph Wheeler's cavalry, with minimal loss. The 26th Iowa was not engaged, for the reserve was not called on. The division of militia, poorly trained and led by militia Brig. Gen. Pleasant J. Phillips, attacked the Federals, who were deployed on the edge of a wood behind breastworks, in badly coordinated assaults across open fields. Repulsed, Phillips retreated, having lost 51 killed, 472 wounded, and scores missing, totaling more than 600 casualties. The Federal casualties numbered 13 killed, 79 wounded, and 2 missing. *O.R.* I-44: 98; Eicher, *The Longest Night*, 765–66.

588. The 26th Iowa advanced on November 24, passing through Irwinton, and crossed the Oconee River on November 26, bivouacking at Irwin Roads. It proceeded on, passing Riddlefield and Summertown, and camping near the Ogeechee River. Major Lubbers reported the men in excellent health. On December 3, Woods's brigade crossed the Ogeechee River and destroyed railroad track and facilities south of Millen for several miles, after which it re-crossed and marched parallel to the river, southeastward toward its mouth, until December 10. On that day the brigade crossed the river near the Ogeechee canal, and marched down the canal toward, and within seven miles of, Savannah, where it bivouacked for the night, ending the marching component of this phase of the campaign. Though the Federals were now within sight of the Atlantic Ocean, Lt. Gen. William J. Hardee had 10,000 men entrenched in formidable fortifications, his troops having flooded the surrounding rice fields, leaving narrow causeways for suitable approach to the city—these of course, as described by Oake, completely enfiladed by well-sighted artillery. *Supplement to the O.R.* II-20: 582; *AGI*, 1865-II: 1168; Eicher, *The Longest Night*, 767.

589. As previously requested, the U.S. Navy, South Atlantic Blockading Squadron, commanded by Rear Admiral John A. Dahlgren, lay anchored offshore, on the lookout for Sherman. The Federal armies needed resupplied with rations, munitions, clothing, and equipment—and would need naval support for the projected attack on Savannah. General Howard made contact with the navy via the Ogeechee River, but Hardee's strong garrison and formidable defenses, particularly at Fort McAllister, commanding the river five miles above its mouth at Ossabaw Sound, blocked any secure linkup. The fort, Sherman believed, would need to be neutralized, if he was to open the river and cement a linkup with the Federal fleet. Sherman, *Memoirs*, II: 193–95; Weigley, *A Great Civil War*, 395.

Brigadier General William B. Woods.
A seasoned veteran in battles from Fort Donelson to Savannah. This future justice of the U.S. Supreme Court assumed command of the 1st Brigade in his brother's (Charles R. Woods) division in January 1865. Brevetted a brigadier general, Woods led the organization on the long march through the Carolinas to Washington, D.C., becoming William Royal Oake's last brigade commander of the war. ROBERT M. COCH COLLECTION

CHAPTER TWENTY-THREE

Christmas at Savannah and Trip Along the Coast to Beaufort

In order to get our supplies it would be necessary to capture Fort McAllister situated on the right bank of the Ogeechee River, and manned by 200 [250] men with about twenty [twenty-four] pieces of artillery, having complete command of the river at that point. Sherman seeing the necessity of carrying the fort before we could get our supplies had ordered [Brigadier] General [William B.] Hazen to assault and capture with his division.[590]

On the morning of December 13th, the day the assault was to be made, in company with two of my comrades I walked over to the 10th Iowa to see my two drafted friends from Iowa, and also to see the assault on the Fort which was about a mile distant, and plainly visible from that point, the intervening distance being covered by a swamp that extended to the coast. On our way we passed a sutler's tent,[591] and seeing that he had shoes for sale I thought I would buy a pair, as I was about bare footed at the time. Selecting a pair of common congress gaiters,[592] such as we usually buy for $1.50 per pair, I inquired the price, and was informed that $7.00 was the lowest he could possibly sell them for. I thought it was rather a stiff price, but looking down at my feet I discovered that one of my large toes was liable to stray away, so I concluded to take the boots.

We arrived at the 10th Iowa a little after noon, and soon found my friends who were glad to see me, but they were heartily sick of army life, and as Coon was then suffering with the sick headache, it made him doubly so. Says he, "Royal, I would give every dollar I am worth if I was only on old Rock Creek, Iowa with Roxy," the latter being his wife, and when drafted was living on Rock Creek, Clinton County, Iowa. Poor Coon, but more of him later.[593]

We now started to get a position where we could view the attack upon the fort, and although the distance was too great to get a good view with the naked eye, quite a fine view could be had by the aid of a glass. Soon we saw a puff of smoke, and heard the boom as the signal gun was fired. Then the guns of the enemy belched forth, and sent their deadly messengers amidst that gallant line of blue as they moved upon the works. They faltered not, and with ringing cheers they spring forward amidst that storm of iron hail, and bursting torpedoes,[594] and planted old glory on the ramparts of the fort. Fort McAllister was ours, and we were in high spirits as we would now get our much needed supplies, and also the mail that had been accumulating for about a month.[595]

Returning to our camp we found our comrades as much elated over the fall of the fort as we were. All the talk was the mail we would get on the morrow, and as we were sadly in need of rations and clothing that was a secondary matter when compared with hearing from our relatives, and friends in the North. The next day the long looked for mail arrived, and the joyful looks and happy smiles that were visible on the countenances of the boys defied description. After reading the letters received we were soon busily engaged in notifying our anxious friends of our safe arrival at the coast.

Soon rumors were afloat that heavy siege guns would soon arrive when an attack would be made on the City of Savannah. On the morning of December 21st our pickets discovered that the enemy had made themselves conspicuous by their scarcity, having evacuated during the night of the 20th leaving us in peaceful possession of the city.[596] Soon the different columns were put in motion, and marched into the city, and went into camp in its outskirts. Thus had we in about thirty days marched 300 miles through the enemy's country carrying a front of 45 miles devastating it of all supplies, and winding up with the capture of Savannah, and whereby fell into our hands 150 heavy guns, 25,000 bales of cotton, and an immense amount of ammunition, and herds of horses, and mules.[597] The City of Savannah, Georgia, was an old town, and has usually been called a handsome one, and if such its beauty can be attributed more to its parks and beautiful shade trees than to its fine buildings. Its streets and parks were lined with fine shade trees chief among the trees being the beautiful willow leafed live oak, and evergreen of exquisite beauty. In the rear of the City was quite a fine park with a fountain while a short distance from the Court House stood a stately and handsome monument erected in memory of Count [Casimir] Pulaski who fell in 1779 in an assault made on that City [at the time it was held] by the British during the Revolutionary War.[598] Our camp was about one mile from the city, and about ten miles from Fort Thunderbolt,[599] which was situated on the bay, and between our camp, and the old fort were some very fine groves of majestic live oaks covered with Spanish moss, which were truly sublime in their grandeur.

On December 24th, in company with John Parker[600] of Company A, the writer took a trip down to the City with the avowed intention of getting something for Christmas dinner on the next day. Visiting some of the large stores, that had opened up, and were doing quite a business, we each secured a very fine military cap, a $2.50 pack of cards, and two pounds each of fine smoking tobacco, when we departed in search of fresh fields. Kind readers it has been so long ago I hardly remember if we paid for the goods or not, but am under the impression they were charged to us. Going down on the wharf we then bought one bushel of oysters in the shell, and some sweet potato pies, paying for them in Confederate money.

Having secured the nucleus for a good dinner we returned to camp, and until bed time were engaged in shelling our oysters, securing about six quarts from the bushel. To say that our Christmas dinner at Savannah, Georgia in 1864 was a good one, and well relished by us after our long march, is but faintly expressing it, and as the grand repast greeted our eyes we thought that even our friends in the North could they have seen it, would have envied us at the time.

During our short stay here, large details of troops were kept busy in building a line of entrenchments on the north [side] of the City. Along about the middle of January 1865 rumors of a move reached our ears. Which way, was the question that naturally suggested itself to us. We certainly would not retrace our steps to Atlanta. Soon our suspense was ended as on the morning of January 21st [actually January 10] we received orders to march to Fort Thunderbolt, and embark on board of a steamer, via Port Royal and Hilton Head, to Beaufort, South Carolina. Soon we were steaming along the coast, and although at that particular part of the coast the scenery is not considered grand, it was particularly pleasing to us after our long and monotonous march in the interior of the country.[601]

We had been on the steamer but a short time when quite a number of the boys began to experience that disagreeable feeling, seasickness, and although it was quite amusing to us that escaped, to watch the fearful grimaces made by our unfortunate comrades, it was anything but fun for them. As we neared Hilton Head where a large fleet of U.S. men of war were lying at anchor, we noticed another steamer following in our wake. As we arrived opposite the fleet, in an instant, as it were, every vessel became a blaze with flags and bunting, while from the mast head like a meteor in the sky floated old glory. As the steamer in our rear arrived opposite the fleet we

Contraband refugees.
Throughout the momentous "March to the Sea" and invasion of the Carolinas, Sherman's troops encountered tens-of-thousands of slaves fleeing bondage who attached themselves to his columns. William Royal Oake mentions these "contrabands" only once at the conclusion of his memoirs. LIBRARY OF CONGRESS

noticed a puff of smoke from one of the ships which was quickly followed by deafening reports as every vessel saluted General Sherman, whom we learned was on board the steamer in our rear.[602]

Continuing on our way we reached Beaufort early in the evening [January 15] and went into camp near the wharf. Beaufort, South Carolina, was quite an important place, from a military standpoint, during the war, but the town itself was small and had that dilapidated appearance common to all Southern towns during the war. It was here as well as other places along the coast, that could be seen the true type of the full blooded African Negro. The low receding forehead, and short kinky crop of wool, together with the broad and flat nose, which would justify a person in placing them in the monkey family rather than human beings.

In taking the sights of the little place an observing person could not but notice the different conveyances in use, as well as the harness used on the horses and mules on drawing the same. The old corn husk collar and wooden back pad, with a chain over it connecting it with the trace chains constituted the entire make up, and the old carts were equally as crude in their construction. The buildings resembled more the cuts we see of the old buildings of colonial times than they did those erected by their progressive neighbors in the Northern States.

The day after our arrival at Beaufort, John Parker, and Peter J. Potter of Company A thought they would engage in the sutler business on a small scale. Out in the bay at anchor about half a mile from the shore were several sloops loaded with sutler goods of all description, and the boys thought by buying some of the same they would make a few dimes by starting a stand on the wharf, close to where the troops that were coming from Savannah by steamer were landing. Getting a boat and rowing out to one of the sloops they inquired the price of apples and various articles, which they thought would suit the tastes of the boys, and would find a ready sale. Being informed that apples were worth $18.00 per barrel they concluded they would buy one barrel as a starter, and if the venture proved a paying one, they would engage in the business on a larger scale. Rowing ashore with their apples it took but a short time to dispose of their fruit and although there were quite a few rotten ones in the barrel their venture netted them $14.00.[603]

Upon learning of their venture I thought I would try my hand at it. Not having much experience in rowing a boat I got two of my comrades, John Simpson, and J. M. Hague to row the boat out to the sloop.[604] Going on board I made known my wants when the owner politely took me over the sloop and showed me the different goods. Selecting a barrel of russet apples I asked to look at them, and taking out the head of the barrel I found them small but sound. Paying for them they were lowered into the boat when we returned to the shore. Taking out the head of the barrel my comrades handed out the apples while I made the proper charge. I don't think it took over half an hour to dispose of the apples, which proved to be very fine, hardly a rotten apple in the barrel, and in footing up I found my barrel of apples brought me $49.50, a net profit of $31.50. Undoubtedly some of my readers may think this story is somewhat fishy, but it is an absolute fact. At this late day I could not tell exactly how we retailed them, but I do know we undersold the dealers in Beaufort.

Early the same evening a little after dark John Parker, came to me saying he wanted to speak to me. Going a little beyond the hearing of our comrades he made known his wants. He had been up in town and had made what he thought an important discovery. One large sutler was doing a thriving business, being crowded with the newly arrived troops, and keeping the proprietor and [all the] clerks busy waiting on them. Parker thought that by watching our chances we might perhaps get a few articles a little below cost. His suggestions I thought were good ones, and met my hearty approval. As a general thing we thought a sutler was in the army to skin the soldier out of what little money they had by charging an enormous price for every little luxury that our needs might crave, consequently we thought it no harm to get their goods below cost if possible. Following Parker we soon arrived at the tent, which just at the time packed with soldiers who were anxiously awaiting their turn to be waited upon, crowding our way into the tent we soon procured a box of fifteen cent cigars and a case of a dozen each of writing portfolios, when we as silently withdrew and returned to camp, and it has always been a question to me whether the proprietor charged the goods or not.

Arriving at camp we proceeded forthwith to treat each one of the company with a good 10 cent cigar, and each of us sold eleven portfolios at $1.50

apiece, one dollar each less than the sutler charged for them.

About an hour before we retired for the night Parker and I were busily engaged in laying plans for the next day, to wit; early in the morning we would purchase about $200.00 worth of sutler's goods of all description, and as troops would be landing all day there were no doubts in our minds but what we could make quite a stake, but alas there is many a slip between the cup and the lip.

Early the following morning [January 16] our regiment received orders to march to Gardners [Garden's] Cross Roads [Corners], about 18 [16] miles north [of Beaufort]. Thus by the stern necessities of war did our well laid plans fail to materialize, and the piles of greenbacks that in our imagination would make us millionaires slipped from our grasp. In a short time after receiving our orders to march we were in line, and marched to our designated camp. The country through which we passed being low and swampy, and at places almost impassible. At this place we lay for several days, and our brief stay here was very unpleasant owing to the continued wet weather.[605]

At a place called Pocalaligo, a few miles north of us were quite a force of the enemy. Consequently, it was imperative on our part to keep a heavy picket line on the main road in our front. About one quarter of a mile in front, on the main road, had been a large frame building, but with the exception of the roof it was all gone. The roof setting on the ground in the same position it did while on the building, and as it was near that point that the pickets on the main road were posted it afforded them comfortable quarters when off duty. About eighty yards in advance of said building, the vidette was posted while on duty, standing at a point where the road made a sharp turn to the right running down through a ravine that was densely wooded on either side.

While encamped at this place it fell to the lot of the writer to be posted as picket at this particular spot, and I will admit that I was for a short time badly scared, and for a brief period of time thought of all the many mean things I had done in my short life. It was about 10 o'clock one cold misty night that I took my position on the post referred to. Now we were allowed to have a little fire on one side, and in the rear of the post where we could go and warm once in a while. The fire was so situated that its reflection

*Christmas at Savannah and
Trip Along the Coast to Beaufort*

shone directly on the bend of the road at the head of the ravine distant about thirty feet. I had been on duty about one hour and a half, when I thought I could hear a horse approaching from the front. In an instant I stepped to my usual place in times of danger, behind a tree, to await results. Every second more distinctly could I hear the approaching footsteps. What was it, I asked myself. I was well satisfied that we were the extreme outpost, consequently it must be rebels. Closer they came, and I said to myself, "Injun what are you going to do, run, yell, or stand your ground." I had about made up my mind to do all, when out of the head of the ravine where the light of the fire shone directly on him, and about thirty feet distant rode a man dressed in a fine gray uniform, the bars on the collar denoting a captain of the Confederate service. In an instant I gained my equilibrium as with musket cocked and at my shoulder pointed directly at him I called, "Halt, who comes there." In an instant he brought his horse to a stand, when for the first time he saw me, and as he looked at the gleaming barrel of a cocked Springfield[606] pointed at his breast and only about thirty feet distant, he answered, "A friend." "Advance friend, and give the countersign," I replied. "I haven't the countersign," he answered, "I am one of Captain Duncan's[607] scouts, and have been outside of the lines consequently had no chance to obtain the countersign." "Then remain where you are until I call the Sergeant of the guard," but at that moment the said officer appeared with the relief guard to take my place. In the meantime I kept my musket pointed directly at him, and kept a close watch on his hands to see that he did not grasp a pair of revolvers that I saw in the holsters of his saddle.

As soon as I was relieved, in company with the sergeant, I approached the scout who from his straight forward manner soon convinced us that he was telling the truth, and upon his dismounting we invited him to the reserve post to partake of a cup of coffee, before continuing on his journey. For the offer he kindly thanked us, saying that he was very hungry. I soon procured some water and in a short time we were enjoying a cup of coffee, sow belly, and hard tack. Then for the first time I took a close look at our friend the scout. I could but admire his coolness, and thought he would be a dangerous foe if cornered. A little above the medium height, while his well knit frame shown to such splendid advantage by his fine, and well fitting uniform, made him, in my estimation, an ideal soldier, while his cool manner showed him to be well fitted for his dangerous vocation as scout. After finishing our midnight repast our scout was escorted to division headquarters.

On January 28th [30th], the army was again in motion, marching in a northerly direction, and on the evening of that day we encamped near Pocotaligo. I well remember being very short of sow belly about this time, all the meat we had been getting was beef, and as all the beef cattle had to be driven on foot, and killed when required, it was what we called blue beef, not a particle of fat being visible in an entire carcass. You could take a piece of it, throw it against any object and it would stick as though it was glued fast. The evening we went into camp here I obtained a requisition from the company commander,[608] and went to the division commissary where I procured a ham by paying 33 cents a pound. It was an expensive luxury, but in those days the cost of an article cut no figure, if we had the money, and the desired article could be obtained.

We were now fully upon the campaign, but the objective point we knew not, although the general opinion was that Charleston would next receive a visit from us. The constant rains that are so usual in the South during the winter season had flooded all the streams, and from the low nature of the ground the roads were almost impassable, and it was no unusual thing to find the creeks half a mile wide, and from one to five feet in depth. Most of the bridges being destroyed by the enemy, it was necessary in many cases for the advance troops to strip or roll up their clothes and wade through, and drive back small bodies of the enemy that were disputing our passage. If my readers should not know how it would feel to be placed in a similar position I would advise them to try wading a stream of water at about 50 degrees of heat and having a minie ball dropping around you every few seconds. I can assure my readers it is hard on the eyes, but a fine place for the beginners to learn the fine art of diving.

On February 7th we reached a small place called Branchville [Bamberg], situated on the Charleston and Augusta Railroad, and about sixty-five miles from the first mentioned place. We lay at this place one day [actually four days] engaged in destroying the railroad.[609] While here we learned from the Negroes that the enemy had evacuated Charleston. At first we could hardly believe such to be the fact, but later found that such was the fact, and that our troops were already in possession of the city.[610] At this place we found a

Christmas at Savannah and
Trip Along the Coast to Beaufort

large shell that had been fired by the Yankees from their gun called the Swamp Angel that was in one of their batteries in the vicinity of Charleston. It had been fired into the city, and had failed to explode for some reason, and the rebels had placed it on board of the cars, and brought it to this place as a memento of the occasion, I suppose. It was amusing to see the boys trying to lift that huge shell of 500 [200] pounds.[611]

On the next day [February 11] we resumed our march, and now that Charleston had fallen [*sic*, the city was still occupied by Confederate forces] the question arose, what next? Soon it was whispered among the troops that Columbia the capital of the State would next receive our attention. And as we were headed in that direction it seemed plausible. On the evening of February 14th we were within ten miles of the capital, and went into camp quite early in the evening in the midst of a disagreeable and cold rain.

On going into camp a heavy picket was placed on the main road in our front. About half an hour after the same had been posted news reached camp that the entire picket post on the main road had been captured by the enemy, who had approached them from the front, and as they were dressed much the same as our own cavalry they were taken for them, and only discovered their mistake when too late. I never saw a more angered man than General [Charles R.] Woods,* our division commander, when he learned the facts, and of the ruse practiced by the rebels to capture our pickets. Soon another detail of seventy men was detailed with instructions to take no prisoners that were dressed in Yankee blue. It was my fortune to be one of the number of the second detail.

The out post was about half a mile in advance of our camp. We arrived at the line a little before dusk and the videttes were at once posted. The reserve being about eighty yards in the rear where they could build a fire as the rain and sleet continued to fall and it was quite cold. Both sides of the road were densely wooded with small timber with a heavy growth of small brush. About 8 o'clock I went on as vidette standing in the thick brush about fifty yards to the left of the road. It was not growing quite cold, and ice had commenced to form on the brush and trees.

I had been on duty about half an hour when I distinctly heard some object moving in the brush directly in front of me and outside of the lines, and from the fact that considerable ice had formed on the brush, whatever

Sherman's troops tearing up railroad tracks.
Soldiers on both sides became amazingly proficient at destroying miles of track and hundreds of bridges and trestles. However, the same troops were just as adept at constructing roads, rail lines, bridges, and trestles. This image shows Union troops tearing up track in Atlanta prior to starting the great "March to the Sea." LIBRARY OF CONGRESS

Method of destroying railroad ties and rails.
Since troops on the march could not carry off the heavy rails, they commonly rendered them useless for reconstructing track by heating them, using the cross ties. The heated rails were then either bent around trees or telegraph poles or simply cast into nearby water to warp them. MEDFORD HISTORICAL SOCIETY

it was made quite a noise. Standing behind a small tree with my musket at full cock and under my gum poncho to keep it dry, I imagined there [was] a whole brigade of rebels after me. The noise grew louder and louder, and I thought, Injun you are a goner this time sure. While I strained my eyes at tempting to penetrate the Egyptian darkness I thought that the reserves eighty yards in the rear could certainly hear my heart beat, [as] nearer came the sound of my imaginary foe. By this time my hair stood straight up. If I was going to do anything I would have to do it quick. I thought about praying, but I had been taught to pray with my eyes shut. I dare not close my eyes, as I had to watch the enemy in front. At that moment the reserve post had replenished their fire, and it blazed up throwing a reflection in my direction, and over me. When lo and behold a few rods in front of, and facing, me stood a mule. After discovering my supposed enemy to be a harmless old mule I suddenly grew brave, and thought that I could whip a whole regiment of rebels, when in fact my hair stood straight up, and I was ready to run but my legs shook so I could not. How I did want to embrace that old mule for getting me out of such a scare.

Christmas at Savannah and Trip Along the Coast to Beaufort

◆ ———————————————— ◆

590. Located on a bluff on the south bank of the Ogeechee River, Fort McAllister was a key to the defenses of Savannah, fifteen miles to the north. Throughout 1862 and 1863, United States warships repeatedly tried, with no success, to subdue the fort with heavy artillery fire. The fort was constructed with dirt and logs, and featured numerous bombproofs and traverses to protect the men and guns from enemy fire. The garrison was commanded by Maj. George W. Anderson. Faust, *Encyclopedia of the Civil War*, 275; *O.R.* I-44-110–11. A graduate of West Point (1855), Hazen was a veteran of numerous western campaigns and battles, including Shiloh, Siege of Corinth, Perryville, Chickamauga, Missionary Ridge, and the campaign for Atlanta. He had recently (August 1864) assumed command of the 2nd Division, XV Army Corps, Army of the Tennessee. Boatner, *Civil War Dictionary*, 390.

591. A sutler was a civilian licensed or permitted to operate a shop at a military camp or post, or in this case moved with the army while on active campaign. Garrison & Garrison, *Civil War Usage*, 243.

592. Oake probably purchased what was known as the "Jefferson boot" or bootee, which was a high quarter shoe called, in its rougher forms, a "brogue" or "brogan." There appears to have been considerable variation in manufacture and style for this laced shoe. Oake's use of the term gaiter is misleading, for a gaiter was a canvas, leather, or rubber leg covering that reached from the instep to above the ankle (about twelve inches) to around mid-calf. Clearly, he purchased his own shoes or boots in any case. Todd, *American Military Equipage*, 70–72.

593. The two friends in the 10th Iowa were Edwin (or Edward) Koons and George Sims. See notes 580 and 581.

594. The earliest land mines were called torpedoes. During the assault, General Hazen lost several men to the mines, which he stated "were exploded by the tread of the troops, blowing many men to atoms...." *O.R.* I-44-110.

595. The assault lasted roughly fifteen minutes. The Confederates suffered 35 men killed and wounded, while Hazen reported 24 men killed and 110 wounded. The fall of the river fort opened Sherman's communication with the Union fleet. Long, *Civil War Day by Day*, 609.

596. Although Sherman maneuvered his left to cut off any escape from Savannah across the Savannah River into South Carolina, he moved too slowly and did not succeed. On December 20, Lt. Gen. William J. Hardee, urged by his superior, Gen. P. G. T. Beauregard, and others to pull out, withdrew his 10,000 troops from their fortifications and marched them across an ingenious pontoon bridge constructed on thirty rice flats (barges), retiring north, without opposition, to link up with other Confederate units. Ibid., 613.

597. In celebration of the important capture, General Sherman sent his famous message to President Lincoln: "I beg to present you, as a Christmas gift, the city of Savannah, with 150 heavy guns and plenty of ammunition, and also about 25,000 bales of cotton." In addition, the Federals seized 800 prisoners, thirteen locomotives, 190 railcars, and three steamers. *O.R.* I-44-783, 786.

598. Oake observed the cast iron fountain in Forsyth Park (then south of town), dating from 1858, one of Savannah's most visible and popular features—then and now—as well as the monument in Monterey Square designed (1853–1855) to commemorate the Polish patriot Casimir

Pulaski. General Pulaski participated in the joint effort of the French and Continental armies to drive British forces from fortified Savannah in 1779. The effort failed, and Pulaski was mortally wounded on October 9, 1779. Roulhac Toledano, *The National Trust Guide to Savannah Architectural and Cultural Treasures* (New York: John Wiley & Sons, Inc., 1997), 137, 151, 171. Oake appears to have based his description of the city of Savannah upon Gen. William T. Sherman's memoirs, which he apparently used extensively when writing his own account of experiences, starting with the Atlanta campaign and carrying on through the March to the Sea and subsequent Carolinas campaign. See Sherman, *Memoirs*, II: 230.

599. Fort Thunderbolt (also known as the Thunderbolt Battery) was one of a series of forts and water batteries constructed on an interior line of defenses at the various water approaches around Savannah. The fort was located along the Wassaw River to guard against attack coming in from the Wassaw Sound. Claudia B. Lamas, "Fortification Survey of Savannah River and Area Waterways, Savannah, Georgia 1861–1865," Lane Library, Armstrong Atlantic State University, Savannah, Georgia, accessed at http://www.hist.armstrong.edu/heritage/ThunderboltCivilWar.htm.

600. Parker, born in Ohio, was 25 when he enlisted on July 8, 1862. A resident of Lowden County, he was promoted fourth corporal on March 24, 1863, and third corporal on April 1, 1863. He was mustered out on June 6, 1865, in Washington, D.C. *Roster* 3: 1086.

601. The regiment boarded the steamer *Crescent*, on January 10, 1865, and embarked for Beaufort. *Supplement to the O.R.* II-20-582.

602. Sherman reported that elements of the Army of the Tennessee, commanded by Maj. Gen. Oliver O. Howard, to which Oake's regiment was assigned in the XV Army Corps, made the initial movement northward to Beaufort to make a lodgment on the Charleston railroad, at or near Pocotaligo. This was accomplished punctually and at little cost. Based on his own report for this period, General Sherman did not depart Savannah until January 22. Therefore, he could not have been present on a nearby steamer when Oake's regiment passed Hilton Head on January 15. The salute fired by the blockade fleet probably was for Secretary of War Edwin M. Stanton, who, accompanied by Quartermaster General of the U.S Army Montgomery C. Meigs and Adjutant General of the U.S. Army Edward D. Townsend, had arrived in Savannah on January 11 to confer with Sherman concerning military matters. Sherman acknowledged that Stanton left by revenue cutter for Port Royal about the 15th of January. This departure could have placed the vessel containing Stanton and his party near Hilton Head on the same day. *O.R.* I-47-I-18; Sherman, *Memoirs*, II: 242, 252.

603. See note 403 for earlier reference to Peter J. Potter.

604. See notes 500 and 501 for earlier references to Hague and Simpson.

605. The regiment with its brigade marched to Garden's Corners on January 16, where it bivouacked until January 30. *Supplement to the O.R.* II-20-582.

606. The weapon Oake now carried was the .58 caliber Springfield rifled musket.

607. The scout encountered by Oake while standing picket was most likely a member of Co. K, 15th Illinois Cavalry, commanded by Capt. William Duncan, assigned the role of escort for Maj. Gen. Oliver O. Howard during the march. Reports show that Duncan's command was quite actively engaged in advance of the army throughout the campaign. *O.R.* I-47-I-22, 46, 200, 201, 203, 204, 206, 208, 214, 215.

608. The commander of Co. A during this period appears to have been Lt. Leander B. Sutton, who was never officially mustered in at the rank of captain. Sutton, born in New York, was 22 and a resident of Canton when he enlisted as third sergeant on July 7, 1862. Promoted second sergeant, March 24, 1863, he was wounded and later promoted first lieutenant on September 2,

1864. He served as captain until June 6, 1865, when he was mustered out with the regiment in Washington, D.C. *Roster* 3: 1095.

609. Since January 30, the 26th Iowa had moved with the army through South Carolina via Andersonville to McPhersonville, from where it marched to Hickory Hill on February 1. There the unit skirmished lightly with Confederate cavalry, suffering no losses, but encountering more difficulty with geographical obstacles such as swamps and rivers. The regiment then moved via Taylor's Mill to Bamberg, thirteen miles west of Branchville, and lay there destroying the railroad, cotton, etc., until February 11, when the troops moved in the direction of Columbia. Sherman's army group, now astride the railroad from Midway to Johnson's Station, divided the Confederates who were in Branchville and Charleston on the east, and near Aiken and in Georgia near Augusta to the west. *Supplement to the O.R.* II-20-582; *O.R.* I-47-I-245; Long, *Civil War Day by Day*, 631–37.

610. Oake's memory and research in preparation of his personal memoir are in error as to the evacuation of Charleston. The city was not evacuated by Confederate forces until the night of February 17, 1865. *O.R.* I-47-I-1049.

611. The Swamp Angel was a 200-pounder (eight-inch) Parrott gun mounted on Morris Island, with which Union forces ineffectively shelled Charleston on August 22–23, 1863. The gun blew up when firing the thirty-sixth round. The damaged gun was later set as a monument in Trenton, New Jersey, where it remains. Boatner, *Civil War Dictionary*, 822.

CHAPTER TWENTY-FOUR

Fight with Hampton's Cavalry and Burning of Columbia

＊ ——————————————— ＊

After my mule scare it was some little time before I regained my composure, and I was very glad when the relief guard came around. Upon returning to the reserve post I made myself a cup of extra strong coffee, that elixir of life, and after partaking of the same was soon under the friendly shelter of my dog tent wrapped in the arms of sleep. Quite early in the morning the troops were again in motion, and in a short time the sound of artillery was heard in our front, and it was evident that the advance had found the enemy who would dispute with us the possession of the capital of the State.

We knew that Wade Hampton's famous Legion of Cavalry[612] was in our front, and would stubbornly resist our further progress. Soon we were halted while the increased artillery fire in front, together with the rattle of musketry told us plainly that our comrades in the advance were having quite a warm time with the rebels. About one mile in advance of us, the road crossed [Little] Congaree Creek, a stream of perhaps twenty feet in width, and on crossing the same the road emerged into a large open field of perhaps one hundred acres in extent. Just across the creek and about a hundred yards from the bridge the enemy had built quite a strong [line of] earthworks, and with their artillery in it were disposed to dispute our passage.[613]

After some sharp firing troops were sent on both flanks of the enemy who fearing that they were about to get in a precarious position, fell back to a position on quite a high ridge on the opposite side of the field, and about one hundred rods from their evacuated earthworks near the bridge. At this particular time our brigade was ordered to the front, and as we crossed the bridge and emerged into the open field a grand spectacle met our gaze when we discovered Hampton's famous legion drawn up in line of battle directly in our front, and about one hundred rods from us, while the intervening distance was an open field, and slightly ascending towards the enemy's position.[614]

Well do I remember that grand and imposing array of cavalry and also my feelings on that occasion. There directly in front of us ready to give us battle was the most famous body of cavalry in the Confederate service. In point of numbers we were about equal and each command seemed anxious for a tilt at arms. As we quickly formed into line and loaded our arms and fixed bayonets there seemed to be a fixed determination on the part of our men to plant Old Glory on the rebel position.

Soon the bugle sounded forward, and with a perfect alignment in that open field the brigade moved forward followed by several pieces of artillery. The ground was perfectly smooth with a slight ascent to the enemy's position. It was a sight well calculated to strike terror into the hearts of those not accustomed to such scenes, to see that line of glittering steel nearly half a mile in length calmly awaiting our approach. As we swept steadily forward we expected every moment to see that magnificent body, of the finest cavalry in the rebel service, hurl itself with the force of a hurricane upon us. Now they commenced to fire upon us, and the spiteful zip of the minie once more greeted us. Steadily that line of blue moved forward in spite of their increasing fire. Our ranks opened while with lightening like rapidity our artillery were in battery, and in an instant poured into the enemy's ranks a deadly fire of shell, which was supplemented by a terrific fire of musketry, as with ringing cheers that line of infantry charged their position.

Again and again in rapid succession the deadly shells were hurled amidst their ranks, while we poured into them the deadly minie. Soon they ingloriously left the field in our possession, and fell back into the timber about half a mile to the rear. We now advanced, and planted Old Glory amidst the dead and dying enemy, who had been so terribly mangled by that storm of lead and iron. Yes we had met the much boasted of Hampton's Legion

[Cavalry Corps] in a fair and open fight, and in less than half an hour had them driven them from a field of their own selection.[615]

We were now ordered into camp for the night within about two miles of Columbia, and little did its citizens dream that ere forty-eight hours their proud city would be a smoldering mass of ruins. It was at Columbia that the first Ordinance of Secession was passed, and dearly would its citizens pay for that treasonable act.

Early the next morning we were on the move in the direction of the city, and upon reaching the Congaree River, about a mile from the city found the bridge that spanned the stream, destroyed by the enemy in order to delay as long as possible our entrance into the City.

Halting a few moments near the approach to the bridge we could see small bodies of the enemy hurrying to and fro in different parts of the city while Captain [Francis] De Gress with two of his twenty-pound[er] Parrotts was stirring them up by dropping a few shots in the neighborhood of the depot, and State House.[616] The Congaree River at this point was about two hundred yards wide, and was formed by the junction of the Saluda and Broad Rivers, about three miles above the City. Not deeming it policy to attempt to cross at this point the troops were put in motion towards the junction of the rivers named, where it was expected we could better gain an entrance to the city.

Arriving at the Saluda factory, about three miles above and situated on that stream, which we crossed on a dam, we pushed on towards a bridge that spanned Broad River, arriving therein the afternoon, but too late to save the bridge, which had been burned by the enemy. The bridge being burned we went into camp on a high plateau of ground on the north of the river, and during the night were annoyed considerably by the bullets of the enemy who were in the proximity in the brush, and timber on the opposite side of the river.[617]

Early the morning of the 17th, the troops, after partaking of their breakfast, were soon in line, and a portion of our regiment was ordered to cross the river in pontoon boats, in the face of a sharp fire, and to drive the enemy back from their position so that a pontoon bridge could be placed across the stream. In a short time we had effected a landing and forced the enemy back, and a pontoon was soon thrown across the river, when the main body of the troops at once commenced crossing, and at once started in the direction of Columbia. When within a few miles of the city we were met by a deputation of the city officials making a formal surrender of the capital.[618]

Soon we came in sight of the city, and as we marched down its principal street, we could but admire its fine buildings that lined both sides of the street. The new State Capital building although in an unfinished condition, was an imposing structure, and its massive walls were but slightly damaged by the twenty pound shots that had been hurled against its solid walls. In proximity to it stood a fine monument that had been erected to the memory of the South Carolina troops that fell in the Mexican war. While marching through the city it was a pleasant, but effecting sight to see the actions of some of our men that had been confined as prisoners by the enemy, but on our entering the city they were at once released, with tears in their eyes and streaming down their faces they were God blessing us for their delivery, and they were ready to smother us with their embraces.

Upon entering the city J. H. Tierney[619] a drummer of our regiment hauled down the rebel flag from the State House, and since the war the writer saw the same flag in the Adjutant General's office in Des Moines, Iowa.

Columbia from the capitol.
This image by George N. Barnard is one of sixty-one photographs in his portfolio documenting Sherman's advance on Atlanta, "March to the Sea," and invasion of the Carolinas. Taken from the South Carolina State Capitol, it records the ruins of Columbia after the holocaust of February 17, 1865. LIBRARY OF CONGRESS

Fight with Hampton's Cavalry
and Burning of Columbia

Marching about two miles out of the city we went into camp, and a patrol guard detailed from the brigade was placed on guard in the city to keep the soldiers within reasonable bounds. As soon as we had stacked our arms many of us started for the city, which was already filled with excited soldiers who were busily engaged in breaking into the many fine stores. Large buildings filled with the choicest of merchandise of every description were broken into, and their contents trampled under foot as so much worthless rage.[620]

As it grew dark, in company with some of Sherman's escort[621] we broke into a large wholesale musical store, and it looked like a sacrilegious act to see the fine instruments that were ruthlessly destroyed, broken into pieces. Large French mirrors that would cost hundreds of dollars would have the butt of a musket or hilt of a sword thrust through them breaking them into fragments. Never will the writer forget that night of February 17th, 1865. The wind blew a perfect gale from the southwest, and quite early in the evening the cry of fire was heard, and soon the citizens illuminated as the lurid flames leaped hundreds of feet in the air fanned by a gale blowing forty miles an hour while the deafening and demoniac yells of the excited soldiers, but added additional terror to the scenes. Some of those in authority made an attempt to use the fire engines and try to subdue the flames, but as fast as the engines arrived upon the scene they were quickly demolished by the excited soldiers who seem determined to prevent as much as possible the subduing of the flames, and not until the whole of the business part of the city was a smoldering mass of ruins was the fire got under control.[622]

On the morning of the 18th it was a sad spectacle that met our gaze, where the day before had stood some of the finest buildings in the state, now all that remained was the black and ruined walls, while on every side could be seen groups of citizens huddled together like sheep. All of their worldly possessions having been swept away in an instant by the fierce conflagration, and in many instances they did not save clothing sufficient to cover their bodies. It was indeed a pitiable sight, and I distinctly remember at the time it reminded me of the description I had read of the capture by the allied forces in Europe during the Peninsular War of the Spanish city of Bagdad [Badajoz],[623] where for a time the city was at the mercy of the excited and drunken soldiers, and where scenes were enacted that rivaled in atrocity the acts of the infamous Rospierre [Robespierre] of France.[624] Of course so far as acts of personal cruelty was concerned Columbia was exempt, but the roaring of the flames mingled with the screams of the defenseless women and children as they fled in terror for their lives from that seething and hissing caldron of living fire, together with the yells of the soldiers, and an occasional explosion of shells made a scene that would never be forgotten by an eye witness of the same.[625] One incident connected with the burning of the city I remember quite well. Soon after we entered the city I was walking along the streets when I saw one of our soldiers sitting on the doorstep of a building, and by his side he had a small basket partly filled with new jackknives and watches, and he was a little under the influence of liquor. I spoke to him and advised him to look out or he might lose them, and sure enough he took a little snooze, and when he awoke some other fellow had his plunder. He was a sadder, but a wiser soldier.

We remained in Columbia the 18th and 19th and before we left the State Arsenal was, entirely demolished, and an immense amount of ammunition contained therein destroyed by hauling and dumping the same into the Congaree River. While the soldiers were engaged in handling the same a shell exploded, the fire from the same igniting a large amount of powder which exploded with terrific force killing sixteen men.[626]

On the morning of the 20th we again resumed our northward march, and during a short halt that we made in the afternoon I witnessed one of the most touching sights I ever saw, and one I never wish to see again. As we were halted in the road an ambulance was directly ahead of us, and all at once out of it rolled a soldier, bound hand and foot and suffering the terrible paroxysms of hydrophobia.

Just at that moment our division commander [General Charles Woods] rode up, and when he saw the soldier rolling upon the ground gave orders for the men to at once place him in the ambulance, taking care he did not scratch or bite them. As the general sat on his horse in the middle of the road it was a terrible sight to see the poor unfortunate bound as he was roll under the horse snapping and frothing at his feet, and although he was rather a small man it required the united strength of all that could get around him to overcome his almost superhuman strength, and again place him in the ambulance. As I watched his sufferings I thought what a relief it would be to him if he could have been shot on the spot, as there was no possible chance of his recovery.

Continuing our march without anything of any particular importance occurring we arrived at the City of Cheraw on March 3rd, and went into camp to await the repairing of the bridge that spanned the [Great] Pedee River at this point. The day after our arrival at Cheraw, I was detailed as picket, being on duty on the south bank of the River, about one mile above the town, Lieutenant John Kane[627] of Company G, 26th Iowa was in command of the brigade pickets. On our post were George M. Lynch and the writer of Company A, and Wm. Gardner of Company I. The lieutenant made his headquarters at our post.

On the opposite side of the river about one mile distant from us was situated a very fine residence, and as none of our troops were on that side of the stream we had every reason to believe the place was teeming with forage, but how to get it was the question. We knew it was strictly against orders for a picket to leave his post even when not on duty, but we were bound to have some forage if possible as our rations were getting low. Approaching the lieutenant I asked his permission for Gardner and I to cross the river and see what we could find, but as I expected he said he could not give us permission, and if we want we would go at our own risk. Being well acquainted with him I knew that he would not report us for leaving the post, although he did not want it said he gave us permission. Discovering an old flat boat, a short distance below us, that was about half full of water we proceeded to bail it out, and after getting two pieces of boards for paddles we started to cross the deep and rapid stream, which was about one hundred yards in width.

After quite a hard task we landed our boat, and grasping our arms started for the house, which we succeeded in reaching in safety, keeping a sharp lookout for stray rebs. About the first thing that greeted our eyes was the large number of Negroes on the premises and as they for the first time saw a live Yankee they acted as if they were spell bound, their eyes sticking out so that a person could hang his hat on them. Approaching one of them I inquired of him what the matter was. He replied, "de good Lawd massa is you uns Yankees." Answering them in the affirmative, they replied, "Good Lawd Massa we thought you all had horns, but you uns look just like Massa's folks." Asking them if there was any rebs around they replied in the negative, and upon our inquiries in regard to forage they told us they would procure us an abundance of the same, and in a short time we had all that half a dozen darkies could carry consisting of chickens, hams, sweet potatoes, apple jack, butter, and milk. When we had secured all that we thought was necessary we pressed into service half a dozen darkies to carry our plunder, and rapidly retraced our steps towards our friends, where after a short time we arrived in safety, being nearly swamped in crossing the river. To say that our comrades were pleased with our success and safe return but faintly expresses their feelings, and I will wager that no part of Sherman's army fared more sumptuously than we did that evening and the next day.[628]

On the next morning in looking up in a large tree that stood on the bank of the river we saw what we thought to be a coon's head sticking out of a large hole in the tree, about forty feet from the ground. Procuring an axe we were soon busily engaged in felling the tree, which fell into the stream, and soon we saw five coons swimming around in the water. Jumping into our old flat boat we procured three of them, two making their escape by swimming to the opposite side of the river.[629]

On the 6th [of March], after being relieved from picket, duty, we returned to camp near Cheraw, and found that the troops had received marching orders. We marched into the city and stacked our arms on a large piece of open ground on the north side of the town and adjacent to the bridge that spanned the river. There to wait until the division preceding us had crossed the bridge. On entering the city we found an immense amount of ammunition together with thirty-six hundred barrels of gunpowder, a good share of which had been dumped into a ravine near the edge of the town. The morning was quite cool, and the boys had built several fires to warm themselves, not knowing of the proximity of the deadly explosives. Our regiment happened to be the nearest to it, in fact only about sixty feet from tons of ammunition and gunpowder. In company with three others I was seated upon the ground playing a social game of cards when all at once quite an explosion took place quickly followed by a second one, which in turn was followed by the most terrific explosion it has ever been my lot to witness. I think I can truthfully say that the First Division of the 15th Army Corps was the most scared body of men I ever saw. Every stack of arms in the division was thrown to the ground by the severity of the shock, while huge volumes of smoke hung like a funeral pall over the frightened soldiers, almost suffocating them with its sulfuric smell, and to add terrors to the scene the terrified and scared mules, and horses belonging to the train, together with a good many of the officer's horses became unmanageable, and went galloping over the field tramping over everything that came in their way.

After the final explosion, and while everything was enveloped in smoke I tried to arise to my feet only to be knocked down by a mule. Again I attempted it, and with the same result, when I concluded to lay quiet until the din and confusion had subsided. Soon the smoke began to clear away, and the scared soldiers could again see each others faces, but still the majority of us were ignorant as to the cause of the explosion, thinking that the enemy had undermined the entire ground upon which we had stacked our arms.

In a short time General Logan and staff, who were on the opposite side of the river at the time of the explosion made their appearance, and I don't think I ever saw the general so excited as on that occasion, as he thought that the entire division was annihilated. In a short time order was restored, and we learned the cause of the accident, and in looking over the ground the mutilated remains of three or four soldiers, that had been blown to atoms, and were unrecognizable, were found, and carefully gathered up and consigned to their last resting place in the bosom of Mother Earth.[630]

Once more we fell in line, and again started on our journey towards the north. On the morning of the 8th our regiment was detailed as train guard, and about noon it began to rain making the roads in a fearful condition, and as we plodded wearily mile after mile through that sticky Carolina mud, wet to the skin and every once in a while helping out of the mud the wagons that had sunk to their axles in the soft and sticky clay, ours was a task that even a Methodist minister would not crave. All day we tiredly plodded through the mud, and at dusk were about eight miles from where the advance troops were encamping, and still the rain fell in torrents. About an hour after dark, being disgusted at the snail's gait at which the wagons were moving, and still about six miles from camp I suggested to George M. Lynch of Company A, that we leave the train and push on a head to camp, which he readily consented to.

Watching an opportunity to leave unobserved by our comrades, we stealthily left our command, and started to pass the long line of heavily loaded wagons that were slowly wending their way through the almost impassable mud. After going about two miles I noticed a house near the road, and suggested going in and resting a while, which my comrade gladly assented to. Entering the house we observed a motherly looking old lady of about sixty years, knitting near an old fashioned fire place, in which burned a cheerful fire giving the place a home like appearance, which brought to my mind the scenes of my boyhood days in old Iowa. As we drew up to the cheerful fire to warm our wet and benumbed limbs my eyes caught sight of a pair of shoes and stockings near me and the closer survey of the room revealed to me the form of a man lying in a bed that stood in one corner of the room. Being almost barefoot I at once made up my mind to swap shoes with the old gentleman that was lying in the bed, and to whom I thought the shoes belonged. Kind readers no doubt some of you will think that it was indeed a heartless act to thus defraud the poor old man of his shoes, but kind friends did any of you take part in that long weary march through the Carolina during the winter months of 1865. Tramping day after day in the mud and water, sometimes waist deep, and sometimes we were barefoot at that. If you did I feel sure you will forgive me. Even in this case I think there were extenuating circumstances, and I figured it out this way. Now I thought the shoes sitting near me were the old man's every day ones and I reasonably concluded that he must have a Sunday pair hid away so there would be no harm in my taking his every day ones. Acting on this supposition I removed my old worn out foot gear, and quietly put my feet inside the old gentleman's shoes, and telling my comrade we had better be going. Bidding the old lady good night, we started on our march towards camp. How the old gentleman felt on learning that his shoes had been stolen I never knew, but a madder man than my comrade I never saw, not because the old man had lost his shoes, but because he had not got them instead of me. Continuing our way through the mud we at last arrived in camp, where after partaking of our usual coffee and hard tack wet through to the skin, we spread our wet dog tent and poncho, and retired for the night.

The next day was a repetition of the preceding day, but towards night the rain ceased to fall. Quite late in the evening when we went into camp we were almost worn out by the long march through the sea of mud.[631]

Fight with Hampton's Cavalry
and Burning of Columbia

Fight with Hampton's Cavalry and Burning of Columbia

612. Oake is mistaken in thinking he faced Hampton's Legion during this action. By this stage in the war, the legion no longer existed, and its troops had long since been assigned to other commands. Wade Hampton, however, had departed Virginia in January 1865, and was in South Carolina, his home state, to look for horses. Hampton had been appointed that day to the rank of lieutenant general and assigned to command the cavalry forces (about 6,000 troopers) covering Gen. Joseph E. Johnston's retreat through South Carolina. The Confederate force encountered appears to have been Butler's division, Maj. Gen. Mathew C. Butler commanding, assigned to Hampton's Cavalry Corps. General Butler was present on the field. The editor could not confirm whether General Hampton was personally on the field, but has no evidence to the contrary. *O.R.* I-47-I-1050, 1065; *O.R.* I-47-III-1199, 1213.

613. Gen. Charles Woods reported that the Confederates employed three pieces of artillery to defend the bridge, four miles south of Columbia. *O.R.* I-47-I-242.

614. The 1st Brigade, Brig. Gen. William B. Woods commanding, had been held in reserve south of the Little Congaree, and did not participate in the action that drove the Confederates from their fortifications south and north of the creek. After the division advanced northward across the stream, another line of battle was formed in the open fields of a large plantation (Colonel Taylor's), the 1st Brigade occupying the left of the division line. The 26th Iowa Infantry, Major Lubbers commanding, was detached and deployed as to skirmish. Ibid., 252.

615. "Butler's division in line of battle was said to be magnificent," wrote Maj. Thomas Osborn, chief of artillery for the Army of the Tennessee. "The front covered more than a mile, on the open field. It was evidently formed with the intention to make a grand charge on us if we showed the least weakness in our disposition...." Osborn states that the cavalry was commanded by Hampton. Richard Harwell and Philip N. Racine, eds., *The Fiery Trail: A Union Officer's Account of Sherman's Last Campaigns* (Knoxville: University of Tennessee Press, 1986), 124.

616. The section of De Gress's battery (Company H, 1st Illinois Light Artillery) unlimbered in the road near the west end of the bridge over the Congaree River. De Gress's guns commanded the main street in the city, where Confederate sharpshooters persisted in firing on the Federals, and some rebel cavalry were seen moving about. The street was briskly shelled, cleared of cavalry, and made untenable. *O.R.* I-47-I-371–72.

617. The Saluda Factory was located on the west bank of the Congaree, three to four miles above (northwest of) the city. The factory produced woolen cloth. Current, *Encyclopedia of the Confederacy*, I: 370.

618. Ironically, even with having ample warning of Sherman's approaching armies, and the presence of nine Confederate generals in Columbia, there was no plan for the city's defense. Resistance to Sherman's advance remained as haphazard as it had been during the previous phases of the march. Wade Hampton, promoted to lieutenant general and placed in command of all Confederate cavalry superceding Joseph Wheeler, was present, as was Gen. P. G. T. Beauregard, who was in overall command of the limited combined forces—though there was practically no infantry on hand to defend the city. Early on February 17, when Sherman's artillery began to shell the city and blue columns pressed up to the riverside, General Hampton retired toward the northern city limits and exited to safety, leaving the mayor, Dr. Thomas J. Goodwyn, to meet the oncoming Federal vanguard and unconditionally surrender the city to

Col. George A. Stone, 25th Iowa Infantry, commanding 3rd Brigade, 1st Division, XV Army Corps. Burke Davis, *Sherman's March* (New York: Random House, 1980), 158; *O.R.* I-47-I-21, 264.

619. John H. Tierney, a native of New Jersey, was 17 years old and a resident of Clinton when he enlisted as drummer on August 13, 1862. He served nearly three years, being mustered out with the regiment in Washington D.C., on June 6, 1865. *Roster* 3: 1102. The editor could not locate documentation to support Oake's claim that John Tierney hauled down a rebel flag from the state house. There were actually two capitols, the old structure and a new, unfinished one. According to Maj. Gen. Giles A. Smith, commanding 4th Division, XVII Army Corps, a detachment of the 13th Iowa Infantry first entered the city and planted two stands of colors, one upon the old capitol and the other upon the new one. In his after-action report of the campaign in the Carolinas, Col. George Stone, 25th Iowa Infantry, who accepted the city's formal unconditional surrender from Mayor Goodwyn, reported that he personally, in the company of another officer, planted the first U.S. flag on the state house. *O.R.* I-47-I-265, 417–18.

620. In his report dated March 26, 1865, Gen. William Woods stated that, at 9 P.M., his 1st Brigade was ordered to relieve Colonel Stone's 3rd Brigade on provost guard duty in the city. "On entering the city I found a large part of the place in flames," he wrote. "I am satisfied by statements made to me by respectable citizens of the town that the fire was first set by the negro inhabitants. A gale was blowing, and the city being chiefly built of wood, the fire was exceedingly hard to control, but by the strenuous exertions of the officers and men of the brigade at least two-fifths of the city was saved from destruction." *O.R.* I-47-I-252.

621. The force assigned as headquarters guard for General Sherman during this period was the 7th Company Ohio Sharpshooters, commanded by Lt. James Cox. Whether it was actually soldiers from this escort organization that Oake was "in company with" is unclear. Ibid., 46. The probability exists that he was mistaken as to the identity of his destructive comrades during what was an extremely confusing and chaotic night for all who participated in and witnessed the controversial events.—Ed.

622. It appears almost certain that Oake actively participated in some of the Federal troops, destructive behavior in Columbia that night. His comment that "Some of those in authority made an attempt to use the fire engines and try to subdue the flames," would also lead the reader to conclude he personally did not assist "those in authority" in battling the blaze.—Ed.

623. The Iberian Peninsular War (1808–1814), known in Spain as the *Guerra de la Independencia*, formed a part of what are commonly referred to as the Napoleonic Wars. Oake is mistaken as to the identity of the location, and is referring to the Siege of Badajoz, Spain (March–April 1812), a fortress commanding Spain's southern gateway. After taking the fortress city by storm, the allied army under Arthur Wellesley, Duke of Wellington, which had sustained heavy casualties, went on a three-day rampage as military discipline collapsed completely, repeating the frenzy of carnage, rape, and pillage to which the army had subjected Ciudad Rodrigo in January 1812. Richard Holmes, ed. *The Oxford Companion to Military History* (New York: Oxford University Press, 2001), 701, 704, 990.

624. This would be the infamous French statesman and "dictator" Maximilien Marie Isidore de Robespierre (1758–1794), who rose to power and reigned supreme over France for three brief months before he followed his several thousand political victims to the guillotine. The despised dictator was toppled after the *coup d'etat* of Thermidor (July 27, 1794) during the early phase of the French Revolutionary Wars (1792–1801). Ibid., 329–32; Chandler, *The Campaigns of Napoleon*, 34; http://www.historyguide.org/intellect/robespierre.html.

625. Often considered the most serious single act of destruction during the war, and perhaps the most controversial, since it is still not known exactly who started the blaze, was the burning of Columbia. The scale of devastation was simply enormous. "I saw property destroyed until I was perfectly sick of it," remarked Lt. Charles S. Brown, of the 21st Michigan Infantry, "& that, for me to say in S.C. is considerable." The current impression is that the fire was simply an accidental element of war. Wade Hampton and his troopers were initially reckless in setting fire to large stores of cotton. However, released Southern civil prisoners, ex-slaves, and some Union soldiers set several other fires throughout the city. Many in this strange multitude were intoxicated by liquor provided by citizens or stolen from storage. Aided by extreme high winds, the fire destroyed roughly a third of the city. "The principal demons in the drama were cotton, whiskey, and wind," concluded historian Bell I. Wiley more than a century later. The Union high command, including Sherman, worked valiantly to extinguish the numerous fires, but the wind on mostly wooden buildings all but made their task impossible. Letter of Lt. Charles S. Brown to "folks" [March or April 1865], Charles S. Brown Papers, 1846–1865, Manuscript Division, Duke University Library; Mark Grimsley, *The Hard Hand of War: Union Military Policy Toward Southern Civilians 1861–1865* (New York: Cambridge University Press, 1995), 202; John F. Marszalek, *Sherman: A Soldier's Passion for Order* (New York: The Free Press, 1993), 324–25; Bell I. Wiley, Foreword, in Marion B. Lucas, *Sherman and the Burning of Columbia* (College Station: Texas A & M University Press, 1976), 13.

626. The Federal troops became careless in dumping wagon loads of captured ammunition in the Saluda River. The deaths of the sixteen Yankee soldiers seemed to delight seventeen-year-old Emma LeConte, daughter of Professor Joseph LeConte of South Carolina College in Columbia, who rejoiced "to think of any of them being killed." Emma LeConte Diary, February 19, 1865, Southern Historical Collection, University of North Carolina.

627. Kane, a native of Ireland, was 21 and a resident of Lyons when he enlisted as fourth sergeant on August 8, 1862. He was promoted first sergeant, October 24, 1862, and second lieutenant, February 27, 1863, and was mustered out with the regiment, June 6, 1865, in Washington, D.C. *Roster* 3: 1071.

628. On the march, Sherman's soldiers were encouraged to forage liberally through Georgia and the Carolinas. These organized foragers soon began to ignore the strict rules of official confiscation procedure. Thousands of men routinely and independently plundered the countryside, ferreting out food, clothing, horses, and valuables from both friendly and unfriendly civilians. These unsupervised forage raids were initially prohibited by numerous commanders; however, the activity was eventually condoned and even encouraged as the nature of the war hardened, and army rations and other essentials grew scarce. During the March to the Sea and throughout the Carolinas campaign, the common name applied to men off foraging as independent raiders was "Sherman's bummers." Interspersed with the bummers on the flanks and in front of the main columns of Federal troops were temporary and permanent Union deserters, Confederate deserters, unscrupulous civilians, escaped slaves, and significant elements of Joseph Wheeler's Confederate cavalry corps, all of them doing a significant amount of jayhawking, or plundering. Therefore, the enormous destruction recorded during the campaign had many perpetrators, and Union soldiers alone were not wholly responsible. Marszalek, *Sherman*, 301–2.

629. These three raccoons evidently ended up either roasted or boiled over the evening cook fire.

630. The accident occurred as the brigade, along with the division, was preparing to move out of its Cheraw camps and cross the pontoon bridge over the Great Pee Dee River. Gen. William Woods reported that a large quantity of ammunition, which had been discarded into a ravine near the road, was accidentally exploded, killing one man and wounding five of the brigade. Gen. Oliver O. Howard, commanding the Army of the Tennessee, stated, "The explosion was very loud and shook the ground for miles. One officer and three men killed, and several men wounded, many quite seriously. The teams were stampeded, and several teamsters were badly injured." Oake is correct in his observation concerning the amount of gunpowder seized in Cheraw. In addition, the Federals took 24 cannon, 2,000 muskets, and 20,000 rounds of infantry ammunition. The carelessness of one soldier cost the lives of several men, and pandemonium briefly reigned. Suspecting sabotage, Sherman thought about ordering the town burned to the ground, when he discovered the accident had been caused by one of his own men. John G. Barrett, *Sherman's March Through the Carolinas* (Chapel Hill: The University Press of North Carolina, 1956), 109–10; *O.R.* I-47-I-202, 253.

631. As Sherman's forces moved north from Cheraw and the valley of the Great Pee Dee River, the period of March 8–12 would prove to be exceedingly laborious for Oake and his comrades. Gen. John A. Logan, commanding the XV Army Corps, reported that "the country was a perfect quicksand." Strong working parties from all the divisions were engaged in corduroying roads and building bridges, for the rains so saturated the ground that the roads were impassable without great labor on behalf of the troops. *O.R.* I-47-I-231–33.

CHAPTER TWENTY-FIVE

High Priced Dinner and a Warm Place at Bentonville

A fter eating our supper and retiring we were soon fast asleep, and in that happy state of unconsciousness, that the good alone can enjoy. About midnight we were startled from our sleep by hearing the familiar call, the long roll being sounded. Soon all was bustle and hurry in camp as the boys more asleep then awake hurriedly began to pack up and prepare for what seemed inevitable. Soon mounted orderlies were moving rapidly from place to place giving orders to prepare to move at a moments notice. What could be the matter, we asked each other. Were we surrounded by rebels, or did we have to make a midnight move in that Egyptian darkness, through that sea of mud that was almost impassible by day light. After marching all day tired and wet, with but about three hours sleep we were in anything but a pleasant mood at being so unceremoniously aroused from our peaceful slumber, and I am afraid many cuss words were used on that occasion.

We were soon in line and as we stood shivering in the cold night air, I thought what a grand thing it was to suffer and die for ones country, on paper.

Soon we received orders to again return to our dog tents as we would remain there until morning, and in a short time we were again sound asleep. It was not until we had resumed our march in the morning did we learn the cause of the midnight alarm the preceding night. It appeared that the cavalry under General Kilpatrick were encamped about six miles to our left, and during the night they had been surprised by the rebels, and driven from their camp, and orders had been sent for a brigade of infantry to go to their assistance, but Kilpatrick in person had rallied his men and finally regained possession of his camp, but with a loss of about 200 men.[632]

After resuming our march the writer with five others was detailed to forage for the regiment. The detail being under the command of that fine soldier Captain James Crozer of Company C 26th Iowa, all being mounted we would at times get quite a distance from the road upon which the troops were marching. About noon, being hungry we stopped at a small plantation to get our dinners. Upon approaching the house (which was a small log house so common in certain sections of the South) we were met by the owner a man of perhaps fifty years of age, to whom we made known our wants, and asking him if it would be convenient for his folks to prepare dinner for us. He answered he reckoned they could, and invited us into the house when he introduced to us his two daughters young ladies of perhaps 20 and 22 years of age , both unmarried. He asked them if they could get us some dinner, which they consented to do, we furnishing the meat and coffee.

The young ladies were soon busily engaged in preparing our meal, and in a short time we were partaking of a solid repast of steaming corn pone and fried ham accompanied by a cup of old Government Java, which we politely invited them to partake of, a privilege they were much pleased with, and highly elated at the thought of once more partaking of a cup of good coffee. After eating our meal and being ready to resume our journey I inquired of them what the charges were for their trouble. The planter replied we could give him what we thought was right. Taking a large roll of Confederate bills from my pocket I handed him a thousand dollar bond, which act seemed to astonish him, and it was quite a little time before he gained breath so as to inform me that it was impossible for him to make change for so large a bill. I informed him that so far as we were concerned it was unnecessary, that we considered ourselves under great obligations to them for so kindly preparing our dinner, and that we insisted on his taking the bill; that we were men of means, and the amount was but a trifle to us. To say that the old man was astonished is putting it mildly, while the two young ladies were completely dumbfounded at the streak of good luck that had befallen them, while their beaming and smiling countenances indicated a desire on their part to embrace the entire outfit (with the exception of the writer.) We now bid them good bye and again resumed our journey, and along towards the evening laden with forage we overtook the marching troops and soon afterwards went into camp for the night.

The next morning, the 11th [12th of March],[633] we were again on the move and in the afternoon entered the town of Fayetteville, situated on the Cape Fear River, and from this point had communication with our Northern friends by the way of Wilmington,[634] as up to this time we had been completely isolated from our friends in the North, as we had neither sent or received any mail since leaving the vicinity of Beaufort on the coast, and many of the boys were bare-footed and sadly in need of clothing after our long and tedious march through the swampy region of the Carolinas.

While at this place I became the possessor of a very fine velvet bound pocket bible, which I now have, and although so many years have elapsed it is in good condition, and I have no doubt if the owners are alive they would be happy with its restoration. It might perhaps interest my readers to know how I became its possessor without stealing it, and for fear some of them might think me sacrilegious enough to steal the word of god I will set them at rest on that score. John M. Hague of my company while out foraging with a comrade secured a parcel done up in a piece of white muslin and upon unwrapping the same, what was his astonishment to find said bible, and officers silk sash and a deck of playing cards. Bringing the same into camp a great many came to look at his fine bible, among them one officer who quickly offered him ten dollars for the book, but Hague refused it but turning to me said, "Injun I will give it to you." Hague being a Catholic he had no particular use for a Protestant bible, and gave it to one that he thought was in need of just such a book. The gift was greatly appreciated by me, and to this day and whenever I see the little book my thoughts revert to that pleasing episode on the banks of the Cape Fear River in North Carolina in 1865. Attached to the inside of the book by silken cords were two cards and two little coils of infants hair and judging from the words written on the cards together with the young lady's signature it is plainly evident that it belonged to a party in the higher walks of life, and as I write this article with that little silken lock of hair before me I wish that to me its history it could unfold. How perhaps even at this moment some fond father or mother with tear dimmed eyes are thinking of the beloved owner of that silken tress, and mourning its loss.[635]

About the 15th, the army having crossed the river, the troops were again in motion in the direction of Goldsboro, and from all indications would soon have a fight or a foot race with the enemy, who were rapidly concentrating all their available forces in our front. After evacuating the city of Charleston, which they did when we cut the Charleston and Augusta railroad at Branchville about fifty-four miles west of Charleston, the enemy's forces had all moved north to intercept us if possible.[636] General Joe Johnston was in command having superseded Beauregard.[637]

It was supposed at the time that the enemy's forces numbered about thirty thousand men, and while it would be impossible to defeat Sherman's army of sixty thousand veterans, they could at least embarrass it to a certain extent as there was no abler officer in the rebel army than wily Joe Johnston, and as our four corps were marching on four parallel roads, Johnston's hope was to catch one Corps before the others could come to its assistance. However if Johnston was wily, Uncle Billy Sherman[638] was equally so, and would not be caught napping.

On the morning of the 16th [of March], comrade T. J. Houston of Company A and the writer thought we would try to get ahead of the advance guard, and by so doing get some forage. Now the orders were very strict against foraging unless on a detail for that purpose, but we thought we would do a little on the side, but we were unlucky in our venture, and were arrested by the advance guard, and had to march with them until we went into camp about 2 o'clock in the afternoon.[639]

On arriving in camp we were taken before Major John Lubbers who was then in command of the regiment. As we were marched up to the major's tent we saluted when the guard reported as having arrested us foraging without a permit, and in advance of the advance guard. The old major looked quite sour, and in his broken German wanted to know, "What for we go forage." We replied, "We thought there was no harm in it, and wanted to get something to eat." He replied, "You don't know vot the orders are huh." "Yes," we told him. "We knew what the orders were if we got caught, but we did not expect to be caught." He replied, "Bunish you for dat." Turning to the guard he said, "Guard, you take dose men with some shobels, and make each vone dig some holes ten feet long dree feet wide and dree feet teep." After getting the shovels and marking the holes the desired size we went to work.

It happened that it was fine digging a kind of a sandy loom, and we soon had the holes dug in a fine shape, and were again taken before the major and saluting him I said, "Major the holes are dug." He dropped his head, and I thought I detected a smile as he said, "Oake you can go to your quarters, but guard take Corporal Houston back and have him fill up dot hole he dug." Poor Houston having taken pains to dig a nice clean hole had to fill it up again, and he was then reduced to the ranks. How glad I was that I was not a Corporal, simply a high private. After the war I frequently met the old major in his home town, Lyons, Iowa, and we used to laugh over it, and the old fellow would say, "Vell Oake, let's take a Lager Peer." Houston never forgave the old major, but if he had not been a non-commissioned officer he would have got off as easy as did the writer. The old major had been a commissioned officer in the German Army and was a strict disciplinarian as are all foreign officers, but a good many of them found out during the Civil War, old country discipline did not work very well when applied to the volunteer service, as a rule the men composing the volunteer army during the Civil War were as intelligent as the officers, and in many cases more so, and while strict discipline might be necessary for the huge armies of Europe, where in some instances they were like a lot of cattle it did not work as well among more intelligent soldiers. Since the war the writer has often met his old comrade Houston, and has had many a laugh over the incident, and I can truthfully say that no better soldier ever marched under the Stars and Stripes than T. J. Houston of Company A 26th, Iowa.[640]

The next day after the arrest of Houston and the writer, we were again pushing our way towards Goldsboro, and upon going into camp in the afternoon near a plantation my old comrade D. W. Swihart (of whom mention has been made several times in this work) and the writer came across a cow that was giving milk, and Swihart was bound to have, if possible, some of the delicious fluid. I myself having been weaned when quite young did not care anything about it, but told my old comrade I would assist him in getting a supply, and by getting the cow in a fence corner I would get her by the horns, and hold her while he milked her into his canteen. The scheme worked admirably for a while. Getting her in a fence corner I managed to secure a firm hold on her horns while Dave squatted down with his canteen in one hand, and proceeded to milk her with the other. The old cow in the meanwhile was watching Dave out of the corner of her eyes. After Dave had got what I thought might be half of a canteen full I relaxed my hold on the horns somewhat, and the cow noticed it, and with a kick and Bah knocked over Dave and the canteen flew about a rod. I ran after the cow, but soon gave it up as a bad job, and when I got back to Dave he was just in the act of picking up his canteen and a madder fellow I never saw, all of his hard earned milk was gone, and while he gave me fits for not holding the cow I could hardly keep my face straight, as I told him how firmly I thought I had hold of her. From the look he gave me, I believe he thought I was lying and I guess he was about right.

On returning to camp he told the boys how near he came to having some milk for his coffee, and would have had it had it not been for Oake, and that d—d cow. On the 20th [21st of March], the 26th Iowa was acting as train guards and along about 9 o'clock it began to rain and in a short time the boom of artillery was heard in front, which indicated that the advance had run up against a snag. The rain continued to fall, and we plodded along in the mud. Soon the increased booming of the dogs of war told us that business in front had begun in earnest. Now we could see a mounted orderly coming from the front, and we received orders to leave the train and push for the front.[641]

Louder and more frequent we heard the cannon in the front. Now the order was double quick to the front, and we started at a rapid pace through the drenching rain, and mud. Soon we began to hear the report of small arms, a certain indication of serious work. As we rapidly approached the field of action, the familiar ping of the minie was again heard, and occasionally some unfortunate could be seen carried from the field of action. As we arrived we were soon in line, and a detail of fifteen men for skirmishers from the 26th was called.[642]

As they advanced to the front they were given a warm reception by the enemy. Upon establishing our lines we at once received orders to build breastworks, and in a short time they were completed, and we awaited further orders. Soon word was brought that nine were wounded and one killed, of the first detail of fifteen skirmishers from the 26th, and another detail of fifteen

High Priced Dinner and
a Warm Place at Bentonville

men was ordered, and it was the writer's fortune to be one of the fifteen.

Our line was formed in a small ravine, while directly in front and distant about one hundred and fifty yards in some thick brush were the enemy. The intervening distance being covered by a growth of quite large timber, and no underbrush, until you approached the place where the enemy's position was supposed to be, and where there was a dense growth of underbrush, making it almost impossible for the eye to penetrate it. As our last detail of fifteen men formed in line behind the works we shook hands with our comrades and bade them good bye, and as the order to advance was given we sprang over the works, and started for the rebs.

As we came into plain view of them they greeted us with a shower of lead. We then returned the fire as with a deafening yell we charged their position, and were met by a murderous fire from ten times our number, and we jumped behind trees to protect ourselves. We for a short time held our position and made it warm for our rebel friends. Soon Captain [William L.] Alexander[643] of the 30th Iowa, who commanded the brigade[644] skirmishers, ordered us to fall back as a strong line of the enemy were about to flank us. I had my gun at my shoulder and resting it along side of a tree, I fired at a big rebel about fifty feet distant. Not waiting to see the result of my shot I turned my eyes, and found our lines had fallen back about three rods, leaving me all alone. In an instant I followed them, and although followed by a shower of bullets I escaped and was soon in my usual position behind a friendly tree, [along] with Captain Alexander.

Kind readers I don't think any minie ball south of the Mason Dixie line could have caught me in going those three rods. I had just loaded my musket, and seeing a rebel, in my hurry forgot to withdraw my ramrod, but blazed away. On proceeding to load I found I was short a ramrod, when looking a little behind me saw one of our soldiers lying dead, and hastened to get the ramrod from his gun, and upon looking at him, discovered him to be Wm. Gardner of Company I, of our regiment, the picket killed out of the first detail of fifteen men. My readers will remember mention of him being made in a former chapter, as being the comrade that left the picket line with the writer, and crossed the Pedee River, after forage, near Cheraw. On looking at poor Gardner my feelings can better be imagined than described, and for an instant I almost forgot my surroundings.[645]

I was quickly reminded of my position as a minie ploughed its way through my shoe, and I quickly regained my friendly tree. After regaining my position behind the tree I took a quick inventory of the damage done my shoe and found that the ball had cut my pants and had made a grove in the heel of my shoe, and from the course it took it must have struck a limb of a tree, and then taken a downward course, and although no great damage had been done it was a close call.

The enemy still kept up a heavy fire, making it quite lively for us, at the same time we were not asleep, and kept them from making any further advance.[646] The rain in the meantime continued to fall and we were completely saturated while the barrels of our muskets were red with rust caused by the continual rain falling on them, while so hot from the rapid firing.

Again we received orders to advance and drive back the enemy. With a cheer we sprang forward from tree to tree, and forced the enemy back a short distance, and succeeded in holding our position until night threw its sable mantle over the field, when with the exception of an occasional shot all was quiet, and the troops could take a rest from the terrible strain they had undergone during the past day.[647]

About 8 o'clock we were relieved by fresh troops, and slowly wended our way back to the main line to partake of some food, that had been prepared for us by our comrades.[648] After eating our supper and drying our clothes some what, we coiled up behind the works, and were soon fast asleep and dreaming of what we thought would be inevitable on the morrow.

Bright and early the next morning we were astir, and after eating our breakfast were ready for the fray. Soon we received orders to move and the line carefully felt its way to the front, but what was the matter? Not a shot came from the enemy. Getting bolder we rapidly advanced on the supposed position by the enemy, only to find they had evacuated their position during the night leaving us masters of the field.[649] Just to the right, and about one hundred yards from where I had been on the skirmish line the day before, we came upon the mutilated and charred remains of three of the enemy that had been wounded and burned in a tent in which they had been lying. It was a sickening sight, and after a glance at them we continued our way through the thick brush to the front, expecting every moment to be greeted with a volley from a concealed enemy.

High Priced Dinner and
a Warm Place at Bentonville

Pushing ahead we soon arrived at the little hamlet of Bentonville, and found that the enemy had escaped us. Upon arriving at the above place, I noticed a couple of our men looking at some object lying on the ground a few rods away. My curiosity being aroused I approached them to see what so drew their attention, and was shocked at the sight I beheld. One of our men perfectly nude and horribly mutilated lay upon the ground while the dis-colored flesh and purple marks around his neck told plainly the cause of his death. Soon we were approached by a Negro, a resident of the place and from him learned the following facts.

It appeared he had been taken prisoner by the enemy and had been asked to give certain information which he had refused to do. They then split his foot between the large toe and the others to the instep to try to compel him to give the desired information, but still he refused. They then cut off his foot, but he still refused. Then they hung him until dead and left him, lying as found by us. Whether or not the Negro told the truth we could not say, but the condition of the unfortunate soldier was just as has been described, and while we were looking at him General Logan and staff rode up, and I think at this time I can see the angry flash of the Generals eye, as he viewed the remains, and heard the Negro's version of the affair.

We remained in camp at this place until the next day when we once more resumed our march for the town of Goldsboro, and arrived at that place on the morning of March 24th, and went into camp to rest, and prepare for the next move. Our march through the Carolinas had been the longest march made by any army during the Civil War, over 425 [485] miles, crossing five quite large rivers, and most of the way through a low and swampy country.[650] The roads made almost impassible by the continued and heavy rains that the South is frequently subject to in the winter and spring of the year. Upon our arrival at Goldsboro a great many of the troops were almost barefoot and sadly in need of clothes. The writer was a little more fortunate as he still had the old mans shoes that he had borrowed, and which proved to wear well. Now that he would soon draw needed supplies I would have returned them if I could have done so.

After being in camp a few days, it became rumored among the troops that during our stay here we would have two hours drill each day. To say that the troops were indignant at having to drill after that long march, and when it was apparent to anyone of common sense that the war was about over, but faintly expresses the feelings of the boys upon hearing that such was actually the fact. For one I told the company commander that I did not think I should drill. He laughed and asked me how I would get out of it. I told him I thought I was going to be sick.

The next morning when the sick call sounded, "Quinine,"[651] with the old timers I fell into line and marched up to the hospital tent and when my turn came the surgeon, George F. Weatherell said, "Well, Oake what in the world is the matter with you." I replied, "I don't know doctor, I feel kinder all over." "Just so, just so," he replied. "Let me look at your tongue." I ran my tongue out about eight inches, he said, "Yes, yes I see, let me feel of your pulse." After feeling of my pulse he smiled and said, "I think I can fix you up, but you will have to remain quiet in your quarters." So he marked me rest in quarters. On returning to camp I told the Company commander that if he wanted guards or pickets I thought I would be able to take my place, but did not feel able to drill, as the surgeon had told me to keep pretty quiet, and had marked me rest in quarters. He replied, "All right," but from the twinkle in his eye I knew he was on to my game.

The next morning, according to the program, the troops marched out to drill, while Robert McLenahan of Company A, M[artin] Davis of Company F and S. M. [F.] Cooper[652] of the 27th Missouri,[653] with whom I became acquainted while in old Libby Prison, and myself, passed our time away playing a social game of draw. After playing a few games George Simms of the 10th Iowa, spoken of as one of the drafted men that came to us just prior to our march to the sea, came to see me, and he was considerably under the weather, in fact at the time he looked a fit subject for the hospital. He said that he felt bad, but thought that if he could get a little whiskey once in a while he thought it would do him good. He being a drafted man and not knowing the ropes did not know how to get it. I told him to wait until we got through with our game, when I thought we could make a raise of the desired article. We soon finished our game when Davis wrote out a requisition and attached the regimental commander's name to it, when taking five canteens we started for the division commissary, distant about a mile, telling our comrades to wait as we would soon be back.

Arriving at the commissary we presented our requisition and was told by the sergeant in charge that he could not let us have it unless the requisition was countersigned by the brigade commander. We told him we could easily get that, but did not think it was necessary. He replied it did not used to be required, but this was an order issued quite recently, and of course he dare not issue it unless the order was complied with. Thanking him we told him we would return to camp and have the requisition properly signed, although it would require a walk of about two miles. Passing around to the tent Davis wrote across the back of the requisition, W. W. Woods,* Brigadier General, Commanding 1st Brigade, 1st Division of 15th Army Corps. We were absent about ten minutes when we returned and again presented the requisition. The sergeant looked at it a moment and said, "All right, boys, you were not long in finding the General." "Oh no," we replied, "We met him on the road a short distance back, and he at once signed it for us." The sergeant's looks told us plainly that he had dealt with just such fellows before. Getting our whiskey we were soon on our way to camp, and I never saw a man more pleased than Simms was upon receiving his canteen filled with the desired article, and many times after that he attributed his quick recovery to that canteen full of whiskey. Poor Simms he was a fine fellow, and I don't want my readers to think that by his wanting a little whiskey that he was a drinking man, as he was very temperate in his habits, but it seemed that it was just what he wanted, and thought it would do him good, and it did. Poor fellow he was killed the first winter after the war by the limb of a tree that he was felling, breaking off and flying back and knocking out his brains.

While lying at Goldsboro the writer had quite a good time playing cards with some of the comrades, who like myself were sick or expected to be sometime. When tired of playing cards we would go out on the drill ground and watch the other fellows drill. While here we drew clothing, and had a regular clean up after our hard campaign. On April 10th we were again on the march, following Joe Johnston's army in the direction of Raleigh, the capital of the state, distant about fifty-six miles.[654]

During our first day's march it rained most of the time and the advance met with considerable opposition from the enemy, but the skirmishers in front (of whom the writer was one) drove them about as fast as the troops could march. Little did the writer know at the time, that it was the last time he would fire a hostile shot at the enemy.[655] The 11th we met with but little opposition, and on the morning of the 12th [of April] as the column was marching along the road, Major Landgrebber [Clemons Landgraeber],[656] of a Missouri Battery, passed along the lines telling the commanders of the different regiments, that it was reported that General [Robert E.] Lee's army had surrendered to General [Ulysses S.] Grant.[657]

I never will forget the excitement of those few moments after receiving the news. The soldiers acted like a lot of escaped lunatics. Hats were wildly thrown in the air, and every man wanted to hug the other fellow. Kind readers you can better judge the feelings of the troops than I can describe them. It did not seem possible that the news could be true. If it were true, it meant that we would soon meet loved ones at home. After four years of the bloodiest war the world ever saw, in which half a million men had lost their lives,[658] it was ended, and not a star had been erased from the glittering folds of Old Glory.

The surrender of Lee meant the collapse of the Confederacy, and an early return to friends in the North. We met with no further opposition from the rebel army, and on April 13th entered the capital of the state and went into camp about one mile from the city. After stacking our arms in company with one or two others we started for a plantation about one mile from camp, thinking that perhaps we could get something in the chicken line.

Arriving at the plantation we found that others had preceded us, and were making it quite lively for the chickens. In a short time we too took a hand in the business and managed to secure a few, together with other forage. Passing near the residence on the plantation and noticing it was entirely deserted I entered it, and found several other soldiers there, but no sign of its occupants. It had evidently been sometime since anyone had been there, but most of the furniture together with a very fine library remained, and also some clothing that was scattered promiscuously around the house.

I at last secured a pair of very fine white pants and a fine velvet vest together with a fine plug hat. Putting on the pants, which I found about six inches too long I then donned the vest, and to put a finishing touch to it put the plug hat over my army cap, and with Webster's Unabridged Dictionary under my arm and with the chickens and other plunder started for camp. It was amusing to see the boys look as I approached camp clad as I was in that ridiculous manner. It was not until I had approached quite close, and spoke

*High Priced Dinner and
a Warm Place at Bentonville*

to them that they recognized me, and then such a shout went up that it was several moments before I could get the floor to explain myself. Finally comrade Leeper of Company H said he would give me two dollars for the pants as they would just fit him, and I quickly told him the garments were his. The plug hat and vest I kept and wore them as long as we remained in camp at this place.

A day or two after our arrival at Raleigh the good news we had heard about the surrender of Lee was confirmed, by an official notice being read to the troops, and also that negotiations were pending between Johnston and Sherman for the surrender of all the rebel forces under the former general's command.[659] On the 25th (I think it was) [actually the 27th of April] an official order from the commanding general was read to the troops announcing the surrender of General Johnston's army, and the end of the war and that in a few days we would start for Washington to be dis-

Ruins of Richmond, Virginia, from the Canal Basin, 1865.
In stark contrast to his first visit to Richmond as a prisoner of war in 1863, a far different landscape greeted William Royal Oake on his return to the captured Confederate capital two years later, when Sherman's victorious army group passed through the city in early May 1865. MEDFORD HISTORICAL SOCIETY

charged.[660] One incident connected with our stay in Raleigh I had almost forgotten to mention and which no doubt hastened the surrender of the rebel army, and that was the news of the assassination of President [Abraham] Lincoln.[661] Upon receipt of that notice, on every hand could be seen groups of soldiers discussing the dastardly outrage, and it seemed to be the wish of the troops to once more engage the rebel army in deadly conflict, and I think that under the circumstances had another battle taken place between the opposing forces no quarter would have been shown so far as the Federal soldiers were concerned. The soldiers were terribly incensed over the cowardly assassination of the President, and a great many of them said that the Southern leaders were directly concerned in the matter and for a while it seemed that nothing but blood would appease their anger.[662] Fortunately General Johnston saw and understood the situation, and knowing the indignation the affair had raised in the Northern troops, wisely surrendered his whole army. The night following the news of the surrender of the rebels, and the termination of the war, permission was given the troops to celebrate the event by firing all the blank cartridges we wished to in honor of the occasion, and for about two hours the darkness was lit up as with electricity by the rapid fire of musketry supplemented by the roar of the numerous pieces of artillery that were with that army of 60,000 men. It was a grand sight, and well fitting the occasion.

In a few days we were again in motion headed for the capital at Washington, [D.C.][663] Soon, all our long and weary marches would be over and we looked forward with joy to again see our friends [in] the North. Then again our thoughts would revert back to the many bloody fields through which we had passed, and we again imagined we could see the cold and mangled remains of beloved comrades as we last saw them ere we consigned them to their last resting place. How we wished they were with us on this happy occasion to enjoy with us the fruits of hardships and suffering, and to be welcomed home by loving hearts and arms that we well knew were ready to receive us upon our return. As those thoughts forced themselves upon us even amidst our great joy at the thought of home and friends a great lump would arise in our throats, and it was impossible to check the falling tears.

After several days march we at last reached Richmond, Virginia,[664] and went into camp on the opposite side of the James River from Richmond. As my readers are aware Richmond is situated on the north side of the James River, while on the south side is the town of Manchester. It was on the south side of the River, about one mile from Manchester, that we were encamped, and while there occurred an incident that is too good to omit, [and] one that the writer will vouch for as being true in every particular.

While encamped here my old comrades, T. J. Houston the fellow that dug the hole, and had to fill it up again, and D. W. Swihart the comrade that tried to milk the cow, were going into the little town of Manchester to make a raid of something to eat, and being a little short of funds they espied a mule which they at once confiscated, and taking it to a citizen in the town and sold it for $35.00, getting the cash for it. All this was well and good and perfectly legitimate if they had stopped there, but I was told by good authority that the same evening they engaged a darkey to re-confiscate the mule. When they again sold the mule for $25.00, and not paying the darkey the twenty-five cents which they agreed to pay him for stealing the mule. I understood the reason they gave for not paying the darkey was that they could not find him. I have no doubt should my old comrades read this they will brand the writer as a base fabricator, but my reputation for truth and veracity is to well known to be refuted by there mere say so.

While lying here, the writer paid a visit to old Libby again, where he had spent so many days in the summer of 1863, and as I stood within its portals I thought if its gloomy walls could talk what tales of suffering and misery it could unfold. As I cast my eyes around the room in which I was confined I thought I could again see the still and quiet form of some comrade lying with some old rags thrown over him, waiting to be carried to his last resting place.

After remaining in camp at Manchester, until May 12th [13th], we were again on the move towards the capital, Washington, and our route took us over the hard fought field of Fredericksburg, evidences of that terrific struggle were still visible on every hand. Buildings in the old historic town were shattered, and torn in every conceivable manner by the storm of iron hail that rained from the contending armies during that bloody struggle.[665]

While on our march there occurred a very laughable incident. In passing quite a large plantation a large number of Negroes were lined up along the side of the road watching the Yankee troops while passing, and as the bands of the various regiments would strike up they would commence to dance. From the little pickininnies up to old gray haired Patriarchs, all were dancing and blessing Massas Lincoln's soldiers. One great stalwart darkey standing near the marching troops drew the attention of comrade Hague of our company, who slipped his bayonet on his gun, and when opposite the darkey made a lunge towards the Negro, and told him to howl. The darkey let out an unearthly yell and the troops in our rear as they came up, and seeing what the matter was would repeat the order to the darkey, and after marching a quarter of a mile we could still hear the darkey yelling, and I sometimes think he is yelling yet.

On another occasion the same comrade made a jump for a darkey as he stood alongside of the road, and the Negro made a break down through the timber at a gait that would beat Dexter's best time in the shade. Over the top of the brush and saplings anyone viewing his trail would think a cyclone had lately passed through the woods. On our march we passed by the home of [George] Washington, Mount Vernon, and all of the troops with reversed arms marched past the last resting place of the Father of our country. The door to the tomb had been thrown open, and the marble caskets containing the remains of the family were in plain view, and the inscriptions thereon could be plainly read. The tomb is situated on a beautiful wooded slope on the banks of the Potomac, a fit resting place for that illustrious character. In passing the tomb my thoughts reverted back to those stirring scenes of 1776, and of the hardships that the soldiers of that period suffered, while wintering at Valley Forge. What would the Father of our Country think could he awaken and see that mighty host of sixty-five thousand armed men passing in review.[666]

After spending a little time in viewing the home of Washington and the surroundings we resumed our march, and went into camp near the City of Alexandria, about 9 miles below Washington City on the Potomac.

While encamped here I visited the old Marshall House, and saw the spot where the gallant Colonel [Elmer E.] Ellsworth fell when shot by that arch traitor [James] Jackson who in turn was killed by Sergeant [Private Francis] Brownell of Ellsworth's Zouaves, an incident that all readers of events of the Civil War are familiar with.[667]

On the evening of May 23rd most of our army crossed Long Bridge, and bivouacked in the streets of the capital preparatory for the [grand] review which would take place on the 24th, with the [grand] review of the Army of the Potomac taking place on the 23rd. The morning of May 24th was a beautiful morning, and the ground was in splendid order for the occasion. The streets were filled with people that had gathered from all parts of the country to see the grandest pageant that the country had or would perhaps ever witness.

Punctually, at 9 A.M., the signal gun was fired, when, led by its general, the army of Sherman started slowly down Pennsylvania Avenue on its grand

John A. Logan and the Army of the Tennessee at the Grand Review.
Participation in day two of the Grand Review of the Armies of the United States was the final highlight of the war for William Royal Oake and the surviving members of the "Clinton County Regiment." It took six and one-half hours for Sherman's 65,000-man fighting force to pass in review. U.S. ARMY MILITARY HISTORY INSTITUTE

review. The crowds of men, women, and children densely lining the side walks almost obstructed the way, while the display of flags and bunting obscured the suns rays. Looking back from the Treasury building to the capital it was a magnificent sight, as in divisions of company formations, that splendid body of men in close columns, and the glittering muskets looked like a solid mass of steel moving with the regularity of the pendulum of a clock. Here indeed was a sight, and one that any soldier participating in, might well be proud of. Here was that invincible army of sixty-five thousand men that had marched, as it were from the Mississippi River through the heart of rebeldom with victory perched upon its banners, seen in its true marching colors in better condition than when on its start, and if necessary ready for four years more of such hardships as they had passed through.[668]

It required six hours and a half for that army to pass the reviewing stand, the Fifteenth, Seventeenth, Fourteenth, and Twentieth Corps, and as General Sherman said, in his estimation, "It was the most magnificent army in existence. Sixty-five thousand men in splendid physique, who had just completed a march of two thousand miles in a hostile country in good drill, and who realized that they were being closely scrutinized by thousands of their fellow countrymen, and foreigners." [669]

The steadiness and firmness of the tread; the careful dress on guides; the uniform intervals between the companies; all eyes directly to the front; and the tattered and bullet-riven flags festooned with flowers all attracted universal attention. Some little scenes enlivened the day and were really laughable, as with some divisions could be seen [numerous] cows, pack mules laden with poultry, hams and some had families of freed slaves along, leading their children. In fact the army appeared as it did when operating on an active campaign in the enemy's country.[670]

Our regiment was mustered out of the United States service in Washington, D. C. on the 6th day of June 1865, and soon afterwards boarded a train for our Iowa homes.[671] We were banqueted most royally in Pittsburgh, and in Chicago we had four hours between trains to enjoy the hospitality of that city. At Clinton, where we had rendezvoused nearly three years previous we were disbanded, and made our way to our various homes as best we could. The writer went on foot and reached home safely, after a service lacking one month of three full years.

High Priced Dinner and a Warm Place at Bentonville

632. This two-hour action at Solemn Grove, or Monroe's Cross Roads, was contemptuously tagged by most Federal infantrymen as "Kilpatrick's Shirt-tailed Skedaddle" or "the Battle of Kilpatrick's Pants," owing to General Kilpatrick's reported state of near undress when his command was surprised. It occurred during the morning of March 10, 1865, as Judson Kilpatrick's three brigades were divided to picket the roads on Sherman's exposed left flank during the night of March 9–10. Confederate Gen. Wade Hampton detected the dispersed deployments of the Federal troopers and had Joe Wheeler's and Matthew Butler's cavalry dash in at daylight. The Confederate horsemen quickly gained possession of the camp of Col. George E. Spencer's brigade, including the house where Kilpatrick and Spencer had their quarters. Kilpatrick escaped on foot into a nearby swamp, and although shaken, he soon rallied the Federal horse-soldiers and counterattacked to reclaim a portion of the horses, wagons, and artillery, and the camp. Kilpatrick reported 4 officers killed and 7 wounded, 15 men killed and 61 severely wounded and several slightly wounded, and 103 officers and men taken prisoner. The Federals reported 80 Confederates killed and a large number of officers and men wounded, and 30 prisoners taken. Listed among the Confederate wounded were Generals William Y. C. Humes, Moses W. Hannon, and James Hagan. Confederate Lt. Col. Joseph F. Waring, commanding the Jeff Davis Legion (Mississippi Cavalry) in the action, thought it was to the enemy's credit they rallied so "promptly after the first surprise." Joseph F. Waring Diary, March 10, 1865, in the Southern Historical Collection, University of North Carolina; O.R. I-47-I-23, 862, 1065, 1130; Barrett, *Sherman's March Through the Carolinas*, 125–30.

633. The 26th Iowa, along with the remainder of William B. Woods's 1st Brigade, advanced from Cheraw, South Carolina, northward on March 5, 1865, and entered North Carolina, moving via Goodwin's Mill, crossing the Lumber River at Gilopolis Bridge and Montpelier, and reaching Fayetteville on March 12. *O.R.* I-47-I-246, 256; *Supplement to the O.R.* II-20-583.

634. Wilmington, North Carolina, had been the last major blockade-running port left to the Confederacy. United States forces assaulted and captured massive Fort Fisher at the mouth of the Cape Fear River on January 15, 1865. With Fisher occupied and ship access to and from the Atlantic cut off by Federal forces, Wilmington was of little importance. Confederate forces under Gen. Braxton Bragg occupied Wilmington until February 22, when they withdrew from the city, abandoning it to the Federal forces. Long, *Civil War Day by Day*, 624, 642.

635. The whereabouts of this Bible is unknown, and Oake does not state the identity of the woman who had owned it.—Ed.

636. Charleston was evacuated by Confederate forces under Lt. Gen. William J. Hardee on the same day that Sherman's forces occupied Columbia, South Carolina: February 17, 1865. Long, *Civil War Day by Day*, 639–40.

637. Johnston was restored to command on February 22, 1865. The new command encompassed two military districts: the Department of Tennessee and Georgia, and the Department of South Carolina, Georgia, and Florida. The troops in North Carolina became part of Johnston's command on March 6, 1865. He would command virtually every Confederate east of the Mississippi except Robert E. Lee's army besieged at Richmond and Petersburg. Johnston's initial orders from his superior, General Lee, were to "Concentrate all available forces and drive back Sherman." *O.R.* I-47-II-1247, 1248; Craig L. Symonds, Joseph E. Johnston: *A Civil War Biography* (New York: W.W. Norton & Company, 1992), 342–43.

638. Oake conveys his admiration and respect for William T. Sherman by using the nickname Uncle. To many of the citizen soldiers who served under the general, Sherman was known simply as Uncle Billy. Garrison & Garrison, *Civil War Usage*, 253.

639. On March 15, 1865, after the entire XV Army Corps had crossed the Cape Fear River, Bvt. Brig. Gen. William Woods reported that he received orders to take charge of and guard the transportation of the corps's several divisions, with the exception of headquarters and regimental teams, twelve ammunition wagons per division, and the ambulances. When organized, the train numbered 550 wagons and extended four and one-half miles in length. With the 1st Brigade as escort, joined by the 90th Illinois, 39th Iowa, and 29th Missouri infantries, the train departed the Cape Fear River opposite Fayetteville on March 16, at 11 A.M. *O.R.* I-47-I-253.

640. Lubbers was not extremely old, but would turn 40 in 1865, making him twenty-two years older than Oake.

641. Oake is nearly correct in his recollections. The brigade escorted the wagon train until 5 P.M., March 20, when it was parked and turned over to Maj. Gen. Joseph Mower, commanding 1st Division, XVII Army Corps, at Buck Creek, eight miles from Dudley's Station on the Goldsboro and Wilmington Railroad. During the four days that Woods's brigade escorted the train, including twenty-four hours for crossing the South River, the troops advanced an average of ten miles a day. In total, the train crossed the South River, Little Cohera and Great Cohera rivers, and Buck Creek. All of the streams were difficult to pass, and the troops were compelled to bridge the first three. General Woods reported that the brigade left the train at Buck Creek at 12 A.M., March 21, and marched until 3 A.M., halted until 6:30 A.M., and resumed the march and rejoined the division about 11 A.M., then three miles from Bentonville. He stated that Confederates were in force and entrenched. *O.R.* I-47-I-253.

642. Woods placed the 1st Brigade, with the 26th Iowa, 27th Missouri, 31st and 32nd Missouri Consolidated Battalion, and 76th Ohio Infantry, on the front line between the 2nd and 3rd Brigades of the 1st Division, leaving the 12th Indiana Infantry in reserve. A force of 100 skirmishers advanced under Capt. William Burch, who was commanding the 31st and 32nd Consolidated Battalion. Ibid., 46, 253. The battle that Oake marched into began on the morning of March 19, when Confederate forces under Joseph E. Johnston attacked Sherman's left flank, comprising the Union Army of Georgia commanded by Maj. Gen. Henry W. Slocum, south of Bentonville. The battle lasted until after dark. Three main assaults by Johnston's army were beaten off. During the evening, the Confederates withdrew to their starting points, and both combatants spent the rest of the night preparing fortifications. The next day, Sherman's right wing under Maj. Gen. Oliver O. Howard, the Army of the Tennessee, arrived to relieve Slocum's left wing. By late afternoon, Sherman's entire force was united in front and on both flanks of the Confederate position. No heavy fighting occurred during the day, but records cite considerable skirmishing along the lines. Long, *Civil War Day by Day*, 654–55.

643. As explained in note 642, Capt. William Alexander did not command the 1st Brigade skirmishers. The 30th Iowa was assigned to the 3rd Brigade (Col. George A. Stone commanding), 1st Division, XV Army Corps. Alexander was a native of Iowa, residing in West Point, when he was appointed first lieutenant of Co. I, 30th Iowa Infantry, on August 8, 1862. He had recovered from being severely wounded at Arkansas Post on January 11, 1863, where the regiment had served in the same brigade as the 26th Iowa, to earn promotion to captain on September 16, 1863. The 30th Iowa was mustered out of service of the United States on June 5, 1865, and departed for Iowa, where Alexander was mustered out August 16, 1865, in Davenport, upon expiration of term of service. *Roster* 3: 1490. Captain Alexander also served as a staff officer under the division commander, Maj. Gen. Charles R. Woods, serving as assistant commissary of musters. *O.R.* I-47-I-67, 248.

644. No record was found to describe the role Alexander played in this combat. He command-ed a company of the 30th Iowa Infantry in Stone's brigade, and may have been detailed to com-mand skirmishers that Stone sent forward. It is apparent that there was considerable confusion on the front, as skirmishers from both the 1st and 3rd brigades commingled in front of Colquitt's lines. General Woods reported that, during the fighting, Captain Burch "received a severe and dangerous wound." Therefore, it is probable Alexander assumed temporary com-mand of Burch's skirmish detail. Ibid., 254.

645. William F. H. Gardner is listed as killed in action at Mill Creek, North Carolina, on March 21, 1865. *Roster* 3: 1059. Similar to Oake's telling of this incident, Civil War memoirs are full of descriptions of the pandemonium experienced in a firefight. Many men would load and fire as quickly as possible, disregarding the prescribed manual of arms and also the steps essential to accurately aim and fire their muskets. Nosworthy, *The Bloody Crucible of Courage*, 586.

646. The Confederates confronting Woods's skirmishers were part of Gen. Robert F. Hoke's division, the left flank of Colquitt's Georgia Brigade, commanded by Col. Charles T. Zachry. Mark L. Bradley, *Last Stand in the Carolinas: The Battle of Bentonville* (Campbell, CA: Savas Woodbury Publishers, 1996), 360. Hereafter cited as *Last Stand in the Carolinas*. Gen. William Woods described the fighting on this front as a "hot skirmish, almost amounting to a battle." *O.R.* I-47-I-253.

647. Initially, Woods's 100 skirmishers under Captain Burch drove off the left flank of the entrenched skirmishers of Colquitt's Georgia Brigade. The Federals immediately began piling up earth to reverse the Confederate rifle pits and make them suitable for their own defense. The Georgians launched a counterattack from their main line and reclaimed the pits. Woods's troops rallied and again drove the Confederates off, only to be driven back once again themselves. General Woods countered this attack by sending in forty fresh troops, enabling his hard-pressed skirmish force to seize the Georgians' pits a third time and hold them. William Woods reported these pits were "within eighty-eight paces of the enemy's main line." Gen. Charles Woods, who had commanded the division, remembered that "the skirmishers" moved "forward in handsome style, driving rebel skirmishers out of their intrenched skirmish pits and forcing them back upon their main works...." Bradley, *Last Stand in the Carolinas*, 360; *O.R.* I-47-I-246, 253–54.

648. In using the word "wend," Oake wants the reader to understand he and his comrades were unhurried in making their shift to the rear. *Webster's Dictionary*, 1117.

649. During the night Joseph Johnston ordered evacuation after receiving reports that Federal forces commanded by Maj. Gen. John Schofield had taken Goldsboro. The battle cost the Confederates 239 men killed, 1,694 wounded, and 673 missing, for a total of 2,606 casualties. Sherman lost 194 killed, 1,112 wounded, and 221 missing, for 1,527 casualties. Historians believe that both counts are probably low. Bentonville resulted in more than 4,100 casualties, making the battle "one of the bloodiest conflicts of the war in 1865." The results were indecisive, with Sherman permitting Johnston to escape with his army intact. Bradley, *Last Stand in the Carolinas*, 404. The casualties sustained by Woods's brigade numbered 1 man killed, and 1 offi-cer and 21 men wounded, for a total of 23 men lost. The 26th Iowa suffered more than a third of the brigade's casualties, losing the 1 man killed (Pvt. William Gardner), and 8 men wound-ed. *O.R.* I-47-I-67. As for retreating, there was little Johnston could do. With nearly 100,000 United States troops in North Carolina, at Goldsboro and in Sherman's army group, Johnston, who now commanded roughly 20,000 effectives, was heavily outnumbered. Long, *Civil War Day by Day*, 655.

650. On March 22, the brigade conducted a reconnaissance, with the rest of the division, to Bentonville. It had retired to the previous day's camp and bivouacked. Moving out about 10 A.M.

on March 23, the division crossed the pontoon bridge over the Neuse River on the afternoon of March 24, moving "leisurely" to Goldsboro, encamping on Rouse's plantation along the New Bern road, and, as had become routine doctrine in the campaign, entrenched their position. The adjutant reported the regiment's discipline fair, weapons worn, and clothing worn out. *Supplement to the O.R.* II-20-583; *O.R.* I-47-I-247.

651. An alkaloid derived from the bark of the cinchona (a genus of trees and shrubs) and used in antimalarial treatments to relieve fever. Oake's use of the word was a common reference made by Civil War soldiers to the standard regimental morning sick call. *Webster's Dictionary*, 178, 820.

652. This soldier was probably Samuel F. Cooper, Co. A, 27th Missouri Infantry. "Detailed Soldier Record for Samuel F. Cooper," http//www.itd.nps.gov/cwss.

653. The 27th Missouri Infantry, commanded by Col. Thomas Curly, had been brigaded with the 26th Iowa Infantry since December 1863, giving Oake plenty of opportunity to become acquainted with some of the Missourians. Dyer, *Compendium*, 498.

654. After a relatively long period of rest at Goldsboro, Sherman's army group took up the march once more, with skirmishing at Boonville, Moccasin Swamp, and Nahunta Station. Long, *Civil War Day by Day*, 672.

655. This last combat experienced by Royal Oake occurred near Nahunta Station, twenty-two miles north of Goldsboro on the Wilmington and Weldon Railroad. Gen. Charles Woods reported that Confederate cavalry, about 1,500 strong, "showed themselves in my front with some boldness." He pushed forward as rapidly as possible, but his skirmishers met with such "determined resistance" at a local crossroads, that the enemy force managed to disengage from the skirmish and retire before Woods could attack with the full force of the division. Woods ordered the division into camp at 5 P.M., astride the crossroads, covering the road west toward Beulah and one north to Wilson, as well as the one his division had been marching and the one leading south toward Pikeville. *O.R.* I-47-I-249.

656. Major Clemons Landgraeber, 2nd Missouri Light Artillery, was not present in North Carolina. A veteran artillery officer with the Army of the Tennessee, he had served in 1864 as chief of artillery for the 1st Division, XV Army Corps, and most recently acting chief of artillery, XVII Army Corps, until January 5, 1865. However, correspondence on the latter date shows that while Sherman's army was quartered at Savannah, Georgia, Landgraeber was ordered to report to the commanding officer of his regiment at St. Louis, Missouri. Additional correspondence reveals him at duty in Missouri in April 1865; therefore, he was not the unknown officer that Oake witnessed passing along the lines reporting Lee's surrender to Grant. By July 1865, Landgraeber was heading west from Omaha, Nebraska, assigned to the Powder River Indian Expedition. *O.R.* I-47-II-17; *O.R.*, I-39-II-554; *O.R.* I-48-II-143, 267; *O.R.* I-48-I-384.

657. Gen. Robert E. Lee surrendered the Confederate Army of Northern Virginia to Lt. Gen. Ulysses S. Grant, General-in-Chief, Armies of the United States, on April 9, 1865, at Appomattox Courthouse, Virginia. Gen. John A. Logan passed down the columns and asked Oake and his comrades, "if they felt a little better." A continuous roll of cheers erupted along the whole line as the general passed each organization. Byers, *Iowa in War Times*, 533.

658. Total deaths in the Civil War for both Federal and Confederate armed forces can be placed at a combined minimum of 623,026, with at least 471,427 wounded, for a total casualty figure of 1,094,453 men who either died during the war or were wounded as a result of war activities (deaths include those mortally wounded who died later). Long, *Civil War Day by Day*, 711.

659. After negotiations at Durham Station, North Carolina, Generals Sherman and Johnston signed a controversial "Memorandum of basis of agreement" on April 19, 1865. Although the agreement ended further fighting in North Carolina, Sherman had dramatically overstepped the limits of his military authority in arranging the agreement's terms, which went far beyond the surrender of Johnston's forces, unnecessarily negotiating peace terms and entering into post-war reconstruction policy between the United States and the Confederacy. On April 24, Sherman learned that President Andrew Johnson had rejected the terms of his "Memorandum" with Joe Johnston, and that he (Sherman) was directed to give forty-eight hours notice to Johnston and then resume hostilities if unconditional surrender could not be obtained. Johnston was immediately sent notice of suspension of the temporary truce. Sherman arranged another meeting with the Confederate general on April 26, at the Bennett House near Durham Station. Final terms of surrender for the soldiers under Johnston's command were signed, using the formula set by Ulysses S. Grant at Appomattox on April 9. Marszalek, *Sherman*, 339–49.

660. Oake is citing Special Field Orders No. 65, Headquarters Military Division of the Mississippi, Maj. Gen. W. T. Sherman, commanding, issued in the field, April 27, 1865, from Raleigh, North Carolina, which announced the further suspension of hostilities and a final agreement with Joe Johnston, which terminated the war as to the armies under his command east of the Chattahoochee River. Forces west of the Chattahoochee would surrender to other United States officials at later dates. On the same day, special field orders were issued from the Army of the Tennessee, instructing the army to march to Richmond, Virginia. *O.R.* I-47-III-322, 324.

661. Sherman had received word on April 17 of the assassination of Abraham Lincoln by the hand of the actor John Wilkes Booth. Booth shot Lincoln in the head while the president and his wife, Mary, were attending a play at Ford's Theater in Washington, D.C., on the night of April 14, 1865. The mortally wounded president died the next morning. Sherman showed the telegram to Joseph Johnston on April 17, at their first Bennett House meeting. On his return to Raleigh, Sherman announced the news of Lincoln's assassination to his army. Although he informed them he did not blame the Confederate army, he did believe the assassination was "the legitimate consequence of rebellion against rightful authority." Marszalek, *Sherman*, 341–43.

662. Sherman's troops were so angry that many desired his surrender talks with Joe Johnston would fail so they could direct their wrath on Johnston's army. Throughout the night, crowds of men milled around, singing "We'll Hang Jeff Davis to a Sour Apple Tree," and searching for some outlet for expressing their emotions. Roughly 2,000 soldiers, the majority of them from John A. Logan's XV Army Corps, actually began to march on Raleigh. An outraged Logan threatened them with artillery and the troubled citizen-soldiers were angrily forced to return to their camps. Marszalek, *Sherman*, 344.

663. On April 27, 1865, the 26th Iowa Infantry was transferred to Colonel Stone's 3rd Brigade, 1st Division, XV Army Corps. The adjutant reported the men's health good, their discipline only fair. The regiment (with the 1st Division) left its camps at Rogers Cross Roads, near the Neuse River, nine miles from Raleigh, on May 1, 1865. *O.R.* I-47-I-77; *O.R.* I-47-III-316, 363; *Supplement to the O.R.* II-20-584.

664. Woods's 1st Division arrived near Petersburg, Virginia, on the afternoon of May 7, 1865. The march northward in extremely warm weather had been brutal. One Wisconsin soldier, John Brobst, wrote, "Many men melted on the march, some fell dead, and some died soon after...." Similar to the majority of accounts of this monumental effort to move tens of thousands of troops roughly 260 miles overland to the Washington area, Oake does not mention the discomfort of the rough cross-country trek, but focuses on the primary purpose of the march—his journey toward being mustered out and proceeding home. Woods's division bivouacked south of the Appomattox River until the morning of May 9, when it marched north, crossing the

Appomattox and moving through Petersburg. In the city, the division passed in review before General Howard, before continuing ten miles beyond the river to a camp on Proctors' Creek. It proceeded on the next day as far as Manchester and bivouacked near the town. It remained in camp there until the morning of May 13. *O.R.* I-47-III-422, 448, 457, 487; William B. Holberton, *Homeward Bound: The Demobilization of the Union and Confederate Armies, 1865–1866* (Mechanicsburg, PA: Stackpole Books, 2001), 24–25. Hereafter cited as *Homeward Bound.*

665. The battle of Fredericksburg, Virginia, was fought in December 1862, when Federal forces from the Army of the Potomac, Maj. Gen. Ambrose Burnside commanding, crossed the Rappahannock River to occupy the town on December 11, preparatory to engaging the Army of Northern Virginia, Gen. Robert E. Lee commanding. Burnside hurled his army against the ably defended Confederate fortifications lining the hills southwest and west of town on December 13. The ill-advised attacks resulted in heavy casualties among the Union forces, and Burnside was forced to withdraw his men across the Rappahannock. Oake viewed the visible signs of this devastation as the division marched through the town on May 17, 1865. The column bivouacked that evening another thirteen miles north on Ossian Creek. Long, *Civil War Day by Day*, 294–96; *O.R.* I-47-III-517.

666. Charles R. Woods's 1st Division departed its camp on the Occoquan River at 4 A.M., May 19, 1865, marching northward along the Alexandria road. General Woods stated that he took advantage of the privilege granted in his orders to move his infantry column to Mount Vernon, while the division wagon train remained on the telegraph road. The troops were marched through the enclosure surrounding Mount Vernon, passing directly in front of Washington's tomb. The column pushed on and camped three miles below Alexandria. Ibid., 533.

667. On May 24, 1861, three regiments of U.S. volunteers crossed the Potomac, by way of the Long Bridge and aboard steamers, to occupy the city of Alexandria, Virginia. Few shots were fired, and the small Confederate detachment in the city quickly departed. This first advance of Union forces against the secessionists in Virginia had been highlighted by the tragic death of 24-year-old Elmer Ellsworth of Illinois, who commanded the 1st Fire Zouaves, or the 11th New York. As his troops rushed toward the center of the city, Ellsworth, with a few of his men, saw a secession flag flying from the Marshall House. Springing up the stairs with two companions, Ellsworth hauled down the flag. On his descent, Ellsworth was confronted by James W. Jackson, the inn's proprietor. Jackson shot and killed Ellsworth before he, too, was fatally shot by Pvt. Francis E. Brownell. Ellsworth's body was taken to lie in state in the East Room of the White House. A law student in the Lincoln-Herndon office, and friend of the president, the youthful colonel immediately became a martyr for the Federal cause. Allan Nevins, *The War for the Union: The Improvised War 1861–1862* (New York: Charles Scribner's Sons, 1959), 46, 146, 179.

668. When the armies finally reached Washington, D.C., the presence of about 200,000 troops in the area placed a logistical strain on army operations. The need to provide water, food, sanitary facilities, and forage, and dispose of manure from thousands of horses and mules, taxed the skills of army quartermasters, commissary personnel, and engineers. At 9 A.M. on May 23, 1865, the Army of the Potomac passed in review down Pennsylvania Avenue, moving in column formation from the capitol to the White House. Review officials had erected stands in front of the White House. One on the south side was reserved for President Andrew Johnson, General Ulysses S. Grant, cabinet officials, and other important guests. The stand on the opposite side of the street was held for the judiciary, members of Congress, and other ticket holders. For the first time since Lincoln's death on April 15, the flag at the White House was at full staff. Holberton, *Homeward Bound*, 25, 27; Long, *Civil War Day by Day*, 689.

669. Sherman, *Memoirs*, II: 377.

*High Priced Dinner and
a Warm Place at Bentonville*

670. Ibid., 378. The earthy appearance of the Army of the West, as it was labeled, caused considerable stir among those in attendance. Sherman's westerners were far more ragged in uniform, considerably more relaxed in their marching order, larger, and more rough-cut than the veterans of the Army of the Potomac. When Sherman dismounted from the parade to take his place on the main reviewing stand, he shook hands with President Johnson, Grant, and other cabinet officials, but refused the hand of Secretary of War Edwin Stanton, who had openly criticized Sherman for his handling of the initial surrender negotiations with Joe Johnston. Marszalek, *Sherman*, 355–57; Long, *Civil War Day by Day*, 690. It is apparent Oake wrote his post-war account of the Grand Review with a copy of Sherman's *Memoirs* close at hand.—Ed.

671. In his final message to the wartime army, dated May 30, 1865, William T. Sherman bid a heartfelt farewell to his men, "with the full belief that, as in war you have been good soldiers, so in peace you will make good citizens; and if, unfortunately, new war should arise in our country, 'Sherman's army' will be the first to buckle on its old armor, and come forth to defend and maintain the Government of our inheritance." *O.R.* I-47-I-45–46.

Epilogue

Through our good fortune, in our youth our hearts were touched with fire...We have seen with our own eyes beyond and above the gold fields, the snowy heights of honor, and it is for us to bear the report to those who come after us.

Oliver Wendell Holmes, Jr.
Memorial Day address, 1884

Just as the Civil War was not fought within a vacuum, the story of William Royal Oake did not end with the close of the war. He joined more than two-and-a-half-million veterans, Union and Confederate, who returned home and began the task of rebuilding their lives in the restructured nation.

Royal had been extremely lucky during his thirty-five months as a soldier. He fought in a total of twenty major battles, engagements, and sieges, smelling powder in numerous actions, affairs, and skirmishes. He was captured and incarcerated as a prisoner of war, and was wounded during his long odyssey as a soldier. Royal twice journeyed across the eastern half of the country—from Iowa to the Atlantic seaboard—thus passing through the Confederacy and returning across the northern tier of states on two occasions, setting foot in at least sixteen states.[1]

The odds against survival had been dim for Royal. The "Clinton County Regiment" departed Iowa with 920 officers and men; an additional 45 recruits joined the organization during the course of the war. From this total enrollment, 6 officers and 70 enlisted men were either killed in battle or died of wounds. Another 4 officers and 213 enlisted men either died of disease, in accidents, while in prison, or of other causes during the war. Thus, the regiment suffered a total of 293 war-related deaths, which is slightly more than 30 percent of those enrolled. A total of 165 officers and men had been wounded. Another 175 members of the regiment were discharged for disability, either for wounds, disease or other causes. This means that 468 men enrolled in the 26th Iowa Infantry were casualties of war, either by death or disability—approximately 48.5 percent of the total enrollment for the war.[2]

The figures and odds for survival within Company A were equally severe. Out of 97 men listed on the company muster rolls during the war, 49 of them either were killed (3), died of wounds (4), died from disease (26), or were discharged for disability (16). Twelve of the company officers and enlisted men, including Royal, were wounded in battle during the conflict; and 6 members of the company, including Royal, had been captured and taken prisoner of war. Thus, Royal's chances had been 50-50 to have died or been discharged for wounds or some disabling disease or accident. Amazingly, only 36 members of Company A, just 37 percent of those carried on the company rolls during the war, were still present with the regiment when it mustered out at Washington, D.C., in June 1865.

One can only assume there was an extremely tearful and joyous homecoming when, still clad in his uniform of blue, Royal marched in on the dusty road from Clinton and finally arrived at the Oake homestead in Bloomfield Township—not to mention a welcomed sigh of relief for the returning veteran.[3]

Royal again assisted his father with the farm, and at some point during the next year, he met and fell in love with Mary Ann Barrick, daughter of William and Elizabeth (Haylock) Barrick, who, like the William Oake family, were natives of England. The Barrick family set sail for the United States in 1847, when Mary Ann, who had been born on June 1, 1846, in Riddlesworth, England, was still an infant. They celebrated her first birthday on the Atlantic Ocean during the voyage to America. William Barrick initially settled the family in Illinois, before moving at some point in 1852 to Iowa, where he established residence on a farm in Waterford Township, located to the east of the Oake homestead in Bloomfield Township. Mary Ann had three brothers, George W. Barrick (five years younger), Alfred A. Barrick (six years younger), and Samuel H. Barrick (thirteen years her junior), and one sister, Charlotte C. Barrick (seven years younger).[4] Royal and Mary were married by Justice of the Peace David M. Neil, at the "Gates" house in the county seat of De Witt, Iowa, on July 15, 1866. The young couple set up residence near the island city of Sabula, in Jackson County, on a track of land Royal had purchased. For the next twelve years he devoted his attention to the work of farming.[5]

Over the course of the next twelve years, five children were born. The first born was a son, named Richard L. Oake, born in Sabula on November 6, 1867; their second child was a daughter, christened Amy,[6] who was born on October 5, 1869, but then tragically passed away days short of her first birthday on September 20, 1870; the third child, another son named William Thomas, was born in Sabula on February 24, 1871; George William, their fourth child, was born September 20, 1873; and Mary Ann gave birth to another boy, Frank Royal Oake, in Sabula on November 15, 1877.[7]

Royal moved his family to east-central Kansas in 1878, establishing a residence in Valley Township, Morris County, along the Neosho River near Council Grove. The United States Federal Census shows his vocation as farming, and Mary's is listed as housekeeping. The three older boys—Richard, William, and George—attended school when possible and, as they grew older, assumed their fair share of farm chores and working the fields.[8] Life in Kansas proved difficult, and in 1881, Royal moved his family once again to Iowa and established permanent residence in Sabula, where his father and mother had moved in 1875 after William senior sold the 160-acre Oake homestead in Clinton County. It was in Sabula, on May 2, 1882, where Mary gave birth to Lottie May, the couple's sixth child.[9]

No longer satisfied with the life of a farmer, Royal plied his skills as a contractor in the island community. Throughout this period of his life, he sold insurance, which provided him "a gratifying measure of success" until he retired from active business. Several fraternal insurance orders were represented in Sabula, and Royal was identified with both the Modern Woodmen of America and the Woodmen of the World, having been a member of the former since around 1878 and the latter since 1883. Being a man of wide general interests, experience, and literary taste, it was during this period when Royal began to write. His stories attracted great interest in the community, and at the encouragement of friends and associates, he authored several columns on early pioneer life in Jackson County and his experiences in the Civil War as feature articles for the local *Sabula Gazette.*

When noted Civil War veteran Benjamin Harrison was elected the president of the United States, Royal was appointed city postmaster and capably discharged his government duties for four years (1890–1894). Throughout his adult life, his political views were as an "unfaltering republican," and his fellow townsmen repeatedly honored him with election to various positions of public trust in the management of city and community affairs. He was elected as city assessor in 1893; was mayor for two years starting in 1894; and was again elected assessor upon completion of his term as mayor. In later years, he would also hold positions of trustee and city councilman, and in one instance, he was a candidate for the local Republican nomination for state representative. However, it was the role of tax assessor that seemed to suit him best, at least in the eyes of the residents of Sabula, and from 1898 until 1914, he won successive reelection to the post of assessor.[10]

As the passage of time carried Royal into middle age, he and Mary began to experience the loss of family and close friends. Mary Ann's father, William, died in Delmar, Iowa, June 8, 1888. Mary Oake, Royal's mother, passed away on July 10, 1893, and was buried in Evergreen Cemetery two miles northeast of Sabula; his father, William, died ten years later on April 30, 1903, at the age of eighty-nine. Elizabeth Haylock Barrick, the mother of Mary Ann Oake, survived her husband by nearly twenty-five years, passing away in Delmar on March 3, 1913. On December 1, 1896, fourteen-year-old Lottie May, after being taken ill with typhoid-pneumonia four days earlier, "passed calmly into that sleep which knows no awakening," the *Gazette* obituary sadly reported the following week. The death announcement for Royal and Mary's daughter cited Lottie as a "bright and intelligent" child, "full of love for her parents and friends and the possessor of a cheerful spirit." Her sudden untimely death came as a great blow to Royal and Mary Ann, who once again experienced the shock and pain of losing another daughter in childhood. They laid Lottie to rest in Evergreen Cemetery, on a family plot located several yards south of where the elder William and Mary Oake lie buried. Royal and Mary Ann would also see the death of their eldest son, Richard, who died on February 6, 1907. At the time of his passing, Richard lived in Puget Sound, Washington, where he had been successfully engaged in a growing business enterprise of producing roofing shingles.[11]

The other three Oake sons were still living successful and productive lives. William Thomas graduated from the College of Physicians and Surgeons of Chicago, where he was elected president of his class of 350 students. He practiced his profession in Elburn, Illinois, where he developed a notable reputation as a successful surgeon. George William lived in the town of Prosser, near Seattle, Washington, where he owned a butchering business; and Frank Royal, who attended Clinton Commercial College, resided in Delmar, Iowa, where he was a successful stock buyer in the small railroad junction city—just two short miles west of the original Oake homestead in Clinton County.[12]

Throughout his post-war life, Royal maintained a close relationship with his old army comrades through his membership in the Grand Army of the Republic (GAR), the Society of the Army of the Tennessee, and the local Jackson County Veterans Association, which he commanded in 1904. The local Sabula GAR was organized in 1883, and was named in memory of Sabula resident and U.S. volunteer Lt. Chauncey Lawrence, who enlisted in the "Temperance Regiment," 24th Iowa Infantry, and was commissioned first lieutenant on August 13, 1862. Lawrence was killed in action during the battle of Champion Hill, Mississippi, on May 14, 1863.[13] Royal served as commander of Chauncey Lawrence Post, No. 163, GAR, in 1908–1909, and again in 1914.[14]

In 1913, Royal decided to write an autobiographical memoir of his war experiences. Perhaps it was something he had wanted to do for years, but for various reasons had not started the task, except to write and publish a series of columns in the *Sabula Gazette*, recounting various events and stories describing the war service of the "Clinton Regiment." Before the close of the year, he set about to writing the draft, using available published documents, memoirs, and war records. Now retired, beyond attending to family and his civic responsibilities, the task of writing the memoir most likely consumed most of his attention throughout the winter of 1913–1914. As spring neared the aging veteran had managed to produce a 400-page manuscript of war recollections describing in full his service as a soldier with the 26th Iowa Infantry. To family and his old comrades, Royal openly expressed an interest in having the memoir published.

On Monday, April 6, 1914, Royal attended the city board of review meeting, where he reported and read over his tax assessment roll to the

William Royal Oake.
This postwar photo of Oake was printed with his obituary in a local Sabula, Iowa, newspaper. Oake makes no mention in his memoirs of having had his photograph made while he was in military service, which proved a popular method of recording for posterity an individual's military service in the war, or providing a lasting keepsake for loved ones at home.

mayor and members of the city council. Three days later, on Thursday, April 9, having lived an eventful, energetic, and productive life of seventy years, one month, and fourteen days since his birth in Dullingham, England, William Royal Oake died. The date of his death is all the more notable, as it marks the anniversary of a significant event from his war experience. On the exact same date, fifty-one years earlier, he was seized as a prisoner of war by Confederate forces while out foraging with a company raiding party along Deer Creek, southeast of Greenville, Mississippi.

The obituary announcement in the *Sabula Gazette* reported, "W. R. Oake was a man of genial and companionable nature and was held in high regard by his numerous friends and associates in Jackson and Clinton counties." It noted he had been a prominent person within the community, and commented on "his popularity" and the great "trust" the residents of the city had placed on him while he had carried out his civic duties through the years, stating he would "be remembered as one of Sabula's progressive and public hearted citizens."[15]

The funeral was held Sunday afternoon, April 12, 1914, at the Methodist Episcopal Church where Royal and Mary Ann had long been members of the congregation. Veterans representing the local Chauncey Lawrence GAR Post attended, and the obituary reported the "church filled to overflowing with friends." Rev. A. N. Conklin delivered the service and paid a beautiful tribute to Royal and his fellow soldiers. A number of hymns were sung to the accompaniment of the piano. Out-of-town family and friends attending were his son William and his wife, Belle, from Austin, Illinois; and son Frank and his wife Bertha Mae from nearby Delmar. Also among those in attendance were Mrs. George Barrick of Winford, South Dakota; Sam Barrick of Sheldon, Iowa; the Honorable James W. Ellis of Maquoketa, Iowa, and Col. F. M. Miles of Miles, Iowa. The body was moved to Evergreen Cemetery, carried to and from the hearse by pall bearers H. L. Benjamin; A. W. Richardson; R. N. Rogers; the Hon. James. W. Ellis, state representative, Jackson County historian, and Civil War veteran; and fellow veterans of the "Clinton Regiment" David W. Swihart and Frank (Francis) Keeley. Royal was laid to rest beside his beloved daughter Lottie May.[16]

Thus the final chapter in the life of William Royal Oake ended. Mary

Ann followed her husband in death on January 19, 1929, and likewise was laid to rest with Lottie May, beside Royal, in the family plot at Evergreen Cemetery. The cemetery, which was "always admired for its beautiful trees," is a pleasant place, peaceful, and serene, surrounded by a heavy forest and far from the bloody fields where Royal witnessed his youth depart and his manhood take root.[17] Visitors will probably not take notice, but across the footpath, west of his gravesite, Royal has a comrade-in-arms from Company A, 26th Iowa Infantry, resting close by, Pvt. David W. Swihart, who died on April 2, 1922, at the age of eighty-four.[18] Together, these two veterans survived numerous trials and witnessed many triumphs while serving with the "Clinton Regiment" during the war. Both escaped the awesome carnage inflicted upon their green regiment during the bloody frontal assault on Arkansas Post, only to be captured three months later on Deer Creek, in Mississippi, and forced to endure confined incarceration while held as prisoners of war at the Vicksburg city jail and later Libby Prison in Richmond. When exchanged and returned to the regiment, each served honorably in the momentous march on Atlanta, the infamous raid to the sea, and the final campaign through the Carolinas. Therefore, it is most fitting these old soldiers rest together, under the evergreens that shade this beautiful "City of the Dead," as if still deployed in skirmish formation upon some eternal field of battle—with many a friendly tree for Royal to fight behind.[19]

CHAPTER NOTES:
Epilogue

➤ ———————————————— ◀

1. The principal military events Royal had participated in were Chickasaw Bayou, Arkansas Post, Greenville raid (Deer Creek), Cherokee, Tuscumbia, Lookout Mountain, Missionary Ridge, Ringgold, Resaca, Dallas, Big Shanty, Kennesaw Mountain, Atlanta, Ezra Church, Siege of Atlanta, Jonesboro, Lovejoy, Savannah, Columbia, and Bentonville. He did not take part in the final sequence of events of the operation to capture Vicksburg, including Jackson, the assaults on Vicksburg (May 19 and 22, 1863), Siege of Vicksburg, or the Siege of Jackson, on account of his capture by Confederate forces at Deer Creek. Joseph Ingersoll. *Iowa and the Rebellion.* (Iowa City, 1866), 538.

2. In preparing his monumental study of losses suffered by United States forces in the war, Lt. Col. William F. Fox considered "Williamson's Iowa Brigade," of the XV Army Corps, composed of the 4th, 9th, 25th, 26th, 30th, and 31st regiments, a "splendid command." The brigade was organized in December 1862, with Brig. Gen. John Thayer in command, who was later succeeded after the Vicksburg campaign by Col. James A. Williamson of the 4th Iowa. When Williamson mustered out in February 1865, he was succeeded by Col. George A. Stone of the 25th Iowa, who commanded the brigade on the march through the Carolinas. *Roster* 3: 1027; Fox. *Regimental Losses.* 515, 519n–20n.

3. *Roster* 3: 1017–1112.

4. The family was found under the name Barrack. Mary Ann is spelled Marrian by the census taker, and Alfred is listed under the name Albert. A search of the *1870 United States Federal Census* cites George and Alfred still at home, but Samuel is not cited as being present in the household, and therefore it must be assumed he had died in childhood. Charlotte is also not listed in the census (reason not determined). Mary Ann married and moved away from the household. Ancestry.com. *1860 United States Federal Census* [database online].

5. A copy of the wedding certificate for Royal and Mary Ann that was made available to the editor notes the couple was married on July 15, 1867. Considering their first child, Richard, was reportedly born in November 1867, this certificate would appear to be in error as to the date assigned. Ellis, *Jackson County*, 2: 588.

6. This first daughter born to Royal and Mary Ann may have been named either Amy B. or Amy E. Oake, as listed in Ancestry.com/MyFamily.com, Inc., 1998–2005. *One World Tree* [database online] search for William Royal Oake & Mary Ann Barrick.

7. Ellis, *Jackson County*, 2: 588.

8. Royal is shown as W. R. Oake, with his age inaccurately cited as 34. Born in 1844, he was actually 36. Mary Ann is also cited two years younger than she actually was. The ages of Richard and William are accurately recorded as 12 and 9 respectively, yet George was 6 and listed as 7, and Frank was 2 and listed as 4—illustrative of the times and conditions affecting how statistical data was collected and hand recorded in the late 19th century. Ancestry.com. *1880 United States Federal Census.* Schedule 1. Inhabitants in Enumeration District No. 139, Morris County, Kansas, June 19, 1880, p. 23.

9. Ellis states the senior Oake moved off the farm in 1876. The obituary account, which appears to have been written by Royal, cites the year his father and mother sold the farm and moved to Sabula as 1875. Ellis, *Jackson County*, 2: 587–88; Obituary, William Oake, *Sabula Gazette.* n.d., probably May 9, 1903.

10. Ellis, *Jackson County*, "History of Sabula, Iowa." Wade Guenther, editor of the *Subula Gazette*, 1: 527–28, 2: 587–88; Obituary, William R. Oake, *Sabula Gazette*, April 18, 1914. Hereafter cited as: Obituary, Wm. R. Oake.

11. The date of death for Richard, cited in the *Gazette* obituary for his father, is reported as February 6, 1907, as opposed to the 1906 date provided in Ellis's biography for William Royal Oake in *History of Jackson County*. Ellis, *Jackson County*, 2: 588; Obituary, Lottie May Oake, *Sabula Gazette*, n.d., possibly December 5, 1896; Obituary, Wm. R. Oake.

12. The residence for William Thomas cited in the *Gazette* obituary for his father is listed as Austin, Illinois. He married Ms. Belle Robinson. George married Ms. Hattie Pratt. His date of death is cited as December 2, 1916. Frank Royal married Bertha Mae Lockard. He died on April 1, 1951, and is buried in Pomona, California. The Oake family genealogy data was collected and provided by Beverly Oake to Farcountry Press. The editor secured additional data on *World Tree Project* and *Family Data Collection* [database online], Provo, Utah; MyFamily.com, 1998–2005; and the numerous *United States Federal Census* records now online. Ellis, *Jackson County*, 2: 588; Obituary, Wm. R. Oake.

13. Chauncey Lawrence is cited as having been born in Portage, Ohio, November 8, 1824, and married Sarah E. Beall in Springfield, Ohio, May 7, 1846. He is cited on the *1850 United States Federal Census* as residing in Springfield and working the trade of carpenter; he and Sarah have a 1-year-old daughter named Kate. The *1860 United States Federal Census* documents the Lawrence family living in Sabula, Iowa, where Chauncey works as a carpenter. Another carpenter by the name of William Bagot (age 28) is cited as living in the household; he appears to have been employed by Lawrence. After the war, Lawrence's body was removed from the Champion Hill battlefield and interred in the Vicksburg National Cemetery, buried in section O, site 4322 (see Ancestry.com: National Cemetery Administration. *U.S. Veterans Cemeteries, ca. 1800–2004* [database online], Provo, Utah; MyFamily.com, Inc., 2005. Original data: National Cemetery Administration. *Nationwide Gravesite Locator*). *Roster* 3: 850, (last name is incorrectly spelled Lawrance); Ellis, *Jackson County*, 1: 537; MyFamily.com Inc., 1998–2005, Ancestry.com – Chauncey Lawrence [database online].

14. Ellis, *Jackson County*, "Jackson County Veteran Association." Harvey Reid, Adjutant, 1: 215, "History of Sabula, Iowa." Guenther, 1: 537, 2: 588.

15. The paper ran the obituary announcement with a photo of Royal that appears to have been taken when he was around 40 to 45 years old. Obituary, Wm. R. Oake.

16. James W. Ellis served in Co. F, 44th Iowa Infantry. He was employed as an insurance agent after the war, and in 1910 authored the two-volume *History of Jackson County, Iowa*, within which he wrote a biography of William Royal Oake, of Sabula, a prominent resident of the county. Obituary, Wm. R. Oake; *Roster* 3: 1070, 1095 (Swihart is misspelled Syhart in *Roster*); *Report of the Adjutant General and Acting Quartermaster General of the State of Iowa. January 11, 1864, to January 1, 1865.* (Des Moines, 1865), 76.

17. "Island City" Sabula. (Sabula: Bicentennial Days Commission, 1976).

18. Ancestry.com. *Iowa Cemetery Records*. Provo, Utah: Ancestry.com, 2000. Original Data: Works Project Administration. Graves Registration Project. Washington, D.C.: n.p.

19. Ellis, *Jackson County*, "History of Sabula, Iowa." Guenther, 1: 528.

Biographical Appendix

❧ ———————— ❧

Nathaniel B. Baker was born in Henniker, New Hampshire, September 29, 1818, attending Phillips Exeter Academy and Harvard (Class of 1839). He read law with Franklin Pierce at Concord until 1842 before establishing his own law practice in the city. From 1841 to 1845, he served as joint proprietor/publisher and editor of the *New Hampshire Patriot.* Baker entered politics as an appointed (Democrat) clerk of the Court of Common Pleas in 1845, and in 1846 became clerk of the Superior Court. Elected to the New Hampshire legislature in 1850, he was chosen Speaker of the House of Representatives and served two terms before winning the gubernatorial election in 1854. His term in office witnessed a fiery legislative session, as resolutions denouncing the Kansas–Nebraska Act (1854) and the Missouri Compromise (1820, 1850) failed to pass, but created considerable debate within the state.

After a year as governor, Baker moved to the "free" state of Iowa, winning election to the Iowa legislature in 1859, before being appointed adjutant general of the state on July 25, 1861, a post he held until his death. As adjutant general, Baker worked directly under Governor Samuel Kirkwood to raise Iowa's quota of volunteers for war service, organizing state regiments and field batteries, outfitting the volunteer personnel with uniforms and equipment, and forwarding the mustered organizations into national service in the United States Army. Baker called the Iowa soldiers his "boys" and watched even the smallest of details concerning the welfare of Iowa volunteers being forwarded to the seat of war.

He married Lucretia Mitchell Tenbroeck (May 10, 1843) and fathered four children. General Baker died on September 11, 1876. Byers, *Iowa in War Times*, 56–58; "A Guide to Likenesses of New Hampshire Officials and Governors on Public Display at the Legislative Office Building and the State House, Concord, New Hampshire, to 1998," http://www.nh.gov/nhdhr/-glikeness/bakenath.html.

Born at Bledsoe's Lick (now Castalian Springs), Tennessee, October 7, 1826, Mexican War veteran **William Brimage Bate**, despite possessing little formal education, had edited a newspaper, served in the Tennessee legislature, and practiced law before being commissioned colonel of the 2nd Tennessee Infantry at the outbreak of the Civil War. Severely wounded at Shiloh and incapacitated for months, he was appointed brigadier general on October 3, 1862, ably commanding a brigade at Stones River, Chickamauga, and at Missionary Ridge. Promoted major general on February 23, 1864, Bate commanded a division, participating in virtually all the engagements fought by the Army of Tennessee in northern Georgia in 1864, from Rocky Face Ridge through Jonesboro. In his memoir, William Royal Oake mistakes Pat Cleburne's division as being the enemy force making a series of May 29, 1864, night assaults at Dallas, Georgia, when instead it was the division commanded by William B. Bate assaulting Gen. John A. Logan's XV Corps's line throughout the evening. After Atlanta was abandoned to Sherman, Bate participated in Hood's offensive into Tennessee, leading his division in the murderous fighting at Franklin and Nashville, and then commanded his troops in opposition to Sherman's march through the Carolinas. He surrendered along with the rest of the Confederate forces under Joe Johnston in North Carolina on April 26, 1865.

Considered an outstanding combat leader, he was wounded three times during the war, having had six horses killed under him in battle. Offered the governorship of Tennessee in 1863, he had refused this civil honor, choosing instead to fight the enemy as long as they occupied his state. He practiced law in Nashville and was elected governor of Tennessee in 1882, and United States senator in 1886, a position he held until his death in Washington,

March 9, 1905. As senator, he was author of a bill (1893) that formally erad-icated remaining Reconstruction legislation from the statute books. Bate is buried at Mount Olivet Cemetery in Nashville. Boatner, *Civil War Dictionary*, 49–50; Ezra J. Warner, *Generals in Gray: Lives of the Confederate Commanders* (Baton Rouge, Louisiana State University Press, 1959), 19–20.

William Royal Oake's association with **Braxton Bragg** stems from his par-ticipation in the battles for Chattanooga in November 1863. A native of Warrenton, North Carolina, Bragg was born on March 22, 1817. A graduate of West Point, he stood fifth out of fifty cadets and was assigned to the artillery. He fought against the Seminoles in Florida, served on the frontier, and won three brevets in the Mexican–American War before tendering his resignation as a lieutenant colonel in 1856 to become a planter in Louisiana. He was appointed a brigadier general in the Provisional Army of the Confederacy on March 7, 1861, and was assigned to command the Gulf Coast from Pensacola to Mobile, being promoted to major general September 12 the same year.

In late March 1862, Bragg assumed command of the Second Corps, Army of the Mississippi, and performed double duty as chief of staff for the army under Albert Sidney Johnston. Bragg led his corps at Shiloh, and upon Johnston's death in the same battle, was appointed a full general in the Regular Army, to rank from April 6, 1862. He replaced P. G. T. Beauregard as commander of the army, which he led in the aborted invasion of Kentucky, August to October 1862, ending in his repulse at Perryville at the hands of the Army of the Ohio, commanded by Gen. Don Carlos Buell. His re-designated Army of Tennessee was again forced to withdraw following a bitter battle at Stones River near Murfreesboro, Tennessee, in early January 1863. After he defeated William S. Rosecrans's Army of the Cumberland at Chickamauga in northwestern Georgia, Bragg lay siege to Chattanooga, but in November, an army group under Gen. Ulysses S. Grant overwhelmed Bragg's army, driving it into northern Georgia. At his own request, Bragg yielded command of the army to Joseph E. Johnston. A close favorite of President Jefferson Davis, Bragg was ordered to Richmond, where he served primarily in the capacity of chief of staff, technically at least, superior to all other general officers in grade, although junior by date of commission, and charged "with the conduct of the military operations in the armies of the Confederacy." When Robert E. Lee was appointed general in chief, Bragg resumed field service in North Carolina, under J. E. Johnston, aiding in contesting Sherman's drive through the Carolinas. The intense debate as to Bragg's military capabilities, which developed while the conflict was still being fought, continues to this day.

His post-bellum activities include service as chief engineer of Alabama, and as a railroad executive. He fell dead in Galveston, Texas, on September 27, 1876; his remains were removed to Mobile, Alabama, for burial. His brother, Thomas, previously a Democratic governor (1854 to 1858) of their native state and a U.S. senator (1859 to 1861), resigned from the Senate when North Carolina seceded in May 1861 and starting in November the same year, would serve briefly as attorney general of the Confederacy, before resigning his cabinet post in March 1862. Boatner, *Civil War Dictionary*, 78–79; Heidler and Heidler, eds., *Encyclopedia of the American Civil War*, James Meredith, "Bragg, Braxton (1817 to 1876) Confederate General," 266–68; Ibid, David S. Heidler and Jeanne T. Heidler, "Bragg, Thomas (1810 to 1872) Confederate attorney general," 268–69; Warner, *Generals in Gray*, 30–31.

Thomas James Churchill was born in Jefferson County, Kentucky, on March 10, 1824. He attended St. Mary's College, studied law at Transylvania University, and served as first lieutenant of the 1st Kentucky Rifles in the Mexican–American War, where he was captured. He settled near Little Rock, Arkansas, becoming a planter and later postmaster of the city in 1861. Commissioned colonel of the 1st Arkansas Mounted Rifles, he rendered notable service at Wilson's Creek, August 10, 1861, and was commissioned brigadier general to rank from March 4, 1862. After fighting under Gen. Edmund Kirby Smith at Richmond, Kentucky, August 30, 1862, Churchill made a valiant defense of the Post of Arkansas (also called Fort Hindman), where William Royal Oake faced his first test of combat, and the 26th Iowa Volunteer Infantry suffered its heaviest single combat loss of the war. Faced with overwhelming odds, Churchill was forced to surrender to the combined National army and navy forces under Gen. John A. McClernand and Admiral David D. Porter when, without his knowledge, some of his men raised the white flag.

Exchanged, Churchill participated in the defense of the Red River valley against Gen. Nathaniel P. Banks in the spring of 1864, and was also engaged in an attack on Gen. Frederick Steele's Union command at Jenkin's Ferry, Arkansas, on April 30, 1864. Promoted major general March 18, 1865, Churchill followed Kirby Smith to Texas and on June 2, 1865, unwillingly surrendered at Galveston as part of the Trans-Mississippi Department—the last Confederate land force to capitulate. From 1874 to 1880, he served as state treasurer of Arkansas and was elected governor in the latter year. He died on May 14, 1905, and is buried in Little Rock. Warner, *Generals in Gray*, 49–50; Boatner, *Civil War Dictionary*, 155.

Irish-born **Patrick Ronayne Cleburne,** a three-year veteran of Her Majesty's 41st Regiment of Foot, is considered by the majority of military historians to have been the most "supremely effective" division commander in the Confederate Army of Tennessee. One of only two foreign-born officers to attain the rank of major general in the Confederate service, Cleburne was born near Cork, Ireland, March 17, 1828. Upon purchasing a discharge from the British army, he immigrated to the United States in 1849, landing at New Orleans. Educated as an apothecary, he eventually settled in Helena, Arkansas, distinguishing himself by remaining in the riverfront community to nurse the sick during a yellow fever epidemic. He practiced law from 1856 until the outbreak of civil war, when he organized a militia company known as the Yell Rifles, serving as their captain. Elected colonel of the 15th Arkansas in 1861, he was promoted to brigadier general on March 4, 1862, and then major general on December 13 of the same year. By 1864, his combative skills had been witnessed on virtually every major battlefield of the western army, having commanded a brigade at Shiloh, Richmond, and Perryville, and a division at Stones River (Murfreesboro), Chickamauga, Missionary Ridge, Ringgold, Resaca, Kennesaw Mountain, Peachtree Creek, Atlanta, and Jonesboro.

A tough disciplinarian, Cleburne held the respect of his soldiers by demonstrating unrelenting courage in combat and a genuine concern for their welfare. He stirred considerable controversy among fellow officers and the Richmond authorities when he formally suggested (by way of a circular paper presented January 2, 1864) the arming of slaves and their muster into military service. Christened "the Stonewall of the West" by Confederate

President Jefferson Davis, Cleburne's death at the battle of Franklin, Tennessee, on November 30, 1864, in the forefront of his troops, proved a tragic loss to the Confederacy. In his memoir, Royal Oake mistakes Cleburne's division being present during the May 29, 1864, night assaults at Dallas, Georgia, when instead it was the division commanded by William B. Bate assaulting the XV Corps's line at Dallas that evening. Cleburne's position on the Confederate line was located four miles to the northwest, where his men anchored the right of Hardee's corps at Pickett's Mill. The most significant confrontation in which the 26th Iowa Volunteer Infantry directly faced Cleburne's division was the pursuit action at Ringgold Gap, Georgia, on November 27, 1864. Boatner, *Civil War Dictionary*, 158–59; Craig L. Symonds, *Stonewall of the West: Patrick Cleburne & the Civil War* (University Press of Kansas, Lawrence, 1997) 158, 181–91; Margaret E. Wagner, Gary W. Gallagher, and Paul Finkleman, eds., *The Library of Congress Civil War Desk Reference* (Simon & Schuster, New York, NY, 2002), 408–9. Hereafter cited as *Civil War Desk Reference*; Warner, *Generals in Gray*, 53–54.

Born in Clinton County near Champlain, New York, on February 3, 1805, **Samuel Ryan Curtis** grew up in Ohio. A graduate of West Point, class of 1831, standing twenty-seventh out of thirty-three cadets, he served one year on the frontier before resigning his commission. Curtis led a productive and varied career as a civil engineer in Ohio, practiced law, served as adjutant general of Ohio, and assumed the colonelcy of the 2nd Ohio Volunteer, which he led with distinction in Gen. Zachary Taylor's army during the Mexican–American War. A post-war resident of Keokuk, Iowa, Curtis continued his engineering career and the practice of law, being elected major in 1856, and in the same year was elected to Congress, serving three successive terms. Mustered into the United States Army as colonel of the 2nd Iowa Infantry May 31, 1861, he was soon appointed brigadier general of volunteers, backdated to rank from May 17, 1861. He commanded a large camp of instruction near St. Louis; later he was in charge of the Southwest District of Missouri.

The following spring, while in command of the Union Army of the Southwest, he defeated the Trans-Mississippi Confederate Army at the battle of Pea Ridge, Arkansas, March 6 to 8, 1862, securing control of Missouri for the Union. For this achievement Curtis was appointed major general of volunteers on March 21, 1862. After a 1,000-mile march through rugged country, he occupied Helena (July 14 to August 29, 1862). When the 26th Iowa Volunteer Infantry was ordered to proceed to St. Louis in October, Curtis commanded the Union Department of the Missouri, until May 1863; then the Department of Kansas, until February 7, 1865; and finally the Department of the Northwest, until July 26, 1865. During this period, Curtis successfully countered Gen. Sterling Price's raid in Missouri and Kansas (September to October 1864). During the latter part of 1865, he served as United States Indian commissioner, and then commissioner to examine the route of the Union Pacific Railroad until April 1866. He died at Council Bluffs, Iowa, December 26, 1866. Boatner, *Civil War Dictionary*, 215; Selwyn A. Brant & Associate Editors, *The Union Army: A History of Military Affairs in the Loyal States 1861–65—Records of the Regiments in the Union Army—Cyclopedia of Battles—Memoirs of Commanders and Soldiers*, 8 vols. & index, (Federal Publishing Company, Madison, Wisconsin, 1908; Reprint, New Material Copyright, Broadfoot Publishing Company, Wilmington, North Carolina, 1998), VIII, 66–67, Hereafter cited as *The Union Army*. Warner, *Generals in Blue*, 107–8.

Samuel Wragg Ferguson was born on November 3, 1834, and was a member of the class of 1857 at West Point, standing nineteenth out of thirty-eight cadets at graduation. Assigned to the dragoons, he participated in the Mormon expedition under Albert Sidney Johnston and saw service in the Washington Territory before resigning on March 1, 1861, as a second lieutenant to join the Confederacy. He served on the staff of Gen. Pierre Gustave Toutant Beauregard, with whom he was attached until after the battle of Shiloh. Promoted to colonel, Ferguson saw a great deal of cavalry service in Mississippi during the Vicksburg Campaign, and it was troopers assigned to his Delta command who captured William Royal Oake and his comrades at Deer Creek on April 9, 1863.

Appointed brigadier general on July 23, 1863, Ferguson commanded a cavalry brigade from then until the end of the war, being assigned to Gen. William H. Jackson's division, Lt. Gen. Leonidas Polk's corps; and after a brief tour of duty in Mississippi, he was engaged on the flanks of Gen. William T.

Sherman's invading army in Georgia and the Carolinas. When Ferguson was being considered for promotion in August 1864, his superior, Gen. Joseph Wheeler, commanding the cavalry corps, Army of Tennessee, "strenuously objected," stating he was a trouble maker and his brigade notorious for desertion. After the war Ferguson studied law and was admitted to the bar, making his post-war home mostly in Greenville, Mississippi. He served as president of the board of Mississippi levee commissioners and in 1885 was appointed by President Chester A. Arthur to the Mississippi River Commission. Ferguson died in Jackson, Mississippi, February 3, 1917, and is interred there. Warner, *Generals in Gray*, 87; Boatner, *Civil War Dictionary*, 277.

Born in New York, **Elijah H. Frank** was twenty-seven years old and a resident of Charlotte, Iowa, in the summer of 1862. His enlistment as first sergeant of Company A, 26th Iowa Volunteer Infantry dates to July 7, 1862 (same date as appears on William Royal Oake's company muster-in sheet). From December 1862 through early February 1863, Frank shared a tent with Oake during the regiment's initial field operations. Frank earned promotion to second lieutenant on February 11, 1863, and shortly thereafter, on February 27, was advanced to the rank of first lieutenant of the company, replacing Lt. Asa Franklin, who had resigned his commission the previous day.

Elijah appears to have performed creditably as a company line officer, and corresponded with family and friends in Iowa, reporting on the activities of the "Clinton Regiment" and the adventures and hardships experienced by his comrades. Nine of his war letters, written from the field to his close friend Katherine Varner of Charlotte, dating from November 3, 1862, to December 13, 1863, survived to be published in the *North Dakota Historical Quarterly* in 1930. Luckily, it is through observations cited in Frank's personal correspondence with Kate that we learn about Royal Oake's embittered emotions concerning the harsh treatment he believed he was subjected to while being held a prisoner of war in Mississippi and Virginia.

By all accounts, Royal Oake and Frank developed a close soldierly bond and friendship, which started with their enlistment in 1862 and matured through shared experiences in the field as tent mates and seasoned combat veterans on numerous campaigns. It was a strong bond, broken only by Frank's unfortunate death. Wounded during the siege of Atlanta, August 12,

1864, Lieutenant Frank developed complications following amputation of his damaged leg, dying two days later on August 14. Frank is buried in the National Cemetery in Marietta, Georgia. *Roster* 3: 1054; "E. H. Frank to Catherine Varner, Charlotte, Iowa, 1862–1863" *NDHQ* 194; Dyer, *Compendium*, 672, 677. Dyer makes one of his rare errors in the masterfully researched *Compendium* by omitting the 26th Iowa Volunteer Infantry from the organizations cited as participating (engaged) in the expedition to the Tallahatchie in which Pvt. John Varner became ill.—Ed.

Samuel Gibbs French was born in Gloucester County, New Jersey, November 22, 1818. A graduate of West Point in 1843, he served garrison duty before seeing action in the Mexican War. Severely wounded at Buena Vista, he earned two brevets in Mexico as an artillery officer before assuming quartermaster duty in Washington and the frontier. Through marriage he acquired a plantation near Vicksburg and resigned from the army in 1856. When Mississippi seceded in January 1861, French was named chief of ordnance for state forces, then a major of artillery in Confederate service in April. Appointed a brigadier general October 23, 1861, he again earned promotion to major general a year later, with his new rank backdated to August 31, 1862.

General French saw intermittent war service in and around Richmond, Petersburg, and Suffolk, and in North Carolina. On May 28, 1863, he was attached to Joe Johnston's forces at Jackson, Mississippi, and a year later joined the Army of Tennessee. He commanded his division in the Atlanta campaign, and at Allatoona Pass, before participating in Hood's Tennessee campaign, where he was relieved from duty prior to the battle of Nashville because an eye infection had rendered him virtually blind. Once recovered from the temporary illness, he served at Mobile until its surrender in April 1865. French lived for another forty-five years, earning a living as a planter before retiring to Florida, where he died at Florala, April 20, 1910. His autobiography, entitled *Two Wars,* was published in 1901. French is buried in Pensacola. Warner, *Generals in Gray,* 93–4.

Born in Point Pleasant, Ohio, on April 27, 1822, **Ulysses Simpson "Sam" Grant** (name officially changed from Hiram Ulysses by clerical error upon entering West Point in 1839) was ranked twenty-first of thirty-nine cadets upon graduation from the U.S. Military Academy at West Point in 1843. As a front-line company lieutenant, Grant earned two citations for gallantry and one for meritorious conduct while serving in the 4th United States Infantry during the war with Mexico (1846 to 1848). His military career took a turn for the worse in the post-war years: while stationed on the Pacific Coast and isolated from his wife, Julia Dent Grant, and young children back in Missouri, he began to drink heavily. Rather than face court-martial, Grant resigned his commission in 1854. For the next six years he struggled to provide for his growing family, failing in a number of business ventures, and eventually took a job as a clerk in his father's leather store in Galena, Illinois.

Initially unable to secure a position in the army when civil war erupted in April 1861, Grant was finally appointed colonel of the 21st Illinois Infantry on June 17, 1861, a position from which he rose rapidly to brigadier general and then to major general. Grant secured the first major National victory of the war when he compelled the "unconditional surrender" of Fort Donelson, Tennessee, in February 1862, inflicting more than 16,000 Confederate casualties (mostly captured). Two months later he secured another bitter victory in the momentous battle of Shiloh, Tennessee, inflicting 10,699 Confederate casualties, but suffering 13,045 killed, wounded, and missing among the National forces. Over the course of the next year, he seized Vicksburg and opened the Mississippi River through a brilliant campaign costing the Confederacy over 10,000 more men killed and wounded, and another 30,000 troops taken prisoner of war. Made supreme commander in the West in October 1863, he conducted the successful relief of National forces besieged at Chattanooga, Tennessee, winning decisive victories at Lookout Mountain and Missionary Ridge. In March 1864, he was elevated to lieutenant general and given command of the armies of the United States. In Virginia, Grant battled Gen. Robert E. Lee's Army of North Virginia southward in a bitter summer campaign to the outskirts of Richmond and Petersburg by June, inflicting awful carnage on his opponent, but suffering even more among his own National forces. After a nine-month siege, Grant forced Lee to evacuate the Confederate capital and on April 9, 1865, received the surrender of the Army of Northern

Virginia at Appomattox Courthouse to end the war. His "ruthlessly realistic common sense," observes biographer William S. McFeely, and "an uneven but remarkable degree of self-confidence enabled Grant to make a very great mark" in the war. This outstanding military accomplishment made him the most successful general Royal would serve under, if only briefly, during the conflict.

After the war, Grant served two terms as the eighteenth president of the United States. His post-presidential years were marked by financial misfortune and bankruptcy. Dying of throat cancer at Mount McGregor, New York, he raced death to complete his memoirs, the publication of which he hoped would provide for his family. He finished the manuscript, but died on July 23, 1885, before the book was published. He and Julia (who followed her soldier in death on December 17, 1902) are buried in an imposing tomb in New York City. Boatner, *Civil War Dictionary*, 352–53; William S. McFeely, *Grant: A Biography* (W. W. Norton & Company, New York, 1981), xiii, 518; Warner, *Generals in Blue*, 183–6.

Born on March 28, 1818, in Charleston, South Carolina, **Wade Hampton** was the son and grandson of veterans of the American Revolution and the War of 1812. A lawyer and member of the South Carolina legislature, Hampton had not championed secession. But when South Carolina seceded he immediately raised a mixed command of infantry, cavalry, and artillery, thereafter known as "Hampton's Legion," and was commissioned a colonel. The legion (brigade) won distinction at First Manassas, where Hampton was slightly wounded. He commanded the brigade during the Peninsula campaign and was appointed brigadier general May 23, 1862. He was wounded a second time at Seven Pines. On July 28, he was assigned command of a cavalry brigade within Jeb Stuart's cavalry corps, and after September 2, was second-in-command to Stuart. Engaged with his cavalry at Antietam, the Chambersburg Raid, and Gettysburg, where he was again wounded, he was promoted major general September 3, 1863. After the battle of the Wilderness (May 1864), he succeeded Stuart (killed at Yellow Tavern) in command of the cavalry corps, Army of Northern Virginia. Hampton ably led the corps, contesting Ulysses S. Grant's Overland campaign to the outskirts of Petersburg. On September 16, 1864, Hampton led an audacious raid, capturing 2,500 cattle from Federal forces laying siege to Petersburg and Richmond. Six weeks later, in an engagement at Burgess's Mill, Hampton's son, Frank Preston Hampton, was killed, and a second son, Wade Hampton, Jr., was wounded. As horses became scarce, he taught his troopers to fight on foot, but in January 1865, he journeyed to South Carolina to purchase remounts.

Appointed lieutenant general on February 15, 1865, Hampton would be one of only three civilians to attain the rank in Confederate service, the other two being Richard Taylor and Nathan Bedford Forrest. Ordered to cover Joe Johnston's retreat, the combative general valiantly parried Sherman's thrust through the Carolinas, which brought him directly into the context of William Royal Oake's war experiences during the campaign. Technically exempt from surrendering when Johnston accepted formal terms from Sherman at Durham Station on April 26, 1865, Hampton urged President Davis to continue the fight west of the Mississippi River. When this scheme failed and Davis was captured by United States forces, Hampton returned to South Carolina. Financially ruined by the war, he entered politics, being elected governor in 1876 and again in 1878, and soon thereafter chosen as a United States Senator, a position he held from 1879 to 1891. Railroad commissioner for Pacific Railways (1893 to 1899), Wade Hampton died at Columbia, South Carolina, April 11, 1902, and is buried there. Boatner, *Civil War Dictionary*, 370–71; Wagner, Gallagher & Finkleman, eds., *Civil War Desk Reference*, 412; Warner, *Generals in Gray*, 123.

Author of *Rifle and Light Infantry Tactics* (1855), adopted as a textbook of the United States Army, **William Joseph Hardee** was born in Camden County, Georgia, on October 12, 1815. After graduating from West Point in 1838, he participated in the Seminole War, trained at the French cavalry school at Saumur, and served on the frontier. Twice promoted for gallantry during the Mexican War, he later served as a major in the 2nd United States Cavalry, commandant of cadets at the U.S. Military Academy at West Point (1856 to 1860), and was eventually promoted to lieutenant colonel of the 1st Cavalry. On leave in Georgia when his native state seceded, Hardee resigned January 31, 1861, and was initially commissioned colonel and soon thereafter brigadier general in Confederate service June 17, 1861.

Hardee served in the western army throughout the war, organizing the original Arkansas Brigade ("Hardee's Brigade") before commanding a Confederate corps at the battles of Shiloh, Perryville, Stones River, and Missionary Ridge, having been advanced to lieutenant general on October 10, 1862. Hardee played a central role in the West, fighting under Joseph E. Johnston and later John Bell Hood, throughout the momentous contest in northern Georgia preceding the fall of Atlanta (September 1864). Placed in charge of the Department of South Carolina, Georgia, and Florida, he commanded an ineffective force that proved powerless before Sherman's relentless march and was forced to yield first Savannah and then Charleston to the invading United States forces. Placed under command of his old friend Joe Johnston in the closing weeks of the war, Hardee unfortunately witnessed the death of his son, Willie Hardee, who died of a wound suffered at Bentonville—Hardee's final performance as a battle commander. A month later, he concluded his war service, surrendering with Johnston's army in North Carolina.

Along with James Longstreet and Thomas J. "Stonewall" Jackson, William J. Hardee, known affectionately as "Old Reliable," was recognized by peers, and since by historians, as one of the outstanding corps commanders in Confederate service. A planter at Selma, Alabama, after the war, Hardee died while making an overland journey at Wytheville, Virginia, November 6, 1873, and is buried in Selma. Nathaniel Cheairs Hughes, Jr., *General William J. Hardee: Old Reliable,* (Louisiana State University Press, Baton Rouge, 1965: Reprinted by Broadfoot Publishing, Wilmington, North Carolina, 1987), 51–69, 292–93; Heidler and Heidler, eds., *Encyclopedia of the American Civil War,* "Hardee, William Joseph (1815 to 1873), Confederate general," 925–26; Warner, *Generals in Gray,* 124–25.

Born in Henry County, North Carolina, December 17, 1804, **Theophilus Hunter Holmes** graduated from West Point in 1829. When he resigned his commission on April 21, 1861, he was one of the fifteen field-grade officers of the line in the old army to cast their service with the Confederacy, having attained the regular rank of major in the 8th Infantry and a brevet citation for gallant service in Mexico. A classmate of Jefferson Davis as cadets at West Point, Holmes was appointed brigadier general by Davis on June 5, 1861, and subsequently commanded the reserve brigade at First Manassas. Promoted major general, October 7, 1861, he was transferred to North Carolina, where he assumed command of a division before returning to Virginia in early 1862 to lead his division during the Seven Days battles. Subsequently assigned command of the Trans-Mississippi Department, July 30, 1862, he was soon promoted lieutenant general, October 10, 1862. Afflicted with chronic deafness, the elderly general had initially declined the command but ultimately accepted the post at the urging of the president.

As a department commander Holmes proved unquestionably mediocre and unequal to his high rank during the winter of 1862 to 1863. He consistently made excuses and failed to effectively coordinate his operations with critical efforts east of the Mississippi River to defend Vicksburg and Port Hudson, the Confederacy's last strongholds on the river. Ridiculed by fellow officers and civilians alike, Holmes asked to be relieved of command and requested the post be assigned to his assistant, Edmund Kirby Smith. Davis acquiesced to his demand on March 13, 1863, but Kirby Smith promptly assigned Holmes to command the District of Arkansas. The old general then led an ill-advised attack on the heavily fortified Federal outpost at Helena, Arkansas, on July 4, 1863. Repulsed, Holmes retreated to Little Rock, temporarily relinquished command, and took to a sickbed. He resigned his post February 28, 1864. For the remainder of the conflict he served in his native state commanding the North Carolina Reserves, consisting mostly of old men and boys. Afterward, he lived out the rest of his life on his farm, dying June 21, 1880. He was buried at Fayetteville. Heidler and Heidler, eds., *Encyclopedia of the American Civil War,* Clay Williams, "Holmes, Theophilus Hunter (1804 to 1880) Confederate general," 989–90; Warner, *Generals in Gray*, 141.

John Bell Hood was arguably one of the best division commanders of the war and experienced perhaps the most spectacular advance of any officer in Confederate service. Born in Owingsville, Kentucky, June 1, 1831, Hood graduated from West Point in 1853. After frontier service in California and Texas, he resigned his lieutenant's commission on April 17, 1861, and joined the Confederate States Army. Hood's boldness, recognized by contemporaries, North and South, was evident in the first two years of the war as he distinguished himself at regimental, brigade, and division command on the Peninsula, at Second Manassas, and Antietam, earning rapid promotion to brigadier general (March 13, 1862) and major general (October 10, 1862). It is doubtful that Robert E. Lee would have attained the successes on the field that he did without Hood's contribution to the combat effectiveness of the Army of Northern Virginia. Hood was twice severely wounded in combat, first at Gettysburg, July 3, 1863, where he lost further use of his left arm, and again at Chickamauga, September 20, 1863, where the severity of the wound forced amputation of his right leg. Hood recovered sufficiently to assume command of a corps in the Army of Tennessee under Joseph E. Johnston in early 1864, was promoted to lieutenant general (awarded February 1, 1864, to rank from September 20, 1863), and would participate in events experienced by William Royal Oake in spring and summer of 1864.

In northern Georgia, the aggressive-minded Hood lacked the proper finesse to excel in the "Fabian" style defensive campaign Johnston practiced against William T. Sherman's invading army group. Frustrated, an impatient Jefferson Davis replaced Johnston with Hood, promoted him to full general with temporary rank, July 18, 1864, and thus elevated the all but crippled Kentuckian over senior officers like Hardee, whom Robert E. Lee advised possessed "more experience in managing an army." "Hood is a bold fighter," Lee told Davis. "I am doubtful as to other qualities necessary." In rapid succession, Hood hurled his troops against Sherman in a desperate attempt to split the larger Federal force and defeat it in detail. At Peachtree Creek, Atlanta, Ezra Church, and later at Jonesboro, Hood suffered heavy, irreplaceable casualties and proved unable to relieve the pressure Sherman exerted on Atlanta. Forced to abandon the city, Hood attempted to sever Sherman's line of supply in northern Georgia. Repulsed at Allatoona Pass, he slipped into Alabama and turned north, carrying an offensive into Middle Tennessee. There, he all but crippled the army in an ill-advised frontal assault on Federal fortifications at Franklin, November 30, 1864, before continuing to Nashville, where his troubled command was shattered by superior United States forces under George H. Thomas in mid-December. Forced to flee southward, Hood was relieved at his own request (January 1865), reverting to his permanent rank of lieutenant general.

Unable to reach Kirby Smith's Confederate force west of the Mississippi, he surrendered to Federal authorities in Natchez, Mississippi, May 31, 1865. He made his post-war residence in New Orleans and authored a memoir, *Advance and Retreat,* before dying of yellow fever, along with his wife and one of their eleven children on August 30, 1879. He was buried at Metairie Cemetery. Robert E. Lee, *The Wartime Papers of R. E. Lee,* eds. Clifford Dowdey and Louis H. Manarin (Little, Brown, & Company, Boston, 1961), 821–22; Richard McMurray, *John Bell Hood and the War for Southern Independence* (The University Press of Kentucky, Lexington, 1982), 116–23; Warner, *Generals in Gray,* 142–43.

Joseph Hooker was born in Hadley, Massachusetts, on November 13, 1814. A graduate of the West Point class of 1837, Hooker demonstrated commendable qualities of leadership and administrative ability, serving in Mexico as a staff officer under Generals P. F. Smith, Benjamin F. Butler, and Gideon J. Pillow. He participated in campaigns commanded by Zachary Taylor and Winfield Scott, winning brevets of all the grades through lieutenant colonel for gallant and meritorious conduct, a record not surpassed by any other first lieutenant in the army. He resigned from the peacetime army in 1853 but reenlisted in 1861 and was commissioned a brigadier general of volunteers on August 6, 1861, to rank from May 17. Nicknamed "Fighting Joe" for his performance during the Peninsula campaign in the spring of 1862, Hooker, who was promoted major general of volunteers May 2, 1862, was never able to live the sobriquet down. At the Seven Days battles, Second Manassas, Antietam (wounded), and Fredericksburg, he exhibited skill in commanding his division and later a corps, and was advanced to brigadier general in the regular army on September 20, 1862.

On January 26, 1863, Lincoln named Hooker to command of the Army of the Potomac. He skillfully improved the morale of the army, which had sharply deteriorated since its defeat under Ambrose E. Burnside at Fredericksburg, and in May 1863 advanced across the Rapidan and Rappahannock against Lee's Army of Northern Virginia. Although he commanded an army half the size of his opponent's, Lee aggressively hurled Stonewall Jackson's corps against Hooker's exposed right flank, roundly defeating the Federal army and forcing Hooker to retreat north. Relieved of command at his own request, just before the battle of Gettysburg, Hooker was soon transferred to the West. In the command of a corps, he fought well under Ulysses S. Grant at Chattanooga, when during the so-called "Battle Above the Clouds" on November 24, 1863, William Royal Oake unknowingly observed "Fighting Joe" in person on the northern slope of Lookout Mountain. Later, under William T. Sherman in the 1864 advance into northern Georgia, Hooker continued to demonstrate his solid qualifications as a combat officer from Mill Creek Gap to the siege of Atlanta. Passed over to command the Army of the Tennessee—when Sherman promoted Hooker's subordinate, Oliver O. Howard, to replace the fallen James B. McPherson, killed at the battle of Atlanta—Hooker again asked to be relieved, and his field service came to an end July 28, 1864. Thereafter, Hooker exercised departmental command as a major general in the regular army until a paralytic stroke forced his retirement in 1868. He died in Garden City, New York, October 31, 1879, and was buried in his wife's hometown, Cincinnati, Ohio. Warner, *Generals in Blue*, 233–35; Boatner, *Civil War Dictionary*, 409.

Alvin Peterson Hovey was born September 26, 1821, near Mount Vernon, Indiana. Orphaned at the age of fifteen, he was in succession a bricklayer, schoolteacher, lawyer, officer of volunteers in the Mexican–American War (although he saw no service), member of the state constitutional convention, circuit judge, and, prior to the outbreak of the Civil War, a justice on the state supreme court—the youngest man ever to serve on the Indiana bench up to that time. Hovey entered the war as colonel of the 24th Indiana Infantry, and after preliminary service in Missouri, he commanded his regiment on the second day of the battle of Shiloh, assigned to Morgan Smith's brigade of Lew Wallace's division. His gallantry during the battle was rewarded with promotion to the rank of brigadier general. By autumn, he commanded a division in Arkansas under Gen. Samuel Curtis, where William Royal Oake briefly served under his command. Later, Hovey led a division in Gen. John McClernand's XIII Corps, Army of the Tennessee, during the Vicksburg campaign. His division experienced heavy combat, especially at the battle of Champion Hill (May 16, 1863), where Ulysses S. Grant gave him great credit for securing the National victory.

In December 1863, Hovey was sent to Indiana to organize new levies of troops being recruited in his home state and act as a go-between for his superior, Ulysses S. Grant, and Governor Oliver Perry Morton. In May, he briefly commanded a division of the XXIII Corps, during the early stage of the Atlanta campaign, but was given a thirty-day leave in June and his division broken up. Until the end of the war, with a brevet promotion (July 4, 1864) to the rank of major general of volunteers, Hovey commanded the District of Indiana. Charged with the recruitment of 10,000 new troops, he accomplished the task by enlisting unmarried men only—these bachelor soldiers quickly became known as "Hovey's Babies." He resigned October 7, 1865, and afterward served as minister to Peru (1865 to 1870), before returning to his law practice in Mount Vernon. He was elected to Congress in 1886, and two years later governor of Indiana. Hovey died in office, in Indianapolis, November 23, 1891, and is buried in Bellefontaine Cemetery, Mount Vernon. Boatner, *Civil War Dictionary*, 412; Warner, *Generals in Blue*, 235–36.

Oliver Otis Howard was born in Leeds, Maine, on November 8, 1830. He graduated from Bowdoin College in 1850 and from the Military Academy at West Point in 1854, ranked fourth in his class. He saw field service in Florida against the Seminole Indians, and from 1857 to 1861 he served as assistant professor of mathematics at West Point. He resigned at the beginning of the Civil War and became colonel of the 3rd Maine Volunteer Regiment. At the first battle of Bull Run, Virginia, July 21, 1861, he commanded a brigade, being promoted brigadier general of volunteers the following September. He served in the Peninsula campaign, and on June 30, during the battle of Seven Pines (Fair Oaks), Virginia, he sustained two serious wounds and lost his right arm. He returned to active service in August 1862, taking part in the Maryland campaign and at Antietam (September 17), succeeding Sedgwick in command of a division and earning promotion to major general of volunteers in November 1862. After the battle of Fredericksburg (December), he was advanced to command of a corps. At Chancellorsville, Virginia, in early May 1863, his XI Corps was routed in a flank attack carried out by Stonewall Jackson. On July 1, 1863, during the first day's battle at Gettysburg, Howard, following the death of John Reynolds, temporarily assumed command of Union forces on the field and subsequently led his corps in the successful defense of Culp's and Cemetery Hills on July 2 and 3, 1863. In late September 1863, the XI Corps was transferred to Chattanooga, Tennessee, to reinforce the Army of the Cumberland, which had been defeated at Chickamauga, and, along with the XII Corps, formed part of Joseph Hooker's command, participating in the attack upon and defeat of Bragg's army at Lookout Mountain and Missionary Ridge. When William T. Sherman, commander of the Military Division of the Mississippi, prepared to invade Georgia in the spring of 1864, the XI Corps merged with the XII Corps to form the new XX Corps, commanded by Hooker, and Howard assumed command of the IV Corps, in George Thomas's Army of the Cumberland. He commanded the corps in all the major actions of the Atlanta campaign, receiving another wound at Pickett's Mill near Dallas, Georgia. Upon the death of General James B. McPherson, killed in action at Atlanta on July 22, 1864, and upon the recommendation of Sherman, Howard was selected to command the Army of the Tennessee. In this capacity, he became the fifth general to command the organization William Royal Oake and the 26th Iowa were assigned to, leading the army in the "March to the Sea" and the invasion of the Carolinas. In March 1865, he was brevetted a major general in the regular army "for gallant and meritorious service in the battle of Ezra Church and during the campaign against Atlanta," and later, in 1893, was awarded the Medal of Honor for bravery at Seven Pines where he had lost his arm. After the war, Howard served as commissioner of the Bureau of Refugees, Freedmen, and Abandoned Lands from 1865 until 1874; in 1872 he was appointed special commissioner to the hostile Apaches of New Mexico and Arizona. From 1874 to 1881, he was in command of the Department of the Columbia, where he conducted the campaign against Chief Joseph and the Nez Perce in 1877 and military operations against the Bannock and Paiute Indians in 1878. Howard served as superintendent of West Point from 1881 to 1882 and then commanded the Department of the Platte (1882 to 1886); the Department of the Pacific (1886 to 1888); and the Division of the East (from 1888 to 1894). Promoted major general in the regular army in 1886, he retired from service in 1894. The establishment of Howard University in Washington, D.C., in 1867 by the Federal government was largely due to

Howard, who was deeply interested in the welfare and education of African Americans. The university was named in his honor, and from 1869 to 1873 he presided over it. In 1895 he helped establish Lincoln Memorial University, in Harrogate, Tennessee, to offer education to the mountain people of the area, becoming president of its board. Howard held honorary degrees from various universities and was a chevalier of the Legion of Honor. He wrote a number of books and articles, among them essays on the Atlanta campaign for the "Battles and Leaders" series in *Century Magazine: My Life and Experience among our Hostile Indians* (1907) and the *Autobiography of O. O. Howard* (2 vols., New York, 1907). Known by contemporaries as the "Christian General," Oliver O. Howard died in Burlington, Vermont, on October 26, 1909. Warner, *Generals in Blue*, 237–39; Boatner, *Civil War Dictionary*, 413–14.

A native Virginian, **Joseph Eggleston Johnston** was a classmate of Robert E. Lee at West Point, graduating thirteen out of forty-six cadets in the class of 1829 (Lee stood second in the class). Wounded five times during the Mexican–American War, Johnston earned repeated brevets. By the outbreak of civil war in 1861, he held the rank of brigadier general and quartermaster in the Army of the United States. Upon the secession of Virginia from the Union, he resigned April 22, 1861, and was immediately commissioned a brigadier in the Provisional Army of the Confederacy. On August 31, 1861, following his solid performance in the decisive Confederate victory at First Manassas in July, he was appointed full general. Johnston being ranked below Samuel Cooper, Albert Sidney Johnston, and Robert E. Lee, however, gave rise to an "acrimonious debate" with President Jefferson Davis, which rendered great disservice to effective unity of command and the Confederate cause. Johnston commanded the Confederate Army of the Potomac (later redesignated the Army of Northern Virginia) and opposed General George B. McClellan in the Peninsula campaign until he was badly wounded in May 1862 at the battle of Seven Pines and the army command passed to Lee.

Johnston returned to duty in November as commander of the Department of the West and was given operational control over both Braxton Bragg's army operating in Tennessee and John Pemberton's army defending Mississippi. Ordered from Tennessee by President Jefferson Davis to retrieve the rapidly deteriorating military situation in Mississippi—with Ulysses S. Grant's National forces threatening capture of Vicksburg—Johnston arrived in Jackson, Mississippi, on May 13, 1863, and immediately abandoned the capital city to Grant's approaching forces. With Vicksburg besieged, Johnston raised a relief force, but did not act aggressively against Grant, who accepted surrender of the fortress city on the July 4.

In the aftermath of Bragg's disastrous defeat in November at Chattanooga, Johnston was assigned command of the Army of Tennessee in December and spent the winter rebuilding the fractured army in northern Georgia. From May 5 to July 17, 1864, he opposed William T. Sherman's drive into northern Georgia, fighting a succession of engagements at Rocky Face Ridge, Resaca, New Hope Church, Dallas, Picket's Mill, and Kennesaw Mountain. However, his strategic withdrawal before Sherman, culminating in the retirement of his army below the Chattahoochee nearly to the northern outskirts of Atlanta, so displeased President Davis, that he relieved Johnston of his command and replaced him with John Bell Hood. One historian has noted that in conducting the retreat south from Dalton to Peachtree Creek, "Johnston demonstrated himself to be at least the equal of Lee as a defensive tactician; whether he possessed other qualifications requisite in an army commander has long been disputed."

General Johnston did not see further action until reassigned by Lee (now commander in chief of all Confederate armies) in February 1865, to oppose Sherman's march through the Carolinas. With a ragged collection of forces, he parried Sherman's movements, fighting at Bentonville, North Carolina, in March, but could not halt the northern invader. Following Lee's surrender to Grant in Virginia, Johnston capitulated to Sherman at Durham Station, North Carolina, on April 26, 1865.

After the war, General Johnston resided in a number of southern cities, where he was engaged in the insurance business. He published his memoirs, *Narrative of Military Operations Directed During the Late War Between the States,* in 1874. Four year later, he was elected to a two-year term from Virginia in the United States House of Representatives; and in 1885, during Grover Cleveland's administration, he held an appointment as commissioner of railroads. Johnston died in the District of Columbia on March 21, 1891, and was buried at Green Mount Cemetery in Baltimore. Faust, ed.,

Biographical Appendix

Encyclopedia of the Civil War, 400–1; Warner, *Generals in Gray,* 161–62.

The war governor of Iowa, **Samuel Jordan Kirkwood** was born in Harford City, Maryland, on December 20, 1813, and spent much of his youth in Washington, D.C. After traveling west, he read law in Mansfield, Ohio, before being admitted to the bar. The young Kirkwood remained a loyal Democrat until 1854, when he broke with the party over Senator Stephen A. Douglas's Kansas–Nebraska bill, which repealed long-standing sectional compromises and reignited the controversial issue of slavery in the western territories. Business interests moved Kirkwood to Iowa City, Iowa, in 1855, where he joined family members and began work as a farmer and miller. Highly regarded for integrity and financial good sense, Kirkwood won election to the state senate in 1855 and was selected as a delegate to the convention that organized the Iowa Republican Party in 1856. A strong supporter of an ever-expanding market economy, he served as a director of the state bank in 1858.

Elected governor in October 1859, Kirkwood and other Iowa Republican Party leaders helped secure the nomination of Abraham Lincoln for president at the 1860 Republican National Convention. When Lincoln's election to the post ignited the initial wave of secession, Kirkwood prophetically pronounced the course Iowa would take in the impending Civil War. "The last man and the last dollar will be given, if needed, for the service of the Government." Unquestionably patriotic, once the flag was fired upon at Fort Sumter, Kirkwood informed the president, "Ten days ago there were two parties in Iowa. Now, there is only one, and that one for the Constitution and the Union unconditionally."

In the early months of the war, Kirkwood was particularly active in organizing and raising Iowa's allotment of volunteers for the United States Army. He had no difficulty in securing an abundance of recruits, but encountered great difficulty in locating sufficient quantities of firearms, while he attempted to overcome logistical difficulties confronting the outfitting of the thousands of state volunteers. When the Iowa Democratic Party split into two factions in 1861, Kirkwood was reelected to a second term as governor. Throughout his tenure in office, he repeatedly urged Lincoln toward emancipation and the use of "black soldiers." Although Kirkwood favored conscription, under his direction Iowa was one of the few states able to fulfill troop quotas without resorting to the draft. After departing the governor's office in 1864, Kirkwood took a brief respite from public service in Iowa City, until 1866, when the state legislature selected him for a one-year term as a United States senator, and in 1876, he was elected to a third term as governor. In 1877, he was elected to a full term in the Senate, concentrating his legislative efforts to secure veteran pensions, create post offices, and monitor foreign diplomacy. In 1881, he resigned from the Senate to serve briefly as secretary of the interior in the James A. Garfield administration. After returning to Iowa, he continued to use his influence to shape party politics until his death in Iowa City, on September 1, 1894. Byers, *Iowa in War Times*, 35, 42; Faust, ed., *Encyclopedia of the Civil War*, 420; Heidler and Heidler, eds., *Encyclopedia of the American Civil War,* "Kirkwood, Samuel Jordan (1813 to 1894), Governor of Iowa," Wallace Hettle, 1128–29.

Known affectionately by his troops as "Black Jack," because of the color of his eyes, hair, and swarthy complexion, **John Alexander Logan** was born in Jackson County, Illinois, February 9, 1826. He attended Shiloh College, and when war with Mexico broke out in 1846 he volunteered for service, being appointed second lieutenant of the 1st Illinois Infantry. He posted a good service record, serving for periods as regimental adjutant and quartermaster. Upon returning home in 1848, he enthusiastically engaged in the study of law, attending the school at Louisville, Kentucky. Elected to the Illinois legislature, he was presidential elector for James Buchanan in 1856, and two years later he was elected to Congress as a Free-Soil Democrat. He won a second term in 1860, while he earnestly supported Stephen A. Douglas's unsuccessful election for president. A staunch pro-war Democrat, Douglas left Congress to fight at First Bull Run as a volunteer in a Michigan regiment. He returned to southern Illinois and recruited the 31st Illinois, being commissioned colonel. He rose rapidly through the ranks and ably demonstrated leadership skills and courage on numerous hard-fought fields, including Belmont and Fort Donelson—where he was wounded, subsequently winning promotion to brigadier general on March 21, 1862—and the advance upon and siege of Corinth, where he commanded a brigade and then a division in the Army of the Tennessee.

During the next year of hard campaigning in Mississippi, through the final operations against Vicksburg, Logan commanded a division in James McPherson's XVII Corps, being promoted to major general on March 13, 1863 (to rank from the preceding November 29). For his services during the grueling siege, where his division exploded a mine in the Confederate works and conducted a desperate assault, he was awarded the Congressional Medal. On December 11, 1863, Logan assumed command of the XV Corps, in which Royal Oake and his "Clinton County Regiment" served. In the operations against Atlanta, Logan served with great distinction, being wounded at Dallas, Georgia, and in assuming command of the Army of the Tennessee—during the heat of battle—when James B. McPherson was killed in action in front of Atlanta on July 22, 1864. Passed over for permanent command of the army, Logan led his corps from the Savannah campaign until the surrender of the Confederate army under Gen. Joseph E. Johnston in North Carolina. After the war ended, Logan served either as a congressman or senator from Illinois almost uninterruptedly until his death on December 26, 1886. In 1884 he had been the unsuccessful Republican nominee for vice president. Buried in Soldiers Home National Cemetery, both contemporaries and later historians consider Logan the "premier civilian combat general" serving in the United States armed forces during the war. Boatner, *Civil War Dictionary*, 486–87; Brant & Eds., *The Union Army*, VIII, 153–54; Warner, *Generals in Blue*, 281–83.

One the most controversial and colorful officers of the war, **John Alexander McClernand** was born in Kentucky near Hardinsburg on May 30, 1812; his family moved to Shawneetown, Illinois, while he was still young. Largely self taught, he was admitted to the bar in 1832 and volunteered as a private in the Black Hawk War. A fiery orator, he proved a gifted politician, serving seven years as an Illinois assemblyman, before being elected to the U.S. House of Representatives as a Jacksonian Democrat in 1843, serving four consecutive terms. Upon the outbreak of war, he resigned his seat and looked to the field of battle to win victories and headlines in his quest for political power.

McClernand wholeheartedly threw his considerable political influence behind the Lincoln administration's war policy, and in a selection calculated to hold southern Illinois democrats to the Union cause, Lincoln appointed him brigadier general of volunteers, ranking from May 17, 1861. In the opening actions of the Mississippi valley campaign, McClernand commanded a division, demonstrating personal bravery and an aggressive willingness to fight at Belmont, Fort Donelson, and Shiloh. He earned a promotion to major general on March 21, 1862. Always politically active, even while leading troops in the field, "he played a subversive role in the army," attempting to supplant George B. McClellan in the East and openly criticizing Ulysses S. Grant's maneuvers in the West.

In October 1862, Lincoln authorized McClernand to raise and command a force for independent operations on the Mississippi River aimed at Vicksburg. The new recruits, raised in the Midwest, were sent to Memphis. There, prior to McClernand's arrival, the War Department instructed William T. Sherman to commandeer the men for his Yazoo River expedition in December. Sherman led the command to defeat on the banks of Chickasaw Bayou, north of Vicksburg, before McClernand arrived and assumed command of operations. On the recommendation of both Sherman and Flag Officer David D. Porter, McClernand conducted the expedition that reduced the Post of Arkansas in January 1863, earning his place in the memoirs of William Royal Oake.

Outranked by U. S. Grant, the department commander, McClernand led the XIII Corps, Army of the Tennessee, as Grant's senior corps commander during the 1863 operations against Vicksburg. Although he performed admirably—with much credit to himself in crucial fighting at Port Gibson and Champion Hill, following a failed assault on Confederate fortifications protecting Vicksburg, May 22—McClernand "furnished the press with a congratulatory order, extolling his men as the heroes of the campaign." The communication had not been cleared through army channels, and Grant relieved him from command on June 19 and sent him home. Still valuable to the Lincoln administration, in February 1864 McClernand was returned to command of the now widely dispersed XIII Corps in Louisiana and Texas and played a minor role in activities associated with Nathaniel P. Bank's disastrous Red River expedition. Taken ill by malaria in May, he returned home, resigning his commission on November 30, 1864, never again fighting in the war.

He resided in Springfield and remained active in Democratic Party pol-

Biographical Appendix

itics but never again sought elected office. In 1876 he served as chairman of the national convention, nominating Samuel J. Tilden for president. A prominent figure in the war, McClernand's place in history has been greatly underestimated in relation to his role as a politician and a sustainer of the Union. Unfortunately, his accomplishments as a combat commander—making no serious blunders and always willing to engage the enemy—were ignored by contemporaries and since by historians. The patriotic politician-turned-soldier remains consistently vilified for ineptness, insubordinate behavior, and for mixing politics with war. He died in Springfield, September 20, 1890, and is buried there. Brant & Eds., The Union Army, VIII, 165; Heidler & Heidler, eds., *Encyclopedia of the American Civil War,* Christopher Meyers, "McClernand, John Alexander (1812 to 1900) Union general," 1277–79: Warner, *Generals in Blue,* 293–94.

James Birdseye McPherson was born November 14, 1828, in Clyde, Ohio. Extremely intelligent and talented, he graduated first in his class from the U.S. Military Academy at West Point in 1853. Commissioned a second lieutenant in the Corps of Engineers, he was appointed assistant instructor of practical engineering at West Point, a compliment never before awarded to a officer so young and inexperienced. Engaged on both coasts in supervising improvements for river, harbor, and seacoast defense, he supervised construction of Fort Delaware and subsequently directed the fortification of the now infamous Alcatraz Island in San Francisco Bay, before being placed in charge of the fortifications of Boston harbor. After war erupted in April 1861, no officer in the United States Army had a more meteoric rise than McPherson. A first lieutenant of engineers as late as August 1861, by October 8, 1862, he ranked as a major general of volunteers, commanding a division of the XIII Corps. In the interim, he served as aide-de-camp to Henry W. Halleck; as chief engineer on the staff of Ulysses S. Grant during operations against Forts Henry and Donelson, the battle of Shiloh, and the subsequent advance upon and siege of Corinth; and as superintendent of railways in western Tennessee and northern Mississippi. Promoted brigadier general of volunteers, August 19, 1862, he soon after participated in the battle of Corinth in October 1862, commanding reinforcements and leading the vanguard of the pursuit against the retreating Confederate force under Gen. Earl Van Dorn, after which

McPherson was advanced to the rank of major general of volunteers.

Assigned to command of the XVII Corps, he continued to serve under Ulysses S. Grant during the successful Mississippi River operation in 1863, seeing significant action at Port Gibson, Raymond, Jackson, Champion Hill, the Big Black River Bridge, and in the assaults upon and siege of Vicksburg. McPherson assumed command of the Army of the Tennessee, in which William Royal Oake and the 26th Iowa Volunteer Infantry were assigned, on March 26, 1864, and thus commanded the army during William T. Sherman's subsequent advance on Atlanta. His inability to aggressively block the retreat of Joseph E. Johnston's Army of Tennessee at Resaca, which might have permitted Sherman to destroy or disperse the opposing Confederate army at the outset of the campaign, proved one of the great missed opportunities of the war; in all probability, it extended the campaign another four months. Throughout the maneuvering ever southward, McPherson supervised his army through the fighting at Pickett's Mill, Dallas, Kennesaw Mountain, and across the Chattahoochee, until he was killed in action, at the age of thirty-five, while attempting to reach his command from Sherman's headquarters during the opening actions of the battle of Atlanta on July 22, 1864. Sherman cried openly "when he viewed the body of his friend laid upon a door torn from its hinges and improvised as a bier." McPherson was buried in the orchard where he played as a child. Greatly favored and admired by his senior officers, Grant and Sherman, McPherson's skill as a combat leader has been sharply criticized by historians, who interpret his generalship lacking in both tactical innovation and aggressiveness. Boatner, *Civil War Dictionary*, 538; Brant & Eds., *The Union Army*, VIII, 171; Warner, *Generals in Blue*, 306–8.

George Washington Morgan was born in Washington County, Pennsylvania, on September 20, 1820. At the age of sixteen, he left college to join in the Texas War for Independence and served as a captain in the army under Sam Houston. He entered the U.S. Military Academy at West Point in 1845 but resigned in his third year because of scholastic difficulty. Thereafter he studied law, and at the age of twenty-six was commissioned colonel of the 2nd Ohio Volunteers, serving in the war with Mexico under Zachary Taylor until March 3, 1847, when he was commissioned colonel of the 15th United States Infantry. Assigned to the army under Winfield Scott,

Morgan was twice wounded at Contreras and Churubusco; on August 20, 1847, he was brevetted brigadier general for gallantry during those battles— an achievement not equaled during the war by an officer so young. When discharged in 1848, he practiced law and farming at Mount Vernon, Ohio, and served as U.S. consul at Marseilles (1856) and minister to Portugal (1858), a post he resigned when civil war erupted in America.

Commissioned brigadier general of volunteers in the Union army, November 12, 1861, he commanded a division in the Army of the Ohio and directed operations that expulsed Confederate forces from Cumberland Gap in June 1862. When he later cut off Kirby Smith's invasion of Kentucky, Morgan abandoned the gap, September 17, 1862, and successfully retired his command and equipment overland to the Ohio River. In December, he commanded a division under William T. Sherman at Chickasaw Bayou, and the XIII Corps during the capture of the Post of Arkansas, where he and Sherman, under John A. McClernand's orders, each commanded a corps. An earlier disagreement between the two—when Sherman found fault with Morgan's handling of his troops in the assault on Confederate fortifications along the Chickasaw bluffs—continued to fester. And prior to the fall of Vicksburg, Morgan, no believer in racial equality, became so dissatisfied with the Lincoln administration's policy of enlisting black men for military service that he tendered his resignation, June 8, 1863. Active in late-war Democratic Party politics, he continued his political career in the post-war years and was elected to the U.S. House of Representatives three times, where he vigorously opposed radical Republican Reconstruction measures. He died at Fort Monroe, Virginia, July 26, 1893, and is buried in Mount Vernon. Boatner, *Civil War Dictionary*, 213, 565–66; Warner, *Generals in Blue*, 333–34.

Quite arguably, the most talented and distinguished of the foreign-born officers to serve in the United States Army during the Civil War was **Peter Joseph Osterhaus**. Born in Coblenz, Prussia (now Germany), on January 4, 1823, he received a military education in Berlin and later became embroiled in the 1848 revolution, which forced him to flee to the United States the following year. He initially settled in Belleville, Illinois, working as a clerk. He later lived in Lebanon, Illinois, before moving to St. Louis, Missouri. Osterhaus entered the Civil War on April 27, 1861, as a major of a Missouri battalion. He fought with the battalion at Wilson's Creek, August 10, and in December was made colonel of the 12th Missouri Infantry. Assigned to Samuel Curtis's Army of the Southwest, he ably commanded a division during the battle of Elkhorn Tavern at Pea Ridge, Arkansas. Appointed brigadier general of volunteers on June 9 1862, he commanded a division in John A. McClernand's XIII Corps, assigned to Ulysses S. Grant's Army of the Tennessee during the Vicksburg campaign, and was wounded at Big Black River. Osterhaus assumed command of the 1st Division, XV Corps, on September 1, 1863, and over the course of the next sixteen months played a direct and significant role in the war experiences of William Royal Oake.

At Chattanooga, Osterhaus and his 1st Division served under Joseph Hooker in the assault on the northern face of Lookout Mountain on November 24, 1863. The next day, at Missionary Ridge, the Prussian "performed magnificently" in directing his command in the attack that drove the Confederate defenders from the southern end of the ridge; and again the next day, November 27, while still attached to Hooker's command, he ably guided his division during the pursuit to Taylor's Ridge at Ringgold Gap. He led the division to further distinction in the subsequent 1864 operations against Atlanta, being promoted major general on July 23, 1864. Sherman opposed this promotion, alleging the Prussian's recent absence from the army was an attempt to lobby for higher rank. Apparently the issue faded from their relationship, for on September 23, 1864, Osterhaus was assigned command of the XV Corps, directing the corps's operations during the celebrated "March to the Sea." On January 8, 1865, he was appointed to the Military Division of West Mississippi, where he served as chief of staff to Maj. Gen. Edward R. S. Canby, who commanded operations that forced the surrender of Mobile, April 12, 1865. A month later, it was Osterhaus that Confederate Lt. Gen. Simon Bolivar Buckner, serving as chief of staff for Gen. Edmund Kirby Smith, surrendered Smith's Trans-Mississippi Department on May 26, 1865.

After the war, Osterhaus alternated residences between St. Louis, where he operated a wholesale hardware business, and France, where he served as U.S. consul in Lyons. In later years he again served in the U.S. consular service, residing in Germany. By Act of Congress, March 17, 1905, he was placed on the retired list of the Regular Army as a brigadier general and continued to receive a military pension until he died in Duisburg, January 17, 1917, three months before the United States declared war on Germany. The old soldier is buried in Coblenz. Boatner, *Civil War Dictionary*, 613; Faust, ed., *Encyclopedia of the Civil War*, 550; Warner, *Generals in Blue*, 352–53.

Of Quaker ancestry, having been born in Philadelphia, Pennsylvania, on August 10, 1814, **John Clifford Pemberton** graduated in the class of 1837 at West Point. An artillerist, he served in the Seminole War and on border duty, before winning two brevets for gallantry in the war with Mexico. Afterward, he served on the frontier fighting Indians, and participated in Albert Sidney Johnston's Utah Expedition against the Mormons. He had a history of advocating states' rights philosophies and forming friendships mostly with Southern-born cadets at the academy. In 1847 he married Martha Thompson of Norfolk, Virginia; his connections undoubtedly contributed further to his decision to resign from the U.S. Army on April 24, 1861, and tender his services to the Confederacy.

His early war service as commander of the Department of South Carolina, Georgia, and Florida hardly prepared him for the rapid promotion he experienced from brigadier (June 17, 1861) to major general, to rank from January 14, 1862, and finally to lieutenant general on October 10, 1862. In command of his coastal department, he counseled the abandonment of Fort Sumter and the construction of other installations, such as Battery Wagner on Morris Island, as the basis for a superior defense of Charleston, South Carolina. At this juncture in the war, with promotion to lieutenant general, he was assigned command of the Department of Mississippi and East Louisiana, an area that embraced the strategic strongholds of Vicksburg and Port Hudson, which defended the only segment of the Mississippi River not yet controlled by United States forces. Hampered by conflicting orders from his superiors at the outset of the campaign, Pemberton was simply outclassed and bewildered by the brilliant strategy employed by Ulysses S. Grant to compel capitulation of Vicksburg and its 30,000 defenders on July 4, 1863.

After being paroled and exchanged as a prisoner of war, Pemberton was unable to secure further duty commensurate with his rank. He resigned his commission of lieutenant general on May 18, 1864, being appointed by

President Davis a lieutenant colonel of artillery. In this capacity, he served faithfully under Robert E. Lee in Virginia until the end of the war. He farmed near Warrenton, Virginia, until moving to Penllyn, Pennsylvania, where he died on July 13, 1881. He is buried in Philadelphia. Boatner, *Civil War Dictionary*, 631; Faust, ed., *Encyclopedia of the Civil War*, 569; Warner, *Generals in Gray*, 232–33.

A native of Pennsylvania, Rear Admiral **David Dixon Porter** commanded the Mississippi Squadron that operated independently but in full cooperation with Ulysses S. Grant's Army of the Tennessee during the pivotal Vicksburg campaign. Born on June 8, 1813, Porter was the son of Commodore David Porter, brother of Commodore William D. Porter, cousin of Union General Fitz-John Porter, and foster brother of David Glasgow Farragut, first admiral of the United States Navy. He sailed with his father to the West Indies to suppress piracy in 1824 and was commissioned Midshipman in the Mexican Navy three years later. He joined the U.S. Navy in 1829, seeing service in the Mediterranean, the South Atlantic, and the Gulf during the war with Mexico.

On April 22, 1861, Porter was named commander, and with his Mortar Schooner Fleet joined Farragut in the advance up the Mississippi, ably assisting his foster brother in the capture of New Orleans in April 1862 by supervising the mortar bombardment and capture of Forts Jackson and St. Phillip. Promoted to acting rear admiral in September 1862, his management of Mississippi River fleet operations proved crucial in the capture of the Post of Arkansas; and his ability to steam transports and gunboats past the shore batteries at Vicksburg secured Ulysses S. Grant the tactical leverage required to place three army corps in the rear of the Confederate garrison, invest the fortress city, and ultimately force its capitulation on July 4, 1863. For his role in the momentous victory, Porter received the thanks of Congress. After a courageous performance by his fleet in the aborted Red River expedition in the spring of 1864, Porter was assigned command of the North Atlantic Blockading Squadron in October 1864, fighting another successful combined operation with Alfred H. Terry's army corps in the capture of the massive coastal installation at Fort Fisher, North Carolina, January 15, 1865. It was here that Porter commanded the largest American fleet ever assembled and received his fourth thanks from Congress.

In 1866, Porter was promoted to vice admiral and later served as superintendent of the United States Naval Academy at Annapolis, Maryland. In this capacity, and later with the Navy Department, he stressed professionalism and rewarded active service among his officers and seamen. Appointed admiral of the navy in 1870, he remained active his entire life until his death in Washington, D.C., on February 13, 1891. He was interred at Arlington National Cemetery. Boatner, *Civil War Dictionary*, 292–95, 661; Faust, ed., *Encyclopedia of the Civil War,* 594–95.

William Stark Rosecrans was born in Delaware County, Ohio, on September 6, 1819, and graduated fifth in his military academy class of 1842 at West Point. Commissioned in the engineer corps, he served for a year constructing coastal fortifications at Hampton Roads, Virginia. He spent the next four years teaching natural and experimental philosophy, and then engineering at West Point. Afterward, he was the superintending engineer at Fort Adams in Newport, Rhode Island, led surveys in New England, and was posted at the Washington navy yard. He resigned his commission as first lieutenant on April 1, 1854. For the next seven years, he applied his military experience to business in Cincinnati, Ohio, where he worked as a civil engineer and architect, and a coal and oil refiner.

With the outbreak of civil war, Rosecrans served as an aide to General George B. McClellan, with the volunteer rank of colonel of engineers. In June 1861, he was simultaneously colonel of the 23rd Ohio Infantry and a brigadier general in the Regular Army, ranking from May 16. Ordered to western Virginia, he commanded a provisional brigade of volunteers, Army of Occupation, at Rich Mountain; upon McClellan's departure to assume command of the Union army, July 23, 1861, Rosecrans assumed command of the Army of Occupation, opposing Robert E. Lee in the operation that drove Confederate forces from the area and initiated erection of the state of West Virginia. In May 1862, Rosecrans was transferred west and commanded the left wing of John Pope's Army of the Mississippi in the advance upon the important railroad junction at Corinth, Mississippi. He succeeded Pope in command of the army, serving under Ulysses S. Grant, as commandant of the District of Corinth. He fought an indecisive engagement against Sterling Price at Iuka, Mississippi, in September, and then successfully repulsed the combined forces of Earl Van Dorn and Price, which attacked Corinth in October 1862. Promoted major general of volunteers on October 25, to rank from March 21, 1862, he relieved Don Carlos Buell in Kentucky, taking command of the newly designated Army of the Cumberland. At the turn of the year, he ably repulsed Braxton Bragg's Army of Tennessee at the titanic Battle of Stones River or Murfreesboro, Tennessee—where losses of almost 25,000 men equaled roughly one-third of the effectives engaged on both sides. Following Bragg's retreat to the Duck River, a general lull plagued operations in Middle Tennessee until late June 1863, when Rosecrans initiated a campaign of maneuver that forced the Confederates to retire from Tullahoma to the fortified railroad center at Chattanooga. Then, after a skillful feint by Rosecrans up the Tennessee, Bragg was forced further south into northern Georgia.

Reinforced by Longstreet's corps from the Army of Northern Virginia, Bragg counterattacked, inflicting a crushing defeat upon Rosecrans at Chickamauga, September 19 and 20, 1863. Rosecrans retreated to Chattanooga, where he was supplanted in command by the arrival of Ulysses S. Grant, commander of the Military Division of the Mississippi, on October 19, 1863. Grant promptly relieved Rosecrans as commander of the Army of the Cumberland, replacing him with George H. Thomas. Three months later, Rosecrans was placed in command of the Department of Missouri, a position he occupied for a year. He then sat out the remainder of the war either awaiting orders or on leave. Called "Old Rosey" by his troops, President Lincoln cited Rosecrans's victory at Stones River—for which he received the thanks of Congress—as being vital to the survival of the Union.

Rosecrans resigned his Regular Army commission, March 28, 1867. Appointed minister to Mexico in 1868, he was relieved from the post when Grant became president in 1869. He then moved to California, residing on a ranch near present-day Redondo Beach. He was elected to the U.S. House of Representatives in 1880, serving until 1885, and rising to chair the Committee on Military Affairs. From 1885 to 1893, he served as registrar to the Treasury. He died at his ranch on March 11, 1898. He remains were reinterred in Arlington National Cemetery in 1902. Boatner, *Civil War Dictionary*, 708; Warner, *Generals in Blue*, 410–11.

Born in Lancaster, Ohio, on February 8, 1820, **William Tecumseh "Cump" Sherman** was the most widely acclaimed of United States military leaders next to Ulysses S. Grant during the Civil War. At the age of nine, he lost his father and was taken in by the neighboring family of Thomas Ewing, a United States senator and cabinet officer. Sherman graduated from the U.S. Military Academy at West Point in 1840, ranking sixth out of forty-two cadets in his class. The young lieutenant served an unexceptional thirteen years of duty on the frontier, stationed in California during the war with Mexico, where he won a brevet of captain for meritorious services. He resigned his commission to become a banker in San Francisco, then a lawyer in Leavenworth, Kansas, before securing the superintendency of the new Louisiana State Seminary of Learning and Military Academy at Pineville (now Louisiana State University at Baton Rouge) prior to the outbreak of civil war.

In January 1861, Sherman was required to accept government weapons recently surrendered by the United States arsenal in Baton Rouge to state forces. Outraged, he promptly tendered his resignation to the governor, declaring, "On no earthly account will I do any act or think any thought hostile…to the…United States." After moving his family to St. Louis, Missouri, he was reappointed to the army with the rank of colonel in the Regular Army, assuming command of the newly organized 13th United States Infantry. Soon after being assigned command of a brigade, he fought in the first major battle of the war at First Manassas, and on August 7, 1861, was advanced to the rank of brigadier general of volunteers. Afterward, he was transferred to the West, serving in Kentucky and then Tennessee, where he commanded a division in the two-day bloodbath at Shiloh; his battlefield actions won him the lasting friendship of Ulysses S. Grant and promotion to major general, to rank from April 6, 1862. Active in operations to secure northern Mississippi and western Tennessee, Sherman directed the expeditionary force that advanced on Vicksburg via the Mississippi River and was repulsed by a reinforced Confederate garrison at Chickasaw Bayou in late December 1862. With the formation of this expedition, throughout the maneuvers and fighting spanning the next two and one-half years of war, Sherman's war experiences became linked with those of William Royal Oake, as the 26th Iowa Volunteer Infantry was permanently attached to the

Army of the Tennessee and assigned to the force (later designated the XV corps) that Sherman commanded at Arkansas Post and as Grant's most trusted subordinate in the victorious Vicksburg campaign of 1863.

Sherman succeeded Grant (promoted commander of all troops in the Western theater, October 1863) in command of the Army of the Tennessee, and directed its participation in the successful series of engagements that defeated Confederate forces besieging Chattanooga in November 1863. He again succeeded Grant, who had been promoted lieutenant general in chief of command of the armies of the United States, March 1864, by assuming command of the Military Division of the Mississippi. As commander of all western United States forces, Sherman conducted an army raid on the Confederate industry and rail communications in Mississippi, advancing from Vicksburg to Meridian (February to March 1864), then returned to northern Georgia, where he directed a massive army group in an arduous four-month summer campaign that culminated in the capture of the city of Atlanta on September 2, 1864. In the fall, he struck out from Atlanta with two armies, conducting an aggressive overland movement to the sea. After forcing the abandonment and surrender of both Savannah and Charleston on the Atlantic coast, he turned his forces northward on an invasion of the Carolinas, which ultimately netted the capitulation of Joe Johnston's western Confederate army at Durham Station, North Carolina, on April 26, 1865, helping to bring the conflict to a close. The army marched north into Virginia, and on May 24, 1865—a year after he and his battle-hardened veterans began their 2,600-mile odyssey through Georgia, the Carolinas, and Virginia—Sherman and his conquering host passed in formal grand review before President Andrew Johnson and Congress in Washington D.C.

Twice tendered the official thanks of Congress during the war, Sherman was elevated to lieutenant general in 1866 and on March 4, 1869, became a full general, serving as general in chief of the army for fourteen years, and the principal administrator of the government policies employed to neutralize armed resistance among hostile Indian tribes and force survivors onto western reservations. His most lasting legacy during this period was the establishment of the army's Command School at Fort Leavenworth. Sherman retired February 8, 1884, and lived in New York City until he died on February 14, 1891. He is buried in St. Louis, Missouri. His provocative *Memoirs of General*

W. T. Sherman (published in 1875) reveals the general's extraordinary mind and problem-solving capabilities, and illustrates his extensive knowledge of the art of war. Boatner, *Civil War Dictionary*, 750–51; Brant & Eds., *The Union Army*, VIII, 235–38; Warner, *Generals in Blue*, 442–44.

Henry Warner Slocum appears in William Royal Oake's memoirs when assigned command of the XX Corps during closing operations against Atlanta, and as commander of the Army of Georgia during the great "March to the Sea" and the raid through the Carolinas. Born at Delphi, New York, on September 24, 1827, Slocum was teaching school when he was appointed to the U.S. Military Academy at West Point in 1848, graduating in 1852. After brief service against the Seminoles in Florida and garrison duty in Charleston Harbor, he resigned in 1856 to practice law in Syracuse, New York. He later served as a state legislator and as an instructor of artillery in the state militia. On May 21, 1861, Slocum was appointed colonel of the 27th New York Infantry and was severely wounded at First Bull Run. Appointed brigadier general of volunteers, August 9, 1861, he served the next three years in the Army of the Potomac, illustrating competence in brigade and division command during operations on the peninsula of Virginia, engaged at Yorktown, West Point, Gaines Mill, Glendale, and Malvern Hill. Promoted major general of volunteers, ranking from July 4, 1862, Slocum commanded the 1st Division, VI Corps, at Second Bull Run, South Mountain, and Antietam, before being appointed to lead the XII Corps. Held in reserve at Fredericksburg in December 1862, Slocum ably led his corps at Chancellorsville and commanded the right wing as "senior major general present on the field" during the crucial battle of Gettysburg in July 1863. When his corps and the XI Corps, under Oliver O. Howard, were sent to serve under Joe Hooker in the relief of Chattanooga, Tennessee, Slocum tendered his resignation to President Lincoln, his relationship with his old army having been strained since his open criticism of Hooker after the defeat at Chancellorsville. The resignation was refused and a compromise reached when Slocum assumed command of one division of his corps to protect the Nashville & Chattanooga Railroad, while the other division served directly under Hooker.

Just prior to Sherman's advance into northern Georgia, Slocum was assigned command of the post at Vicksburg, serving from April 20 to August 14, 1864. He then returned to Georgia to succeed Hooker, who had asked to be relieved when Oliver O. Howard, his junior in rank, was promoted to succeed McPherson in command of the Army of the Tennessee. Slocum arrived on the outskirts of Atlanta to lead the XX Corps during the final weeks of operations. When Sherman marched six corps against the Macon Railroad south of the city in late August, Slocum was left north of the city to guard communications. When Confederate forces left their entrenchments around Atlanta to engage Sherman, Slocum threw his corps directly into the city and accepted its surrender on September 2, 1864. Given command of the newly designated Army of Georgia (made up of the XIV and XX Corps) on November 11, 1864, Slocum participated in operations at Savannah, Averasboro, Bentonville, Goldsboro, and Raleigh, until the surrender of Confederate forces under Joseph E. Johnston. After resigning September 28, 1865, he served three terms in the U.S. House of Representatives, and was a member of the Board of Gettysburg Monument Commissioners. General Slocum died in Brooklyn, New York, April 14, 1894, and is buried in Green-Wood Cemetery. Brant & Eds., *The Union Army*, VIII, 241–42; Warner, *Generals in Blue*, 451–53.

A native of Bucks County, Pennsylvania, born on April 28, 1815, **Andrew Jackson Smith** became one of the premier generals in the U.S. Army during four years of field service in the Western theater during the Civil War. A graduate of the U.S. Military Academy at West Point in 1838, Smith was appointed a second lieutenant with the 1st Dragoons. For the next twenty-three years, he served almost exclusively in the West fighting Indians, was posted in California during the war with Mexico, and attained the rank of major on May 13, 1861. Appointed colonel of the 2nd California Volunteer Cavalry at the outbreak of civil war, he resigned in November to become chief of cavalry under General Henry W. Halleck in Missouri. Four months later, he was appointed brigadier general of volunteers on March 17, 1862. Smith directed cavalry operations under Halleck during the advance upon and siege of Corinth, Mississippi, until after the strategic transportation hub was evacuated by P. G. T. Beauregard.

After brief service as commander of forces at Covington, Kentucky

(September to October 1862), and another month-long appointment commanding the 1st Division, Army of the Ohio, in field operations in Kentucky (October to November 1862), Smith was stationed in Memphis, Tennessee. Assigned to command one of the four divisions organized under William T. Sherman, he participated in the Yazoo River expedition in late December, being engaged at Chickasaw Bayou. He commanded a division in the XIII Corps in the operation against the Post of Arkansas, which was carried by assault January 11, 1863. Engaged under Ulysses S. Grant in the winter and spring of 1863, he led the 10th Division, XIII Corps, at Port Gibson, Champion's Hill, and Big Black River, as well as during the assaults upon, siege, and capture of Vicksburg. In March 1864, he assumed command of the XVI Corps, Army of the Tennessee, which was detached to the Department of the Gulf. Under General Nathaniel P. Banks, Smith led his corps during the Red River campaign, being engaged at Fort DeRussy, Pleasant Hill, and Cane River.

Appointed major general of volunteers May 12, 1864, Smith directed raids in western Tennessee and into northern Mississippi, where he decimated Confederate forces under Stephen D. Lee and Nathan B. Forrest at Tupelo on July 14, 1864. Transferred to Missouri to aid in the pursuit of Sterling Price, his detached corps, Army of the Tennessee, was then sent to reinforce George H. Thomas at Nashville, where Smith played a decisive role in the defeat of John Bell Hood on December 15 to 16, 1864. Reassigned to the Department of the Gulf, February 1865, he closed out the war directing his XVI Corps, which he now referred to as "the lost tribes of Israel," on account of its extensive wanderings during the war. Smith's "career attracted little notoriety compared to that of many of his colleagues," wrote one historian. "Nevertheless, he was one of the most competent division and corps commanders in the service." Brevetted a brigadier general in the U.S. Army for Pleasant Hill and Tupelo, and major general for Nashville, he was appointed colonel of the 7th United States Cavalry in 1866, serving for three years before resigning when President Grant appointed him postmaster of St. Louis in 1869. He later served as city auditor and commander of a Missouri militia brigade, before his death on January 30, 1897, with interment at Bellefontaine Cemetery. Boatner, *Civil War Dictionary*, 768; Warner, *Generals in Blue*, 454–56.

Milo Smith was forty-three years old when he accepted Gov. Samuel Kirkwood's appointment to be colonel of the 26th Iowa Volunteer Infantry. A local resident of Clinton, Smith was born in Shoreham Township, Addison County, Vermont, January 25, 1819. The industrious young man left home at the age of seventeen and spent the next twelve years teaching at schools in Vermont, New York, and later Illinois. In 1848 he altered his course to begin a prominent career as a surveyor and railroad engineer, earning appointment as chief engineer and superintendent in 1852 of the Elgin State Line Railroad in Illinois. Smith later journeyed to Iowa in 1855, where he secured an appointment as chief engineer and superintendent of the Chicago, Iowa, & Nebraska Railroad, the position he held when Governor Kirkwood commissioned him to organize and command of the 26th "Clinton County" Infantry Regiment in the summer of 1862.

Smith was twice wounded in combat—first on January 11, 1863, during the initial battle he and the regiment were engaged in at the Post of Arkansas. "No officer...behaved better, or did better fighting on that battle field, than Col. Milo Smith and his regiment," wrote Brig. Gen. John M. Thayer, Smith's brigade commander, to Governor Kirkwood. The second wound came just four months later, as he directed the regiment's movements during Grant's May 22 assault on Vicksburg. Although he suffered from these injuries, Smith remained in the field during the forty-seven-day siege of the city; during the final two weeks of the investment, he briefly performed double duty in directing his regiment and commanding the 3rd Brigade, 1st Division, XV Corps, until the surrender of the Confederate garrison on July 4, 1863.

Transferred with the Army of the Tennessee to help break the siege of Chattanooga, Smith led the regiment through engagements in November at Lookout Mountain, Missionary Ridge, and Ringgold Gap. The next year, Smith and the 26th Iowa Volunteers participated in Sherman's momentous advance on Atlanta and the infamous "March to the Sea." Over the course of next year—from December 14, 1863, to January 21, 1865—Smith commanded the 1st Brigade, 1st Division, XV Corps (which included the 26th Iowa Volunteer Infantry) on three occasions for a total of eight months, his last service as brigade commander encompassing the battles of Atlanta, Ezra Church, and Jonesboro, and the subsequent "March to the Sea."

Smith resigned January 28, 1865, taking leave from the regiment as it lay in camp near Beaufort, South Carolina, and returned to civilian life in Clinton. Besides resuming his railroad interests, he operated a farm implement business, served as vice president of the Clinton National Bank, and owned a city hotel. In 1887, Smith was appointed a commissioner for the Soldier's Home in Marshalltown, Iowa, and was elected superintendent of the home, holding the position for five years. Active in the Grand Army of the Republic and the Society of the Army of the Tennessee, the old veteran died in Clinton, February 28, 1904. Byers, *Iowa in War Times,* 201; *The Biographical Record of Clinton County, Iowa,* (S. J. Clarke Publishing Co., Chicago, 1901), 34–39; *Report of Proceedings of the Society of the Army of the Tennessee,* Meeting XXXV, Cincinnati, 1905, "In Memoriam," 276.

The elder brother of Union Gen. Giles A. Smith, **Morgan Lewis Smith** was born March 8, 1821, in Mexico, New York. His family soon relocated to Jefferson County, where Smith grew to manhood, leaving home at twenty-one. For the next two decades, he wandered through various vocations: schoolteacher in Indiana; a professional soldier, serving as sergeant and drill instructor in the Regular Army for five years (1845 to 1850) under the assumed name of Martin L. Sanford; and, from 1850 to the outbreak of the war, a riverboat-man on the Ohio and Mississippi. He recruited and organized the 8th Missouri Infantry, consisting mostly of St. Louis waterfront rowdies whom Smith converted into excellent soldiers as the regiment's first colonel (commissioned July 4, 1861), until he was assigned command of a brigade in the assault on Fort Donelson. Assigned to a division commanded by Lewis Wallace, Smith's brigade was heavily engaged on the second day of fighting at Shiloh, and saw action during the advance and siege of Corinth.

Promoted to brigadier general on July 16, 1862, Smith was badly wounded during Sherman's Yazoo expedition in the bitter engagement at Chickasaw Bayou at year's end (December 1862). Incapacitated, he did not return to duty until the following October 1863. At Chattanooga, during battles fought to relieve the besieged city in November, Smith commanded the 2nd Division of the XV Corps, continuing to lead the division during the 1864 Atlanta campaign. He assumed temporary command of the corps during the battle of Atlanta (holding the appointment for a week), when his corps commander, John A. Logan, briefly took command of the Army of the Tennessee after Gen. James B. McPherson was killed in action on July 22. Severe aggravation from his old Chickasaw Bayou wound forced him from further active service in the field on August 5. Upon return from sick leave, he was assigned to command the military District of Vicksburg, and held the post from September 27, 1864, until June 22, 1865. He did not wait to muster out and resigned his commission on July 12, failing to receive a brevet promotion to major general. Appointed U.S. consul general to Hawaii, he served in Honolulu until Ulysses S. Grant took office. Smith then moved to Washington, D.C., where he engaged in various business interests. He died suddenly on December 28, 1874, while traveling to Jersey City, New Jersey. He is buried in Arlington National Cemetery. Boatner, *Civil War Dictionary*, 773–74. Warner, *Generals in Blue*, 459-60.

Frederick Steele was born January 14, 1819, in Delhi, New York. He graduated from the U.S. Military Academy at West Point in the class of 1843, ranked nine positions behind fellow classmate Ulysses S. Grant. With service on the frontier, and as a veteran of the war with Mexico, where he won two brevets for gallantry, Steele was appointed major of the 11th United States Infantry, and saw early combat in the Civil War in command of a battalion of regulars at the battle of Wilson's Creek, August 10, 1861. Named colonel of the 8th Iowa Infantry, September 23, 1861, and brigadier general of volunteers, January 29, 1862, he commanded the District of Southeast Missouri until May 14, 1862, and a division of Samuel Curtis's Army of the Southwest, taking part in operations in Arkansas, which resulted in the capture and occupation of Helena.

Steele commanded one of the four divisions Sherman used in the expedition to the Yazoo River in December 1862, commanding the division to which the 26th Iowa Volunteer Infantry and William Royal Oake was assigned. He directed the division in the attack along Chickasaw Bayou and in the subsequent assault on the Post of Arkansas, January 11, 1863, where the 26th Iowa Volunteer Infantry recorded the heaviest loss of life sustained in battle by the regiment during the war. Steele continued to command the 1st Division of the XV Corps throughout the next seven months of field

Biographical Appendix

operations waged by Ulysses S. Grant against Vicksburg, and supervised the raid from Greenville into the Mississippi delta, where William Royal Oake was taken prisoner of war in April 1863.

Promoted major general of volunteers, March 17, 1863, to rank from the preceding November 29, in the aftermath of the surrender of Vicksburg, Steele was placed in command of all United States forces in Arkansas. He marched inland from the Mississippi, driving through the state to capture Little Rock on September 10, 1863. The following spring, he marched his command overland, fighting several severe engagements in the southwestern portion of the state in direct support of Nathaniel P. Banks's aborted ascent of the Red River. From February to June 1865, he led a division under Edward R. S. Canby in operations against Mobile, and at the close of hostilities with the Confederacy was sent to Texas and did not muster out of volunteer service until 1867, meanwhile having been appointed colonel of the 20th United States Infantry. He had earned brevets to brigadier general, United States Army, for Vicksburg and Little Rock, and to major general in recognition for his war service. A year later, while commanding the Department of Columbia, he was on leave at San Mateo, California, when an attack of apoplexy caused him to fall from a buggy he was driving. Steele died on January 12, 1868. He is buried in Woodlawn Memorial Park, Colma, California. Boatner, *Civil War Dictionary*, 794–95; Warner, *Generals in Blue*, 474–75.

John Milton Thayer was born January 24, 1820, in Bellingham, Massachusetts. Raised on a farm, he gained his early education in district school and taught school himself before graduating with honors in 1841 from Brown University in Providence, Rhode Island. He studied law and began a practice in Worcester, Massachusetts. Thayer also served as a lieutenant in the local militia until 1854, shortly after passage of the Kansas–Nebraska Act. He then moved his family to Nebraska Territory, where he acquired farmland near Omaha. He was soon commissioned the first brigadier general of the territorial militia and quickly demonstrated military skill as an Indian fighter. As a result, he was unanimously elected major general of state forces by the legislature in 1855, continuing to hold the position until the outbreak of civil war. In 1859, when conflict erupted between white settlers and the Pawnees, Thayer led the successful campaign that captured the entire tribe, forcing the members onto a reservation.

Thayer's military experience placed him in great demand when hostilities erupted in April 1861. On July 21, 1861, he was appointed colonel of the 1st Nebraska Territorial Infantry, taking creditable participation in the battle and capture of Fort Donelson and the battle of Shiloh, where he ably commanded a brigade in Lewis Wallace's division through both combats. On October 4, 1862, Thayer was appointed brigadier general of volunteers, but the Senate failed to confirm his nomination. He was reappointed and confirmed to the rank on March 13, 1863. Assigned command of a brigade in the division led by Gen. Frederick Steele, he led his troops, which included Royal Oake and the 26th Iowa Volunteer Infantry, in the assaults along Chickasaw Bayou (December 1862) and in the subsequent attack on the Post of Arkansas, January 11, 1863.

In the momentous operation Ulysses S. Grant waged against Vicksburg in 1863, Thayer continued to serve under William T. Sherman and led the 3rd Brigade, 1st Division, XV Corps, in which the 26th Iowa Volunteer Infantry was attached, until August 1, 1863. He then accompanied General Steele into Arkansas, assuming command of the District of the Frontier, with headquarters at Fort Smith, on February 22, 1864. He participated in Steele's Camden expedition, organized to support Nathaniel P. Bank's ascent of the Red River, and remained in Arkansas for the duration of the war. Promoted brevet major general of volunteers for war service, his resignation was approved by the War Department on July 19, 1865. An "ardent and active radical" Republican, he served four years as United States senator, until 1871; was appointed governor of the Wyoming Territory by President Grant, serving from 1875 to 1879; and in 1886 was elected governor of Nebraska, serving three successive terms until 1892. He retired to private life in Lincoln, where he died March 19, 1906, being interred in Wyuka Cemetery. Boatner, *Civil War Dictionary*, 834; Dyer, *Compendium*, 498; Warner, *Generals in Blue*, 499–500.

One of the ablest and most successful military commanders in the Civil War was **George Henry Thomas**. Born in Southampton County, Virginia, on July 31, 1816, Thomas had begun the study of law when friends secured him an appointment to the U.S. Military Academy at West Point in 1836. He graduated in 1840, ranking twelfth in a class of forty-two, among whom were future general officers William T. Sherman, Richard S. Ewell, Thomas Jordan, and John Getty. Thomas served in the artillery for fifteen years, was stationed at coastal forts, and participated in operations against the Seminoles and in the war with Mexico, where he was brevetted for gallantry at the battles of Monterey and Buena Vista. When the 2nd United States Cavalry was created in 1855, he became one of its first majors, with superiors such as Albert Sidney Johnston, Robert E. Lee, and Major William J. Hardee. In this capacity, Thomas served almost constantly on the Indian frontier in Texas until civil war erupted in April 1861.

A native Virginian, Thomas flatly refused an offer by Virginia Governor Thomas Letcher to resign his commission and become chief of ordnance of the state's forces. By virtue of Johnston and Lee joining the Confederacy, Thomas was advanced to lieutenant colonel and colonel three weeks following the bombardment of Fort Sumter. His sisters disavowed him until the end of their days for his decision to remain in the United States Army and serve the Union. He commanded a brigade under Gen. Robert Patterson in the Shenandoah during the campaign of First Manassas. He was appointed brigadier general of volunteers on August 17, 1861, and was transferred to the West, where he served throughout the entire war.

In Kentucky, he commanded the Union forces that defeated the Confederates under Felix K. Zollicoffer at Mill Springs in January 1862. He was assigned command of the 1st Division, Army of the Ohio, under Don Carlos Buell in the overland march to Tennessee. Promoted major general of volunteers, to rank from April 25, 1862—and first under Henry W. Halleck, then under Buell, and finally under William S. Rosecrans—he served with distinction in the advance upon and siege of Corinth, and the battles of Perryville and Stones River; he staved off disaster at Chickamauga in September 1863 when he rallied broken commands around his corps on the crest of Horseshoe Ridge and held his ground against overwhelming odds until late afternoon, retiring unmolested to Chattanooga. There, on the orders of his new superior, Ulysses S. Grant, supreme commander of Union forces in the West, Thomas was named commander of the Army of the Cumberland, replacing Rosecrans, and promoted brigadier general in the Regular Army on October 27, 1863. A month later, in the hard-fought battles for Chattanooga, his army stormed the heights of Missionary Ridge on November 25, driving the Confederate Army of Tennessee under Braxton Bragg from the formidable position.

In the subsequent advance into northern Georgia and the capture of Atlanta (May 5 to September 2, 1864) Thomas's Army of the Cumberland constituted half of William T. Sherman's entire army group in the field. After the occupation of Atlanta, when John Bell Hood moved through northwestern Alabama into middle Tennessee, Thomas was detached by Sherman north with some 35,000 troops to Nashville, and once there was reinforced with an additional 35,000 men transferred from other commands. On November 30, 1864, a portion of his command repulsed an ill-advised frontal assault by Hood on the Federal breastworks at Franklin; and two weeks later, Thomas delivered Hood a crushing defeat on the outskirts of Nashville, during two brutal days of fighting on December 15 and 16, 1864, hurling the shattered remnants of the Confederate Army of Tennessee into northern Alabama. On January 16, 1865, he was promoted major general, United States Army, to rank from the date of the battle of Nashville. In March he received the thanks of Congress. Thomas continued in command of the Department of the Tennessee until 1867. He was assigned at his own request to command the Division of the Pacific, with headquarters in San Francisco, and the following year died of a stroke in his office on March 28, 1870. He is buried at his wife's hometown of Troy, New York, in Oakwood Cemetery. Nicknamed the "Rock of Chickamauga" for his heroic stand on Horseshoe Ridge, September 20, 1863, General Thomas, along with his superiors William T. Sherman and Ulysses S. Grant, form the triumvirate that many historians acknowledge won the war to preserve the Union. Brant & Eds., *The Union Army*, VIII, 267–69; Warner, *Generals in Blue*, 500–2.

James Alexander Williamson plays a prominent role in the war experiences of William Royal Oake, as his 4th Iowa Infantry was often brigaded with and fought alongside the 26th Iowa Volunteer Infantry from December 1862 to December 1863; and Williamson served intermittently as brigade commander during this period. He service during the war was marked by "a fearlessness and an eagerness to learn," as he rose from first lieutenant to brevet major general of volunteers despite the fact he had no previous military experience.

Born on February 8, 1829, in Adair County, Kentucky, Williamson spent his early childhood in Indiana and his teenage years in Keokuk County, Iowa. He graduated from Knox College in Galesburg, Illinois, and returned to Lancaster, Iowa, to study law and begin a practice. He relocated to Des Moines and played a prominent role in the movement that shifted the state capital from Iowa City to Des Moines. A staunch Democrat, he served as state party chairman and was a delegate to the 1860 Baltimore convention that nominated Stephen A. Douglas for the presidency.

After initial service as adjutant of the 4th Iowa (whose colonel was Grenville M. Dodge), Williamson was elected lieutenant colonel in April 1862 and became its colonel in July. In March 1862, he fought with the regiment at Elkhorn Tavern (Pea Ridge) under Samuel Curtis; then garrisoned the Federal outpost at Helena, Arkansas, during the summer and fall of 1862, where he assumed command of the regiment; then participated in the hard fighting at Chickasaw Bayou under William T. Sherman, where his regiment lost 112 men killed and wounded; and participated in the subsequent capture of the Post of Arkansas under John A. McClernand. His regiment, along with the 26th Iowa Volunteer Infantry, was assigned to Steele's 1st Division, Sherman's XV Corps, fighting in the pivotal operation waged by Ulysses S. Grant against Vicksburg. Prior to the surrender of the fortress city, Williamson was compelled to take a leave of absence because of ill health. After returning to duty, he was assigned command of 2nd Brigade, Osterhaus's 1st Division, Army of the Tennessee, September 1, 1863, directing brigade operations during the fighting waged for the relief of Chattanooga, including the "Battle Above the Clouds" engagement on Lookout Mountain (November 24), the storming of Missionary Ridge (November 25), and the pursuit action at Ringgold (November 27).

Williamson led his brigade during the advance on Atlanta in 1864 and was in nearly every battle and skirmish of the movement. At the battle of Atlanta on July 22, his participated in the Union counterattack that recovered De Gress's Illinois Battery, the skirmishers from his brigade being the first to reach the position. After the fall of Atlanta, Williamson was assigned command of the 3rd Brigade, 1st Division, XV Corps, leading it during the "March to the Sea." Shortly after the capture of Savannah, he was appointed brigadier general of volunteers, January 15, 1865. He left the army briefly to return to Iowa and, during the summer, again served under Grenville M. Dodge, briefly commanding the District of Missouri. Brevetted major general of volunteers for gallant conduct during the war on March 13, 1865, he mustered out of service, August 24, 1865, having been wounded five times during the war. He became an active Republican, serving as a delegate to the National Convention in 1868, associated himself with the promotion of the Union Pacific Railroad, and served five years as a commissioner to the General Land Office; in 1881 he became a commissioner of the Atlantic & Pacific Railroad (predecessor of the Santa Fe Railroad) and was president of the railway when he retired in 1892. On January 15, 1895, he was awarded the Medal of Honor "for having led his regiment at Chickasaw Bluffs against a superior force strongly entrenched and holding his ground when all support had been withdrawn." General Williamson died while on summer retreat in Jamestown, Rhode Island, September 7, 1902, and is buried in Rock Creek Cemetery, Georgetown. D.C. Brant & Eds., *The Union Army*, VIII, 302–4; Warner, *Generals in Blue*, 564–65; Boatner, *Civil War Dictionary*, 928–29; Dyer, *Compendium*, 498–99.

The relationship of Gen. **Charles Robert Woods** with the war experiences of William Royal Oake dates to November 1862, when their respective regiments participated in operations in the Mississippi Valley; later, beginning in February 1864 until the close of the war, Woods served almost constantly as either Oake's brigade commander or his division commander. Born on February 19, 1827, in Newark, Ohio, Charles R. Woods was the younger brother of William Burnham Woods, who would also wear the stars of a general officer in the war and play a prominent role in the war memories of Royal Oake. Raised on a farm with a limited tutored education, Woods was appointed to the U.S. Military Academy at West Point in 1848. Upon graduation four years later, he served routine duty as an infantry officer in Texas and Washington until 1860. His first Civil War service was as commander of troops sent on the chartered steamer *Star of the West* to relieve Fort Sumter. Unsuccessful, the mission earned famed for being the instance when the first hostile shot of the war was fired.

After a brief service on quartermaster duty, Woods was commissioned colonel of the 76th Ohio Infantry on October 13, 1861, and briefly participated in operations in western Virginia, before his regiment was transferred to the Western theater. There Woods ably led his troops during the battle and capture of Fort Donelson and at bloody Shiloh, being assigned to Lewis Wallace's division of Ulysses S. Grant's army. In the subsequent advance on Corinth in May 1862, he was briefly advanced to brigade command. Later, during William T. Sherman's expedition to the Yazoo River, resulting in the battle at Chickasaw Bayou, and in the ensuing movement to seize the Post of Arkansas, Woods was again in charge of his old regiment. He continued this command through the initial operations against Vicksburg until he was advanced to the command of the 2nd Brigade, Peter J. Osterhaus's 1st Division, Sherman's XV Corps. On August 4, 1863, Woods was formally promoted to brigadier general of volunteers. In September he assumed command of the 1st Brigade in Osterhaus's division, leading it in battles for Chattanooga in November and during the celebrated advance against Atlanta, where, for a month during the summer siege of the city, while General Osterhaus was away on a leave of absence, he briefly commanded the 1st Division, XV Corps, now led by John A. Logan, and subsequently assumed temporary direction over the 3rd Division, XVII Corps. Woods's gallant conduct and leadership during the series of hard-fought engagements, which began with Lookout Mountain and continued with the advance into northern Georgia, ending with the surrender of Atlanta, won him the brevet rank of colonel in the Regular Army.

Returned to command of the 1st Division on September 23, 1864, Woods permanently replaced Osterhaus, guiding the division in the pursuit of John B. Hood into Alabama, and then embarked on Sherman's infamous "March to the Sea" and the advance through the Carolinas that followed. He received his third brevet promotion on November 24, 1864, to major general of volunteers, and later earned a fourth brevet to the same rank in the regular service "for gallant and meritorious service" at the conclusion of the war. Throughout the remainder of 1865 and 1866, Woods held department commands in Alabama and Georgia during the initial period of Reconstruction. Mustered out of volunteer service as a result of the reorganization of the United States Army in July 1866, he became lieutenant colonel of the 33rd Infantry. Failing health forced his early retirement in 1874, having been promoted colonel of the 2nd United States Infantry the same year.

He retired to his estate near Newark, Ohio, dying there on February 26, 1885; he is buried in Cedar Hill Cemetery. Brant & Eds., *The Union Army*, VIII, 306–7; Dyer, *Compendium*, 498, 518; Warner, *Generals in Blue*, 571–72.

Two and one-half years older than his brother Charles, **William B. Woods** was born at the family farm in Newark, Ohio, on August 5, 1824. Extremely intelligent, he studied for three years at Western Reserve College and then attended Yale, graduating in 1845 as valedictorian of his class. Admitted to the Ohio bar in 1847, he possessed great oratorical skill, which served him well in his practice of law and his interest in politics. Aligned with the Democratic Party, he was elected mayor of Newark in 1855. Initially opposed to the extreme executive policies practiced by the Lincoln administration following the outbreak of the Civil War, he delayed, but eventually followed his brother into military service, ultimately shifting his allegiance to the Republican Party.

In February 1862, Woods was commissioned lieutenant colonel of the 76th Ohio Infantry, the regiment commanded by his younger brother Charles. Engaged with the regiment at bloody Shiloh, his creditable war experiences paced those of Charles, whom he continued to serve under in the advance upon Corinth, in the swamps at Chickasaw Bayou, and in the assault on the Post of Arkansas, where he was slightly wounded on January 11, 1863. When Charles was assigned command of the 2nd Brigade, 1st Division, XV Corps, on May 22, 1863 (during the operation Grant waged against Vicksburg), William assumed the reins of command for the regiment and led the troops during the grueling forty-seven-day siege of the city. In September, after his brother was promoted to brigadier general, Woods was advanced to the colonelcy, and continued to command the regiment, which remained permanently assigned to the 1st Brigade, 1st Division, XV Corps, through the engagements fought for the relief of Chattanooga in November, then guiding it successfully through the spring and summer 1864 advance on Atlanta, fighting at Resaca, Dallas, Atlanta, Jonesboro, and Lovejoy Station.

After the pursuit of Hood into Alabama, Woods led his troops in the march from Atlanta to Savannah, and on January 21, 1865, assumed command of the 1st Brigade in his brother's division. As brevet brigadier general, he led the brigade through the long march through the Carolinas. In this capacity, he served as Royal Oake's last brigade commander of the war. Toward the end of the fighting in North Carolina, he briefly commanded the division for a handful of days in early April, and on May 31, 1865, was commissioned brigadier general of volunteers, and also was brevetted major general. After participating in the Grand Review in Washington, D.C., he mustered out of service on June 16, 1865.

He settled in Alabama after the war, speculating in land. In 1869, President Grant appointed him a United States circuit court judge for the area encompassing Georgia and the Gulf states. He resided in Atlanta for eleven years, providing a sensible, firm, and moderate hand to adjudicating racial issues that arose during Reconstruction. In 1880, President Rutherford B. Hayes appointed him associate justice of the United States Supreme Court. Woods died in Washington, D.C., May 14, 1887, and is buried near his brother, who preceded him in death two years earlier, in the Cedar Hill Cemetery in Newark, Ohio. Brant & Eds., *The Union Army*, VIII, 307–8; Dyer, *Compendium*, 498; Warner, *Generals in Blue*, 572–73.

Index

Index entries for chapter notes are indicated by the page number, followed by the letter n and the note number.

Page numbers for photographs appear in italics.

Index

Lovejoy Station 257, 261n556
Lubbers, Maj. John 38, 53–54n60, 178, 266–67, 268n576, 309–10, 325n640
Lumber River 324n633
Lynch, George M. 298
Lynn, Pvt. James 73, 82n176
Lyons, IA 131

Macon & Western Central Railroad 240n521
Macon Railroad 253n546
MacQuigg, Asst. Sur. William 37, 52n38
Magill, Lt. Col. Samuel G. 37, 41–42, 51n33
Mahar, Pvt. David 75, 87n228
Maher, Pvt. William 74, 84n199
mail 272, 278
Manigault, Brig. Gen. Arthur M. 234n514
March to the Sea 269–73, *270, 280,* 304n628
Marietta, GA 222n494, 222n496
Markland, Sgt. Sylvester 75, 86n223
Marks, Pvt. William 76, 88n247
Martensen, Pvt. Paul S. 75, 85n212
Mason, Lt. John W. 100, 102, 106n301
McAlister, Corp. Archibald 76, 88n250
McCahill, 2nd Lt. Philip 38, 54n68
McCauley, Pvt. Samuel 76, 87n238
McClellan, Gen. George B. 268n574
McClenahan, Sgt. Robert 71, 81n164, 232
McClernand, Gen. John A. *32,* 46, 60n119, 364–66
McDill, 2nd Lt. James 37, 53n56, 73
McDonald, Pvt. John 76, 87n239
McDonnell, Pvt. John 74, 84n200
McDonnell, William 147, 155n399
McDowell, Pvt. George A. 73, 83n185
McLain, John 43–44, 60n115
McLaughlin, Pvt. Alanson 76, 89n261
McLeish, Chap. John, Jr. 37, 52n40
McLenahan, Sgt. Robert J. 260, 266–67, 315
McPherson, Maj. Gen. James 183, 191n445, 195, 199n462, *209,* 230, 234n510, 366–67
Mead's Guerillas 179n432
medical care 187–88, 203–4, 211, 315, 327n651
Meier, Pvt. Anton 75, 85n213

Meigs, Qrtrmster Gen. Montomgery C. 290n602
Merrell, Capt. Nathaniel A. 38, 53n57, 74
Merrimac 126, 134n354
Military Division of Mississippi 139n369, 151n375
Miller, James 118
Miller, Pvt. Leonidas 104, 108n318, 129, 131, 209–11, 212n478
Milliken's Bend 44, 46, 61n126, 92–94
Missionary Ridge 141, 144, 146, 151–52n378, 154n391, 154n394
Mississippi Cavalry Regiment 108n321
Mississippi Delta 106n298
Monitor 134n354
Monroe's Cross Roads 324n632
Montague, Thomas 39, 55n80
Moon's Station 262n561
Moore, Brig. Gen. John C. 152–53n385
Morgan, Gen. George W. 45, 367–68
Morgan, Pvt. Sydenham W. 76, 88n246
Morse, Pvt. Langdon 77, 91n281
mortars 97n294
Mower, Maj. Gen. Joseph 325n641
Moyses, Pvt. James G. 77, 90n278
Mullett, Pvt. Myron J. 75, 87n231
Murry, Patrick 160–61, 166n408–9
muskets 40

Nahunta Station, NC 327n655
New Hope Church 206n469–70
New York 125–26, 133n351
night assaults 196–98, 199n464
9th New York Infantry 133n352
Nye, Capt. Charles M. 38, 54n69, 108n314
Nyrop, Pvt. Wilhelm 74, 85n209

Oake, Amy 333, 339n6
Oake, Frank Royal 333, 335, 339n8, 340n12
Oake, George William 333, 335, 339n8, 340n12
Oake, Lottie 334–35, 337
Oake, Mary 334, 335
Oake, Richard L. 333, 335, 339n8, 340n11
Oake, William 334, 335
Oake, William Royal 11–28, 33–35, *36,* 48n11, 49n13, 135, 138n364, 144, 152n384, 331–38, *336*

Schmutz, Pvt. Paul 75, 86n215
Schnack, Pvt. Detleff 75, 86n218
Schroder, Pvt. August W. 73, 83–84n189
Schultz, Pvt. Johann H. 75, 86n216
seabiscuit 227, 228n503
Selma, AL 117, 120n336
76th Ohio Infantry 191n443
Shadna Church 253n547
Shaffer, Corp. Henry L. 73, 82n178
Sheridan, Maj. Gen. Philip H.
    153–54n390
Sherman, Maj. Gen. William T. 44,
    45–46, 60n119, 151n375, 153n387,
    183, 190n438, *194*, 230-31, 234n512,
    234n514, 327–28n659, 328n660,
    330n670, 330n671, 374–76
Shields, Pvt. Richard 77, 90n276
Ship's Gap 259, 263n568, 263n571,
    268n572, 268n573
Shoup, Brig. Gen. Francis Asbury 222n497
Shoupades 217–19, 222n497, 222n498,
    231
Siege of Badajoz 296–97, 303n623
signal flags 258, 262n563
Simpson, John 224, 228n501
Simpson, 1st Corp. Horace 103, 104,
    108n317
Sims, George 270–71, 274n580, 315–16
Sinkey, John 73, 82n171
skirmish lines *185, 202*
skirmish pits 204–5, 206n473, 207–8,
    216
skirmishers 152n381
Slocum, Maj. Gen. Henry W. 249,
    325n642, 376–77
Smith, Col. Milo 36, 37, 39, 56n86, 69, 70,
    191n443, *225*, 228n502, 240n523,
    379–80
Smith, Gen. A. J. 45, 377–78
Smith, Gen. Morgan L. 45, 46, 380–81
Smith, Maj. Gen. Giles A. 303n619
Smith's Landing 106n299
Snake Creek Gap 183–84, 191n444, 259
Snodgrass, Sgt. Hugh 73, 82n172
Solemn Grove 324n632
South River 325n641
Spencer, Col. George E. 324n632
squads 101, 107n312
St. Louis, Missouri 39
Stanley, Pvt. Omar H. 75, 86n221

Stanton, Edwin M. 290n602, 330n670
Star Fort 262–63n565
Stearns, Corp. John E. 76, 88n242
Steele, Gen. Frederick 45, 46, *98*, 99,
    107n307, 110, 381–82
Steele, 1st Lt. John L. 38, 54–55n73, 149,
    155n402
Steinhilbert, Pvt. George 75, 86n217
Stevens, Corp. Ahira 75, 86n224
Stevenson, Maj. Gen. Carter L. 107,
    152–53n385, 153n387
Stone Mountain 233n504
Strong, Lt. James W. 40, 57n97
Strong, Pvt. Levi 177, 179n435
Stuach, Pvt. William Stewart 74, 84n201
Sugar Valley 191n447
Sun Flower River 110
supply lines 99, 269, 274n577, 274n578,
    277, 278
sutlers 277, 282–83, 289n591
Sutton, Lt. Leander B. 290–91n608
Svendsen, 1st Lt. Edward 38, 54n61, 74
Swamp Angel 286, 291n611
Sweeny, M. P. 58n105
Swift, William H. 175–76, 179n433,
    185–86
swifts 202–3, 206n468
Swihart, Pvt. David W. 104, 108n319,
    112–13, 129, 136, 204, 207, 216,
    243–44, 310–11, 320, 338
Symons, Pvt. John C. 73, 83n183

Tallahatchie River 42, 59n111
Taylor's Mill 291n609
Taylor's Ridge 191n444, 259
Ten Mile Home 131, 134n361
Tenbroeck, Lucretia Mitchell 342
Tennessee Quick Step 112, 119n324
10th Regiment Iowa Infantry 271,
    274–75n583
Texas Railroad 44, 61n127
Thayer, Brig. Gen. John M. 46, *66*,
    382–83
13th Army Corps 44
Thomas, Maj. Gen. George H. 141,
    151n375, 154n394, 185, 192n450,
    383–85
Thomas, Pvt. Charles A. 73, 83n180
Thomas, Pvt. Edward P. 77, 90n267
Tierney, J. H. 295, 303n619

A native "jayhawker" and graduate of the University of Kansas, **Stacy Dale Allen** is a twenty-year veteran of the United States National Park Service. Currently Chief Park Ranger at Shiloh National Military Park, Stacy manages interpretation, law enforcement, resource management, and historic preservation programs at the famous West Tennessee Civil War site, which also stewards prehistoric cultural resources associated with Shiloh Indian Mounds National Historic Landmark and a new National Civil War Interpretive Center located in Corinth, Mississippi.

Author of numerous articles on the Civil War, Stacy has prominent contributions in seven books and served as researcher/preparer on several National Park Service historic resource studies and management documents, including the Civil War Sites Advisory Commission Report on the Nation's Civil War Battlefields; Siege and Battle of Corinth Special Resource Study; and the Vicksburg Campaign Trail Feasibility Study. Recent publications include "Corinth: Crossroads of the Western Confederacy" and "Shiloh! A Visitor's Guide," both published by *Blue & Gray Magazine;* and an essay on General Lew Wallace in Grant's Lieutenants: "From Cairo to Vicksburg," Steven E. Woodworth, editor, for the University Press of Kansas.

Stacy is married to Diane Woodford of Savannah, Tennessee. They have two children and five grandchildren.